Eating and Being Eaten:
Cannibalism as Food for Thought

Edited by

Francis B. Nyamnjoh

Langaa Research & Publishing CIG
Mankon, Bamenda

Publisher:
Langaa RPCIG
Langaa Research & Publishing Common Initiative Group
P.O. Box 902 Mankon
Bamenda
North West Region
Cameroon
Langaagrp@gmail.com
www.langaa-rpcig.net

Distributed in and outside N. America by African Books Collective
orders@africanbookscollective.com
www.africanbookscollective.com

ISBN-10: 9956-550-96-5

ISBN-13: 978-9956-550-96-8

© Francis B. Nyamnjoh 2018

About the Authors

Chapter 1

Francis B. Nyamnjoh is a professor of Social Anthropology at the University of Cape Town, South Africa. His most recent books include *#RhodesMustFall: Nibbling at Resilient Colonialism in South Africa* (2016) and *Drinking from the Cosmic Gourd: How Amos Tutuola Can Change Our Minds* (2017).

Chapter 2

Andreas Buhler is a Ph.D. candidate in Social Anthropology at the University of Cape Town. He is doing research on the relationship between entrepreneurship and land. His previous research was on the housing crisis in Cape Town.

Chapter 3

Dr Artwell Nhemachena teaches Sociology at the University of Namibia. He has studied Sociology and Social Anthropology. His current areas of research interest are Relational Ontologies, Sociology and Social Anthropology of Science and Technology Studies, Decoloniality and Transformation. He has published eight books and several book chapters and journal articles.

Maria B. Kaundjua teaches Sociology at the University of Namibia. She holds a Masters Degree in Population and Development Studies. She is involved in research on Sexual and Reproductive Health, Demographic Studies, Climate Change, Environmental Health and Development. She has published a number of journal articles.

Chapter 4

Walter Gam Nkwi holds a Ph.D. from the University of Leiden. He has published books, articles in journals, book chapters and encyclopaedias. He is currently the Secretary General in the Faculty of Engineering and Technology and also a Senior Lecturer in the Department of History, Faculty of Arts, University of Buea, Cameroon.

Chapter 5

Ayanda Manqoyi is a Ph.D. Student in anthropology at the University of California, Davis, in the United States of America. His research interest is to understand how the family obligation, known in South Africa as 'black tax', mediates when one ascends to institutionalised middle class.

Chapter 6

Veronica D. Masenya, is a social scientist and a graduate of the University of the Free State, South Africa. She holds a B.A. degree, B.A. Honours Degree (Anthropology) and M.A. Degree (Sociology). She is currently a Ph.D. candidate and her research focuses on 'funerary practices in contemporary Bloemfontein, South Africa'.

Chapter 7

Dominique Santos was born in Cape Town, bred in Johannesburg and buttered in London. Her Ph.D. explored the intersections of popular music and experiences of social change amongst various multi-racial communities in South Africa. She currently lives in Bloemfontein, where she is a post-doctoral fellow at the University of the Free State.

Chapter 8

Moshumee T. Dewoo has spent the last decade researching post-independent African modes of identification specifically as these relate to access to political power. She has written and published various pieces on the subject and is currently focused on the case of the 'Nasyon' community in Mauritius, with the intent of submitting her primary findings thereon by way of a Ph.D. thesis to complete at the University of Cape Town.

Chapter 9

Akira Takada is currently an associate professor at Kyoto University, Japan. His academic interests include language socialisation and the transformation of ethnicity. He has published many books and articles, including *Narratives on San ethnicity: The cultural and ecological foundations of lifeworld among the !Xun of north-central Namibia* (2015).

Table of Contents

Foreword ix
Harri Englund

1

Introduction: Cannibalism as Food for Thought 1
Francis B. Nyamnjoh

Introduction.. 1
There is more meat to cannibalism than meets the eye....................... 4
Compassionate Cannibalism 18
Being Human as Eating and Being Eaten.................................... 39
Humans and Animals as two sides of the
same Cannibal Feast.. 41
Cannibalism in Camouflage.. 52
Contributions to this Volume: an Overview................................ 62
Conclusion 68

2

The Violence of Translating People into Cannibals: The Man-Eating Anthropologists 99
Andreas Buhler

The violence of translating people into cannibals 99
Anthropology, cannibalism and colonial violence...................... 101
The problematic notion of cannibalism 104
The ethnography of cannibalism:
representing the other 109
Ethnography and the violence of
making a text from data.. 118
Cannibalism: beyond the modern world
and towards a new anthropology 120

3

Incorporated or Cannibalised by Posthuman Others? Sanctions and Witchcraft in Contemporary Zimbabwe 127

Artwell Nhemachena & Maria Kaundjua

Introduction 128

The Capture and Cannibalisation of Zimbabwe:
on the Imperial Leviathan 133

Luring and Incorporating 'Delicious'
Africa in a Cannibalistic World:
Zimbabwe and Sanctions 142

Conclusion 148

4

**'The Body of Christ? Amen':
Christianity and the Cannibalisation of the Bamenda Grassfielders (Cameroon)** 157

Walter Gam Nkwi

Introduction 157

Eating up Traditional Rulers: the Projection
and Delegitimisation Argument 164

Ex-soldiers or 'Fernando Po Repartees' and
the Licence to Consume Grassfielders 171

The Ex-servicemen and Cannibalism
Consuming and being Consumed:
'Love' and 'Sex' in the Church Compounds 175

Domestication of Western Christianity by the
Bamenda Grassfielders 183

Conclusion 190

5

Researching Cannibalising Obligations in Post-apartheid South Africa 197

Ayanda Manqoyi

Introduction 197

Background on Black Middle Class in South Africa 198

Cannibalising Black Middle Class 202

Cannibalising Obligations 205
Media on Cannibalising Black Tax 208
Citizenship and Cannibalism 212
Cannibalising Systemic Obligations 214
Conclusion 215

6

Lehu la gago le ya mphidisha
'your death nourishes me' 223
Veronica Dimakatso Masenya
The investment of 'life' 235
The saga of human ashes 240
Conclusion 245

7

Rainbow Nation of the Flesh 255
Dominique Santos
The Kitchen 259
Appetisers 265
Main Course 268
Dessert 271
Gluttony 272
In Lieu of a Conclusion:
After Dinner Mint, Coffee & Brandy 278

8

My African Heart: The Obscure Gourmandise
of an Enlightened Man 283
Moshumee T. Dewoo
Introduction 283
The Pale Tale of Extraction 285
The Path of the Dying Heart 291
Conclusion 298

9

Consumerisation of cannibalism in contemporary Japanese society 309

Akira Takada

Introduction 309
Exploiting the suicidal 312
Fantasising reality and realising the fantasy 315
Fetish to rawness 320
Consumerisation of cannibalism 323
Concluding remarks 328

Index 333

Foreword

Cannibalism is freshly palatable to scholarly tastes. Much more than a source for puns of variable ingenuity, cannibalism uncoupled from its connotations of human beings devouring human flesh has great potential to re-engage some of the most profound questions in what it means to be human. Once consigned to the dustbin of anthropological (or racist) fantasies, cannibalism has in recent years attracted new critical thinking, much of it philosophical or essayist in nature. To that body of scholarship the present volume adds a rich set of impassioned studies of intellectual history and current life-worlds. The promise here is not only to subject a rethought cannibalism to the rigours of empirical analysis, worthwhile as such an effort undoubtedly is. The promise is also to chart ways in which the understandable horror evoked by cannibalism can be qualified by the recognition that human beings necessarily partake of the lives of others, whether human or non-human. The challenge is to identify moral resources in the rethought cannibalism.

The promise and the challenge appear less startling if an important piece of disciplinary history is borne in mind. Reaching beyond the tiresome scapegoating of anthropology for crimes committed by incomparably more powerful agents of history, the present volume reminds us of how often the elementary structures of kinship have turned out to be its *alimentary* forms. In other words, the well-documented uses of means of sustenance in making people feel related to one another underline the close connection between eating, being eaten and being human. Equally well-known and widespread are the metaphorical links made between sex and food. Sigmund Freud's forays into the darkest recesses of intimacy might also have been prefigured by certain aspects of witchcraft and sorcery the world over. Those closest to oneself are also those capable of inflicting the greatest pain.

The present volume, spearheaded by Francis Nyamnjoh's remarkable essay, takes an important step further from merely bemoaning the misrepresentations of various others by European colonial powers. If the studies assembled here did little more than restate the humanity of a narrowly-conceived cannibalism's victims, they would themselves reassert victimhood as the register in which the debate on cannibalism has to be conducted. Instead, Nyamnjoh develops his key observation that 'to feed on someone's life chances is tantamount to feeding on someone's flesh' into a far more challenging proposition than what is possible within the identity-obsessed campaigns of the twenty-first century. He throws down the gauntlet of *incompleteness* to confront the clamour of identities, victims, reparations. The idea that we all start out by being complete as persons and human beings perpetuates the kind of ethics and politics in which the only hues are black and white. The cry for incompleteness grows louder than the politically correct clamour of our own times. It asserts incompleteness as the condition of the powerful no less than of those whom they prey upon. It heralds the arrival of another ethics and politics.

Harri Englund
Cambridge
17 April 2018

Chapter 1

Introduction: Cannibalism as Food for Thought

Francis B. Nyamnjoh

Introduction

The present essay notes, with regret, that even among its non-Western critics, understandings of cannibalism have continued to be narrowly framed and articulated around a rather disturbingly parochial Eurocentric index of consumption and of what it means to be human. It invites the reader to critically interrogate presuppositions that proliferate around cannibalism as an essentially negative indulgence and practice that diminishes the humanity of both the eater and the eaten, and therefore to be viscerally and rationally opposed in the interest of real or imagined ideals of purity, cleanliness, decency and palatability of 'cultured' and 'civilised' beings (Douglas 2001[1966]). It challenges scholars to explore innovative ways of thinking about cannibalism, predicated upon keeping prejudices and expectations of modernity in check, as well as seeing in such expectations and prejudices a disguised form of cannibalism. Within the call for innovativeness, it should be possible and epistemologically significant to analyse cannibalism in the strict sense (as something 'strange', 'unsettling' and 'outside' our expectations of generosity on the possibility of a common humanity and equality of access to human dignity) without invoking notions of primitive savagery, *but also* without a feeble and stifling political correctness (Lindenbaum 2004).

The essay brings into conversation past and present articulations, representations and understandings of and around cannibalism in the interest of pointing attention to the veiled, disguised and mostly invisible dimensions of cannibalism in the many a so-called modern and civilised society that we inhabit and love to show off as trophies in human progression from primitivism and barbarism to liberalism as the pinnacle of tolerance and inclusivism. In this connection, the essay suggests that we could enrich our understanding of Western modernity, by thinking of it as underpinned by a quest for superiority and supremacy through the cannibalisation of the non-Western 'Other'. Such cannibalisation has taken the form of enslavement and extractive colonialism in the past, and in the present, it takes the form of sweatshop labour extractive capitalism, the repressive policing of the mobility of the non-Western 'Other', and the opportunistic trafficking (in whole or dismembered) of those reduced to the indignities of life as human waste and as wasted humanity by Western modernity and its chainsaws of Frankenstein industrialisation, commodification, globalisation and trivialisation (Barker et al. 1998; Hulme 1998). In the form of neoliberalism and globalised consumerism, those who do not qualify to be consumed all too easily find themselves consumed by irrelevance and the stark invisibility of whatever humanity they may claim or aspire to.

The essay argues for recognition of *cannibalism as a normal way of being human as open-ended composites*,[1] and for assuming the ethical and moral implications and obligations of a universe, a cosmology and ontology informed or dictated by this recognition. In an interconnected world characterised by eating for sustenance, self and collective protection, projection and reproduction, one (humans and non-humans alike) cannot eat, ad infinitum, without the risk of being eaten in turn, and/or the possibility of eating oneself up into bare existence and, ultimately, extinction. This calls for constant awareness of the centrality and importance of cannibalism in our daily quests for and processes of being and becoming. Such awareness is an imperative first step in the process of how best to harness the reality and potentiality of cannibalism in its multiplicity of forms and manifestations in the interest of all and sundry, regardless of race, place, culture, class, gender, sexual orientation and generation. Once we recognise the ubiquity of cannibalism in all its guises and disguises, we are compelled, in all humility, to confront the question of an all-inclusive ethics and morality of a flexible, nuanced, complex, interconnected, bridging humanity articulated from the vantage point of *incompleteness* as the norm (Nyamnjoh 2017[2015]a, 2017b) – a morality and an ethics

2

that privilege boundary crossing in the negotiation of moral dilemmas and the cultivation of moral sympathies and inclusive moral compasses (Englund 2015a, 2015b; Nyamnjoh 2015a). Put differently, if cannibalism is a normal way of being human as a dynamic and flexible reality, then it is in our individual and collective interest to develop a carefully negotiated and delicately navigated moral and ethical order of self-preservation that is founded on inclusiveness informed by the myth of wholeness, the humility of *incompleteness* and the reality of interconnections of interacting fluidities.

The tendency thus far has been to dodge or tiptoe around this question by defining cannibalism too narrowly, and by outsourcing or projecting it onto purportedly inferior others, while taking attention away from our own cannibalism and its resultant anxieties in the name of civilisation and pretensions to a superior moral order. In research, to define is to confine, and to predetermine the outcome is to direct attention to certain aspects by taking attention away from other aspects of our subject of enquiry. If cannibalism is not explored and understood in its fullness, we might not know when, as Travis-Henikoff (2008: 243) puts it, we are over-consuming and risking running out of food, family, friends or enemies. This highlights the need for us to curb our enthusiasm for cannibalisation through a careful balance between our cravings for proteins and profits as a way of life (Harris 1977; Sahlins 1978) and the imperative for reproduction, social and otherwise, not only of the fittest and the human, but of all and sundry, humans and non-humans.

Notwithstanding arguments in favour of 'contingency cannibalism' informed by the recognition of and subscription to 'superhardcore survivalism' (Takada 1999; see also Esteban 2016), such potentials to harness cannibalism are best explored not within the modernisation or civilisational Darwinian logic of survival of the fittest and winner takes all or giant compressor syndrome. The most promising framework for such harnessing lies with the logic and framework of *incompleteness* (Nyamnjoh 2017[2015]a, 2017b), which, along with its ethics and morality of conviviality, recognises our mutual entanglements and manglements as humans, one and all, seeking sustenance in full awareness that cannibalism and cannibalisation are, in one form or other, the only game in town, a necessary evil. What opportunities for an ethics of conviviality are there when we all recognise that no one has the monopoly of cannibalism and cannibalisation? That no single being, culture or civilisation can have the last laugh in the game of cannibalism? That as eaters and eaten we all survive together or we perish together? In our cannibalistic indulgence, there is hardly room for such extravagant assertions as: 'Everyone for themselves, and God for us all.' Let's not delude ourselves. We all are in it together, our *Cannibalism Ubuntu* boat: we either perish as one or we survive as one.

There is more meat to cannibalism than meets the eye

Among humans cannibalism[2] – 'the act of any life form consuming others of its own kind' (Travis-Henikoff 2008: 56) or seeking externalisation of the self through the internalisation of others of its kind (Viveiros de Castro 2014[2009]: 176) – is a universal attribute of being and surviving as human through hierarchical relationships of power and seeking distinction at all costs through claims of and aspirations to fulfilment (Jooma 1997, 2001; Carbonell et al. 2010). As Travis-Henikoff remarks of the Asmat of New Guinea, among whom 'Anyone, at any time, was a possible target', headhunting and cannibalism served to define 'boundaries, expanding victorious villages and depleting, or totally destroying, a losing group. At all times, every village was potentially at war with every other village' (Travis-Henikoff 2008: 240). To be alive and stay alive is to admit and embrace the cannibal reality – however in your face or disguised – of that very fact.

As a lifelong game of eating and being eaten, cannibalism is practised by all and sundry, to various degrees through relationships and social interactions, be this horizontal or vertical. In love or in hate, fear or fascination, everyday life and relationships or ambitions of dominance, cannibalism comes in handy, and has always done so, since ancestral times, making of us all, without exception, 'descendants of cannibals' (Travis-Henikoff 2008: 93) and

4

perpetrators of cannibalism. '[T]here are cannibals lurking in all of our ancestral closets', argues Travis-Henikoff, with 'recent DNA studies' in support (Travis-Henikoff 2008: 189), and there is no reason to assume that cannibals are confined in the ancestral closets, if we were to take cannibalism seriously beyond its literal and primary connotation of eating the flesh of another human. To eat *'la viande des autres'* (Geschiere 1995) might be its obvious public face, but cannibalism as a practice is far more of an insinuating and insidious part and parcel of everyday life and social processes than meets the eye or tickles the palate. Taking others in as food for the body, the mind and the soul is not confined to ingesting them through the mouth. The consuming passions of our cannibalism need more than the mouth (real or imagined) in their quest for fulfilment.

We cannibalise those we love, just as we do those we hate, and not always literally, as a study of white labour and black slave labour in the makings of American capitalism would suggest (Fitzhugh 1988[1960]). This point is echoed by another study of 'cannibal democracy', which shows how blackness is selectively cannibalised through an insistence on whitening up in the making of racialised citizenship in the Americas, Brazil and the USA in particular (Nunes 2008). The idea of cannibal democracy could also be extended to depict forms of government that thrive on institutions and on structures and practices of dissemblance that eat up the very populace whom they are purportedly enshrined to protect. As individuals and collectivities, many of us have somehow fallen prey to the idea that we succeed best (or delude ourselves that we are successful) when we literally, symbolically, metaphorically or indirectly eat up rivals and enemies and/or make a meal of fear and those we claim to love.

To literally kill a person in order to feed on the resources and opportunities made available to us by their death amounts to cannibalism, regardless of whether we actually make a meal of the dead person's body. To feed on someone's life chances is tantamount to feeding on someone's flesh – either way, one is depleted, diminished, cannibalised. Similarly, to reduce a person to a degradable, shameful, acute and passive level of dependency and

5

powerlessness – to a bare existence stripped of self-worth, personhood and agency – by one's exceedingly predatory claims of entitlements to power, privilege, resources and the bodies and energies of others in a given context, such as film producer Harvey Weinstein allegedly did to women who came hunting for fame, dignity and agency in Hollywood,[3] amounts to cannibalism.

At a personal and individual level, such cannibalism takes the form of freezing the humanity of others at sub-zero temperatures, so we can eat up their life chances with a numbed sense of guilt. In societal and cultural terms, cannibalism comes with denying ourselves the uncontained animalism and monstrosity we effusively imagine and project onto others through the drama of fear and fascination, so we may make game of others without feeling the weight of the screaming desperation of severed prey to which we have reduced others. Reducing others – be they individuals, communities, cultures or ways of life and systems of value – to a ridiculous defensiveness and to a fate worse than death amounts to nothing less than cannibalism gone rogue. With cannibalism, instant death might not always be the worst form of extraction, as dying by degree is equally and often more effective in feeding cannibalistic appetites for much longer terms.

Naked or clothed, cannibalism is part and parcel of the everyday in a world (primitive or traditional, modern or civilised) animated by and framed around *ambitions of completeness* and the zero sum games of winner takes all that go with such ambitions (Nyamnjoh 2017[2015]a, 2017b). It is cannibalism's ubiquity and capacity for presence in simultaneous multiplicities that pushes Claude Lévi-Strauss (2016[2013]) to argue emphatically, as did George Fitzhugh (1988[1960]) before him, that in one form or another, 'we are all cannibals', regardless of our excited claims to being modern, of our often exaggerated displays of revulsion when cannibalism features in our conversation menus, and of whether or not the humans we consume are served through our palates, injected, inserted as transplants or grafted onto our bodies.

Cannibalism need not be a cultural or a normative practice in the society where it occurs to qualify as such, ranging as it does from the ritual to benign, from medicinal to gastronomic

(Lindenbaum 2004; Travis-Henikoff 2008; Brown 2013). In our ambitions of *completeness* through autonomy-seeking behaviour (Nyamnjoh 2017[2015]a, 2017b), we would have few successes to report, let along celebrate and enshrine, if there was little room for cannibalism in our lives, covert or overt, symbolic or metaphorical. The very idea of society as a network of interconnecting and interacting hierarchies, let alone civilisation, is absolutely unthinkable without cannibalism in one form or other. We may all be cannibals, but cannibalism is far from being an indiscriminate act. Each cannibal has a hierarchy of desirability and *raison d'être* for their cannibalism. When we go out shopping for the real or metaphorical meal of the day, what are we most likely to put in our shopping baskets? What are we most likely to ignore? What reasons do we readily or reluctantly avail ourselves of for the choices we make or fail to make? If we were in a position to pick and choose whom we ingest or incorporate in one form or another, how would we go about our business of cannibalisation?

To build a society and champion a civilisation is to spill blood,[4] often savagely, and to make mincemeat of others, their ideas, moral and ethical order, especially of those who think differently and pose a serious challenge to our ambitions of dominance and its absolutes, and to our truth claims (Diop 1991; Bourdieu 1984, 1996; Barker et al. 1998; Elias 2000; Harrison 2008). Yet, paradoxically, the more we crave fulfilment through pretensions to modernity and civilisation, the greater our tendency to outsource and disguise our cannibalism, keen as we are to claim and maintain illusions and delusions of superiority in love and in hate through willing away any direct or obvious forms of cannibalism and the repulsive violence associated with it.

Many who think, talk and refer to cannibalism with visceral revulsion seem to limit it to the physical or literal act of ferociously making a meal of the flesh and bones of others – an evil act or practice often associated with primitive savages living dangerously like wild animals at the margins of humanity and human civilisation, and needing to be stamped out at all costs (Watson 2006; Avramescu 2009; Metcalf 2014). Even among us ethnologists, anthropologists and archaeologists renowned for our readiness to bend over backwards with understanding and in celebration of 'cultural relativism', ethnographic evidence (Johnson 1993) and the suspension of any and all value judgement against the morality of any given culture (Petrey 2005: 116), there is a good measure of lingering unease when it comes to making a case for tolerance and accommodation of cannibalism and its cultural logics (Lumholtz 2009[1889]; Arens 1979; Hulme 1998; Takada 1999; Aubry 2002; Lindenbaum 2004; Petrey 2005; Turner II 2008). As Caroline Aubry remarks of herself and fellow anthropologists, 'We might like to think of ourselves as open-minded and adventurous, but we nevertheless still recoil at the thought of eating human flesh. Cannibalism … still represents a limit to cultural relativism' (Aubry 2002: 433).

The tendency, *a priori*, even among such scholars of relativism, is to represent and relate to real or imaginary cannibals and cannibal cultures as less than human, animalistic and ruled by basic instincts. Reacting to a statement that 'Several academics and scholars have written and loudly proclaimed that human cannibalism has never been practiced except for instances of starvation', Erima Henare, a Maori man whose ancestors practised cannibalism, retorted, 'That is absurd! … Someone should eat them; they could take notes posthumously' (Travis-Henikoff 2008: 109–110). The 'blanket disbelief in ritual cannibalism' by some scholars seems intended to counter the equally 'blanket condemnation of precontact indigenes as blood thirsty savages' by European explorers, both of which are often uncritically internalised and reproduced by certain scholars (Petrey 2005: 114). Could such an overly sensitive or politically correct disposition by scholars of either blanket account for a measure of symbolic cannibalism – consuming the dynamic nature of the practices and social experience of those studied and rendering them into shells of themselves in the name of cultural relativism, on the one hand, while paying lip service to the very same cultural relativism by insisting on political correctness on the unsettling dimensions of the lives and stories of the communities of their ethnographic curiosities, on the other?

Few anthropologists are ready to argue publicly and seriously, the way Beth Conklin does, that, whatever their personal or cultural revulsions, scholars should not ignore 'the possibility that people different from themselves might have other ways of being human, other understandings of the body, or other ways of coping with death that might make cannibalism seem a good thing to do' (Conklin 2001: 6). Her rare plea for scholars to accept and put cannibalism in perspective is supported by Mikel Burley (2016) and by Claude Lévi-Strauss in a short essay, one of his most recent before his death, *We Are All Cannibals* (2016[2013]). This essay makes the call to hunt for cannibalism beyond the confines of its stereotypical hunting grounds, by arguing in material culture terms that if things or possessions are technologies of self-extension for a person, then dispossession, repossession and dispersal of a person's material accumulations or extensions amount to cannibalisation of that person, regardless of whether the person is physically dead or seemingly alive.

Even the idea of gift exchange ceases to be confined merely to the circulation of material substances: it is a form of cannibalism, and could and should be understood in terms of eating the other up by degree in little gift parcels, in lieu of making an instant, once and for all, meal of the person, in the manner of a boa constrictor. Eating up is not only a multivariate practice and process. It takes myriad forms, and is often far more intricate than meets the eye, even as gazing is a spectacular form of eating up the other.

In anthropological practice for example, as anthropologists who may or may not be interested in cannibalism as a subject of ethnographic research, we are all too aware of how much cannibalisation of our informants, their histories and stories, intimacies and local knowledges would apply to us who, often with inconvenient and intrusive technologies of observation and lack of reflexivity and positionality, frequently study down or around the poor in remote localities and locations, in the interest of promoting our personal careers, discipline and/or making a difference in the lives of the poor and the powerless (Nyamnjoh 2012, 2015b; Gordon 2013). And if we were indeed in the company of cannibals, seeking to immortalise their rapacious savagery with our cameras, how often do we stop to ask ourselves questions such as: 'Where does the heart of darkness lie, in the fleshy body-tearing rites of the cannibals or in the photographing eye of the beholder exposing them naked and deformed piece by piece to the world?' (Taussig 1987: 117).

Such cannibalisation may not always be mitigated by the fact that anthropologists have already recognised that ethnographic praxis is fundamentally premised on the time and generosity of others, that it may often be awkward and uncomfortable, and that the gift of friendship may be the best form of reciprocity an anthropologist can marshal in order to 'repay' their interlocutors. It is not often that we feel or allow ourselves to feel cannibalised in turn by those we encounter in the field, who might want to take us into confidence as a bridge, translator or facilitator for taking to the wider world – on their own terms – their own creativity and its outputs or whatever other end they seek to achieve by associating with an anthropologist they perceive, rightly or wrongly, to be well-connected and well-suited for their purpose (Schwarcz 2017). If, as I have argued, cannibalism is dispersed and often part and parcel of ordinary human beings and doings in contemporary life, rather than an exceptional practice performed only by primitive 'savages' in the past, then surely, such cannibalistic tendencies must seep into ethnographic praxis, since the discipline of anthropology does not stand outside the societies it seeks to comment on. Instead of sweeping under the carpet our own cannibalism as anthropologists, it is worth looking into whether and how anthropology itself might be considered a form of cannibalism (or, at least, as having cannibalistic tendencies), but one that desperately seeks to present itself as productive, invigorating and crucial to unsettling routine assumptions about the anthropologists and their interlocutors.

Beyond anthropology, just imagine how much eating we as humans do of others, with our eyes and ears mostly, thanks to the global proliferation of instant multipliers of visual and oral images of spectacle and the spectacular by information and communication technologies such as the television, the computer, the internet, cell and smart phones, large and gigantesque video projection, and social media platforms such as Google, Facebook, Whatsapp, Twitter, Instagram and Snapchat. Such cannibalisation entails opening oneself to being cannibalised in turn, not only by other humans, but by the ultimate facilitators and 'macdonaldisation' of consumer cannibalism – the technological companies for the mass production and circulation of desire. In this regard, Amazon, Apple, Facebook, and Google, the four most important tech companies, have each 'embedded themselves in our lives, hugely influencing us by playing to our basic human instincts: from the eternal human search for answers to our need for love'[5] (see also Galloway 2017). Their lure and allure tempt us to indulge without relent as the prisoners of desiring greed that we all are. As the controversial and scandalous harvest of the personal data of over 87 million Facebook users in the USA by Cambridge Analytica – a firm linked to former Trump adviser Steve Bannon, which compiled user data to target American voters – shows,[6] these tech companies could fall prey to or connive with third party public relations and/or political campaign companies, who are willing to go to extreme lengths, however unethical, to serve the propaganda and ideological interests of their clients and sponsors.[7]

Imagine how much consumption of celebrities and their jaws-dropping sizzling photos and videos – in a manner not dissimilar to how predators of the wild feast on their prey – we would otherwise go without, were it not for this global proliferation of and instant gratification for desire made possible by these cannibalising magic multiplier technologies and tech companies? Maggie Kilgour has written of 'a veritable boom of cannibal literature, film and criticism' in the West since the late 1960s, making of 'the cannibal … a major modern mythical figure' of a 'consumer society' uneasy about its own material appetites' (Kilgour 1997: 19). As Jennifer Brown has argued, the entertainment industry of music, film, literature and television offer a popular menu of cannibalism delights for millions of customers, from snacks to five course meals (Brown 2013). In December 2011, as part of a TV show meant to provide 'serious answers to stupid questions' two Dutch TV presenters, Valerio Zeno and Dennis Storm, 'ate pieces of each other's flesh in front of a live television audience', in response to the question: 'What does human flesh taste like?' (Van Beers 2012: 65).

When accusations of cannibalism are literal and confined to the real or imagined actual ingestion of the flesh and bones of other humans, such accusations are usually a ploy for something else. During the unequal encounters of the past between the West and the rest, for example, claims and accusations of cannibalism served as the perfect excuse for enslavement, colonisation, exploitation and forceful Christianisation and Westernisation (Arens 1979; Barker et al. 1998; Hulme 1998; Gustav 1999; Valsiner 2000; Conklin 2001: 4; Obeyesekere 2005; Watson 2006; Sewlall 2006; Travis-Henikoff 2008: 102–103; Avramescu 2009; Rothera 2009; Mackintosh 2011; Brown 2013: 17–53; Wankier 2016). As Gananath Obeyesekere (2005: 1) puts it, the often dramatised accounts or 'cannibal talk' of man-eating natives as part of a repertoire of Western obsession with 'savagism' was a 'colonial projection providing a justification for colonialism, proselytism, conquest, and sometimes for the very extermination of native peoples' (Obeyesekere 2005: 1). Cannibalism was then and now, 'the ultimate charge' that a group of people so labelled deserved not only the status of savages worthy of extermination, but that you who had labelled them thus were authorised to do the exterminating (Kilgour 2001: vii).

In many an instance, colonialism was justified by presenting prospective colonies as virgin territories awaiting the embrace (passionate or tentative), enchantment, consummation and domestication – cannibalisation so to speak – by the benevolence of expansionist enlightenment penetration spearheaded by European settler masculinities. In other words, the colonising, enslaving and dispossessing West failed to notice the irony of its very own cannibalisation of non-Western 'Others', their labour, bodies, creative energies and material riches, while actively claiming real or imagined cannibalism amongst those it sought to annihilate literally, socially and metaphorically.[8] How could they not see that their craving for total and absolute control over the colonised – body, mind and soul – was nothing short of cannibalism (Brown 2013)? Would they be surprised, subsequently, to learn that the tools of self-extension, ownership and control (books, media and ideologies of superiority, disinformation and misinformation) we use to cannibalise spectacularly end up cannibalising us in turn (Debord

1990)? How can we be surprised when we – in the manner of trigger-happy, bloodthirsty, control freaks – have learnt repeatedly, that our mass produced man-hunting killing machines and weapons of mass destruction are just as cannibalising when turned inwards against our communities, our loved ones and ourselves, as they are devastatingly cannibalistic towards our prey, our enemies and those against whom we go to war?

In their cannibalistic endeavours the penetrating, colonising and enslaving Europeans were aided and abetted by tools of self-extension such as popular literary traditions that feasted like scavengers on fictitious encounters with avid cannibals in which male Western adventurers were intended to prove their manhood and bravado and affirm that they had, in Indiana Jones-like fashion, 'indeed travelled into the wildest, most dangerous and exotic realms of human existence' (Conklin 2001: 5; see also Lumholtz 2009[1889]; Célestin 1996; Gill 1999; Rawson 1999; Guest 2001b; Blythe 2003; Obeyesekere 2005; Brown 2013). Drawing on her study of the legitimating literature of the colonial encounters between the English adventurers and their constructed cannibals of distant lands in India, Africa and elsewhere, Jennifer Brown concludes:

> The colonial adventure fiction from *Robinson Crusoe* to *Tarzan* thrived on gleeful descriptions of savage cannibals and the dashing heroics of the English men pitted against them. Driven by a need to justify imperialism and to glorify Englishness, these books built on a long tradition of labelling the enemy or Other as cannibal. By reducing the natives to animal status, the colonialists could rape the land with impunity and label themselves civilizers. However, beneath all of these heroics was a creeping anxiety. Joseph Conrad questioned the rapacity of the colonial system itself and shed a glimmering light on the not-so-attractive appetites of the supposedly civilized imperialists (Brown 2013: 215).

Given the contested nature of empirical information pertaining to pre-European and precolonial forms of sacrificial anthropophagy or cannibalism, many an endogenous people and community find themselves often at the mercy of unsubstantiated 'cannibal talk' (Obeyesekere 2005: 257). Repeatedly represented as cannibals by invasive Europeans in the past, some native communities, such as the Maori of New Zealand, eventually developed a strategy of identifying themselves as cannibals as a form of deterrence or 'a weapon of the weak' (Obeyesekere 2005: 52–56).[9] Similarly, under German colonialism the Maka of eastern Cameroon earned a reputation as 'hardened cannibals' (Geschiere 1997: 33–34), a reputation which they eventually accepted and learnt to play upon to their advantage. Thus, when during one of his field work visits Dutch anthropologist Peter Geschiere invited a Maka village elder to eat at his house, the elder started the meal with this 'shocking' affirmation: 'It's good. Before we ate whites. Now we eat with them.' (Geschiere 1997: 28). In the face of such self-serving mythical accounts of cannibalism, it is hardly surprising that many a scholar, especially from the non-West, has tended to be rather sceptical of any reported matter-of-fact accounts of cannibalism and to demand rigorous scrutiny of the purported evidence (Arens 1979; McGowan 1994; Salmon 1995; Hulme 1998; Conklin 2001: 6; Kilgour 2001; Obeyesekere 2005; Petrey 2005; Watson 2006; Langfur 2014a, 2014b; Lévi-Strauss 2016[2013]; Metcalf 2014). This is especially the case when, in the absence of credible documentary evidence, claims of cannibalism are attributed to archaeological sources (Barber 1992; Salmon 1995; White 2001; Carbonell et al. 2010), which might offer evidence 'that some humans (or human corpses) have been treated with a certain lack of respect' but not necessarily *proof* that 'the flesh of the humans whose bones have been discarded in the village dump actually had been eaten by village residents' (Abler 1980: 311). The closest to evidence of cannibalism, in findings and conclusions by archaeologists, among whom cannibalism remains 'a contentious issue' (Bello et al. 2016: 739) and 'virtually all the evidence has a measure of ambiguity and is capable of alternative interpretation' (Green 1998: 169) would read more or less as follows:

Results: The frequency of cut marks at Gough's Cave exceeds 65%, while it is below 1% in the Serbian sites, and no human tooth marks and only one case of percussion damage have been observed on the three Serbian collections. The distribution of cut marks on human bones is comparable in the four assemblages. Cannibalized human remains, however, present a uniform cut mark distribution, which can be associated with disarticulation of persistent and labile articulations, and the scalping and filleting of muscles. For secondary burials where modification occurred after a period of decay, disarticulation marks are less common and the disarticulation of labile joints is rare. The micromorphometric analyses of cut marks on human and non-human remains suggest that cut marks produced when cleaning partially decayed bodies are significantly different from cut marks produced during butchery of fresh bodies.

Conclusions: A distinction between cannibalism and secondary treatment of human bodies can be made based on frequency, distribution and micromorphometric characteristics of cut marks (Bello et al. 2016: 721).

William Arens, for example, argued that Europeans, who dramatised the cannibalism of the non-Western societies and cultures they sought to conquer, Christianise and Europeanise, would be hard pressed to point to any concrete examples, beyond their prejudices and overly fertile imagination of their long-distance travellers (sailors, merchants, soldiers and missionaries) and writers, where cannibalism was an effectively institutionalised and socially accepted practice (Arens1979, 1998; Petrey 2005: 114–118; Watson 2006: 15–16; Estok 2012; Brown 2013: 4–5). In South Africa, missionary obsession with, preconceptions and appetites for cannibalism and fascination with the slaughter and consumption of humans were instrumental in shaping both the form and the content of the narratives of their African informants about their beliefs, cultures and socialities (Delius 2010). As Hal Langfur has argued in relation to European encounters with indigenous communities in Brazil, the primary goal was 'conversion' of the natives as 'the ultimate confirmation for colonists that their mission was just, that the natives, given the right conditions, might be guileless lambs, willing – even eager – to submit themselves to church and crown'. In this connection, 'cannibalism was only the most disturbing of behaviors invoked to condemn them as savages, to legitimate their slaughter, to justify their enslavement and the seizure of territory' (Langfur 2014a: 5).

Uncomfortable, perhaps understandably, with the raw, cannibalistic violence characteristic of Western encounters with non-Western worlds, Arens, if only to drill home his point that a morbid fascination with cannibalism says more about the rituals of the fascinated than those of the fascinating (Brady 1982; Mar 2016: 325), did not hesitate to throw whatever baby there may have been in claims of cannibalism out with the bathwater of Western insinuations, stereotypes and extravagant exaggerations on cultures of ritual and rampant cannibalism among non-Western peoples in distant places (Abler 1980; Sahlins 2003). As a strategic ploy to draw attention to the contentious nature of texts pregnant with exaggerations, prejudice and innuendo and offering a powerful licence for radical alterity and stereotyping with impunity, Arens most certainly had a point. His point was especially worth marking if one takes into account these words by Jennifer Brown on the unrelenting fascination with cannibalism in the West: 'cannibalism in our culture is not simply indicative of our obsession with it, but also highlights the sheer pleasure we take in it, hearing about it, contemplating it, fantasizing about it' (Brown 2013: 2). When it is not supposedly real cases of humans eating humans that are depicted, it is fantasised cases of zombies, werewolves and Dracula-like vampires feasting on human blood to ensure a regular menu of fears (ranging from the racial and the psychological to the political, economic and territorial) and fascination with cannibalism and the enduring ties between the human and the beastly in the civilised cultures and creative avenues of self and collective cultivation of the West (Brown 2013: 10).

That said, why is William Arens's discomfort so understandable? So relatable? Was he utterly disgusted by the highly ideologically driven, thinly substantiated and palpably questionable arrogant claims of superiority brandished by European scholars in their monologues on Europe and its thirst for conquest? Did the fact that the inadequately documented overly sensationalised cases of cannibalism are overwhelmingly about the non-Western world,

16

and that the documenting is mostly from the outsider standpoint of the European adventurer and mostly by European scholars exacerbate his disgust (Petrey 2005)? Was Arens further disgusted by the fact that scholars and the ruling elite of the global south (products of the colonial world in many regards) actively participate in the reproduction and perpetration of colonialist narratives, imagery and practices of cannibalism in its many forms, reifying the terror of their purported barbarism and cannibalistic nature as constructed in Western literary, anthropological and related representations (Taussig 1987; Marcelin 2012)? Was Arens's whole purpose to, as Marshall Sahlins suggests, create doubts about the 'apparent "truths"' of cannibalism 'by arguing that their status as truths is derived from the regime of power on whose behalf they have been constructed', and through this, 'to assume the moral high ground' as defenders of the indigenous peoples against the the predatory excesses of an invasive West (Sahlins 2003: 3)?

Why are we so defensive, so eager to distance ourselves from cannibalism even when we have little or no evidence to the contrary (Takada 1999: 23-29), and despite the ever surging enthusiasm of archaeological findings using more sophisticated scientific techniques of authentication (White 2001)? Could the reason be the persistence of European eagerness to keep shifting the goalposts of a common, universal humanity even through standards of measure dictated by its own subjectivities in past encounters engineered and propelled by various crusades of *missions civilisatrices* (Devisch 1996, 2017)? In other words, could the reason for our being overly defensive be that even among its non-Western critics, understandings of cannibalism continue to be narrowly framed and articulate around a rather limited Eurocentric idea of consumption and of what it means to be human? Still in different words, could the rest of the world be guilty of seeking recognition and representation for its own humanity within the very narrow parameters or frames of reference imposed by the very Eurocentrism that licensed the violation and debasement of that humanity from the outset of unequal encounters?

If alternative cosmologies, ontologies and epistemologies silenced systematically by the zero sum logic of Eurocentrism were to replace or at least enter into serious conversation with the prevalent Eurocentrism, would our approach to cannibalism maintain the same unease, discomfort and defensiveness that William Arens so eloquently expresses and with which many of us identify?

Put differently, would our understanding and approach to cannibalism change were we to stop whitening up (becoming assimilated, incorporated or cannibalised by whiteness and its reductionist indicators of being human), or at least doing so rather sheepishly (Devisch 1996, 2017)? If we were to seriously challenge the skewed Eurocentric understanding in which our cannibals are always from the next geography (be it continent, region, country, town, village, ethnic or racial community) (Brady 1982; Rawson 1999: 168–169, 183–184; Valsiner 2000),[10] could we be more accommodating of the fact that cannibalism is part and parcel of being and becoming human, in the fullness of the challenges confronting our creative imagination? In this connection, Brown (2013: 12) notes that even when the cannibal is provided for within the boundaries of the Western nation, as opposed to the colonial jungles of yesteryear, the tendency remains to depict them as 'outside the boundaries of the civilised modern city'. Could Arens's unease with cannibalism, an unease shared by many a non-Western intellectual, be accounted for by a zero-sum model of civilisation that privileges appearances, the imaginary and differentiation over and above the experiential and the messiness of its everyday articulations?

Compassionate Cannibalism

Given its self-assumed status as the gendarme of global taste in humanity, why does the West display such sanitised disclaimers *vis-à-vis* its own histories and practices of cannibalism? Why is it much keener to accept histories of state violence, bloody wars of genocidal proportions and violent encounters, slavery, colonialism and myriad forms of rabid imperialism, but not the cannibalism that may have gone with or resulted from such conflicts? And in what way, exactly, is the consumption of human life in serial killing not cannibalism even if the serial killer does not literally eat the human flesh harvested and objectified (Lefebvre 2005)? In the West's crusade against cannibalism, its enlightenment pursuits through civilising missionaries seldom saw or see cannibalism in compassionate, let alone, universal terms (Devisch 1996, 2017). The dominant discourse is that cannibalism is the affliction of non-Western contexts, the savage barbarism of many a primitive culture, at the heart of many a savaging civilising mission (Arens 1979; Gill 1999; Lindenbaum 2004; Kirkaldy 2005; Obeyesekere 2005; Metcalf 2014).

William Arens, in *The Man-eating Myth*, took to task the provability, prevalent in anthropological circles, of anthropophagy or what is popularly known as cannibalism since Christopher Columbus' 15th century voyage of 'discovery' of the Caribbean and related geographies (Arens 1979) – a voyage that purportedly led to the discovery of people who were 'both not quite monsters, and also not quite fully human' (Williams 2012: 243). Arens challenged the proliferation of allegations of cannibalism despite the 'weak or imperfect observation standards' of the studies and publications claiming such proliferation (Brady 1982: 606). As Brady puts it, Arens saw a discipline such as anthropology to 'feed on cannibalism', given the zealousness with which it committed itself to think about, study, write about and draw sustenance from publishing on cannibals, almost as if its very existence as a discipline and as a source of employment depended on the complementary existence of the cannibal (Brady 1982: 597–598).

Arens argued that cannibalism, as extravagantly represented in creative and scholarly accounts of European encounters with the rest of the world, was pure fabrication, a figment of European imagination, and a projection of Europe's civilisational claims and its ambitions of conquest and dominance over nature and other cultures. Arens's book generated and continues to generate heated controversy (Arens 1979). While many scholars have taken issue with his sweeping and categorically dismissal of cannibalism, few would question Arens's challenge to scholars to authenticate and substantiate more and with actual empirical evidence than merely to claim, evoke or insinuate the existence of cannibalism and its normalcy in many a so-called primitive society prior to contact with the prescriptive evangelical enlightenment gaze of Europe (Lindenbaum 2004). Those motivated or propelled by such abstract ideological representations of cannibalism failed and continue to fail to see it as a reflection of love and emotional ways of coping with loss, death and bereavement in some cases.[11]

Such is precisely how Wari' Amazonian Indians of Brazil reportedly saw cannibalism, prior to contact with the prescriptiveness of 'Western Civilisation' between 1956 and 1969. According to Conklin, whose historical ethnography is a subtle, patient and carefully negotiated conversation between the etic and the emic, Wari' were driven by compassion when they 'disposed of the bodies of their dead ... by eating the roasted flesh, certain internal organs, and sometimes the ground bones' (Conklin 2001: xv).[12] They were appalled by the horrifying barbarism of simply letting their dead rot away unattended in the 'cold, wet, and polluting' ground through burial (Conklin 2001: xviii).

Similarly, the Fore of New Guinea consumed their dead as a sign of affection and respect for the deceased and as the 'the best way in which to process their grief'. Reportedly, the Fore preferred consuming their dead to ensure that 'the dear departed could be forever with the consumer in body and spirit', truly blended and mangled up together in love, 'as opposed to burying the body in sugar-cane gardens, to rot and decay ... in the cold, wet ground' (Travis-Henikoff 2008: 99).

It is worth noting, however, as Zita Nunes has argued, that cannibalism is a deeply ambivalent practice, an ambivalence accounted for by the fact that 'cannibalism possesses only through loss'. Be it in love or in hate, she argues, ingestion or incorporation invariably results in losing, more or less permanently, that which one is ingesting, incorporating, assimilating and using to reassert oneself. As she puts it, 'While incorporation may be conceived of as a strategy against loss (as in melancholia) or to pay homage to the desired qualities in an adversary, it requires violence to a loved or desired and feared object, leading to its destruction' (Nunes 2008: 12). But if no loss is ever complete because no ingestion or incorporation is ever wholly total, what becomes of 'the remainder', 'the indigestible residue', 'the inassimilable', 'the excrement', that is either rejected by the eater, resists being eaten or cannot be absorbed (Nunes 2008: 13–14, 32)? What are the resultant anxieties and conflicts of cannibalism that produces rejects, remainders and residues – malcontents? Is there reason in the argument that repulsion derives from habit, that all flesh is nourishing, and that there is nothing extraordinarily different in eating human flesh from eating chicken (Avramescu 2009: 103)?

Of Europe or the West Rawson remarks:

> Cannibalism cannot be contemplated among 'us', even in our supposedly most clear-sighted and ruthless exposures of ourselves, except in a metaphorical form. The possibilities of a literal application to 'ourselves' as distinct from others are a matter of endlessly fascinating speculative self-implication and tease, but usually blocked, in the last analysis, by strategies that range from soft-pedaling evasions or circumventions, as in Montaigne, to barefaced denial (Rawson 1999: 183).

Rawson adds:

> It is indeed probable that a geo-political history of empires could be written by charting the successive places where a dominant culture located its cannibal other. The common factor in the long history of cannibal imputations is the combination of denial of it in ourselves and attribution of it to 'others', whom 'we' wish to defame, conquer, appropriate, or 'civilize' (Rawson 1999: 184).

Kilgour observes that '[t]raditionally … cannibalism has served as the image of absolute difference – the strict boundary that divides the civilized from the savage, the human from the monstrous' (Kilgour 1997: 20).

If cannibalism is quite simply primitive savagery at its most repulsive that reflects 'the world beyond the fence' (Hubinger and Lucie Svatoňová 1991), and civilisation all about moving away from cannibalism and the backwardness it purportedly represents, and if Europe or the West, the self-elected champion of 'modern

21

civilisation', has not always been modern or civilised (Kilgour 1997; Tiffin 2007), then the question deserves to be asked: Whatever became of Europe's cannibalism when Europe became enchanted by the magic of civilisation and modernity? How exactly would Europe convince us it went about avoiding the status of 'civilised barbarism' in its bloodthirsty violence and quest for civilisation away from the dark ages (Diop 1991; Uhlir 2016)? Did its modernity, like witchcraft, cannibalise its cannibalism? Was its cannibalism repressed to its unconscious? Was it outsourced in the manner of a capitalist with a giant nose for cheap labour? To whom – the state as an agent of absolute cruelty perhaps? The rest of the world as one big fantasy space (Barker et al. 1998)? Did Europe's cold temperate climate (as opposed to the hot tropics) become its saving grace, as some like Montesquieu[13] had the habit of arguing? Did Europe's unilineal evolutionary modernism materialise to camouflage the dark sides of its cultural pretensions? To disguise and drive underground its cannibalism? With what consequences? Or did Europe in its modernist pretensions simply learn to take attention away from the cannibalism that is unshakably at the core of that very same modernity with a big 'M' and civilisation with a capital 'C'? Has Europe's obsessive claim to divine inspiration, science and rationality blinded it to the very reality of fear of and fascination with darkness and the dark sides of its insistent claims to modernity and civilisation? What do we make of the proliferation of discourses of cannibalism in a Europe that is all too eager, in Pontus Pilate fashion, to wash its hands of cannibalism (McGowan 1994: 415)?

The answer may well lie in the fact that 'civilisation conceals its own forms of savagery' (Kilgour 1997: 19) by overplaying binary oppositions that take attention away from its inextricable entanglements with savagery and its active and persistent involvement with the production, fetishisation and demonisation of the cannibal 'Other' (Watson 2006: 91–97). As Mikely Burley argues, it is only by relying 'on an unduly constrained conception of what cannibalism consists in: by overlooking the variety of forms that the eating of human beings can take' and by neglecting 'the heterogeneity of ways of being human', can one contend that cannibalism is a mere myth or be categorical in claiming that one lives in a cannibalism-free context and social system (Burley 2016: 500).

Perhaps this myopia and concealment would account for why crusaders against cannibalism, especially in the West, do not appear to see cannibalism in the current pervasive commodification of the human body, the boom in surgery tourism and proliferation of implanted and transplanted body parts among humans (Shilling(2012[1993]; Scheper-Hughes 2000, 2001a, 2001b, 2004; Van Beers 2012). Such transplantations and implantations yield individuals of composite body parts,[14] individuals who would otherwise be reduced to bare life were it not for the flesh, organs and bodily substances harvested from other humans, dead or alive, friend or foe, citizen or alien, and/or were they ever expected to pay back their debts by returning the borrowed body parts. What a paradox that such compositeness is not satisfactorily acknowledged within the logic of ambitions of *completeness*, binary oppositions and bounded singularities from which it materialises (Kilgour 1997; Tiffin 2007; Nyamnjoh 2017[2015]a, 2017b)!

Yet, it is glaringly cannibalism when a 'modern' and 'civilised' people and society in the 21st century condones the savage dismemberment of corpses and the harvesting of the choicest body parts from living humans for the bodily repairs of other humans. If it is compassion, it is hardly compassion of the Wari' type. Why is it desirable to prop up defective bodies and spent anatomies with body parts harvested from the dead, or illegally from poorer and often defenceless persons whose deplorable lives at the margins are as good as food for the vultures of fortune (Scheper-Hughes 2000, 2001a, 2001b, 2004; Masquelier 2000)?[15] In the case of Europe's early modern medicinal cannibalism, 'the vast majority of the corpses which supplied fat and flesh were those of the poor', who 'were far more likely to be executed and far less likely to be securely buried, if buried at all' (Sugg 2013: 833). In what way is the medical cannibalism of today – implanting and transplanting body parts harvested from others to save lives – different from the consumption of human flesh to save lives that was actively labelled cannibalism and campaigned against by the colonising West during its encounters with the non-West? As Takada rightly observes, 'Ironically, the Western civilisations that moved decisively to quell cannibalism in the last century now lead the world in the new forms of cannibalism' (Takada 1999: 134).

This normalisation of the industry of bodily repairs with the vital substances and organs of others is well illustrated by the story of Jemima Layzell, a 13-year-old girl whose decision to donate her organs in response to a battery of persistent appeals reportedly helped a 'record eight people to live' when her family donated her organs following her unexpected death in 2012 from a brain aneurysm.[16] This is how Jemima Layzell's body parts were harvested and consumed following her death:

> Jemima's heart, small bowel, and pancreas were transplanted into three people. Two people received her kidneys. Her liver was split and transplanted into another two people, while her lungs were transplanted into one patient. The eight recipients included five children, who came from all over England.[17]

There is a booming global market with a monster appetite and demand for human bodies and body parts, which body harvesters, not always acting legally or within the bounds of morality, work tirelessly round the clock to satisfy. Few health services the world over think twice before going hunting or appealing for body parts (Scheper-Hughes 2000, 2001a, 2001b, 2004; Noble 2011) and, in South Africa for example, it is not uncommon for the body parts of the poor in a public hospital morgue to be harvested without the knowledge or consent of their family or relations (Scheper-Hughes 2000: 199). The National Health Service Blood and Transplant unit of the UK is reportedly actively promoting sensitisation conversations within families to follow in Jemima's footsteps, 'because a shortage of donated organs is costing hundreds of lives every year'.[18] According to Rachel Naylor of the BBC, by October 2017, there were reportedly 6,406 people on the transplant waiting list across the UK, a situation further compounded by the fact that the families of the deceased sometimes block the donation of theirs organs despite their having registered to have them donated. As she put it, 'Organs from 505 registered donors could not be made available for transplant in the last five years because of objections from relatives'.[19] Many would be hard pressed not to see this and the growing proliferation of transplantation as cannibalism (Noble 2011). In the USA, where the yearly waiting list for human organ transplants runs easily into tens of thousands (Chae and Cooper 1997), when people go to get a driver's licence, they are given the option of checking the 'organ donor' box and have that designation appear on their licence.

Nancy Scheper-Hughes, who has written extensively on the growing global trafficking in human bodies, whole and in parts for medical consumption (Scheper-Hughes 2000, 2001a, 2001b, 2004), has called the phenomenon variously as 'the new cannibalism',[20] as 'late modern cannibalism' (Scheper-Hughes 2001a) and as 'neo-cannibalism' (Scheper-Hughes 2001b, 2001c).[21] Jemima's parents reportedly found the decision to deliver her corpse for medical cannibalisation hard to make.[22] Medical cannibalism seems increasingly like a global rhizome of vultures determined to scavenge away indiscriminately at dead, dying and impoverished bodies, for any flesh, bone or fluid to prop lives up. Are we increasingly headed for a future of 'the production of clones created specifically for providing spare body parts' (Takada 1999: 134), as well as a future of 'victimless cannibalism' through consumption of human muscle cells grown for food by use of in vitro meat technology (Schneider 2013: 1023)?

'Cannibalism exists. Cannibalism will continue as long as people exist', proclaims Shiguro Takada (1999: 133). To Claude Lévi-Strauss, who believes that we are all cannibals and that the reality of cannibalism must be perceived in all its ramifications, there are no sacred places and spaces or no-go areas for cannibalism, regardless of the purported level of development of a society. Defining cannibalism as the practice of 'intentionally introducing into the bodies of human beings parts or substances from other human bodies', Lévi-Strauss (2016 [2013]: 88) challenges us to approach our curiosity about cannibalism with open- and nimble-mindedness. Like others scholars (Rawson 1999; Lindenbaum 2004; Travis-Henikoff 2008; Brown 2013), Lévi-Strauss sees cannibalism as practised the world over in various ways and in different forms, and for different reasons. To Lévi-Strauss:

> Cannibalism can be practiced to meet nutritional needs (in times of scarcity or because of a taste for human flesh); it can be a political act (punishment for criminals or revenge against one's enemies); it can have a magical function (assimilation of the virtues of the deceased or, on the contrary, the casting out of their souls); or it can be part of a ritual (a religious cult, a feast of the dead or coming-of-age ceremony, or a rite to assure agricultural prosperity). Finally, it can be therapeutic, as attested by many prescriptions in ancient medicine and in Europe itself in the not-so-remote past. Injections of pituitary gland and grafts of human brain matter indisputably belong to that last category, as do organ transplants, which have become common practice (Lévi-Strauss 2016[2013]: 87–88).

As Zita Nunes observes, eating has its risks, and 'It is not always possible to keep what is perceived to be harmful outside of the body', as always present is 'the danger of an inadvertent taking into the body – through contagion, for example – that could lead to the destruction of the body' (Nunes 2008: 37–38). Lévi-Strauss illustrates his point with deaths in Great Britain, New Zealand, the United States and France, among women and children reportedly injected with 'hormone extracted from human pituitary glands ... or grafts from the brain membranes of humans' (Lévi-Strauss 2016[2013]: 85), and draws parallels with similar deaths in the 1950s from a mysterious virus 'kuru' that attacked the central nervous systems of New Guinean (specifically the Fore of Okapa) women and children thought to have been caused by their involvement with cannibalism (see also Tiffin 2007; Lindenbaum 2008, 2009).[23] Noting that among the Fore, the 'act of eating the corpse of certain close relatives was a means of demonstrating affection and respect' (Lévi-Strauss 2016[2013]: 85), Lévi-Strauss describes how the women[24] went about making a meal of their beloved corpse, their treatment of which might have resulted in the infection of their young children:

The flesh, viscera, and brains were cooked; the bones were ground up and served with vegetables. The women were in charge of cutting up the corpses and of the other culinary operations, and they were particularly fond of these macabre meals. It may be supposed that they became infected while handling contaminated brains and that they infected their young children through bodily contact (Lévi-Strauss 2016[2013]: 85).

Commenting on the same people and practice, Travis-Henikoff adds:

> The butchering of the corpse was performed away from the village, often in the women's sweet potato gardens where up to 40 women and children would gather for the event and subsequent feast. After de-fleshing the bodies with bamboo knives, Fore women used stone axes to disarticulate the body, cracking the long bones for the extraction of marrow and the cranium for the brain. Every single part of the body was consumed but for the teeth and bile sack. Sexual organs went to the closest kin of the opposite sex.
>
> When all meats, organs and offal had been processed and eaten, the remaining bones, and bone pieces, were placed by the fire pit. After a week or so of slow roasting, the bones would be pounded in bamboo containers and the resultant 'salt' would be sprinkled over cooked vegetables, offering a healthy dose of calcium. In the end there were no remains whatsoever to be found of the cannibalism that had taken place (Travis Henikoff 2008: 100–101).

Whether 'performed for reasons of survival, revenge, ritual mourning, religious realization or culinary satisfaction' (Travis-Henikoff 2008: 295), or done inadvertently by contamination (such as a person eating an animal or a fish that has eaten a person,[25] or the foetus eating the mother in the womb through the placenta as happens with all unborn children) (Avramescu 2009: 130), cannibalism is cannibalism, Lévi-Strauss insists, regardless of what route one adopts in consuming the other. Whether we consume the

27

other as a hard core meal of flesh and bone, or in the softer forms of bodily fluids (blood, sweat, urine, semen, breast milk, saliva, breath, tears or faeces)[26] or as ashes following cremation,[27] it all amounts to cannibalism. As Lévi-Strauss puts it rhetorically, there is little justification in limiting cannibalism to the ingestion of human flesh, when a human being can be consumed in many other ways:

> … what essential difference is there between the oral route and the blood route, between ingestion and injection, for introducing into an organism a little of the substance of another? People will say it is the bestial appetite for human flesh that makes cannibalism horrible. They will then have to restrict their condemnation to a few extreme cases and omit from the definition of cannibalism other attested cases, where it is imposed as a religious obligation, often performed with repugnance – revulsion even – expressed as faintness and vomiting. The distinction some would be tempted to make between a barbaric and superstitious custom on the one hand, a practice grounded in scientific knowledge on the other, would hardly be convincing either. Many uses of substances drawn from the human body, scientific from the standpoint of the ancient pharmacopoeia, are considered by us to be superstitions. And after a few years modern medicine itself proscribes treatments, formerly believed to be effective, because they have turned out to be useless if not harmful. The distinction appears to be less sharp than one would like to imagine (Lévi-Strauss 2016[2013]: 86).

In case you were in doubt, doubt no more: kissing and sexing are cannibalism too, following Lévi-Strauss above. Bodily fluids are involved and exchanged.

The history of global cannibalism and its variants in Europe is well documented (Takada 1999; White 2001; Price 2003; Lindenbaum 2004; Obeyesekere 2005; Travis-Henikoff 2008; Avramescu 2009; Noble 2011; Wilby 2013; Tsai 2016), leading Turner II to conclude that 'Europeans were rather good at cannibalism' (2008: 20), and still very much are, in various guises, including in music, film, literature and television (Brown 2013).

Even if confined purely to its medicinal dimensions, Europe indeed has a rich history of cannibalism (Noble 2011; Sugg 2006, 2013). In his essay, *Of Cannibals*, Michel de Montaigne – generally perceived, however contested, as 'a Renaissance purveyor of the concept of cultural relativism' (Johnson 1993: 153), who was keen to disabuse his fellow Frenchmen and Europeans of the tendency for radical alterity in defining and confining cannibalism among the so-called barbarians of the non-Western societies of distant geographies while turning a blind eye on far worse barbaric extremities of their own[28] – pointed out that so-called cannibals did not eat human flesh for the sake of nourishment but usually in extreme cases of revenge, just like his very own French ancestors did when besieged by Caesar in the city of Alésia (Montaigne 1943[1580]: 84–86); see also Célestin 1996: 54–57; Johnson 1993; Rawson 1999; Lefebvre 2005: 46; Williams 2012).[29]

Medicinal cannibalism has a long history in Europe, where prior to the 18th century, it was common practice for 'physicians … to use human flesh in all sorts of ways for our health, applying it either inwardly or outwardly' (Montaigne 1943[1580]: 85). As Gordon-Grube affirms, in the 16th, 17th and 18th centuries, medicinal 'cannibalism, involving human flesh, blood, heart, skull, bone marrow, and other body parts, was not limited to fringe groups of society, but was practiced in the most respectable circles' (Gordon-Grube 1988: 406). Corpse medicine was richly tolerated and highly valued, Richard Sugg argues, adding that at the same time that Europeans began to wonder at and revile the cannibals of America, 'the cannibals of Europe began their most systematic, widespread and profitable use of the human body', with 'the most privileged and educated Europeans … swallowing or applying human flesh, fat, bone and blood as medicine' (Sugg 2013: 825), the best supplies of which came in the form of mummies (Noble 2011), especially from Egypt (Sugg 2006). While executed prisoners were a main source of body substances, of particular efficacy was blood 'drunk immediately after the death of the person from whose body it was taken', and of especial potency was 'the blood of those who died violently in their prime' (Conklin 2001: 9). The harvesting, storage and consumption of human blood through transfusions of various kinds and bone marrow through transplants is an institutionalised practice in hospitals throughout Europe and globally. There is documentary evidence that Europe's practices of medicinal cannibalism such as the smearing of human wounds with fat extracted from human corpses followed Europe in its adventures into new worlds, even though Europe has done everything to erase its practices of consuming human body substances from its collective self-image (Conklin 2001: 11). As Louise Noble argues:

> By constructing the medical violation and consumption of human bodies as a desirable practice, early modern medical discourse offers a complex understanding of what it means for one human to consume the body of another. Corpse pharmacology constituted socially sanctioned ingestion of the human body, and the cannibalistic imagery produced by the medical treatment and deployment of corpses provided a useful tool for the early modern literary imagination. The attractiveness and effectiveness of cannibal imagery has much to do with its resemblance to the cannibal act itself. Embedded in competing discourses of cannibalism – symbolically suggestive as they are – is the prospect of the literal: that there are, somewhere in the world, humans who eat other humans (Noble 2011: 9).

Sugg draws our attention to the paradox of Europe's history of medicinal cannibalism when he remarks:

> Looking at traditional European attitudes to the 'savage' cannibals of the New World, few would have guessed that the real cannibals – those operating a vastly more widespread, systematic, commodified and proto-scientific form of man-eating – were in fact the Europeans themselves (Sugg 2013: 831).

Could such commitment to save lives with body parts borrowed – in the manner of the skull who borrows body parts in order to activate itself into a human being and transition into 'The Complete Gentleman' worthy of the attention of the most beautiful woman in the world, in Amos Tutuola's *The Palm-Wine Drinkard* (Tutuola

1952) – from the dead and even the living, a long-standing practice in Europe, possibly have something in common with proliferating stories in urban Africa of the harvesting and trafficking in body parts to feed the ever surging demands of the African 'traditional medicine' industry (Travis-Henikoff 2008: 275–286)?[30]

In rural and urban Africa, stories proliferate in newspapers and social media of cannibalism in all its forms as suggested by Lévi-Strauss above, from the harvest and ingestion of human flesh (from heart to genitals and the head) and human bodily fluids (semen, blood (menstrual and otherwise), urine, etc.)[31] to the strategic blending of human organs with various medicinal plants and portions for potency and related occult practices (Geschiere 1997, 2013; Masquelier 2000; Moore and Sanders 2001; Niehaus 2001; Nyamnjoh 2001; Wasserman 2010; Samba 2012). Ritual cannibalism in the form of human sacrifices for social and political healing feature every now and again in reports on wars of resistance and liberation, on secret societies or cults and initiation ceremonies of a cultural and religious nature (Ellis 1999; Richards 2009).

Is one tradition and practice of medicinal cannibalism more compassionate than the other, or is one form of compassion more sanitised, more ethical, more rational, more scientific, more civilised, more modern and, therefore, more authoritative and legitimate? How do both forms of medicinal compassionate cannibalism compare with the cannibalism of transubstantiation practised by the Catholic Christians among us, when at the sacrament of the Eucharist we eat the body and drink the blood of Jesus Christ, son of God, in communion, however real or symbolical (Kilgour 1990; McGowan 1994; Price 2003: 26–44; Travis-Henikoff 2008: 127; Noble 2011: 3; Duggan 2013; Callander 2014), even as the doctrine of resurrection of the body of the dead would portray the cannibal as a most diabolical anti-Divinity figure (Avramescu 2009: 135; see also McGowan 1994)? Is it a coincidence that in 2nd century Europe the perceived 'deviant diet' and 'religious practices involving human sacrifice' of Christians occasioned accusations of cannibalism against them (McGowan 1994: 427)?

As Travis-Henikoff reminds us, in the Christian Bible, while the 'overt acts of cannibalism are confined to the Old Testament, the New Testament commands the practice of symbolic cannibalism to all who believe in Christ' (Travis-Henikoff 2008: 125). This is evidence, she argues, that actual and symbolic cannibalism are two sides of the same coin and of the same moral and ethical quandary, for:

> As human beings our emotional reactions are basically similar to one another, and while one group may actually eat of the flesh of the dead, believing that doing so will allow their loved ones to continue their existence on the other side, others partake symbolically and emotionally in order to be at one with their god and gain eternal life (Travis-Henikoff 2008: 128).

Again, we are reminded of the argument by Lévi-Strauss, that cannibalism is cannibalism, symbolic or real, direct or indirect, virtual or otherwise, in Europe or elsewhere, among the supposedly primitive or the incredibly modern.

Understood in these terms, a description of cannibalism such as the following may have far more in common with hard- and soft-core pornography, with prostitution and pimping or selling bodies to eat, and with the technologically enhanced predatory voyeurism of global consumer television and social media than meets the nakedness of the yearning civilised eye. Indeed, if we are able to factor in as virtual, visual, voyeuristic or symbolic cannibalism the exploits of the global industries of desire and virtual reality (modelling, advertising, sex, sea, sand and entertainment, tourism, music, film, art creation and consumption, etc.) media and social media (including platforms such as Facebook, Instagram, Snapchat, WhatsApp, etc.), vulture-like celebrity spotting by endlessly fascinated paparazzi with preying lenses,[32] and superstars spectacularly chased and gobbled up like snacks by famished fandoms, the passage below by Travis-Henikoff, although initially written as a description of hard-core cannibalism among purportedly primitive savages, could easily and eloquently speak for any of the present day innovative forms of cannibalism. Food is food – be it for the belly, the mind and the soul or for the senses of the body, and be it solid, liquid, virtual or intangible – and food everywhere has its ethics, it sociality, and its politics. The text, informed by a string of outsider accounts in a context of unequal encounters between different categories of eaters and eaten, predators and preys, reads:

> Early writers, and later, professors, government officials, historians, clergymen and immigrants, observed that the Australian Aborigines thoroughly enjoyed human flesh, though some claimed the shunning of brains. Of male carcasses, the thigh was considered the choicest portion, whereas the breasts of a woman were most favored for their fat content. But the most sought after morsel was kidney fat or the kidneys themselves, which were regarded as the center of life. If a man was cannibalized out of revenge, the killer would carry some of the victim's flesh around with him in a 'basketwork', or 'dilly-bag', for good luck and strength. The flesh was rolled up in grass, and it was said that if a man felt weak in body or mind he would take out the flesh of his enemy and take a bite, thus feeding both mind and body while protecting himself from the spirit of his enemy (Travis-Henikoff 2008: 185–186).

As Friedman observes, 'Dismembered bodies, just as pornography, incite disgust at one level but canny attraction at another forbidden level' (Friedman 1991: 155).

David Pfennig has argued that 'Cannibals often must decide between investing in personal reproduction (by engaging in indiscriminate cannibalism) or "helping" a relative to reproduce (by not eating that relative)' (Pfennig 1997: 667). The text by Travis-Henikoff above suggests that cannibalism is far from being an indiscriminate act, even in terms of the actual eating of the eaten. Each cannibal or community of cannibals has a hierarchy of desirability, with choice and means. When we go out shopping or hunting for the meat of the day, what we are most likely to put in our hunting bags or shopping baskets, and what we are most likely to reject if we have the choice and means to pick and choose what we ingest, depends very much on the tastes that we have cultivated, the prestige and power that those tastes confer, and our personal or collective moral and ethical subscriptions and commitments.

Is there anything in common, directly or indirectly, between cannibalism inspired by the imperative to save, repair or renew lives, in modern or traditional medicine, with other forms of cannibalism (hair and body part transplants and implants, for example) undertaken to make one look more beautiful, more pleasing to the eye? How, for instance, does the consumption of human hair, harvested from women as part of religious ritual or forcefully by treasure hunters seeking a quick buck, such as depicted by Chris Rock in his 'Good Hair' documentary,[33] compare with compassionate medical cannibalism? Temples in India and other parts of Asia have found in African American and black women globally a 9 billion Dollar market for the hair of dead people, those routinely shaven for religious purposes, and others whose hair is harvested illegally (Nyamnjoh and Fuh 2014; Tarlo 2016).[34] As Emma Tarlo (2016) shows in her ethnographic study on the entangled web of the secret lives of hair, we consume hair in a rich variety of ways, ranging from wearing it on our heads, to eating it as food, through using it in cosmetics, clothes, ropes, personal and public collections.

Whatever similarities there are or not, compassionate cannibalism is as relevant, justifiable and justified in the 21st century, regardless of geography or purported level of civilisation, as it was in our distant pasts. Reasons for compassionate cannibalism need not always be the same, the world over. Among the Wari' prior to contact with Western prescriptivism, for example, 'cannibalism was done out of compassion for the person who was eaten, and ... for the bereaved relatives, as a way to help lessen their sorrow' (Conklin 2001: xvii–xviii). '[E]ating the dead was a social obligation considered necessary to ensure or promote collective well-being, not just the well-being of the individuals who ate the flesh.' (Conklin 2001: xxviii) Beth Conklin argues that compassionate cannibalism was pleasing to the spirit of the dead person and seldom for the self-gratification of the living, that only exceptionally did Wari' eat their own close blood relatives or spouses, and that they usually allowed those who had married into the family to assume the compassionate duty of eating up the dead, however nauseating. Not to eat for whatever reason, she argues, was tantamount to insulting the dead person's family and memory (Conklin 2001: xvii–xviii). Beth Conklin elaborates:

> Cannibalism used to be the normal treatment for all Wari' who died of any cause, except for a few circumstances in which bodies were cremated rather than eaten. In some funerals, especially funerals for children, all or most of the flesh was eaten. In funerals for adults and adolescents, often only part of the flesh was consumed (and the rest was burned), because the corpse was not roasted until two or three days of crying and eulogizing had passed, by which time it was nearly too decayed to stomach. Even then, Wari' still considered it important to consume at least some of the corpse. They did not eat their dead because they liked the taste of human flesh, nor because they needed the meat. Rather, they ate out of a sense of respect and compassion for the dead person and for the dead person's family (Conklin 2001: xvi).

Conklin contrasts funeral or mortuary endocannibalism among Wari' with accounts of similar practices by Melanesians, whose cannibalism, purportedly, was primarily motivated by a desire to retrieve and recycle the vital substances and energies contained in the bodies of the dead. As she explains, Melanesians had a shared:

> ... belief that cannibalism primarily benefited the individuals who ate the corpse, and the belief that the corpse contained substances or vital energies that needed to be recaptured and recycled into the bodies of those who consumed it. By eating pieces of the corpse, the dead person's relatives kept these vital elements circulating in their own bodies and kin group, in a kind of closed economy of body elements (Conklin 2001: xxviii).

According to Conklin, this Melanesian variant has heavily and disproportionately influenced Anglo-American theorists, who 'have tended to assume that incorporation – the idea of eating a corpse as a way for living people to absorb the dead person's vital energies or body substances – was always the motive behind mortuary cannibalism' (Conklin 2001: xxviii). Within the Melanesian interpretive tradition, some anthropological studies of cannibalism in Papua New Guinea associate the 'ritual devouring of morsels of one's enemies on the battlefield' with seeking 'to dominate and destroy them supernaturally' (Beidelman 1983: 934; see also Eve 1995). Conklin argues that:

> In contrast to endocannibalism in Melanesia, which aimed to preserve, perpetuate, and redistribute elements of the deceased, South American endocannibalism more often had the objective of *eradicating* the corpse in order to *sever* relations between the dead person's body and spirit, and between living people and the spirits of the dead (Conklin 2001: xxviii).

The contrast notwithstanding, there is absolutely no reason why the motivation to retain the vital life substances of the body of the deceased cannot co-exist with the motivation that eating the body would save it from decay and lessen the mourner's grief. Just as eating does not have to be a direct ingestion or incorporation of flesh to qualify as such, as studies of sexual cannibalism such as necrophilia, the act of having sex and deriving sexual pleasure from a corpse practised, among others by gravediggers and mortuary attendants, would attest (Aggrawal 2009). Consuming desire as 'a total human phenomenon' and a form of elevation or absorption into a superior life (Friedman 1991: 155–156) could lead one to kill those they crave, make love to their corpse and make a meal of their choicest body parts, as the following account by Jonathan Friedman of a young Japanese male doctoral student and a young female Dutch French literature student in Paris makes evident:

> In 1984 a young Japanese student completing a doctoral degree in Paris met a substantially larger young Dutch girl in Paris to study French literature. The two became good friends, but the Japanese man had more amorous designs on young woman. Time and time again he tried to seduce his friend, but to no avail. She insisted on a pure friendship relation. One evening he invited her to dinner at his

36

place and wasted little time in murdering her and making love to her still luke-warm corpse. Following this first taste of love, he, not without finesse, carved her body, separating the inedible portions, the head and innards, from the delicacies such as breasts, thighs, sirloin, and filet. After enjoying a rather brusque meal of raw flesh, he packed the waste portions in heavy-duty garbage bags and deposited them in the Bois de Boulogne. He carefully packed the delicacies into his refrigerator and, in the ensuing weeks, indulged himself in lonely banquets steak *saignant*, stews, and other tasty morsels. Needless to say, he was soon covered by the police, and like the proud witches and cannibals of old he confessed willingly to his deed (Friedman 1991: 154).

The young Japanese not only willingly confessed to his deed, he added that he had always desired being able to eat a pretty young girl with whom he was in love. 'His consumption of her body was also the consummation of his love.' (Friedman 1991: 154) Even in the adult entertainment industry where resolving the tension between consumption and consummation is not a primary focus, it is not uncommon for eating to be associated with more than just oral ingestion, as the following exchange from the documentary *After Porn Ends*, illustrates: 'That's a tasty little pussy you've got', observes the male actor; 'Why don't you come over and taste it', replies the female actress.[35] '[T]he eating of human beings, or parts of human bodies, need be neither violent nor contemptuous.' (Burley 2016: 500) The creativity that feeds the horror movie industry, where 'having an old friend for dinner' is part of the menu (Bellamy 2014: 6),[36] does not suggest otherwise (Lefebvre 2005; Brown 2013; Bellamy 2014). Indeed, every now and again, in ordinary everyday interactions between parents and children, and among lovers, one comes across statements such as 'You smell good enough to eat'.

Cannibalism can be incentivised both by love and by hate, by fascination and by fear. Not all cannibalism practised by Wari' was compassionate. They also reportedly ate the enemy corpses of war captives. While the 'manner in which they roasted and consumed their own dead conveyed honor and respect for the person who was eaten', the manner in which 'they handled and ate enemy corpses explicitly marked the enemy as a nonperson and expressed hostility and hatred' (Conklin 2001: xxiii). Cannibalism as freezing the 'Other' out of a common humanity and rendering them into enemies as a justification or impetus to prey on them in the manner of animals of the wild has been the subject of abundant, albeit contentious, literature and theorisation (Taussig 1987; Célestin 1996; Guest 2001b; Obeyesekere 2005; Lefebvre 2005; Avramescu 2009; Brown 2013; Fairhead 2015; Ng 2015; Mar 2016) and provides the substantive metaphorical fodder for this essay. However, as Conklin rightly argues, to see cannibalism only in destructive terms as a process of ingestion or incorporation of a fellow human being is to miss out on its creative, transformative and dissociative dimensions (Conklin 2001: xxvii). She elaborates:

> Cannibalism was not just a destructive act; it also was a creative act. Besides eradicating the corpse, the ritual in which the eating of the dead occurred presented mourners with dramatically new images as they watched their loved one's body be cut up and roasted, much like game, divided into pieces that progressively became less and less identifiable, more and more similar in appearance to animal meat. This is another piece in the puzzle of Wari' funerary cannibalism: it made graphic statements about the loss of human identity and the destiny of the human spirit, and about meat-eating and the relations among people, and between humans and animals, through which food is produced and exchanged (Conklin 2001: xxi).

The fact of rendering the meat of the corpse 'less and less identifiable, more and more similar in appearance to animal meat' is very significant, and resonates with how so-called witches are known to behave in some African circles, for example. In many an African community, where real and imagined cases of rampant cannibalism were the subject of many a contentious publication prior to and during colonialism, one is more likely in the postcolonial context to come across accusations of witchcraft and occult practices than encounters with the consumption of human flesh in any direct and matter-of-fact manner (Geschiere 1995,

1997, 2013; Ashforth 2000; Moore and Sanders 2001; Niehaus 2001; Kirkaldy 2005; Mavhungu 2012).

Those who fail to see 'the body as a place where relationships are formed and transformed' and where ties are tightened and loosened, are reluctant to provide for the sort of compassion and emotional attachments to intimate others, as a justification for the all-consuming sociality of the living mourning the dead (Conklin 2001: xxi), and/or divining ever innovative ways of eating the other up without appearing to do so.[37] They see cannibalism as little more than a fringe or dying practice, limited to those whom civilisation has left behind, to those steeped in problematic occult beliefs and practices, and to those caught in situations of extreme hunger, fury and vengeance, overpopulation and effusive religious enthusiasm or stuck between a rock and a hard place where extreme necessity supposedly knows no law, such as wars, shipwrecks and being lost in the wilderness (Avramescu 2009: 85; Brown 2013: 6–7; Fairhead 2015; Esteban 2016).[38] How does such insistence and persistence in depictions of 'cannibalism … [as] a potent symbol of savagery' (Comaroff and Comaroff 1991: 123) square with the reality of the consuming passions and squirming appetites of being human as a dynamic process of being sensitive to the opportunities and opportunisms of nature and nurture in conversation?

Being Human as Eating and Being Eaten

If we are *what* we eat (Gabaccia 1998; Reynolds 2009) or *whom* we eat (Tsai 2016), then we can understand why cultural identities tend to be dictated by dietary taboos around eating and the eaten, and distinctions between insiders and outsiders can take the form of what and how one eats (Goody 1982; Nyamnjoh and Rowlands 2013; Klein and Murcott 2014). In this context, as Kilgour puts it, 'cannibalism provides an image for the construction of clear boundaries between groups: "we" are civilized and eat nicely, "they" are barbaric and eat savagely; "we" eat normally, "they", perversely' (Kilgour 1997: 20). It could, as well, amount to the blurring of boundaries and to dramatising 'the danger of drawing boundaries too absolutely' or 'not drawing them at all' (Kilgour

2001: viii), when the traditionally eaten begins to eat the eater (Callander 2014). Reynolds seeks to portray this turning of the tables, in her study of literary cannibalism among francophone writers as an aggressive and transgressive act aimed at desacralising and neutralising the oppressive authorial supremacy of European imperialism (Reynolds 2009). It is thus of interest, to explore how representations of cannibalism have historically enforced and dissolved identity boundaries and their ideological accoutrements, and the extent to which such representations could be said to give voice to the diverse marginal groups which they are intended to silence, to question the dominant ideologies they are evoked to support, and to shed light on the predicament of a shared humanity between cannibals and their victims if both are perceived and represented as absolute opposites (Guest 2001a).

In the game of life characterised by unequal encounters between individuals and cultures compelled to share places and spaces like scorpions in a lidded basket, it would appear that the question is not so much whether cannibalism is possible but rather who is eating whom, how and why, and the power relations that render such eating or being eaten visible and invisible in particular ways and contexts (Geschiere 1997, 2013; Ellis 1999; Guest 2001a, 2001b; Lindenbaum 2004; Avramescu 2009). Little wonder that the mission to civilise so-called savages (within and between societies) is sometimes presented as an education of culinary practices, meant to dictate not only what is eaten but how it is eaten. As Wankier demonstrates in her analysis of popular travel accounts of imperial England, this logic permeated and propelled 'consuming narratives' of 16th and early 17th century encounters between European adventurers and conquerors and the non-European 'Other' they systematically represented as inferior from *what* and *how* they ate (Wankier 2016). This is the case in the encounter between Robinson Crusoe and Friday – or the purported meeting between savage cannibalism and a cannibalising civilisation – in Daniel Defoe's novel, when the former uses the purported delights of English cooking[39] to impress the latter to give up human flesh (Jooma 1997, 2001; Avramescu 2009: 173). In other words, as a 'consuming explorer' or an 'exploring consumer' Robinson Crusoe

(Kilgour 1997: 22) uses English cooking as bait to lure Friday to the colonial butchery of his culturally informed sense of self and being human. The power relations implicit in eating and being eaten, as well as in determining who eats what, how and why, leads Mackintosh to draw the following conclusion on the political significance of representations of cannibals and carnivores in *Robinson Crusoe*:

> ... [T]he question of who (or what) may eat what (or whom) is shown to be inseparable from the broader questions raised by the novel around sovereignty, conquest and citizenship. Killing and eating a body, whether animal or human, is a direct expression of power; so too is dictating what others may or may not eat. Most obviously, cannibalism is used by Crusoe as a justification for his conquest and suppression of the native population; as a corrective to their unnatural appetite, he teaches the savages to slaughter and eat goats (Mackintosh 2011: 24).

Mackintosh further argues that, as a necessary step the eventual enslavement or destruction of his savages, Crusoe condemns their 'inhumanity' while reinforcing his own humanity (Mackintosh 2011:39; see also Jooma 1997, 2001). Despite such concerted efforts at creating and maintaining rigid distinctions between humans and animals, Europeans and cannibals, eaters and the eaten, the realities of encounters and interactions between categories result in inextricable interconnections and fluidities (Mackintosh 2011: 39). This leads Mackintosh to conclude: 'A colonial project which begins by asserting the difference between humans and animals ends by collapsing it, revealing that under the colonial gaze, some humans at least have been animals all along.' (Mackintosh 2011: 25)

Humans and Animals as Two Sides of the Same Cannibal Feast

In many a non-Western postcolonial context where Christian and colonial ethics and morality have become part of a complex of civilisational repertoire, the language of eating and being eaten

41

continues to be used during accusations and counter accusations on involvement in witchcraft, not in any direct sense, but through indirections such as the negative and violent words people employ in addressing one another, or in talking about others in their absence. Words are powerful, and words can kill, one hears repeatedly. Attitudes and behaviour matter and, without actually being physically violent towards someone, confrontational attitudes and callous indifference to their person and their humanity is considered violent and violating enough to amount to killing and making a meal of them. Every now and again, one comes across a statement such as: '(S)He sucked the life out of me', suggesting that the person making the statement has been eaten up, and is as good as dead. Even when those accused of having eaten another up to the point of rendering them dead in real terms by means of witchcraft own up to doing so, it is seldom a case of consuming human flesh directly. In the Cameroon Grassfields it is believed that witches have the capacity to transform themselves and their prey into animals before preying upon the latter – hence the characterisation of such eating as mysterious, beyond matter-of-fact (Samba 2012). Just like the Wari' in Conklin's ethnography, when witches gather and decide to make a meal of someone, usually a family member or an intimate other, that person is magically transformed to the animal of choice of the witches gathered, before they proceed to make a meal of the person. In other words, even when someone is actually eaten up, he or she is seldom eaten up as human flesh; he or she becomes a meal only indirectly by assuming the guise of the meat of an animal which humans treat as game and are familiar with as food.

Carlos Fausto seems to suggest something similar in his discussion of cannibalism in an Amazonian context and cosmology where the dichotomies and dualisms between humans and animals are often blurred in attitudes and practices around food and eating (Fausto 2007). Beth Conklin adds that 'in Amazonian cosmologies, cannibalism mediates the human spirit's transition from life to death, from mortal human to a new immortal identity in the afterlife'. Among the Yanomami, for example, 'every death is seen as an act of cannibalism in which the human soul is devoured by a spirit or an enemy', while among the Araweté (Tupian speakers of Pará) of Brazil, the popular belief is that 'at death, human spirits are cannibalized by the gods, then rejuvenated and transformed into gods themselves' (Conklin 2001: xxvi; see also Maranhão 1998; Vilaca 2000; Burley 2016).

As Suzanne Oakdale reiterates in her review of Conklin's *Consuming Grief*, among the Wari', 'human life is bound up in a series of cannibalistic exchanges with the animal world', with 'several species of animals believe to have human souls', and with the same animals in a position to 'provide humans with the safest and most nourishing meat, but also ultimately "eat" the souls of the Wari', causing death' (Oakdale 2004: 184). Wari's cosmology of interconnection and circulation between humans and animals does not stop with death, as relationships of 'reciprocity and predation between souls with animal bodies and human bodies' (Oakdale 2004: 1984) are expected to continue in life and death: 'After death, human souls can then take on animal bodies (usually white-lipped peccaries) and offer themselves as game to feed their living relatives – a sign, read by the living, that the dead still care for them.' (Oakdale 2004: 184)

Hence Conklin's conclusion: To 'live as a fully civilized human being is to act as both predator and prey, eater and eaten, in a cosmic dynamic' (p. 195, cited in Oakdale 2004: 184; see also Vilaca 2000) of myriad interconnections, entanglements and manglements among humans, animals, nature, super-nature and culture. This belief and action in accordance with the 'nondifferentiation between humans and animals' is, according to Eduardo Viveiros de Castro, 'virtually universal' in Amerindian cosmology. A cosmology in which *being human* (and not *being animal*) is what both humans and animals share as a common origin. Hence, to Amerindians, any animal is capable of humanity and 'animals have a human, sociocultural inner aspect that is "disguised" by an ostensibly bestial bodily form', which makes *being human or being an animal much more than meets the eye* (Viveiros de Castro 2004: 464–468). Within this logic, Viveiros de Castro argues, one understands:

... why death in Amazonia involves being transformed into an animal: if the souls of animals are conceived as possessing a primordial human corporeal form, then it is logical that human souls would be conceived as having the posthumous form of a primordial animal, or as entering a body that will eventually be killed and eaten by the living (Viveiros de Castro 2014[2009]: 155–156).

These intersections, interconnections and continuities between humans and animals are even more compelling if one takes DNA measurements seriously – as, for instance, 'the DNA of chimpanzees is 95 per cent to 98.7 per cent the same as that of humans', depending on the measurements used, even if such ambiguities have no place in law, where animals are systematically treated as inferior to humans who are equally subjected to legal hierarchies and discriminations[40] (see also Van Beers 2012).

Similar beliefs in cannibalism, zombies and the transformation of human beings into animals for food and hunting for food are reported in Haiti, where eating and feeding are a central organising principle of life and social relations (Bourguignon 1959; Marcelin 2012). As Alex Mackintosh observes in relation to cannibalism and animal slaughter in Daniel Defoe's novel *Robinson Crusoe*, the cannibal and the carnivore are far more bound together than they might appear (Macintosh 2011). Indeed, beliefs in transmutation and transubstantiation between humans and animals and things that blur the boundaries between human and non-human, natural, cultural and supernatural are widespread across Africa and the African diaspora (Bourguignon 1959; Zulaika 1993; Ellis 1999; Thornton 2003; Richards 2009; Marcelin 2012; Fardon 2014), as well as among other non-Western cultures around the globe (Miller 1995; Podruchny 2004).

Cosmologies and ontologies informed by the fluid interconnections and ambiguities between humans and animals, and by beliefs and practices whereby 'humans and animals can turn into each other by temporarily taking on one another's bodies' for greater potency and efficacy (Willerslev 2004: 629) are far more commonly held in the non-Western hemisphere than is the tendency in canonical dualistic Western thought to articulate personhood and animalhood through radical dichotomisation between the human and the animal, the cultural and the natural (Willerslev 2007: 12). Commenting on alterity, identity and difference in tales of hospitality and cannibalism along the Southern Silk Route linking China, Burma and India, Lucien Miller remarks: 'Regarding food or its lack, the association between eating meat and human flesh is frequently intimated, and the bridge linking carnivore and cannibal is crossed, especially in tales where human protagonists identify with animals and birds' (Miller 1995: 142).

In the writings of the Nigerian storyteller, Amos Tutuola, where humans can transform themselves into just about anything – from animals to plants, through insects, creepy-crawlies, water and air – and regain their human form as need be, we are introduced to universe of interconnections between the human, the animal and the non-human, the world of human agency and the bush of ghosts, the visible and invisible, nature, culture and supernature, that would suggest that the mere act of eating anything (including drinking water and breathing) implies the possibility of eating a human being, in one form or another (Nyamnjoh 2017b). In Amos Tutuola's universe of infinite interconnections and entanglements, a universe shared in popular beliefs and perceptions of reality across Africa:

> Everyone and everything is malleable and flexible, from humans and their anatomies, to animals and plants, gods, ghosts and spirits. Anything can be anything. People and things adopt different forms and manifest themselves differently according to context and necessity. Something transformed can regain the state that preceded its transformation. A thing can double itself, and the double becomes the thing and the thing the double. A shadow is not always only a shadow, just as a thing is not always only a thing. Masters are servants and servants are masters. Humbling ambiguity is the order of the day. Gods are humans and humans are gods. Spirits assume human forms, and humans can transform themselves into spirits, animals and plants. Sometimes a creature combines multiple forms of being – half-human and half-animal or half-plant, half-god, half-ghost, half-spirit, half-male or half-female, etc. – and assumes the consciousness akin to each form, even as it retains the consciousness of its form of origin to

facilitate reverting. It is a universe of agency ad infinitum, one in which structures exist only to the extent that they can be humbled by the agency of those who make structures possible (Nyamnjoh 2017b: 136–137).

An analysis of *The Texas Chainsaw Massacre* series as a genre of cannibal films in the USA reveals an interconnection between food, class and power, in which the cannibal is variously portrayed as a starving member of the working class who eats humans to survive, to the cannibal as an embodiment of a warrior class where being a good soldier depends on being a cannibal, through the cannibal as a member of the middle class whose cannibalism is an expression and endorsement of unfettered capitalism (Bernard 2011). Rogue capitalism – capitalism without a human face – amounts to cannibalism gone wild (Lefebvre 2005).

The centrality of eating and feeding, and the possibility of death being only temporal given the likelihood of the dead person being turned into a zombie and revived to keep alive the cycle of eating and being eaten, speaks of cannibalism more as a process of nibbling and dying by degree than an instance of a five course meal of a freshly dismembered human. It is dangerous and indeed threatening to social reproduction, to swallow others in whole – (in the manner of the boa constrictor) only to stay immobilised by the weighty burden of what one has taken in – instead of eating in measured portions, and in tune with the need for a careful balance between the need to eat and the obligation to avail oneself to be eaten.

It would appear eating as religion and eating religiously might hold the key to understanding cannibalism not only among the Aztecs – who 'understood themselves to dwell within an eating landscape, and ... reciprocated by eating the gods who ate them' (Carrasco 1995: 459) – as David Carrasco (1995) suggests, but to understanding cannibalism in its dynamic complexities, indirections and ambivalences globally. If we provide for cosmologies and ontologies of interconnection and conviviality between the human, the natural and the supernatural, how does the idea of the human, the animalistic and the divine co-existing in an entangled and mangled sense in the same body, the same mind and indeed, the same soul, configure or reconfigure our understanding of and attitudes to cannibalism? Put differently, how is our thinking informed or influenced by the realisation that humans can transform themselves into animals and animals into humans, just as the gods/divine can inhabit the bodies of humans and animals (Bourguignon 1959; Zulaika 1993; Maranhão1998; Moore and Sanders 2001; Niehaus 2001; Thornton 2003; Willerslev 2004; Fausto 2007; Sanders 2008; Marcelin 2012; Nyamnjoh 2017b)? And to what extent does the dominant literature on cannibalism framed largely around assumptions and presumptions of ontologies and epistemologies of dualism and binary opposition, do justice to the realities of cannibalism seen through the prism of permanent and open-ended interconnections and continuous transformations between nature and culture, animal and human, natural and supernatural, eating and being eaten (Willerslev 2004, 2007; Tiffin 2007; Nyamnjoh 2017b)? How are technological advances that make it possible for human heart, liver and other cells and embryos to be grown in pigs, for example, and then transplanted in humans who need the relevant body parts replaced, likely to further complicate the distinction between humans and animals, cannibals and carnivores (Chae and Cooper 1997)? Put differently, how does the persistence of cannibalism in so-called modern societies problematise, contest or even annihilate the myth of autonomous independent entities or categories (be these individuals, societies, cultures or civilisations), with clearly differentiated boundaries between the self and the other, us and them, insiders and outsiders, nature and culture (Kilgour 1997: 21)? There is much to chew on in Kilgour's conclusion that 'The horror of cannibalism lies not in its figuration of radical otherness and difference but in its embodiment of undifferentiation and the disappearance of the principle of alterity' (Kilgour 1997: 35).

The indirect forms of consumption of the human alluded to above are also evident in newer or more modern forms of witchcraft, where the violence is not meant to result in an immediate and final death, but rather in a form of death by degree. In such instances, witches who decide to kill someone are more likely to opt for soft and prolonged death, than going for instant death and finitude. When that option is made, the person targeted may disappear from their home community and familiar circles through a soft death and soft burial to reappear elsewhere in a distant land where he or she is a little known stranger, and where he or she is made, forced or compelled to slave away like zombies for the gratification and enrichment of the witch that has implanted him or her in that distant location, and controls his or her senses and willpower. The targeted person is usually considered dead by the community he or she has left behind, but the witch knows him or her to be alive (even if only barely), and is in constant contact with the person to collect the earnings from his or her toil and sweat (Bourguignon 1959; Ardener 1996; Geschiere 1997, 2013). Could there be a connection between this form of witchcraft and the Arab and European raids for slaves and for labour to work in distant lands and distant plantations that many an African villager in the hinterlands of the continent could only dream nightmarishly and mourn about? Could such raids have led the Africans who stayed back to consider the men and women caught in the raid as lost to the cannibalism of the raiders?

Even among Wari' who reportedly used to practise cannibalism as a normal compassionate way of disposing of the dead, the younger generation are, since burials were introduced and normalised by crusading outsiders, keen to distance themselves from the 'forest' ways and curious customs of their grandparents that allowed for eating the dead (Conklin 2001: xix). With the death, passing or sacrifice of the strange customs of their grandparents, one is curious to find out what symbolic and/or other modern forms of cannibalism have been developed or adopted by Wari' of the 21st century in replacement for both the compassionate and hostile cannibalism of yesteryear.

Thus, beyond the obvious cases of cannibalism motivated by compassion, medical or symbolic, exceptional or mainstream, should we really, in the 21st century, be absolving ourselves and our purportedly modern civilisation of cannibalism that lightly? Do old habits die that easily? If cannibalism was really as widespread prior to contact with Europe or the West as is often reported, are we to believe that those who allegedly practised it gave up so easily? Without a fight? If colonialism itself has proved so resilient despite the advent of the postcolony, why are we so keen to suppose that the cannibalism practised before colonialism simply vanished once the colonial missionary, state and government legislated against it? If cannibalism points to a lack of civilisation as Daniel Defoe may be said to suggest in *Robinson Crusoe* (Jooma 1997, 2001; Macintosh 2011), how do those who have acquired some measure of civilisation police and watch over their precious civilisation to avoid slipping back into cannibalism (Montaigne 1943[1580]; Célestin 1996: 28–62; Hulme 1998; Uhlir 2016)? Put differently, if the cannibalism one has given up, under duress or freely, in favour of civilisation is always lurking at the margins of that civilisation, posing a constant danger and always attempting to undo the civilisation, how does one ensure that the cannibalism at the frontiers or margins of a cherished civilisation is policed with vigilance? Can one categorically rule out the possibility of vulnerability however fireproofed a civilisation is in its fortification against cannibalism?

As Merrall Price observes, it is a paradox that 'as allegations of cannibalism function to place the accused outside the borders of civilization, they simultaneously work against themselves, reaffirming the humanity of the accused' (Price 2003: 25). Thus, if we suppose that cannibalism in its multiple forms did not simply disappear but was driven underground and continues to manifest itself through various indirections, would it not be of interest to document such indirections? If cannibalism has become, or was always a chameleon, are we not curious to know how, where and why it has camouflaged itself in the interest of continuing with business as usual even when the circumstances are proving unusual?

The same argument on the resilience and multifaceted dimensions of cannibalism applies to Europe or the West, and its tendency to rush into claims of absolutes in rupture with tradition and embrace of modernity and civilisation as evidence of the absence or scarcity of cannibalism within its ranks. If mobility and its technologies have expanded and proliferated around the world beyond their narrow confines during the age of European voyages of discovery, conquest and territorial expansionism, and if it is a lot easier for the traditionally immobilised 'native savages' and their purported exoticism to move flexibly across rural, urban, national, regional, transnational and continental boundaries and borders, should it surprise anyone that the so-called 'mobile natives' move with their cultures and logics of practice, influencing and being in turn influenced in the process by the cultures and logics of practice of the 'civilised moderns' they encounter in their mobility, home and away (Célestin 1996; Lindenbaum 2009; Nyamnjoh 2013)?

And should we be surprised if – thanks to the flexibility and mutuality of mobility and the resilience of the fact of a common humanity despite hierarchical relationships of power and dominance informed by race and geography, among other things – the various realities and imaginaries on and around cannibalism were to blend together and become inextricably entangled and mangled up creatively around the conundrum of eating and being eaten (consumed and being consumed) as a marker of the contingencies of being and becoming in a universe of a multiplicity of universal particularisms (Ranger 2007)? Whether or not influenced by mobile 'native savages' of yesteryear, it is possible, in the 21st century, for a European cannibal to take advantage of the latest information and communication technologies to advertise with detailed specification whom he or she would like to prey upon. An example in this regard is the case of a 41-year-old German computer technician, Armin Meiwes, whose horror-films-fuelled 'childhood fantasies of eating school friends' developed between the ages of 8 and 12 pushed him to advertise 'on the internet for a well-built male prepared to be slaughtered and then consumed'. A 43-year-old man, named Bernd-Jurgen Brandes, answered the advert in March 2001. Meiwes took the volunteer to his home in Rotenburg, cut off, flambéed and ate Brandes's penis before stabbing him repeatedly in the neck, dissecting the corpse and eating some of it. Meiwes was subsequently tried and sentenced to life imprisonment in what was termed 'Germany's first cannibalism case'.[41] This leaves one to wonder what the Hitler-engineered antisemitism and its attendant holocaust or what the massive killings in World War II and the genocide unleashed upon the

Herero people of Namibia under German colonialism amounted to if not as pogroms or as orgies of spectacular collective violence – ritual cannibalism – at the service of ambitions of racial supremacy and dominance.

Drawing on such metaphor of resilient cannibalism to understand the dynamics of cultural encounters in Brazil, it has been suggested that far from copying foreign influence, indigenous Brazilian populations have tended rather to ingest, digest and absorb such foreign influences 'as a precondition for the creation of a new, more independent national civilisation' (Nunes 2008: 11, 32). This effectively suggests that in situations of mobility and encounters of people and cultures, a new civilisation can only truly materialise through multiple acts of cannibalism, in one form or another, and with or without its ambivalences.

Is it not thinking the unthinkable to perceive civilisation and modernity as a form of large-scale institutionalised cannibalism? Indeed, is not the very idea of progress and development only meaningful thanks to the cannibalisation of that which one is progressing or seeking to develop away from? Take the case with the Aborigines of Australia, who may have been labelled cannibals by the encroaching white man but who since the landing of Captain Cook, suffered one indignation after another, including mass killings and decimating dispossession (Travis-Henikoff 2008: 188–189). Is not power and privilege built around and marinated by spurious ideologies of superiority or supremacy of race, place, class, culture, religion, gender, age and sexuality, inter alia, successful only to the extent that those perceived and represented as inferior within the scheme of things are systematically cannibalised socially, politically and economically? It takes cannibalism in one form or another to dispossess, debase and impoverish *en masse* entire social categories and groups of being specifically defined and confined for the purpose of being seen and treated as disposable humanity.

Guaranteeing a life of sumptuous superabundance for some means a death sentence and annihilation for others. Just as a war is no less a bloodbath simply because it has been outsourced to drones, cannibalism is no less the eating up of someone and their vital energies by labelling or signposting it as development, progress, civilisation or in the interest of the nation-state. As Avramescu argues, due to a revision of mores in Europe with the enlightenment, the dismemberment of the human body was no longer seen as a spectacle worthy of a civilised nation. Even before, butchers in the Middle Ages, who used to carry out for neighbours their activities in public places such as communal courtyards and street sides, found themselves banished to abattoirs in order to keep bleeding flesh out of the public gaze. It is possible that with these developments and heightened sensitivities and sensibilities to dismemberment of bodies and blood-dripping flesh, cannibalism was thrust into the shadows and the underground of collective representations. The cannibal, turned citizen, becomes an exceptional figure whose monstrous fascination with the morbid is domesticated, cultivated and professionalised, among others, by surgeons and performers of autopsies whose consumption of corpses is not necessarily literal, and who do so on the basis of the expertise for which they earn a living (Avramescu 2009: 49).

Cannibalism in Camouflage

Limiting cannibalism to its literal and predictable dimensions is to ignore cannibalism in camouflage, mutable and capable of materialising in myriad guises, places and spaces (Kilgour 1990; Lefebvre 2005; Brown 2013), be these in personal or institutionalised relationships. It amounts to ignoring cannibalism as a guise or a metaphor mobilised 'to make sense of different fears' (Jancovich 2013: x) and fascinations. Limiting our understandings of cannibalism amounts to us outsourcing to scapegoats the reality of our very own cannibalism and the cannibalism of our institutions and normalised ways of life, something which at a point in history was practised by Britain when it exiled its criminals to places such as Australia, to dwell and exercise their criminal-mindedness among purportedly inhuman savages and cannibals (Avramescu 2009: 48).

The British did more than outsource its criminals to other geographies. They outsourced their most dehumanising stereotypes and caricatures to other races, other bodies and/or anatomies defined and confined as amoral, beneath humanity and desperately needing redemption by divine intervention. Even apparently upright, sophisticated and self-critical British adventurers, officers, facilitators and chroniclers of encounters with the Other were not unknown to be guilty of (re)activating and projecting onto this Other the vile fantasies of 'grim tales of witches, ghosts, ogres, and bogeymen that ate human flesh' into which they had been socialised right from their nursery years (Obeyesekere 2005: 29). As Harry Sewlall observes, colonial representations in popular literature reinforced taken-for-granted stereotypical portrayals of the non-European Other as savage, childlike simpletons and cannibals, thereby serving not only to claim moral superiority and 'justify conquest and genocide', but also to reveal the cannibalistic side of the human nature of the conquering, genocidal and colonising European (Sewlall 2006: 171).

In failing to see cannibalism in our institutionalised journalism, political rhetoric, religious fundamentalism and everyday speech as modern humans and social actors, we fail as well to see how we could use language to eat up people's perceptions and sensibilities, and sometimes, but not always, their lives, as well as to eat ourselves up (Chesbro 1990). This is to miss out on the fascinating creativity and subtlety with which cannibalism ensures continuity for itself and ourselves despite our proclaimed limitation in imaginative capacity in its regard (Lefebvre 2005; Brown 2013; Ng 2015). Mislabelling and signposting wrongly makes it possible for our cannibalism to get away with orgies of massacres. Humanity can ill afford the keeping up of appearances by allowing cannibalism to pass for what it is not. If civilisation, modernity, citizenship, nationality and the sovereign nation-state are not possible without the cannibalisation of others through a rigid reproduction of difference that flies in the face of the universality of sameness, what purpose and whose interests are served by a deaf insistence on such labels as a hard currency? Who stands to benefit from the cannibalisation of whom from constantly shifting goalposts of tolerable mobility, citizenship, belonging, morality and ethics?

It is cannibalism out of control when, consumed by hatred and bigotry, we seek to make outsiders of obvious insiders, and aliens of fellow humans, using such spurious excuses as race, nationality, ethnicity, geography, culture, religion, class, gender, sexuality, generation or other categories such as migrant. When we act to diminish the life chances of others (such as the rescinding by the Trump administration in the US in late 2017 of the Deferred Action for Childhood Arrivals (DACA) of the Obama administration) – a move that stands to affect an estimated 800,000 Dreamers (those who arrived the US as infants or were born in the US of illegal 'alien' parents, and are classified as 'undocumented' immigrants)[42] – what else could it be but cannibalism? What is it about the United States of America if not racialised cannibalism that, as a study reported in *The New York Times* shows, even in the 21st century, 'Black boys raised in America, even in the wealthiest families and living in some of the most well-to-do neighborhoods, still earn less in adulthood than white boys with similar backgrounds'? Indeed, 'White boys who grow up rich are likely to remain that way', while 'Black boys raised at the top, however, are more likely to become poor than to stay wealthy in their own adult households'.[43]

There are deep historical roots of unequal encounters to the racialised cannibalism of the United States of America. To paraphrase George Fitzhugh, who was writing in the context of racialised American capitalism and the hierarchies of labour – devalued black slave labour and more competitive white labour – his provocations and anti-abolitionism aside, respectable as we may appear (as masters or as slaves without masters in a highly racialised capitalist setting as the United States of America), we are 'cannibals all', when we do not labour or are successfully trying to live without labour on the unrequited labour of others – those whom in our purportedly respectable eyes are often low, bad and disreputable people (Fitzhugh 1988[1960]: 16), while simultaneously rendering our toiling zombies, black, white, brown and yellow, socially and politically invisible, non-existent or quite simply, less than human, be they obviously enslaved or apparently free labour.

Averting such cannibalisation of the labour of others, be it targeted at enslaved Africans of yesteryear or at aliens and Dreamers in present-day America, requires the careful balance between work and leisure, dependence and independence, moral particularism and universalism, which Amos Tutuola proposes in

54

the story of the palm-wine drinkard. For the drinkard to qualify to 'do no other work more than to drink palm-wine ... from morning till night and from night till morning' since the age of ten requires an opposite or a complement in the person of 'an expert palm-wine tapster' who 'had no other work more than to tap palm-wine every day' (Tutuola 1952: 7). To be absolutely independent of work, the drinkard requires absolute dependence on the work of the tapster. In other words, it takes moral insensitivity and making mincemeat of any kind of leisure and autonomy due the tapster to make possible the sort of independence and overindulgence in pleasure and leisure craved by the drinkard. This is not dissimilar to the situation under 'corporate cannibalism' championed by 'corporate cannibals' driven by greed as creed (Elkington 1997), where ordinary clients and even employees of corporate institutions, who often find themselves without much alternative to the bloodthirsty appetite by corporations to privilege profits over people, are bound to feel 'naked among cannibals' (Hand 2001: 130). Using insider knowledge of Australian banks, Graham Hand affirms, 'There are a lot of cannibals out there, especially in international finance' (Hand 2001: 130).

Thus, to limit cannibalism simply to butchering and eating someone else, raw or cooked, is to ignore at one's peril more insidious and often more devastating forms of cannibalism that insinuate themselves into our everyday personal and institutional relationships. In the case of the United States and Brazil, for example, it amounts to ignoring the hierarchies of intersection between race and democracy informed by histories of slavery and unequal encounters between blacks and whites that are best understood in terms of racialised cannibalism and its hierarchies of ingestible and digestible humans (Nunes 2008). In a democracy where 'The consuming body ... is not only racially marked as white, but also gendered as male', it is of essence not to situate cannibalism, *a priori*, as a homogenous, equally available and accessible opportunity to eat and be eaten, but rather, to seek to understand 'Who is eating whom?' (Nunes 2008: 34). Katherine Martinez echoes this point in her discussion of cannibalism as a highly gendered patriarchal phenomenon in which men and masculinists propensities are privileged in the literal and metaphorical consumption and control of women's and feminised male bodies (Martinez 2011).

Cannibalism has no sacred or secret places. Cannibalism is a truly universal phenomenon in its materialisation and in the fantasies, fears and fascinations it inspires (Montaigne 1943[1580]; Fitzhugh 1988[1960]; Takada 1999; Lefebvre 2005; Lévi-Strauss 2016[2013]; Brown 2013; Bellamy 2014). 'It can rear its ugly head whenever people are schooled to think of others as less than human, during wars, or when a lack of resources bring forth survival tactics inherent within the form (Travis-Henikoff 2008: 230).' As Europeans were busy categorising Africans as cannibals, they in turn were perceived by the Africans they encountered as cannibals. In the Belgian Congo, for example, where the Congolese thought the white colonialists sometimes ate the Congolese people, 'the imagined threat of cannibalism often lingered just beneath the surface of both sides of the colonial interchange' – a situation compounded by the practice of cutting the body of the living or the dead to make visible the internal bits and pieces for medical reasons (Au 2017: 296).

The Europeans may not have literally eaten pieces of their colonised Congolese subjects, 'But they did cut off, extract and send away blood, lumbar fluid, tumours and so forth, consuming them in the process of medical research' (Au 2017: 311).[44] In his study of Maka society during contact with Europe and under the wild rubber economy, Geschiere remarked that the use of cannibalism as a trope for othering was not the monopoly of the colonising European, as the Maka drew on it to good effect in labelling the Germans they encountered as cannibals (Geschiere 1997: 27–34). During the transatlantic slave trade, the 'chilling fear of being killed, eaten by white cannibals, crushed to make oil, or ground to make gunpowder' often drove some of the human cargo on ships bound for labour in the Americas to jump into the sea (Thornton 2003: 274). In the eyes of enslaved Africans, to be eaten up was a process in which the actual ingestion of human flesh was only a detail. As John Thornton puts it:

Consuming the bodies of the enslaved was but one of many symbols of avarice and selfishness, and in the context of the slave trade could clearly be applied to or expected of the Europeans who manned the slave ships and delivered the Africans to their American masters. Indeed, the link between slavery and cannibalism might be made even if the slaves were not immediately eaten on arrival ... for the accusation and rumors of the events were as important as any demonstrated proof (Thornton 2003: 281).

We are all cannibals when, through our vacuous claims of superiority or supremacy we act, socially, politically, economically and culturally to make life impossible for others, defined, in our estimation, as morally inferior or not quite like us. Such cannibalism is not confined to meat eaters.

Even vegans who indulge in the stifling of life possibilities for others are cannibals. Apart from the moral and ethical debates that sometimes inform options and choices in vegetarianism in opposition to carnivorousness (Irvine 1989), it could be argued, in addition to symbolic, metaphorical and indirect cannibalism claimed here, that vegetarians are cannibals in another sense: where and when buried corpses decompose and serve as nutrients for the vegetables that are fed vegans, that is no less an act of cannibalism merely because of its indirection. Vegetarians are also cannibals if one takes seriously cosmologies and ontologies of interconnection and conviviality that favour a composite and fluid idea of being human in intersection, entanglement and manglement with nature and supernature. Within such a universe where everything and everyone is present in simultaneous multiplicity, to eat at all, regardless of what one eats, is to eat to some degree, a fellow human being.

Eating others up through state or government policies and practices that defy expectations of a common humanity is cannibalistic. Just as it is cannibalism, regardless of our free market rhetoric of consumer sovereignty, for corporations to make a creed of greed with life threatening implications for ordinary consumers and employees. It is cannibalism, when in the name of belief and religion, one is determined to hate and violate the dignity of others who do not share our religion and beliefs in a manner that surpasses even the excesses of the devil and its well-oiled appetite for mischief. And it is cannibalism as well, when one works one's way up the ladder to assume the position of a prophet in a church one has created or joined much more as a business for preying on converts and congregants than as an institution for praying, saving lives, nourishing souls and bringing people, big and small, closer to one another and to the divine.

A cannibalism free society is a utopian society of the type imagined by Catalin Avramescu in these terms that echo Jean-Jacques Rousseau's fantasy of the unfettered freedom of noble savage (Dunn 2002):

> Let us imagine a society where all are equal and free, where there are no punishable offences and no state authority, where private property is unheard of and each has sufficient according to his needs, where there is no money, where people are healthy and robust and live to over a hundred, where there is no need to work, where the most diverse pleasures are enjoyed … and from whence religion has been banished (Avramescu 2009: 213).

Is it not a paradox that it is precisely the sort of societies that have come closest to this *egalitarian ideal* of a moral community in being and in consumption, its necessity and violence (Englund 2015a, 2015b; Nyamnjoh 2015a) that have been most accused of and castigated for real or imaginary cannibalism within the narrow human-flesh-eating low-intensity variant of what it truly means to consume the other in human terms? This question should however not be seen to imply that pre-colonial societies were egalitarian and free of violence, or that they were an exception to the paradox of limitless production and relentless consumption for which capitalism is renowned. Not only does capitalism have an appetite for labour, it thrives on consuming the labourer's time and in extracting surplus-value and accumulating profit from the labourer's energies (Barker et al. 1998). In this sense, 'savage consumption' as the epitome of ultimate possessiveness and the logical end of human relations could be seen as characteristic both of cannibalism and capitalism. Little wonder that Karl Marx saw capitalist production as cannibalistic in its capacity to endlessly feed off the living blood of labour, likening the capitalist to a 'vampire, werewolf, or parasite forever feeding off the lifeblood of the proletariat' (Lefebvre 2005: 48).

Nor should the question be seen as an uncritical endorsement of the notion of thriving, happy 'natives' (such as Jean-Jacques Rousseau's noble savages (Dunn 2002)) prior to colonialism, which in former settler colonies such as South Africa and Zimbabwe, often emerges in everyday discussions around the violent expulsion of white settlers (since they arrived and ruined everything) and underpin ahistorical calls to go back to the pre-colonial 'good old days'. It is equally worth reiterating, as William Arens has argued, that beyond the tenuous documentary evidence often tainted by the prescriptive euphoria and ambitions of dominance of the European conqueror, 'there is no sure way of knowing if the locals were indeed eating their friends and/or enemies on a customary basis before Europeans conquered them' (Arens 2003: 18; see also Arens 1979). As Salmon argues in support of Arens, to found a major anthropological claim on 'hearsay and biased evidence' is hardly a vindication of participant observation as '*the* method', par excellence, of anthropological enquiry (Salmon 1995: 129–131).

In purely relative and comparative terms, there is evidence to the effect that some societies, moral communities, social organisations and philosophies of personhood, ownership and control of resources are more amenable to ideas of inclusive success than others (Englund 2015a, 2015b; Nyamnjoh 2015a). Those societies and communities are *more likely but not exclusively* to be peripheral to or at the margins of Western civilisation and modernity than otherwise.

That notwithstanding, it should be possible to deconstruct and disarticulate cannibalism and the problematic meanings attached to it without recourse to a utopian past prior to colonialism and its attended accusations of cannibalism.

We should be very wary of the notion that any society, whatever the depth of its moral sensitivities and sensibilities, can be fully egalitarian, peaceful, and free of violence – even as we believe that this is an ideal we must strive toward. Violence (and affects such as anger, rage, jealousy and humiliation, which often configure or are attached to it) is part of the human condition of eating and being eaten. To deny individuals and societies this inclination toward violence (however implicit or explicit it may be) is to deny them the sustenance, possibilities and contradictions of being human through (contentious, conflictual and often unequal) relationships with nature, other humans and supernature. It also produces an unusable and unsustainable ground on which to conduct politics and the organisation of more liveable societies or moral communities. We must beware of any individual or society who thinks its heart and mind is evil free, which is insulated from or pretends not to notice its evils. This begs the question: How could civilisation and its accoutrements survive another day if consuming the other was reduced merely to devouring flesh and gnawing with savage ferocity the bones of others, raw or cooked? The fact that teeth rot, even or perhaps especially in a civilised context, must mean an alertness to ever creative and innovative ways of incorporation to attend to our eternal hunger for self and collective externalisation.[45] This reality makes a flexible and inclusive understanding of cannibalism all the more compelling, as the business of eating and being eaten must go on, with or without teeth. Could low intensity and obviously limited understanding of cannibalism, cannibals and consumption have been invented or instrumentalised to give European capitalism its boundless ferocious appetite and its zero-sum logic of winner-takes-all, a well-pampered head-start to their ambitions of superiority and dominance, at home and away (Mackintosh 2011)? Does it not lead eventually to inverted cannibalism? Could cases of invented cannibalism, cannibals and cannibal 'tribes' determined to keep European penetration, missionaries and Christianisation ploys at bay have been used to drum up mass hysteria and fanaticism in support of Europe's purported enlightenment cause within its own societies and around the globe?

Put differently, did Europe brand cannibalism, cannibals and cannibal communities as a way of rationalising its obscenities to make them palatable and liveable? An excuse for outsourcing the gruesome monstrosities of the civilisation it claimed onto those defined *a priori* as less-than-human savages trapped at the state of nature and desperately seeking redemption even at the risk of imperial wars of conversion, conquest, slavery and colonialism (Taussig 1987; Lyon 1995; Berglund 1999; Pettey 2003; Macintosh 2011; Duggan 2013; Ng 2015)? If so, then accusing socially, culturally and geographically distant others of cannibalism was intended, the way a hunter would, to harvest enough red meat (in the form of reckless exploitation of labour and resources, and widespread racialised dispossession and debasement the world over) to feed European capitalism's appetite and ambitions of dominance. The hunt is reincarnated through modern day institutions purporting to maintain world financial stability, even purporting to maintain 'peace and order', without always making evident, for whom exactly (George 1990; Nyamnjoh 2015a).

Those who in the prescriptive gaze of a penetrating Europe do not qualify as human or are perceived as not fully human (Arens 1979; Lindenbaum 2004; Obeyesekere 2005; Mackintosh 2011; Fairhead 2015) are in every regard fair game for the gnawing teeth or dentures of the treasure hunters of predatory European capitalism (Lefebvre 2005; Mackintosh 2011). Little wonder that enslaved Africans in the Americas repeatedly used ideas of cannibalism to come to terms with their exploitation by their white owners (Thornton 2003).

In light of such tenacious determination to make a meal of others – body, mind and soul and their material extensions[46] – should it surprise anyone that European capitalism has successfully rendered invisible through myriad forms of incorporation every other mode of social organisation, philosophy of life and personhood (Barker et al. 1998)? '[T]he unsavoury truth ... [is] that the white man was always cannibalistic', concludes Jennifer Brown. Be it in the colonies or at home in the West, '*we* are rapacious, cannibalistic aggressors', she insists (Brown 2013: 14). And we should all accept the fact, adds Derek Petrey, for it is only when 'we accept the reality of cannibalism, historical and current, European and non-European ... [that] we may move past it to understand the people who practice it and the systems of meaning involved in its practice' (Petrey 2005: 120). To move past cannibalism and to understand the people who practise it, and the meaning they bring to bear on their actions, is to recognise that eating and being eaten is human and universal. It is also to provide for a truly inclusive universal ethics and morality that underpin our reality of eating and being eaten. Such morality and ethics – which should determine when cannibalism is within the bounds of the tolerable and the point at which cannibalism goes out of control and endangers the very ideals of life, social reproduction and a universal humanism – are neither assumed nor imposed with an imagined hierarchy of humanity, moral and ethical orders. Rather, they are to be carefully negotiated with required sensibility and sensitivity to the fact that in our game of cannibalism, no one and no people have the monopoly of cannibalisation and of creative improvisation in its regard.

Contributions to this Volume: an Overview

Many of the issues raised in this essay are taken up and developed further in the contributions that follow.

In *Chapter Two,* Andreas Buhler discusses how cannibalism has been written about, especially by anthropologists, and in what way anthropologists may be considered cannibals as well. Through various ethnographic texts, Buhler shows that the construction of the cannibal was an integral part of justifying the structural violence of colonialism. Tales of cannibalism were used by the colonial regimes to reduce people to the savage other. Anthropologists have since worked to dispel the savage/civilised binary, but have also become trapped by it. The writing of an ethnographic text could be in itself a form of cannibalism where the specificity of a culture and the humanity of people are savaged and devoured. To Buhler, much of the academic debate on the existence or non-existence of cannibalism has in the end reduced local people and their histories to be either European colonialist creations or the products of traditions stripped of all history prior to unequal encounters with a colonising Europe. In this debate, any notion of agency is stripped from research subjects, and the structural violence of colonialism is reproduced in academic texts in often unproblematised ways.

Using Zimbabwe as a case study, Artwell Nhemachena and Maria Kaundjua, in *Chapter Three*, discuss the ways in which that country has been cannibalised and incorporated into the (neo-)imperial world since the colonial era. The chapter examines the figures and figments of the cannibal in colonial historical perspective. It also draws on contemporary discourses of posthumanism and the attendant contemporary discourses on ethics to map out the terrain of cannibalism in the envisaged and emergent post-human world. Thus, with insights from colonial history in which the African humanistic ethics of *hunhu/unhu*, as enshrined in *Ubuntu and Chivanhu*, were destroyed in favour of colonial cannibalism, this chapter spells out the implications of the envisaged and emergent posthuman ethics, including 'ethics of care' and 'ethics of vulnerability'. Underscoring ways in which posthumanistic transnational corporations, institutions and some foreign governments cannibalise Africa, and Zimbabwe in particular, Nhemachena and Kaundjua shed light on the duplicities of 'ethics of care' and 'ethics of vulnerability' that are foregrounded within Western academies even as Africa is being cannibalised in a world that has since deposed and disposed of African humanistic ethics. In the light of associations of cannibalism with witchcraft in Zimbabwean epistemologies and ontologies, the authors argue that (neo-)imperial contrivances at incorporating Africa constitute logics of cannibalistic witchcraft, however cloaked in discourses of 'ethics of vulnerability' and 'ethics of care'. In this regard, the practices of sanctioning the other are as much aspects of witchcraft and sorcery as they are of any other sanctions that are designed to sap the vitalities of the targeted entities or nations.

Walter Gam Nkwi, in *Chapter Four*, focuses on the cannibalisation of the Bamenda Grassfielders of Cameroon by colonial Christianity. He argues, however, that the Bamenda Grassfielders were not uncritical recipients of colonial Christianity, and shows how in the process, Christianity was in turn cannibalised by the Grassfielders and their belief systems, through a process of active domestication. By extension, the encounter between European Christianity and African indigenous religions was not a case of one way cannibalism, even if that is what the Europeans aimed for and thought they were achieving. It was a case of mutual cannibalisation. The result being that African Christianity is not exactly a mirror image of Western Christianity, as the latter has been chewed, digested and blended into the religious and cultural anatomy of the Grassfielders. Put differently, the vital force of colonial Christianity has, over the years, been ingested and used to strengthen the indigenous belief systems and practices of this region of Cameroon and Africa. If Western Christianity arrived with ambitions of eating up the Grassfielders and their indigenous religions and religiosities, its gastronomic ambitions and appetites were met and tamed by an equally strong determination on the part of the local population to survive culturally, collectively and individually, an ambition which was achieved by eating up Western Christianity in turn. Nkwi's chapter and argument thus shed light on and critiques the tendency towards an overly narrow concept of cannibalism that tended to accompany European colonial missionary incursions in Africa. This process of mutual consumption by the competing religions is testament to the fact that cannibalisation should not be confined to its literal meaning of eating the flesh of another human being. There are several dimensions of cannibalism encapsulated in the everyday activities and relationships of all and sundry.

In *Chapter Five*, Ayanda Manqoyi, discusses cannibalism through the prism of what in post-apartheid South Africa is commonly referred to as 'Black Tax'. As a metaphor 'Black Tax' describes the various obligations to home and host communities among black middle-class (even if not always exclusively confined to this class) men and women living in post-apartheid South Africa. As Manqoyi puts it, the liberal template prescribes a form of cannibalism that sacrifices family and extended relations as conditions to ascend to the status of black middle class in contemporary South Africa. He argues that intellectual institutions and the media have tended to treat as anathema cultures and practices of inclusive success that encourage attempts to provide for bridging across individual success and collective success as part and parcel of being black and middle class in South Africa. Consequently, obligations to kin and kith are depicted as a hindrance to individual success and, paradoxically, to the economic growth of the country. The emphasis is often on status and conspicuous consumption as the relevant forms of identity making and class authentication. In such neoliberal fixations with categories and the glitter of appearances of achievement, there is little patience beyond formalities with providing for an ethics of care and inclusion, despite life-threatening vulnerabilities. However, Manqoyi argues and substantiates empirically, despite the construction of an exclusionary post-apartheid society, the black middle-class South Africans are constructing notions of success that seek to repair relationships by including family and extended networks struggling from a history of extractive colonialism and apartheid policies. Any efforts to prescribe reductions indexed to institute black middle class cannibalises long-standing African philosophies of collective success.

Veronica Masenya's contribution – *Chapter Six* – complements Manqoyi's by touching on other aspects of cannibalism as South Africa grapples with its post-apartheid predicaments. 'Savage' and 'inhuman' or nothing, Masenya argues, cannibalism continues to exist in the so-called 'modern' South African society in both obvious and indirect ways. It manifests itself in everyday activities in various forms conveyed in literal and/or metaphorical meanings. This is portrayed in oral communication mechanisms such as proverbs inherited from the lived experiences of generations past and present, who have used such proverbs as tools to guide, teach, reflect, praise and critique human actions. The chapter is centred on a proverb drawn from the Sepedi language of South Africa that expresses the nuanced deeds of cannibalism: '*Lehu la gago le ya mphidisha*', translated into 'your death nourishes me'. Like the general (mis)conception of cannibalism, this proverb is marked with negative connotations, highlighting situations where the demise of one becomes a source of gain for another. The chapter is rich in ethnographic insights and evidence on the currency of cannibalism and cannibal relationships drawn from a wide range of situations from '*muti* killings' to smoking cremated ashes, through inheritance dynamics and funeral insurance scandals. The scenarios in this essay highlight the direct and indirect manifestations of nuanced forms of cannibalism as practices which see some social bodies nourished by the deaths of others. While death and funerary practices might in the past have nourished communities through the social rituals that accompany death, incorporation into consumer capitalist society creates conditions where 'nourishment' is read as enrichment at the expense of others, rather than nourishment for the benefit of the community as a whole. This essay will lead us to consider how the proverb's interpretation shifts in contexts where bodies and social practices are commodifiable.

If one were still in doubt that there is much more to cannibalism than the incorporation of human flesh, literally, Dominique Santos, in *Chapter Seven*, dispels that doubt convincingly. Her chapter explores the social world of an upmarket lap-dancing club in Sandton, Gauteng Province, South Africa, in the first decade of the 21st century. The lap-dancing club is a site in which the bodies of young women are prepared and consumed by customers who are primarily men. In turn, these women consume the money and social opportunities offered by the men. As the club attempts to tap into the expanded demographic of the consumers of lap-dancing bodies during the beginning of the era of Black Economic Empowerment (BEE), racialised tensions over resources emerge as girls compete to eat and be eaten.

In *Chapter Eight*, Moshumee Dewoo writes richly and figuratively about 'Enlightened Man', and his propensity to project unto others his cannibalism while doing everything to conceal the violent fact of his essentially cannibalistic nature and culture. She is deeply critical of how such projections and disguises have been used to justify the extractive extravaganza *vis-à-vis* Africa, Africans and African resources by the predatory Enlightened Man from the Enlightened Soil of Europe. Lurking beneath the surface of the purported Enlightenment, is what Dewoo describes as the monster gorging away at Africa's Heart (natural resources), that vital part of another body in a manner mirroring the extractive policies, strategies and endeavours of the periods of enslavement and colonialism. She uses 'this truth' to debunk the sort of deceitful and terribly limited conversations and practices that have prevailed around the fact of cannibalism, often to the credit of the

Enlightened Man of Europe and to the detriment of everyone else, especially the dispossessed and silenced sons and daughters of the African soil.

As the crowning grace of our barbecue of cannibal delights, Akira Takada, in *Chapter Nine*, sheds light on a foreshadowing of cannibalism in Japan through three case analyses. (1) In 2017, a young man was arrested following the discovery of nine dismembered bodies. Most of the victims were girls who were considering suicide. The background for this case includes a desire for symbolic death among youngsters and the Japanese sex industry's exploitation of an amateur aura in young girls, as the suspect was a broker who recruited girls to the sex industry. (2) In the Japanese pop scene, the term 'idol' is used to refer to young starlets. Their admirers often buy dozens of their CDs in exchange for a ticket that provides them with the opportunity to shake hands with these idols. The idols are prohibited from having intimate relationships in their private lives. In these practices, a recursive interplay between fantasising reality and realising the fantasy may be detected. (3) *Nama* is a Japanese term that indicates rawness, nudity or bareness, and the condition of being live or alive. It is used favourably in advertisements for commodities or fashions, such as raw meat (*nama niku*), bare legs (*nama ashi*) and live music (*nama ensou*), and is intended to be interpreted by the general public as they see fit. For example, one could opt to have raw meat in the company of bare legs and the sound of live music. Many people make fetishes of these items, which has increased their symbolic value in this highly industrialised and consumerised society. These cases reflect a consumer culture that is sustained by extremely complex systems of material production, product distribution, and information circulation. Takada argues that in an effort to overcome the persistent sense of 'incompleteness' present in their daily lives, the Japanese may be generating a new form of cannibalism.

Conclusion

The essays in this volume make a case for cannibalism as a universal reality and preoccupation. Whether motivated by need, greed or both, cannibalism requires attention in all its guises and disguises. In this introduction, I have argued that cannibalism must not escape intelligent scrutiny and complex analyses when it comes to the Western world as well as the world Westerners have sought to make and remake in their giant compressor image, need and greed. However, to recognise that we are ultimately all cannibals should not be seen and treated as incompatible with the utopia of justice, equality and freedom, if such utopia is not conceptualised and pursued as an absolute quest for absolutes. Thus, the following questions: In chewing, ingesting and digesting this essay on cannibalism, how best do we 'disregard the overwhelmingly negative stereotypification of the cannibalistic act without averting our gaze from the actuality of the practice' (Petrey 2005: 120)? What exactly would change, ethically, morally and otherwise, if we were to take seriously the fact that cannibalism is normal, that we are all cannibals, and that life, society, civilisation or modernity in whatever form or guise is not thinkable, not to mention feasible, without factoring in cannibalism in one form or another? How would we go about the business of putting together an ethics and moral order sanctioned by the understanding that every hierarchy is cannibalistic, wittingly and unwittingly? How would we account for the reality of interconnections, malleability and compositeness of being human – a reality informed by a cosmology and an ontology in which anything can be anything à la Tutuola (Nyamnjoh 2017b)? If the utopia of justice, equality and freedom is only meaningfully pursued within a framework of interconnections, interdependencies and conviviality, how do we pursue it in recognition of the reality of a humanity that fulfils itself through a compositeness and fluidity of form, and by eating and being eaten?

Put differently, what would a truly normalised and de-ideologised understanding and provision for cannibalism in our lives and relationships as individuals, societies and communities look like? For one thing, we would desist from defining and confining cannibalism to its so-called hardcore, shocking, disgusting, revolting and fascinating dimensions that are to be found among retarded backward-looking primitive savages and lawless societies yet to embrace modernity and civilisation in a serious way.

We would, for example, not confine to the metaphorical the association made by French Jesuit priest François Garasse in 1623 between cannibalism and Epicureanism by which he sought to highlight the Epicureans' perceived 'transgressive, animal-like behaviour based on immanent desire as opposed to civilised behaviour guided by external law' of 'the civilised, Catholic, and human community';[47] nor should we take as merely a figure of speech the mutual accusations of cannibalism between Protestants and Catholics in 17th century France (Duggan 2013: 463–464).

We would also desist from reluctantly conceding cannibalism in our sanitised urban modern civilised geographies only to criminal-minded deranged individuals, devilish secret societies steeped in occult beliefs and practices, those trapped or stranded in extremely difficult situations (such as caught betwixt and between in the middle of nowhere and vulnerable to extreme starvation with little access to normal civilised food), and in fantasy spaces of creative imagination gone wild (such as film and fiction production and related cultural entertainment industries).

Equally, we would go beyond enlivening our speech and writing with cannibalism and cannibalisation as metaphorical verbs, adjectives and nouns of little consequence,[48] while reserving our most pejorative bile for the purportedly serious cases of cultural and ritual cannibalism deemed to be practised by the backward cultures of some backward races and backward geographies. Even then, in modern times, some food choices, such as being carnivorous or meat-eating are seen as masculinising, while others such as being a vegetarian are perceived to emasculate, feminise and subvert masculinity or cannibalism in camouflage (Estok 2012).

We would take more seriously the broad spectrum of cannibalism in its nuanced complexities as need and greed entangled, and be better able to see it even in camouflage, especially in places and spaces where our current obsession with and projection of cannibalism in its most basic form has tended to render cannibalism invisible, or to envelope it in metaphors and symbols (Kilgour 1990). It would, above all, re-insert, emphatically, the interconnections and interdependencies between being an animal, a person and a spirit – interconnections and interdependencies which the fixation in our evolutionary, linear, zero-sum game approach to modernity and civilisation with the emergence and cultivation of the singular, unified, autonomous self has tended to de-emphasise, to delegitimate and to render invisible.

Invisibility does not translate to non-existence. Thus, far from distancing itself from barbarism through acts of denialism and invisibilisation of cannibalism (Hubinger and Lucie Svatoňová 1991), Western civilisation is a mere shadow of its true self without its barbarism. It simply cannot afford to stifle or succeed cannibalising its cannibalism. Equally, it simply cannot content itself by outsourcing such cannibalism to the creative industries and the medical world of implants, transplants and infusions. And so let's all affirm, once and for all: '*We are all cannibals; we've always been!*'

With this admission in mind, if we provide for the potential for cannibalism driven by love or hate or both, and by need, greed or both, we have a framework within which people display in their human closets even in disguised forms and templates, their complex and multifaceted liaisons with cannibalism. With this should come as well understanding and providing for the moral economy of cannibalism as a universal reality and preoccupation. We would understand, for example, that gifts or tributaries are a form of postponement of the ultimate sacrifice – human and the self – which enables the gift giver and payer of tributes to stay alive, because, like Abraham in the Bible, they have found a ram to serve as a sacrifice so Isaac might live another day. The more personal the gift or tribute and the more history it has accumulated as an extension of the self, the more likely it is to appear and thus be accepted as a worthy substitute, double or lookalike of the gift-giver or tribute-payer by the receiver. Because of such gifts and tributes, we have become used to eating others up mostly indirectly, through things and proxies, rather than directly, in the superficial manner we have come to understand cannibalism. Yet, aren't forbidden treasures meant to be eaten in hiding, especially if there is a risk of being eaten in return if found out? In this regard, it could be argued that the history of humankind and its ambitions of superiority and civilisation *vis-à-vis* the non-human, the subhuman and the less-than-human is one of exploring ever creative and innovative ways of disguising and camouflaging the persistence of humanity's savage cannibalism.

As we gather from Conklin's (2001) ethnography on compassionate cannibalism among Wari', cannibalism often entails the removal of the person being consumed from the category of the human. This is interesting for two reasons. Colonialism and capitalism are underpinned by the removal of a person from the category of the human so that their bodies and labour can be exploited by the colonial state or the capitalist system (Taussig 1987). A similar removal seems to be taking place in the Amazon, but toward other ends, and, perhaps most importantly, only after the person has passed away. So, while both these worlds engage in this removal, their way of doing so is animated by very different motives, desires, needs and outcomes. This renders needless questions about whether cannibalism should or should not end. Rather, what should be highlighted and promoted are the forms of cannibalism which do not entail extinguishing the life of another. There should be a way to avoid throwing the cannibal baby of need out with the cannibal bathwater of greed.

If the idea of cosmologies and ontologies of interconnection and conviviality between the human, the natural and the supernatural is to be taken seriously, there is a need to problematise the category 'human', instead of thinking of it as settled. For, if bounded categories are mythical, then the category 'human' must be mythical too. This calls for putting on the chopping block and making mincemeat of bounded conceptions of the human and being human. In this regard, the idea of all-encompassing cannibalism provides a stepping-stone towards a new understanding of humanity or life itself. Inspired by popular African and Amerindian cosmologies and ontologies of interconnection and conviviality, one can envisage a continuous (and indeed unstoppable) cannibalistic flow of bodily substances into and through individual bodies (both human and non-human) which almost seems like a single force, a river of sorts, or a confluence of rivers, where individuals float into and through each other in a way that is neither individual nor collective. In this regard, what is needed is a universally derived and sustained morality and ethics of cannibalism. One that recognises and provides for the human as open-ended as well as for the reality of eating and being eaten, and thus the need for a carefully negotiated and navigated balance of appetites and ambitions of predation amongst humans and between humans and non-humans. Ultimately, needed is an ethics informed by an eternal awareness of and alertness to the fact that in a universe peopled by the ambitions and politics of consumption, appetite and taste (both literally and metaphorically), the hunter can very easily and without warning, become the hunted, and the hunted the hunter.

Mobility in quest for opportunities and sustenance makes cannibalism in its multiple dimensions a permanent feature on the landscape and experience of our humanity in its flexibility and intricacies. Mobility, its hungers and thirsts, and the encounters it engineers between different peoples, cultures, societies and social categories almost always entail some form of cannibalism as a means of bringing new kinds of civilisational and societal structures into being, with and despite hierarchical relations of power and privilege (Ranger 2007; Geschiere 2009; Nyamnjoh 2013). The cannibalism of different cultures, languages and ways of being and doing that is attendant to mobility and its quests seems productive, transformative, and (re)inventive – and one of the most vital aspects of what it means to be human as a composite and fluid reality in a dynamic world of myriad interconnections and enchantments. To nourish and cherish such a productive form of cannibalism requires not only a compassionate generosity to let in and accommodate the stranger knocking at the door of our personal and civilisational certitudes (Cohen 2017) but, also and more importantly, a deliberate effort to reach in, identify, contemplate, understand, embrace and become intimate with the stranger within us, individuals and societies alike (Simmel 1950; Harrison 2008; Devisch 2017; Lategan 2018). This is something to hold on to, ethically and morally, even as we expel those forms of cannibalism that are premised on notions of superiority, dominance and often sterile greedy ambitions of *completeness.*

Endnotes

1 Fluid, dynamic and pieced together from a plurality of beings through intricate encounters, negotiation and navigation of myriad identity margins. See Dave Mann's review of Todd Gray's 'Pluralities of Being', titled 'Piecing Together Pluralities of Being', http://www.jhblive.com/Reviews-in-Johannesburg/events/piecing-together-pluralities-of-being/109324, accessed 15 March 2018.

2 The word 'cannibal' is said to have originated from a corruption in 1492 by Christopher Columbus of the word 'Carib', the name of an Amerindian people in the Caribbean islands mischievously introduced to Columbus by their neighbours as 'man-eaters' (Arens 1979: 45; Brady 1982: 603–604; Rawson 1999: 168; Lefebvre 2005: 46; Rothera 2009; Williams 2012: 242–243) a point that leads Claude Rawson to argue that in a sense, 'cannibalism' did not exist before 1492 (Rawson 1999: 168). However, existence should not be conflated with naming. Perhaps aware of the origins of the word, some scholars insist on a distinction between cannibalism, when used in relation to humans, and anthropophagy, the Greek word for 'man-eating'. When the distinction is made, cannibalism is seen as 'essentially a fantasy that the Other is going to eat us', and anthropophagy as 'the actual consumption of human flesh' (Obeyesekere 2005: 14). In this essay, cannibalism is used to connote both the actual eating of human flesh and fantasies of eating other humans, being eaten by other humans,and being seen to eat other humans. Eating is understood in its most inclusive and elastic sense to imply consumption in general, directly and indirectly, actually, symbolically, metaphorically and in fantasy – such as often featured in children's literature by the likes of Roald Dahl (Piatti-Farnell 2010). It draws attention to the culturally cultivated ideas around eating and being eaten, and being human not as a reality that is unambiguously and categorically distinct from being something else (animal or spirit), but as a crossroads or meeting point of converging and diverging possibilities of identification. The question

ultimately arises: what does it mean to eat up another when that other is often a composite of many things, ranging from the natural (an animal), to the palpably human, to the supernatural?

³ For a report on the unfolding story of how, allegedly, Harvey Weinstein used his position of power and privilege as a Hollywood film producer to sexually harass, have sex and sometimes rape actresses and would be actresses in his circles, see, 'Harvey Weinstein: More women accuse Hollywood producer of rape', http://www.bbc.com/news/world-us-canada-41626563, accessed 15 October 2017. The allegations and accusations have multiplied, and along with them came allegations about other Hollywood celebrities. Reporting on another allegation concerning Kevin Spacey, the BBC noted in passing that Harvey Weinstein 'has been accused by more than 50 women of a range of allegations ranging from rape to sexual harassment'. See 'Kevin Spacey apologises over Anthony Rapp "sexual advance" claim', http://www.bbc.com/news/world-us-canada-41799026, assessed 30 October 2017. Others accused include celebrity newscasters such as Matt Lauer of NBC. See, for example, Yohana Desta, 'Graphic, Disturbing Details of Matt Lauer's Alleged Sexual Misconduct: A bombshell Variety report alleges Lauer gave one female colleague a sex toy, and more', https://www.vanityfair.com/hollywood/2017/11/matt-lauer-sexual-misconduct-allegations, accessed 3 December 2017. As some women in the Metoo movement have argued, this is not about the addiction to sex and power of one individual or of Hollywood and Congress as institutions; it is about the abuse of power by a masculinity in crisis that has convinced itself that absolute power is only possible through the unmitigated harassing, bullying, pestering and preying on – cannibalising – others, women and men alike.

⁴ It is worth bearing in mind, as Louis Herns Marcelin argues, that:

Blood is one of the most evident and recurrent metaphors in human societies. Its plasticity and openendedness seem to allow it to transcribe a complexity of meanings inscribed in a sum of domains, from ethnophysiology to moral attribute, from magic to sacrifice, from personhood to organizing principle of social organization and representations of power relations. Blood may be simultaneously and variously envisioned as a source of power renewal (sacrifice or cannibalism), a keynote in the language of power (violence or repression), a fundamental statement that articulates a cosmovision of alterity (us vs. them), and a principle of legitimization of specific forms of domination and privilege (lineage, kinship, imagined communities, and patriarchy) (Marcelin 2012: 255).

[5] See the BBC, 'The four companies that shape our lives: Apple, Amazon, Facebook and Google: these four companies enormously influence our lives. Is that good or bad?',
http://www.bbc.com/capital/story/20171208-the-four-companies-that-shape-our-lives, accessed 8 December 2017.

[6] See Carole Cadwalladr and Emma Graham-Harrison, 'Revealed: 50 million Facebook profiles harvested for Cambridge Analytica in major data breach',
https://www.theguardian.com/news/2018/mar/17/cambridge-analytica-facebook-influence-us-election; and Matthew Rosenberg, Nicholas Confessore and Carole Cadwalladr, 'How Trump Consultants Exploited the Facebook Data of Millions',
https://www.nytimes.com/2018/03/17/us/politics/cambridge-analytica-trump-campaign.html, accessed 23 March 2018.

[7] See Casey Newton, 'Mark Zuckerberg apologizes for the Cambridge Analytica scandal',
https://www.theverge.com/2018/3/21/17150158/mark-zuckerberg-cnn-interview-cambridge-analytica, accessed 23 March 2018.

[8] If the controversy caused by Bruce Gilley in a 2017 article extolling the virtues of colonialism, castigating anti-colonialism and its extremities, and making a case for the recolonisation of countries where development has been stalled by widespread violence, mass killings, endemic corruption and greed (Gilley 2017), among other things, the reasoning, projections and double standards displayed by European colonisers since first contact are still very much around, informing apparently scholarly and academic discourses as much as they do pronouncements by politicians and the logic and practices of big Western corporations. The controversial article was not the first by Gilley on the theme of the positive contributions of colonialism to the colonies and the colonised. In 2016 he published an article the title of which speaks for itself, 'Chinua Achebe on the Positive Legacies of Colonialism' (Gilley 2016). For an idea of the reaction Gilley's

2017 article attracted, see Colleen Flaherty's 'Is Retraction the New Rebuttal?',
https://www.insidehighered.com/news/2017/09/19/controversy-over-paper-favor-colonialism-sparks-calls-retraction.WcKc0IDN3P4.email, accessed 30 September 2017.

[9] This open admission, even if not intended to be taken seriously beyond the invasive European circles for which it was meant as a deterrent, raises the question: Since cannibalism (as literal flesh-eating or as structural violence) is often concealed or rendered mythical and unknowable, what does the *overt* identification as a cannibal, or as having a cannibalistic history, reveal or tell us about the past and present socio-political conjunction?

[10] An example worth chewing on in this regard is provided Gananath Obeyesekere of the first encounters between Captain Cook and the Hawaiians: 'from the very first visit: Cook thought that the Hawaiians were cannibals; and the Hawaiians thought that it was the British who were out to eat them!' (Obeyesekere 2005: 26), making the question not so much who is or is not a cannibal, but rather, whose representation of cannibalism carries more visibility and authority where, especially in a context of unequal encounters. Seen in this light, it is hardly in books written or documents archived by Europeans on first encounters and colonialism that one should expect to find what the so-called 'natives' truly thought of the Europeans they encountered. Given Europe's ambitions of dominance, and active investment in seeking justifications for violence and violation of those it encountered in its treasure-hunting globetrotting, should it surprise anyone that its claims of cannibalism among the people it encountered were more fantasy and fiction, and more of an exaggeration of whatever reality of anthropophagy there may have been? The unequal power to document, archive and ensure sustainability of the victor's account in such encounters meant that the British would pass onto its reader the following account: 'while the British believed that the cannibalism they imputed to the savage was real, the imputation of the savage that the British were cannibals must surely be a fantasy because the British knew that they (the British) were not cannibals!' (Obeyesekere 2005: 28).

[11] Beth Conklin (2001: xxiv) refers variously to this form of compassionate cannibalism as endocannibalism (the eating of kin after

their natural or accidental death), mortuary cannibalism and funerary cannibalism, which she contrasts with the cannibalism targeted at those outside of one's group or intimate circles – revenge victims and outsiders or enemies – usually termed exocannibalism. Other forms of cannibalism include autocannibalism, which 'covers everything from nail biting to torture-induced self-consumption', survival cannibalism, which 'is driven by starvation', ritual cannibalism, which 'occurs when members of a family or community consume their dead during funerary rites in order to inherit their qualities or honor their memory', and pathological cannibalism, which is practised mostly by 'criminals who consume their victims' (White 2001: 60). Jeff Blomster (1984) discusses 15 non-mutually exclusive reasons for cannibalism, namely: ritual, religion and sacrifice, magical purposes, gustatory, ancestor worship, way of disposing of the dead, show respect or to humiliate an enemy, political, celebrate victory and other special events, protein, control population growth, justice, psychological, symbolic, survival.

12 Beth Conklin elaborates that the Wari' 'always ate the flesh, but sometimes they also consumed the bone meal mixed with honey' (2001: xxv). She add that almost everyone who died was eaten, regardless of their age or status' (2001: xxvi).

13 See his *Spirit of the Laws*, Book 14.

14 A sort of United Nations of human body parts that brings to mind the story of The Complete Gentleman in Amos Tutuola's *The Palm-Wine Drinkard* (1952), who becomes the most handsome and the most beautiful man in the world only by borrowing body parts to activate himself from a bare skull to a fully-fledged human. In other words, his claims to any humanity materialise only in his capacity to eat up the body parts of others. That same humanity melts away as soon as he is compelled to return the body parts that he has borrowed.

15 A survey published in 2001 by Margareta Sanner, of feelings and ideas of patients in Sweden about receiving transplants of different origins, indicated an ambivalence in attitudes to having a foreign organ in one's body. However, 'Most individuals were willing to accept at least one organ', that 'Animal organs were the least preferred', and that a hierarchy of organ preferences existed in which organs from a relative were most preferred, and organs from an animal the least preferred, for 'rational, magical, and analogy thinking' reasons (Sanner 2001: 19).

[16] https://www.theguardian.com/society/2017/sep/08/donated-organs-of-13-year-old-girl-help-record-eight-people-to-live, accessed 08 09 2017.

[17] https://www.theguardian.com/society/2017/sep/08/donated-organs-of-13-year-old-girl-help-record-eight-people-to-live, accessed 08 09 2017.

[18] https://www.theguardian.com/society/2017/sep/08/donated-organs-of-13-year-old-girl-help-record-eight-people-to-live, accessed 08 09 2017.

[19] See Rachel Naylor, 'Hundreds of families block organ donation', http://www.bbc.com/news/health-41671600, accessed 19 October 2017.

[20] See Nancy Scheper-Hughes, 1998, 'The New Cannibalism', http://pascalfroissart.free.fr/3-cache/1998-scheperhughes.pdf, accessed 6 October 2017.

[21] See also, Nancy Scheper-Hughes, *Neo-Cannibalism, Organ Theft, and Military-Biomedical Necropolitics*, http://www.endslavery.va/content/endslavery/en/publications/acta_20/scheper_hughes_panel.html, accessed 26 November 2017.

[22] https://www.theguardian.com/society/2017/sep/08/donated-organs-of-13-year-old-girl-help-record-eight-people-to-live, accessed 08 09 2017.

[23] If Jared Diamonds is to be believed, the affected babies were those who 'made the fatal mistake of licking their fingers after playing with raw brains that their mothers had just cut out of dead kuru victims awaiting cooking' (Diamond 1998: 198).

[24] For a discussion of the centrality of gender and the role of women in mortuary or funerary cannibalism (necrophargy) in Papua New Guinea, see Ilka Thiessen (2001).

[25] As Helen Tiffin puts it, 'Carnivory in general reminds us that though we are the meat consumers, we are ourselves potentially meat'. She adds: 'When a shark is caught, we are thus also obsessed with the contents of its gut, especially when it, so very rarely, contains human remains. [...] Sharks, who have the capacity, if rarely the inclination, to eat us can, potentially, expose us as the flesh of which we are composed, and their ability to ingest our meat – like ours theirs – makes them too proximate in terms of self-exposure and self-reflection, obliging us to exaggerate their differences through the very similarity we are reluctant to

acknowledge: their apparent "savagery" in "attacking" prey as against our "civilized" dining' (Tiffin 2007: 20).

26 See Jean-Pierre Warnier (1993) for an example of how the balance between consumption and reproduction both as a biological and social function is carefully navigated and negotiated through the transmission of the bodily fluids of the cannibalising and cannibalised 'container king' in the Cameroon Grassfields, where the circulation of life depends very much on how people are able to feed and feed from their ancestors (Nyamnjoh and Rowlands 2013).

27 Graham Harvey recounts the fascinating case of Wally Hope, founder of Stonehenge People's Free Festival, who was cremated following his death in 1975 and whose 'ashes were scattered and partially consumed within the sacred circle of Stonehenge and he became an ancestor' (Harvey 2004: 263).

28 See, for example, Scott Juall's essay on Jean de Léry, who believed that the French who set out to conquer the supposed savages and cannibals of Brazil were often far more barbaric than the latter (Juall 2008).

29 Montaigne recounts how, after treating their prisoners for a long time with utmost hospitality, the captors tie the prisoner's arms and kill him with swords, in full view of an assembly. The captors then proceed to 'roast him and eat him in common and send some pieces to their absent friends', an act not be mistaken as committed because the killers seek 'nourishment', but rather, as an act of 'extreme revenge' (Montaigne 1943[1580]: 84).

30 See for example, a widely commented report in South African mainstream and social media in September 2017 of cannibalism and traffic in human body parts, https://www.timeslive.co.za/sunday-times/news/2017-08-26-dark-secrets-of-poor-villagers--tired-of--eating-human--flesh/, accessed 28 September 2017.

31 On October 11, for example, it was reported that a night curfew had been imposed by the Malawian government following the killing of five people in the south of the country, rumoured for drinking human blood as part of magic rituals; see BBC, 'Malawi curfew over 'vampire' killings', http://www.bbc.com/news/world-africa-41574608, accessed 11 October 2017. According to Joanne Lu of UN Dispatch, these 'attacks are alarmingly reminiscent of a sharp increase over the last couple years of

attacks on people with albinism, whose bones and body parts are believed to bring good luck in witchcraft rituals'; see https://mg.co.za/article/2017-10-20-00-vigilante-vampire-slayers-haunt-malawi, accessed 23 October 2017. Commenting on an earlier draft of this essay, Malizani Jimu notes: 'There is confusion in that the situation started as if those accused were for blood for medical use, then it turned for magic. Even the killing of albinos a year or so ago was preceded by stories of body parts hunters who at one time targeted women only, before men became the target ... all for charms. There was a time we had numerous road accidents involving minibuses or combis and they were also associated with blood collectors as well.'

[32] If paparazzi are driven by love, it is the love of sharks for blood. Princess Diana, described as a magnet and one person industry for paparazzi and the media, was an excellent example in this regard. For details on how Princess Diana was virtually assaulted, savaged and preyed upon by paparazzi for most of her life as a princess, including the very final moments that led to her death in August 1997, see 'My Mother Diana (Royal Family Documentary) – Real Stories', https://www.youtube.com/watch?v=BvR7vOx3ZBk&t=1828s, accessed 26 December 2017; 'Prince Harry Points Finger of Blame on Paparazzi for Princess Diana's Death', https://www.youtube.com/watch?v=uvi970LFh0g, accessed 26 December 2017; 'Diana's Legacy: How Her Death Shaped How William Handles the Paparazzi', https://www.youtube.com/watch?v=Yaa_qzIgwr0&t=26s, accessed 26 December 2017; 'How Diana tricked the paparazzi with her HANDBAGS as "cleavage bags" to protect her modesty', https://www.youtube.com/watch?v=CQhDSjwXJsI&t=28s, accessed 26 December 2017. https://www.netflix.com/watch/80141959?trackId=15035895&tctx=2%2C0%2Cb07c1d6e-6f8b-4006-8763-b026ed0e0f33-8843563, accessed 1 January 2018.

[33] C. Rock, L. Crouther, C. Sklar, J. Stilson, (writers) & J. Stilson, (director), 2009, Good Hair [Documentary], USA: HBO. Good Hair is a documentary that Chris Rock embarked upon when his four-year-old daughter asked him, 'Daddy, how come I don't have good hair?'. The film details the extent to which African American women are ready to bend

over backward financially, and in terms of physical pain and time, to look beautiful in accordance with the American ideal: 'the straighter the hair, the prettier one looks', making black women who stick to their natural hair losers in the beauty game. Chris Rock concludes: What matters is not what his daughter has on her head, but what is in it.

34 C. Rock, L. Crouther, C. Sklar, J. Stilson (writers) & J. Stilson (director) 2009. Also see: OPRAH.com, 2009, 'Chris Rock on the billion dollar black "good hair" industry', CNN [online], 4 November 2009, available at http://edition.cnn.com/2009/LIVING/homestyle/11/04/o.chris.rock.g ood.hair/, accessed 18 October 2017.

35 See *After Porn Ends* 1 & 2 by Bryce Wagoner and Andy Weiss,
https://www.netflix.com/watch/70242063?trackId=15035895&tctx =2%2C2%2Cb07c1d6e-6f8b-4006-8763-b026ed0e0f33-8843563 &
https://www.netflix.com/watch/80141959?trackId=15035895&tctx =2%2C0%2Cb07c1d6e-6f8b-4006-8763-b026ed0e0f33-8843563, accessed 1 January 2018.

36 Desmond Bellamy explains his choice of thesis, 'Having an old friend for dinner', as 'taken from a double entendre in the final scene of the film *The silence of the lambs* (Demme 1991) in which the newly escaped 'pure psychopath' cannibal, Hannibal Lecter, is planning to kill and eat his former jailer' (Bellamy 2014: 6).

37 A case could be made on the rampant cannibalism of Fast Food Executives (if not the whole industry), who barely pay their employees a 'living wage', and overburden their customers to death with junk food. And similar case could be made of the business of 'development' as well, touting 'development' for the 'underdeveloped' while eating on those 'being developed' and becoming overdeveloped to the point of ripping at the seams.

38 Some studies that trace the beginnings of cannibalism to times of excruciating starvation seem to lend credence to this train of thought (Travis-Henikoff 2008; Avramescu 2009; Esteban 2016), with Shiguro Takada prescribing, provocatively, what he terms 'Contingent cannibalism' for such dire situations of extreme hunger and the risk of protein deficiency (Takada 1999), as practiced by Japanese soldiers in the Philippines during World War II (Esteban 2016). Reportedly, among the Australian Aborigines for example, 'During times of starvation, older

women were treated, killed and consumed in the same manner as game, and if a person was seriously injured, he too was killed and eaten. Infant cannibalism was widespread and many tribes consumed all firstborns to ensure the future fecundity of the mother' (Travis-Henikoff 2008: 184). Further examples of starvation induced cannibalism reportedly took place during World War II (Travis-Henikoff 2008: 219-230).

[39] Never mind those who think the English have no cuisine to delight anyone about beyond the traditional Fish 'n Chips.

[40] See G. Donald, McNeil Jr, 'When Human Rights Extend to Nonhumans', http://www.nytimes.com/2008/07/13/weekinreview/13mcneil.html, accessed 26 November 2017.

[41] See 'German cannibal tells of fantasy', http://news.bbc.co.uk/2/hi/europe/3286721.stm, accessed 11 November 2017.

[42] See 'Daca Dreamers: Trump outlines demands for new deal', http://www.bbc.com/news/world-us-canada-41548363, accessed 9 October 2017. Indeed, it has been noted that merely by defining and confining, the problematic methodologies used to measure and classify the world over are able to render invisible (read cannibalised) some 350 million people, according to an article by Sean Coughlan published by the BBC, adding that the undocumented and invisible who fall below the demographic radar, often consist of the poorest of the poor 'families growing up in places where censuses and administrators do not reach' and who live in sprawling slums around some cities in the developing world. Equally invisible are homeless or nomadic and missing populations, such as unwanted refugees driven over borders by political violence. See Sean Coughlan, 'The 350 million people who don't even exist', http://www.bbc.com/news/business-41730606, accessed 26 October 2017.

[43] See Emily Badger, Claire Cain Miller, Adam Pearce and Kevin Quealy, 'Extensive Data Shows Punishing Reach of Racism for Black Boys', https://www.nytimes.com/interactive/2018/03/19/upshot/race-class-white-and-black-men.html, accessed 20 March 2018.

[44] This, of course, should not be taken to imply that Africans encountered by Europeans prior to and during the slave trade and colonialism did not have local technologies of exploring the effects of

82

bodily organs and substances, such as the vernacular public autopsy in the highlands of Cameroon, discussed by Matthieu Salpeteura and Jean-Pierre Warnier (2013).

[45] It is hardly surprising therefore, that in 21st century Britain, 1,000 dentists should be concerned enough about the escalating number of rotten teeth in the country to publish a letter in the *Daily Telegraph* sounding the alarm on a 'national health disaster' in dentistry. The letter complained about how inadequate prevention and untreated patients were forcing Britain to rely on charity from the developing world. An excerpt of the letter read:

Not only does rotten teeth remain the number one medical reason for any young child being admitted to hospital, but third world-based dental charities are expanding here from previous years and large American charities are looking to come to the UK as our inadequate dental systems are now an international disgrace (See 'Dental crisis leaves Britain reliant on charity from the developing world',
http://www.telegraph.co.uk/news/2018/01/02/dental-crisis-leaves-britain-reliant-charity-developing-world/, accessed 2 January 2018.).

[46] What difference is there between murder and killing someone's soul? Or between making a meal of someone's flesh and eating up, debasing or obliterating the fruit of someone's creative imagination? Not much, in effect, but you might think differently, and be morally and ethically inspired accordingly, on what a world is possible when eating flesh or the body, is not the same as eating the mind or eating the soul of another.

[47] To Garasse, according to Duggan, cannibalism connotes any behaviour perceived to be excessive, such as 'excessive eating, drinking, and sex', but with the idea of excess goes the idea of lack. One overly indulges in eating, drinking and sex, because one lacks the cultivated stability and predictability of willpower to tame such appetites (Duggan 2013; 469). Thus:

In creating analogies between Epicureans and cannibals, Garasse uses direct comparisons with cannibals (who are like animals); he associates them with animals (many of which are cannibalistic) and

83

focuses not only on *what* they eat but also, and perhaps more importantly, on *how* they eat, all of which serves to dehumanize Epicureans and to exclude them from the civilized community of good, God-fearing Catholics (Duggan 2013: 468).

The metaphor of cannibalism is a thin disguise of what Garasse really thinks of Epicureans. Duggan explains:

> By drawing on the figure of cannibalism, Garasse could construct the Epicurean as an ontologically inferior being who fails to transcend his animality, which is manifest in his uncontrolled appetites that drive him to roam from tavern to tavern. The danger represented by the Epicurean resides not only in his challenge to Catholic alimentary practices but also in his ability to seduce, devour, incorporate innocent youth into his heretical body. This incorporation occurs figuratively through the diffusion and inculcation of heterodox beliefs, and physically through the sexual practice of sodomy, of man 'devouring' man (Duggan 2013: 477).

[48] On how cannibalism as metaphor allows one to get away with murder, the following comment by Claude Rawson is worth contemplating: 'The cannibalism of the French, in Montaigne's account, is worse than the Brazilian cannibals' real man-eating, but it remains after all metaphorical, and therefore not so bad as the real thing. In this, it resembles the Eucharist, which may not be called metaphoric but may not be allowed to be anything else' (Rawson 1999: 179). Even when writers broach the theme of cannibalism, the tendency is to resort to 'circumnavigation, ambiguity, hinted denials, melodramatic horror or the nervous joke', instead of the otherwise remarkable sober factuality that tends to characterise the rest of the narrative (Rawson 1999: 187). Indeed, the drift to metaphor as a way of taking attention away from literal cannibalism is remarkable in the arsenal of metaphors with cannibalistic connotation in circulation. Rawson illustrates this drift into metaphors on the unspeakability that surrounds cannibalism thus: 'when, for example, lovers call their beloved sugar or honey, or experience a devouring passion; or when a woman is called a dish; or when retiring Speakers of the United States House of Representatives say their congressional colleagues are cannibals; or when a tyrant or a conquering nation swallows up its victims; or when we batten on one another in our personal relations; or when

mechanics cannibalise a car for spare parts; or when literary theorists use cannibal language to mean whatever literary theorists mean' (Rawson 1999: 188). To this could be added other cannibal metaphors in circulation in the world of sports and in industries of desire such as advertising, tourism and adult entertainment.

References

Abler, T. S. (1980) 'Iroquois Cannibalism: Fact Not Fiction', *Ethnohistory*, Vol. 27(4): 309–316.

Aggrawal, A. (2009) 'A New Classification of Necreophilia', *Journal of Forensic and Legal Medicine*, Vol. 16: 316–320.

Ardener, E. (1996) 'Witchcraft, Economics and the Continuity of Belief' in Ardener, Shirley (ed.): *Kingdom on Mount Cameroon: Studies in the History of the Cameroon Coast, 1500-1970*, Oxford: Berghahn.

Arens, W. (1979) *The Man-eating Myth: Anthropology and Anthropophagy*, New York: Oxford University Press.

Arens, W. (1998) 'Rethinking anthropophagy' in F. Barker, P. Hulme, and M. Iversen (eds): *Cannibalism and the Colonial World*, Cambridge: Cambridge University Press: pp. 39–62.

Arens, W. (2003) 'Cannibalism Reconsidered Responses to Marshall Sahlins', *Anthropology Today*, Vol. 19(5): 18–19.

Ashforth, A. (2000) *Madumo: A Man Bewitched*, Chicago: University of Chicago Press.

Au, S. (2017) 'Cutting the Flesh: Surgery, Autopsy and Cannibalism in the Belgian Congo', *Med. Hist.* Vol. 61(2): 295–312.

Aubry, C. (2002) 'Consuming Grief: Compassionate Cannibalism in an Amazonian Society (review)', *Anthropological Quarterly*, Vol. 75(2): 433–436.

Avramescu, C. (2009) *An Intellectual History of Cannibalism*, Princeton: Princeton University Press.

Barber, I. (1992) 'Archaeology, Ethnography, and the Record of Maori Cannibalism before 1815: A Critical Review', *The Journal of the Polynesian Society*, Vol. 101(3): 241–292.

Barker, F., Hulme, P., and Iversen, M. (eds) (1998) *Cannibalism and the Colonial World*, Cambridge: Cambridge University Press.

Beidelman, T. O. (1983) 'Reviewed Work: The Ethnography of Cannibalism by Paula Brown and Donald Tuzin', *Anthropos*, Bd. 78(5–6): 933–936.

Bellamy, D. (2014) 'Having an Old Friend for Dinner: Cannibalism Goes to the Movies', B. Media (Hons) thesis, Southern Cross University.

Bello, S.M., Wallduck, R., Dimitrijević V., Zivaljević, I., Stringer, C.B. (2016) 'Cannibalism versus Funerary Defleshing and Disarticulation after a Period of Decay: Comparisons of Bone Modifications from Four Prehistoric Sites', *American Journal of Physical Anthropology*, 161: 722–743.

Berglund, J. (1999) 'Write, Right, White, Rite: Literacy, Imperialism, Race, and Cannibalism in Edgar Rice Burroughs' *Tarzan of the Apes*', *Studies in American Fiction*, Vol. 27(1): 53–76.

Bernard, M. (2011) 'Cannibalism, Class and Power', *Food, Culture & Society*, Vol. 14(3): 413–432.

Blomster, J. (1984) 'Reasons for Cannibalism and Evidence in Pre-Historic Man', https://repository.wlu.edu/bitstream/handle/11021/32340/W LURG38_ArchPapers_Blomster_1984.pdf?sequence=1, accessed 26 November 2017.

Blythe, H. L. (2003) 'The Fixed Period (1882): Euthanasia, Cannibalism, and Colonial Extinction in Trollope's Antipodes', *Nineteenth-Century Contexts*, Vol. 25(2): 161–180.

Bourdieu, P. (1984) *Distinction: A Social Critique of the Judgement of Taste*, Cambridge, Massachusetts: Harvard University Press.

Bourdieu, P. (1996) *The State Nobility*, Cambridge: Polity.

Bourguignon, E. (1959) 'The Persistence of Folk Belief: Some Notes on Cannibalism and Zombis in Haiti', *The Journal of American Folklore*, Vol. 72(283): 36–46.

Brady, I. (1982) 'Review Articles: The Myth-Eating Man: *The Man-Eating Myth: Anthropology and Anthropophagy*. W. Arens. New York: Oxford University Press, 1979. vii + 206 pp. $9.95 (cloth)', *American Anthropologist*, Vol. 84(3): 595–611.

Brown, J. (2013) *Cannibalism in Literature and Film*, New York: Palgrave Macmillan.

Burley, M. (2016) 'Eating Human Beings: Varieties of Cannibalism and the Heterogeneity of Human Life', *Philosophy*, Vol. 91(4): 483–501.

Callander, J. K. (2014) 'Cannibalism and Communion in Swift's "Receipt to Restore Stella's Youth"', *SEL Studies in English Literature 1500–1900*, Vol. 54(3): 585–604.

Carbonell, E., Cáceres, I., Lozano, M., Saladié, P., Rosell, J., Lorenzo, C., Vallverdú, J. Huguet, R., Canals, A., and Bermúdez de Castro, J. M. (2010) 'Cultural Cannibalism as a Paleoeconomic System in the European Lower Pleistocene: The Case of Level TD6 of Gran Dolina (Sierra de Atapuerca, Burgos, Spain)', *Current Anthropology*, Vol. 51(4): 539–549.

Carrasco, D. (1995) 'Cosmic Jaws: We Eat the Gods and the Gods Eat Us', *Journal of the American Academy of Religion*, Vol. 63(3): 429–463.

Célestin, R. (1996) *From Cannibals to Radicals: Figures and Limits of Exoticism*, Minneapolis: University of Minnesota Press.

Chae, S. J. and Cooper, D. K. C. (1997) 'Review Article: Legal Implications of Xenotransplantation', *Xenotransplantation*, 4: 132–139.

Cohen, R. (2017) 'Strangers and Migrants in the Making of African Societies: A Conceptual and Historical Review', *Fudan Journal of the Humanities and Social Sciences* DOI 10.1007/s40647-017-0203-x.

Chesbro, G. C. (1990) *The Language of Cannibals*, New York: The Mysterious Press.

Comaroff, J., and Comaroff, J. L. (1991) *Of Revelation and Revolution: Christianity, Colonialism, and Consciousness in South Africa*, Volume One, Chicago: Chicago University Press.

Conklin, B. A. (2001) *Consuming Grief: Compassionate Cannibalism in an Amazonian Society*, Austin: University of Texas Press.

Debord, G. (1990) *Comments on the Society of the Spectacle*, New York: Verso.

Defoe, D. (2007) *Robinson Crusoe*, Oxford: Oxford University Press.

Delius, P. (2010) 'Recapturing Captives and Conversations with "Cannibals": In Pursuit of a Neglected Stratum in South African History', *Journal of Southern African Studies*, Vol. 36(1): 7–23.

Devisch, R. (1996) '"Pillaging Jesus": Healing Churches and the Villagisation of Kinshasa', *Africa*, Vol. 66(4): 555–585.

Devisch, R. (2017) *Body and Affect in the Intercultural Encounter*, Bamenda/Leiden: Langaa RPCIG/African Studies Centre, Leiden.

Diamond, J. (1998) *Guns, Germs and Steel: A Short History of Everybody for the Last 13,000 Years*, London: Vintage.

Diop, C. A. (1991) *Civilization or Barbarism: An Authentic Anthropology*, New York: Lawrence Hill Books.

Douglas, M. (2001[1966]) *Purity and Danger: An Analysis of the Concepts of Pollution and Taboo*, London: Routledge.

Duggan, A.E. (2013) 'Epicurean Cannibalism, or France Gone Savage', *French Studies*, Vol. LXVII(4): 463 – 477.

Dunn, S., (eds) (2002) *The Social Contract and the First and Second Discourses: Jean-Jacques Rousseau*, New Haven: Yale University Press.

Elias, N. (2000) *The Civilizing Process*, Oxford: Blackwell.

Elkington, J. (1997) *Cannibals with Forks: The Triple Bottom Line of 21st Century Business*, Oxford: Capstone Publishing Limited.

Ellis, S. (1999) *The Mask of Anarchy: The Destruction of Liberia and the Religious Dimension of an African Civil War*, London: Christopher Hurst.

Englund, H. (2015a) 'Forget the Poor Radio Kinship and Exploited Labor in Zambia', *Current Anthropology*, Vol. 56(11): S137–S145.

Englund, H. (2015b) 'Multivocal morality Narrative, Sentiment, and Zambia's Radio Grandfathers', *Hau: Journal of Ethnographic Theory*, Vol. 5(2): 251–273.

Esteban, R. (2016) 'Cannibalism among Japanese Soldiers in Bukidnon, Philippines, 1945–47', *Asian Studies: Journal of Critical Perspectives on Asia*, Vol. 52(1): 63–102.

Estok, S. C. (2012) 'Cannibalism, Ecocriticism, and Portraying the Journey', *CLCWeb: Comparative Literature and Culture*, 14.5 (2012): https://doi.org/10.7771/1481-4374.2138.

Eve, R. (1995) 'Shamanism, Sorcery and Cannibalism: The Incorporation of Power in the Magical Cult of *"Buai"*, *Oceania*, Vol. 65(3): 212–233.

Fairhead, J. (2015) *The Captain and 'the Cannibal': An Epic Story of Exploration, Kidnapping, and the Broadway Stage*, New Haven: Yale University Press.

Fardon, R. (2014) *Tiger in an African Palace and Other Thoughts about Identification and Transformation*, Bamenda: Langaa.

Fausto, C. (2007) 'Feasting on People: Eating Animals and Humans in Amazonia', *Current Anthropology*, Vol. 48(4): 497–530.

Fitzhugh, G. (1988[1960]) *Cannibals All! Or Slaves Without Masters*, edited by C. Vann Woodward, Cambridge, Massachusetts: The Belknap Press of Harvard University Press.

Friedman, J. (1991) 'Consuming Desires: Strategies of Selfhood and Appropriation', *Cultural Anthropology*, Vol. 6(2): 154–163.

Gabaccia, D. R. (1998) *We Are What We Eat: Ethnic Food and the Making of Americans*, Cambridge, Massachusetts: Harvard University Press.

Galloway, S. (2017) *The Four: The Hidden DNA of Amazon, Apple, Facebook, and Google*, London: Portfolio.

George, S. (1990) *A Fate Worse than Debt: The World Financial Crisis and the Poor*, New York: Grove Press.

Geschiere, P. (1995) *Sorcellerie et Politique en Afrique: La Viande des Autres*, Paris: Karthala.

Geschiere, P. (1997) *The Modernity of Witchcraft: Politics and the Occult in Postcolonial Africa*, Charlottesville: University Press of Virginia.

Geschiere, P. (2009) *The Perils of Belonging: Autochthony, Citizenship and Exclusion in Africa and Europe*, Chicago: University of Chicago Press.

Geschiere, P. (2013) *Witchcraft, Intimacy, and Trust: Africa in Comparison*, Chicago: University of Chicago Press.

Gill, D. (1999) 'The Fascination of the Abomination: Conrad and Cannibalism', *The Conradian*, Vol. 24(2): 1–30.

Gilley, B. (2016) 'Chinua Achebe on the Positive Legacies of Colonialism', *African Affairs*, Vol. 115(461): 646–663.

Gilley, B. (2017) 'The case for colonialism', *Third World Quarterly*, DOI:10.1080/01436597.2017.1369037.

Goody, J. (1982) *Cooking, Cuisine and Class: A Study in Comparative Sociology*, Cambridge: Cambridge University Press.

Gordon, R. J. (2013) 'Not Studying White, Up or Down, but Around Southern Africa: A Response to Francis Nyamnjoh', *Africa Spectrum*, Vol. 48(2): 117–121.

Gordon-Grube, K. (1988) 'Anthropophagy in Post-Renaissance Europe: The Tradition of Medicinal Cannibalism', *American Anthropologist*, Vol. 90(2): 405–409.

Green, M. (1998) 'Humans as Ritual Victims in the Later Prehistory of Western Europe', *Oxford Journal of Archaeology*, Vol. 17(2): 169–189.

Guest, K. (2001a) 'Introduction: Cannibalism and the Boundaries of Identity', in: K. Guest (ed.) *Eating Their Words: Cannibalism and the Boundaries of Cultural Identity*, New York: State University of New York Press, pp. 1–9.

Guest, K., (ed.) (2001b) *Eating Their Words: Cannibalism and the Boundaries of Cultural Identity*, New York: State University of New York Press.

Gustav, J. (1999) *The Images of Savages: Ancient Roots of Modern Prejudice in Western Culture*, New York: Routledge.

Hand, G. (2001) *Naked Among Cannibals: What Really Happens Inside Australian Banks*, Crows Nest: Allen & Unwin.

Harris, M. (1977) *Cannibals and Kings: The Origins of Culture*, Glasgow: Fontana/Collins.

Harrison, F. V. (2008) *Outsider Within: Reworking Anthropology in the Global Age*, Urbana: University of Illinois Press.

Harvey, G. (2004) 'Endo-cannibalism in the Making of a Recent British Ancestor', *Mortality*, Vol. 9(3): 255–267.

Hubinger, V. and Svatoňová, L. (1991) 'Svět Za Ohradou / The World Beyond the Fence', *Český lid*, Vol. 78(1): 1–12.

Hulme, P. (1998) 'Introduction: The Cannibal Scene', in F. Barker, P. Hulme, and M. Iversen (eds) *Cannibalism and the Colonial World*, Cambridge: Cambridge University Press, pp. 1–38.

Irvine, W. B. (1989) 'Cannibalism, Vegetarianism, and Narcissism', *Between the Species*, Vol. 5(1) Article 4: 11–17.

Jancovich, M. (2013) 'Foreword', in J. Brown, (author), *Cannibalism in Literature and Film*, New York: Palgrave Macmillan, pp. ix–x.

Johnson, N. B. (1993) 'Cannibals and Culture: The Anthropology of Michel de Montaigne', *Dialectical Anthropology*, Vol. 18: 153–176.

Jooma, M. (1997) 'Robinson Crusoe Inc (Corporates): Domestic economy, Incest and the Trope of Cannibalism', *Lit: Literature Interpretation Theory*, Vol. 8(1): 61-81.

Jooma, M. (2001) 'Robinson Crusoe Inc(orporates): Domestic Economy, Incest, and the Trope of Cannibalism', in: Guest, K. (ed.): *Eating Their Words: Cannibalism and the Boundaries of Cultural Identity*, New York: State University of New York Press, pp. 57–8).

Juall, S. D. (2008) '"Beaucoup plus barbares que les Sauvages mesmes": Cannibalism, Savagery, and Religious Alterity in Jean de Léry's Histoire d'un voyage faict en la terre du Brésil (1599–1600)', *L'Esprit Créateur*, Vol. 48(1): 58–71.

Kilgour, M. (1990) *From Communion to Cannibalism: An Anatomy of Metaphors of Incorporation*, Princeton: Princeton University Press.

Kilgour, M. (1997) 'Cannibals and Critics: An Exploration of James de Mille's "Strange Manuscript"', *Mosaic: An Interdisciplinary Critical Journal*, Vol. 30(1): 19–37.

Kilgour, M. (2001) 'Foreword' in K. Guest (ed.): *Eating Their Words: Cannibalism and the Boundaries of Cultural Identity*, New York: State University of New York Press, pp. vii–viii.

Kirkaldy, A. (2005) '"There is no meat that tastes better than human flesh!" Christian Converts' Tales of Cannibalism in Late Nineteenth-century Sekhukhuneland', *Historia*, Vol. 50(2): 25–61.

Klein, J. A. and Murcott, A. (eds) (2014) *Food Consumption in Global Perspective: Essays in the Anthropology of Food in Honour of Jack Goody*, Basingstoke: Palgrave Macmillan.

Langfur, H. (2014a) 'Introduction: Recovering Brazil's Indigenous Pasts' in H. Langfur (ed.): *Native Brazil: Beyond the Convert and the Cannibal, 1500–1900*, Albuquerque: University of New Mexico Press, pp. 1–28.

Langfur, H. (ed.) (2014b) *Native Brazil: Beyond the Convert and the Cannibal, 1500–1900*, Albuquerque: University of New Mexico Press.

Lategan, B. C. (2018) 'In Praise of Strangeness. Exploring the Hermeneutical Potential of an Unlikely Source,' *Stellenbosch Theological Journal* Vol. 4(1): (in press).

Lefebvre, M. (2005) 'Conspicuous Consumption: The Figure of the Serial Killer as Cannibal in the Age of Capitalism', *Theory, Culture & Society*, Vol. 22(3): 43–62.

Lévi-Strauss, C. (2016[2013]) *We Are All Cannibals and Other Essays*, New York: Columbia University Press.

Lindenbaum, S. (2004) 'Thinking about Cannibalism', *Annual Review of Anthropology*, Vol. 33: 475–98.

Lindenbaum, S. (2008) 'Review: Understanding Kuru: The Contribution of Anthropology and Medicine', *Philosophical Transactions: Royal Society B*, 363, 3715–3720.

Lindenbaum, S. (2009) 'Cannibalism, Kuru and Anthropology', *Folia Neuropathol*, Vol. 47(2): 138–144.

Lumholtz, C. (2009[1889]) *Among Cannibals: An Account of Four Years' Travels in Australia and of Camp Life with the Aborigines of Queensland*, Cambridge: Cambridge University Press.

Lyon, P. (1995) 'From Man-Eaters to Spam-Eaters: Literary Tourism and the Discourse of Cannibalism from Herman Melville to Paul Theroux', *Arizona Quarterly: A Journal of American Literature, Culture, and Theory*, Vol. 51(2): 33–62.

Macintosh, A. (2011) 'Crusoe's Abattoir: Cannibalism and Animal Slaughter in Robinson Crusoe', *Critical Quarterly*, Vol. 53(3): 24–43.

Mar, T. B. (2016) 'Performing Cannibalism in the South Seas' in Kalissa Alexeyeff and John Taylor (eds) *Touring Pacific Cultures*, Acton: Australian National University, pp. 323–331.

Maranhão, T. (1998) 'The Adventures of Ontology in the Amazon Forest', *Paideuma: Mitteilungen zur Kulturkunde*, Bd. 44, pp. 155–168.

Marcelin, L. H. (2012) 'In the Name of the Nation: Blood Symbolism and the Political Habitus of Violence in Haiti', *American Anthropologist*, Vol. 114(2): 253–266.

Martinez, K. (2011) 'Gendered Consumptions: Cannibalism as a Form of Patriarchal Control', *The Rutgers Journal of Sociology*, Vol. 1(1): 89–109.

Masquelier, A. (2000) 'Of Hunters and Cannibals: Migration, Labor and Consumption in the Mawri Imagination', *Cultural Anthropology*, Vol. 15(1): 84–126.

Mavhungu, K. (2012) *Witchcraft in Post-Colonial Africa: Beliefs, Techniques and Containment Strategies*, Bamenda: Langaa.

McGowan, A. (1994) 'Eating People: Accusations of Cannibalism against Christians in the Second Century', *Journal of Early Christian Studies*, Vol. 2(4): 413–442.

Metcalf, A. C. (2014) 'The Society of Jesus and the First Aldeias of Brazil' in H. Langfur (ed.): *Native Brazil: Beyond the Convert and the Cannibal, 1500–1900*, Albuquerque: University of New Mexico Press, pp. 29–61.

Miller, L. (1995) 'Southern Silk Route Tales: Hospitality, Cannibalism and the Other', *Merveilles & contes*, Vol. 9(2): 137–169.

Montaigne, M. (1943[1580]) 'Of Cannibals' in Donald M. Frame (translator), *Michel de Montaigne, Selected Essays*, New York: Walter J. Black, pp. 73–92.

Moore, H. L. and Sanders, T., (eds) (2001) *Magical Interpretations, Material Realities: Modernity, Witchcraft and the Occult in Postcolonial Africa*, London: Routledge.

Ng, L. (2015) 'Cannibalism, Colonialism and Apocalypse in Mitchell's Global Future', *SubStance*, Vol. 44(1): 107–122.

Niehaus, I., (with Eliazaar Mohlala) (2001) *Witchcraft, Power and Politics: Exploring the Occult in the South African Lowveld*, London: Pluto Press.

Noble, L. (2011) *Medicinal Cannibalism in Early Modern English Literature and Culture*, New York: Palgrave Macmillan.

Nunes, Z. (2008) *Cannibal Democracy: Race and Representation in the Literature of the Americas*, Minneapolis: University of Minnesota Press.

Nyamnjoh, F. B. (2001) 'Delusions of development and the enrichment of witchcraft discourses in Cameroon' in H. Moore, and T. Sanders (eds): *Magical Interpretations, Material Realities: Modernity, Witchcraft and the Occult in Postcolonial Africa*, London: Routledge, 28–49.

Nyamnjoh, F. B. (2012) 'Blinded by Sight: Diving the Future of Anthropology in Africa', *Africa Spectrum*, Vol. 47(2–3): 63–92.

Nyamnjoh, F. B. (2013) 'Fiction and Reality of Mobility in Africa', *Citizenship Studies*, Vol. 17(6–7): 653–680.

Nyamnjoh, F. B. (2015a) *C'est l'homme qui fait l'homme: Cul-de-Sac Ubuntu-ism in Côte d'Ivoire*, Bamenda: Langaa.

Nyamnjoh, F. B. (2105b) 'Beyond an Evangelising Public Anthropology: Science, Theory and Commitment', *Journal of Contemporary African Studies*, 33(1): 48–63.

Nyamnjoh, F. B. (2017[2015]a) 'Incompleteness: Frontier Africa and the Currency of Conviviality', *Journal of Asian and African Studies*, Vol. 52(3): 253–270.

Nyamnjoh, F. B. (2017b) *Drinking from the Cosmic Gourd: How Amos Tutuola Can Change Our Minds*, Bamenda: Langaa.

Nyamnjoh, F. B., and Fuh, D. (2014) 'Africans Consuming Hair, Africans Consumed by Hair', *Africa Insight*, Vol. 44(1): 52–68.

Nyamnjoh, H. and Rowlands, M. (2013) 'Do You Eat Achu Here? Nurturing as a Way of Life in a Cameroon Diaspora', *Critical African Studies*, Vol. 5(3): 140–152.

Obeyesekere, G. (2005) *Cannibal Talk: The Man-Eating Myth and Human Sacrifice in the South Seas*, Berkeley: University of California Press.

Oakdale, S. (2004) 'Review: Consuming Grief: Compassionate Cannibalism in an Amazonian Society. Beth A. Conklin. Austin: University of Texas Press, 2001. 317 pp.', *American Anthropologist*, Vol. 106(1): 183–184.

Petrey, D. (2005) 'Write about All of This: Concerning Cannibalism Revisionism', *Chasqui: revista de literatura latinoamericana*, Vol. 34(1): 13–123.

Pettey, H. B. (2003) 'Cannibalism, Slavery, and Self-Consumption in Moby-Dick', *Arizona Quarterly: A Journal of American Literature, Culture, and Theory*, Vol. 59(1): 31–58.

Pfennig, D. W. (1997) 'Kinship and Cannibalism', *BioScience*, Vol. 47(10): 667–675.

Piatti-Farnell, L. (2010) 'A Tour of the Cannibal Quarters: Industrial Fantasies and Carnivorous Appetites in Roald Dahl's Fiction', *Otherness: Essays and Studies* 1.1,

http://www.otherness.dk/fileadmin/www.othernessandthearts.
org/Publications/Journal_Otherness/Otherness__Essays_and_
Studies_1.1/A_Tour_of_the_Cannibal_Quarters_01.pdf,
accessed 2 November 2017.

Podruchny, C. (2004) 'Werewolves and Windigos: Narratives of
Cannibal Monsters in French-Canadian Voyageur Oral
Tradition', *Ethnohistory*, Vol. 51(4): 677–700.

Price, L. M. (2003) *Consuming Passions: The Uses of Cannibalism in Late
Medieval and Early Modern Europe*, New York: Routledge.

Ranger, T. (2007) 'Review Article: Scotland Yard in the Bush:
Medicine Murders, Child Witches and the Construction of the
Occult: A Literature Review', *Africa*, Vol. 77(2): 272–283.

Rawson, C. (1999) 'Unspeakable Rites: Cultural Reticence and the
Cannibal Question', *Social Research*, Vol. 66(1): 167–193.

Reynolds, F. V. (2009) 'Literary: Cannibalism: Almost the Same, but
Not Quite/Almost the Same, but Not White', PhD
Dissertation, Graduate School of Arts and Sciences, Harvard
University, Cambridge, Massachusetts.

Richards, P. (2009) 'Dressed to Kill: Clothing as Technology of the
Body in the Civil War in Sierra Leone', *Journal of Material Culture*,
Vol. 14(4): 495–512.

Rothera, E. C. (2009) '"Since This is a Horrible Thing to Think
About": European Perceptions of Native American
Cannibalism', *The Gettysburg Historical Journal*, Vol. 8: 1–34.

Sahlins, M. (1978) 'Culture as Protein and Profit', *The New York
Review*, November 23, pp. 45–53.

Sahlins, M. (2003) 'Artificially Maintained Controversies: Global
Warming and Fijian Cannibalism', *Anthropology Today*, Vol. 19(3):
3–5.

Salmon, M. H. (1995) 'Standards of Evidence in Anthropological
Reasoning', *The Southern Journal of Philosophy*, Vol. XXXIV: 129–
145.

Salpeteura, M. and Warnier, J.-P. (2013) 'Looking for the Effects of
Bodily Organs and Substances through Vernacular Public
Autopsy in Cameroon', *Critical African Studies*, Vol. 5(3): 153–
174.

Samba, P. M., (2012) *Witchcraft, Magic and Divination: Accounts from the Wimbum Area of the Cameroon Grassfields*, Bamenda: Langaa.

Sanders, T. (2008) *Beyond Bodies: Rainmaking and Sense Making in Tanzania*, Toronto: University of Toronto Press.

Sanner, M. A. (2001) 'People's Feelings and Ideas about Receiving Transplants of Different Origins – Questions of Life and Death, Identity, and Nature's Border', *Clinical Transplantation*, 15: 19–27.

Scheper-Hughes, N. (2000) 'The Global Traffic in Human Organs', *Current Anthropology*, Vol. 41(2): 191–224.

Scheper-Hughes, N. (2001a) 'Bodies for Sale – Whole or in Parts', *Body & Society*, Vol. 7(2–3): 1–8.

Scheper-Hughes, N. (2001b) 'Commodity Fetishism in Organs Trafficking', *Body & Society*, Vol. 7(2–3): 31–62.

Scheper-Hughes, N. (2001c) 'Neo-Cannibalism: The Global Trade in Human Organs', Special Issue on The Body and Being Human, *Hedgehog Review*, Vol. 3(2): 79–99.

Scheper-Hughes, N. (2004) 'Parts unknown: Undercover Ethnography of the Organs-trafficking Underworld', *Ethnograpy*, Vol. 5(1): 29–73.

Schneider, Z. (2013) 'In Vitro Meat: Space Travel, Cannibalism, and Federal Regulation', *50 Houston Law Review*, Vol. 50(3): 991–1026.

Schwarcz, L. M. (2017) 'I was Cannibalised by an Artist' in João Biehl and Peter Locke (eds): *Unfinished: The Anthropology of Belonging*, Durham: Duke University Press, pp. 173–196.

Sewlall, H. (2006) 'Cannibalism in the Colonial Imaginary: A Reading of Joseph Conrad's "Falk"', *Journal of Literary Studies*, Vol. 22(1–2): 158–174.

Shilling, C. (2012[1993]) *The Body & Social Theory*, Los Angeles: Sage.

Simmel, G. (1950) 'The Stranger' in Kurt Wolff (Trans.): *The Sociology of Georg Simmel*, New York: Free Press, 1950, pp. 402–408.

Sugg, R. (2006) '"Good Physic but Bad Food": Early Modern Attitudes to Medicinal Cannibalism and its Suppliers', *Social History of Medicine*, Vol. 19(2): 225–240.

Sugg, R. (2013) 'Medicinal Cannibalism in Early Modern Literature and Culture', *Literature Compass*, 10/11: 825–835.

Takada, S. (1999) *Contingency of Cannibalism: Superhardcore Survivalism's Dirty Little Secret*, Boulder, Colorado: Paladin Press.

Tarlo, E. (2016) *Entanglement: The Secret Lives of Hair*, London: One World Publications.

Taussig, M. (1987) *Shamanism, Colonialism, and the Wild Man: A Study in Terror and Healing*, Chicago: Chicago University Press.

Thiessen, I. (2001) 'The Social Construction of Gender. Female Cannibalism in Papua New Guinea', *Anthropos*, Bd. 96, H. 1, pp. 141–156.

Thornton, J. (2003) 'Cannibals, Witches, and Slave Traders in the Atlantic World', T*he William and Mary Quarterly*, Vol. 60(2): 273–294.

Tiffin, H. (2007) 'Foot in Mouth: Animals, Disease, and the Cannibal Complex', *Mosaic: An Interdisciplinary Critical Journal*, Vol. 40(1): 11–26.

Travis-Henikoff (2008) *Dinner with a Cannibal: The Complete History of Mankind's Oldest Tabo*, Santa Monica: Santa Monica Press LLC.

Tsai, Y.-C. (2016) 'You Are Whom You Eat: Cannibalism in Contemporary Chinese Fiction and Film', PhD Dissertation, University of California, Irvine.

Turner II, C. G. (2008) 'Foreword' in Carole A. Travis-Henikoff, *Dinner with a Cannibal: The Complete History of Mankind's Oldest Tabo*, Santa Monica: Santa Monica Press LLC.

Tutuola, A. (1952) *The Palm-Wine Drinkard*, London: Faber and Faber.

Uhlir, K. K. (2016) *Civilized Barbarism: Cannibalism and Rome in Coriolanus and Titus Andronicus*, Honours Thesis in English, Washington and Lee University.

Valsiner, J. (2000) 'Social Consumption of Cannibals', *Culture & Psychology*, Vol. 6(1): 88–96.

Van Beers, B. (2012) 'TV Cannibalism, Body Worlds and Trade in Human Body Parts: Legal-Philosophical Reflections on the Rise of Late Modern Cannibalism', *Amsterdam Law Forum*, Vol. 4(2): 65–75.

Vilaca, A. (2000) 'Relations between Funerary Cannibalism and Warfare Cannibalism: The Question of Predation', *Ethnos*, Vol. 65(1): 83–106.

Viveiros de Castro, E. B. (2004) 'Exchanging Perspectives: The Transformation of Objects into Subjects in Amerindian Ontologies', *Common Knowledge*, Vol. 10(3): 463–484.

Viveiros de Castro, E. (2014[2009]) *Cannibal Metaphysics: For a Post-Structural Anthropology*, Minneapolis: Univocal Publishing.

Wankier, A. M. (2016) 'Consuming Narratives: Food and Cannibalism in Early Modern British Imperialism', PhD Dissertation in History, University of California Irvine.

Warnier, J.-P. (1993) 'The King as a Container in the Cameroon Grassfields', *Paideuma*, Bd. 39: 303–319

Wasserman, H. (2010) *Tabloid Journalism in South Africa: True Story!*, Bloomington: Indiana University Press.

Watson, K. L. (2006) 'Encountering Cannibalism: A Cultural History', unpublished MA Thesis, Graduate College of Bowling Green State University, USA.

White, T. D. (2001) 'We Were Cannibals', *Scientific American*, Vol. 285(2): 58–65.

Wilby, E. (2013) 'Burchard's *strigae*, the Witches' Sabbath, and Shamanistic Cannibalism in Early Modern Europe', *Magic, Ritual, and Witchcraft*, Vol. 8(1): 18–49.

Willerslev, R. (2004) 'Not Animal, Not Not-Animal: Hunting, Imitation and Empathetic Knowledge among the Siberian Yukaghirs', *The Journal of the Royal Anthropological Institute*, Vol. 10(3): 629–652.

Willerslev, R. (2007) *Soul Hunters: Hunting, Animism, and Personhood among the Siberian Yukaghirs*, Berkeley: University of California Press.

Williams, W. (2012) '"'L'Humanité du tout perdue?'": Early Modern Monsters, Cannibals and Human Souls', *History and Anthropology*, Vol. 23(2): 235–256.

Zulaika, J. (1993) 'Further Encounters with the Wild Man: Of Cannibals, Dogs, and Terrorists', *Etnofoor*, Vol. 6(2): 21–39.

Chapter 2

The Violence of Translating People into Cannibals: The Man-Eating Anthropologists

Andreas Buhler

The violence of translating people into cannibals

The first thing most people think about when they hear the word 'cannibal' is the brutal killing and then the eating of a fellow human being as portrayed in movies and books. For many this will also conjure up the image of a non-western other living on the fringes of the 'known world' (Avramescu 2009). The idea of consumption is taken to mean the devouring of human flesh. Yet as Francis Nyamnjoh argues in the introduction to this book, the consumption of humans means more than just the eating of human flesh, and to some degree we all consume human beings in one way or another. The charge of cannibalism is most commonly used to dehumanise those seen as 'threatening the social order' (Kilgour 1998: 239) or to create a dichotomy between civilisation and barbarism (Avramescu 2009). Acknowledging that we are all consumers of humans in different ways helps us to accept the notion that our humanity is shared and universal. Recognising our own cannibalistic practices makes us better at acknowledging and accepting the diverse ways in which one can be human. To this end, I argue in this chapter that the colonialist discourse translated people into cannibals as a tool for creating an image of the savage other. I follow the argument on cannibalism to further show how, through the violence of translation and our historical relationship with the colonial project (Asad 1973; Mafeje 1976), we as anthropologists are also cannibals and consumers of human lives.

To substantiate this argument will demand an analysis of how the cannibal is understood in western enlightenment thinking, which has deeply shaped anthropology as a discipline, and how this thinking has affected the production of academic knowledge. In engaging with

99

this problem my literature research has not so much been to find ethnographic accounts of cannibalism, of which there are plenty, but to find narratives that illuminate aspects of cannibalism as imagined in western thought and as utilised in colonialist conquest. The focus of this chapter is therefore how cannibalism has been written about and in this pursuit it speaks to how the discipline of anthropology goes about consuming people in research and writing. Conducting ethnographic research can in itself be an act of violence or exploitation. If cannibalism is about the making and projections of the self through ingesting other people, as Nyamnjoh suggests in the introduction of this book, then the anthropologist is certainly a cannibal. We devour the lives of the participants in our research projects and the essence of who they are to establish ourselves and our identities in our professional (and personal) lives.

The debate between Obeyesekere (1992, 1998, 2005), Arens (1979 1998) and Sahlins (1983, 1995) about cannibalism, colonialism and representation is illuminating in showing both how cannibalism has been written about and how we as anthropologists can devour the subjects of our research. Over the three decades' long debate the academic discourse on cannibalism has changed drastically. In recent years the writing and research methods of anthropology have become increasingly ethical and humane. Yet it is important to remember that no matter what, we are consumers of people in our professional lives, and that we must make the choice of whether we devour our research subjects with the care of a funeral rite (Conklin 2001: xv) or in the reckless and uncaring manner of capitalism (Phillips 1998: 185), which has devoured millions without a thought.

The chapter also reflects upon the violent nature of translating peoples' lives into academic texts. Cultural translation was from the 1950s a common way for anthropologists to refer to their own profession (Asad 1986: 142), so there is no doubt that translating peoples' lives is at the core of what we do. The kind of violence that is the focus of this chapter is the structural violence of colonialism and the violence of anthropological translation of social lives into texts. By structural violence I mean violence that 'is exerted systematically – that is indirectly – by everyone who belongs to a certain social order' (Farmer 2004: 307). Using the concept of

100

structural violence as an analytical tool is useful in uncovering the violence of colonialism and to uproot the inner workings of the processes that perpetuate that violence. Especially this is true for the more subtle forms in which colonial violence is perpetuated as is the case in how we write about cannibalism.

Galtung (1990) divides violence into three expressions: structural, cultural and direct violence. Structural violence has exploitation at its centre, cultural violence is used to justify and legitimise violence and direct violence is the physical acts of violence like killing and maiming (Galtung 1990). Farmer (2004) argues that these three expressions of violence could all be seen as forms of structural violence. Structural violence inherently tries to justify itself and is also a factor in any form of direct violence. This approach to structural violence is useful to my analysis, as the notion of cannibalism in the colonial discourse was both a result of and legitimacy for structural violence and a justification for the usage of direct violence.

Anthropology, cannibalism and colonial violence

Altering history 'is perhaps the most common explanatory sleight of hand relied upon by the architects of structural violence' (Farmer 2004: 308). The earliest anthropologists can be said to be complicit in the colonialist project as they legitimated the conquest by coining the colonised peoples as the early stages of societal evolution (Ferguson 2005: 141), and thereby propping up the mission to civilise. While later anthropologists tried to break with the early evolutionist perspective, they were still holding on to the dualism of primitive/civilised and traditional/modern and in doing so reinforced the notion of societies as ranged on an evolutionary ladder. Anthropologists were also complicit in colonialism by not really critiquing or sometimes even taking into account the presence of colonial conquest; it was after all colonialism that enabled some of the early groundbreaking ethnographic research such as that of Malinowski's study of the Trobriander Islands (Mosse 2006: 936). The methods of ethnographic research were inextricably linked to – and in many ways complicit in – the structural violence of colonialism (Mafeje 1976: 317) and, as I elaborate on later in this chapter, it is a link that still haunts anthropology as a discipline today.

It is in this aspect of anthropology's complicity in the structural violence of colonialism that I see the concept of translation to become important. This image of anthropology as complicit is historically reproduced by the anthropological technique of writing in the ethnographic present and which has continued to deprive the subjects of anthropological research of any agentic capability and modes of change. The cannibal has become a category that immediately creates an image of the people described and attributes to them the moral and historical contents of that category. Obeyesekere (2005) argues that the colonial discourse on cannibalism has informed and shaped any subsequent discourses on the topic. As soon as the notion of the cannibal is invoked, the people spoken about are translated into a certain discourse with the moral judgments that are attached. With cannibalism it seems that even the most open-minded struggle to reserve judgment and disgust, and it is most often seen as the depth of human depravity (Burley 2016: 485). Colonialist notions such as savage or primitive will often automatically follow on from this. In translating the colonised people into savages, the violence of colonialism is excused as a mission to help the presumed helpless and irrational natives.

In line with this argument Rosman and Rubel (2003) state that: 'Hierarchy, hegemony and cultural dominance are often said to be reflected in translations, especially those which were done during the colonial period', and they argue further that 'these features are also said to be present in translations, which are being done now in the postcolonial period' (Rosman and Rubel 2003: 6). The translation of culture, from the subjects of research projects to academic texts, which is central to the anthropological pursuit, reflects the dominant systems of power. Anthropological research cannot therefore be divorced from colonial discourses which continue to be reproduced still. Cannibalism continues to be a label reserved for certain peoples and practices and once evoked translates people into primitives both in the colonial and the post-colonial period. The translation of people into savages, robbing them of their humanity, was an integral part in the structural violence of colonialism, and was intended to cover over the violence of colonialism and to deny the humanity of the colonised. This was done to bridge the enlightenment paradox between its humanistic ideals and the brutality of colonial conquest, a paradox that has been at the centre of anthropological research as well. So while Europeans were devouring human lives at an unprecedented scale they were constantly throwing accusations of cannibalism at the very people being devoured.

Creating images of cannibals was an act of translating local people into savages in need of being saved from the natural state that they live in, how this seeks to hide the violence and exploitation of colonialism and for architects of structural violence to moralise their own actions. It becomes a mission to civilise and save rather than to conquer and exploit. In the colonialist discourse the two sets of concepts so seemingly far apart become the same, saving is conquering and civilising is exploiting. Violence and translation are part of the same process of domination. People are translated into savages being described as cannibals which in itself is a violent act by the translator, and, at the same time, this translation becomes integral in excusing and hiding the structural violence of colonialism and global capitalism.

In ethnographic texts based on sources from people closely related to the colonialist project, the image of the cannibal savage is reproduced. These accounts are in turn used to write ethnographies on cannibalism, and when reproduced without a critical engagement with the concept of cannibalism also tend to reproduce with it the colonialist discourse on the people colonised. The ethnographer's mission is to collect data and information which capture peoples' lives and freeze them in a moment in time. This means that people's lives are the lifeblood and what gives nourishment to the discipline of anthropology and to the individual anthropologist's academic career. Interestingly this makes the anthropologist himself into a cannibal of sorts. But what is really meant when the term 'cannibal' is invoked? Before I move on, it becomes pertinent to unpack what it actually means to name someone a cannibal.

The problematic notion of cannibalism

The term 'cannibal' is presumed to be derived from the Spanish name that the colonialist conquerors gave to the local people living in the Caribbean during Christopher Columbus's expedition. 'Cannibal' is itself derived from *Canibales*, the Spanish name used for the local Carib people, at the time of Columbus's arrival in the Americas (Hulme 1998). It is therefore a term which from its inception is tied to one of the earliest colonialist encounters. It has later been invoked in many colonialist encounters; in fact the colonialist presence seems to bring out the cannibals in numbers (Banivanua-Mar 2010). The reason I have chosen to focus on cannibalism is because it is illuminating of the process in which colonialist and post-colonialist discourse around notions of the exotic other. The anthropological debates around the notion of cannibalism further serve to highlight the ethical dilemmas of doing ethnographic research. It is, as I will argue later, one of the strongest forms of othering, as it immediately creates boundaries of who belongs where and creates dichotomies of us and them.

To understand how people were translated into savages I will first have to understand how western thinkers thought of and described cannibalism. What did cannibalism mean in the western imagination? In *An Intellectual History of Cannibalism*, Avramescu (2009) shows how different thinkers in western philosophy and science saw the cannibal morally and geographically, and how this thinking is deeply entrenched in the notion of a binary divide between civilised and savage.

Jerry Phillips (1998) shows how the cannibalism traps the colonised local people into a dangerous other. This image is created in effort for the capitalism and colonialism to invoke hostility and resentment against the victims of these systems of dominance, or to create a moral pretence for exploitation. Cannibalism was an integral part of the Spanish colonialist creation of the Caribbean peoples into savages and in turn obscured the true savagery of the colonialist conquest (Phillips 1998: 191). This is shown in the ultimatum that Cortés gave the local peoples he encountered: 'to warn and command them not to worship idols, or sacrifice human beings and eat their flesh' (Phillips 1998: 192). It was clear that if they did not commit to these terms they would all be killed.

The notion of the cannibal is therefore not only interlinked with the beginning of colonialism, but is also strongly related with the exotic other. These are both prominent elements in the history of how western thinkers viewed cannibalism. Focusing on thinkers like Thomas Hobbes, John Lock, Adam Smith, David Hume and many others, Avramescu (2009) gives a comprehensive analysis of the different dominant theoretical perspectives on cannibalism of the European enlightenment period. He (Avramescu 2009) further shows the conceptions intellectuals at the time had of the cannibal as both a real world phenomenon and a literary figure. This shows not only how people were made into savages by creating notions of cannibalism, but also what imagery was invoked when people spoke of the cannibal. This is an issue that follows discourses on cannibalism today still, while academics try to portray cannibalism as something morally relativistic it still contains the perspective and moral judgement of the enlightenment age.

Avramescu (2009) identifies three stages of cannibalism in western thought: first as a creature of natural law, second as a diabolical retort and third a creature of circumstance and education. All three stages are fitted into colonialist notions of the savage other. The cornerstone of the enlightenment scientific thought was the notion that the world should be viewed through a lens of fundamental opposites. Outside the boundaries of civilisation there had to be a brutal and grotesque figure, the opposite of the civic man (Avramescu 2009: 8). The cannibal was before and during the enlightenment period described as the uncontrolled state of man that has become a part of nature, nature here seen as a binary opposite to culture. The idea that a person or people could be civil was therefore countered with the opposite notion that some people had to be savages. This is a binary that continued to be prominent in 20th century anthropology, most obviously so in much of the early ethnographic research in which the anthropologist is seen as rational/modern and the research subjects as cultural/traditional.

The 17th and 18th century thinkers saw cannibalism only as a morally just act when it was of the absolute necessity (Avramescu

2009). This would be in a situation where the survival of a group depended on the killing and eating of another human being, such as if people were adrift at sea without supplies. It would then be the natural law of survival rather than the civic law that should guide people's actions. The peoples that then practised cannibalism as a part of the norm rather than exception were seen as breaking both civic and natural law and therefore men of nature and were seen as primitive. The cannibal, in eating human flesh when not a necessity, could only be explained by being so alienated from the rules of man that the rules of nature had to be inverted. It then follows that people practising habitual or continued acts of cannibalism are seen as part of nature and therefore savage and the opposite of adhering to the civic laws of man. In a time when more rights are given to the supposed rational individual the natural man is, in the moral philosophy of the 18th century, stripped of his rights as a rational actor as he cannot be trusted to not abuse his rights (Avramescu 2009: 45).

The natural man was at one point seen as a weak being and the absence of society is inscribed in him (Avramescu 2009: 72). This view was however contradicted by other thinkers who argued that the savage was a dangerous animal or beast. The high point of torture and cruelty was the devouring of the flesh of one's victims; in the early accounts written by Christopher Columbus the cannibal is described as a monster, a man with the head of a dog (Avramescu 2009: 78–86). 'During the Enlightenment, the cannibal thus acquires one of the attributes of the Devil, that of being the incarnation of extreme evil' (Avramescu 2009: 89). The view of the cannibal moves from this image to one of a domesticated monster, a kind of man, but not really, a trainable beast of sorts. The natural man or the cannibal then becomes understood as both child that has been inhibited by growing up in the wild and needs to be trained, and a savage and threatening beast that needs to be conquered (Avramescu 2009: 91). The colonised peoples are seen as alternatively as these two representations, sometimes the beast that needs to be defeated and sometimes the child that needs to be taught.

The explorer James Cook saw himself as a father of both his crew and the peoples that he encountered. They had to listen to his orders or else be disciplined, but this was not done with the intent of conquest, but of nurturing a so called civilised society and any resistance could not be tolerated (Obeyesekere 1992). Cook and other explorers were practically the first ethnographers who recorded on the peoples and customs they encountered. For instance it was an explorer on board Columbus's ship that wrote about the first reported case of supposed cannibalism in the New World (the account was based on an abandoned village). The discourse of these adventurers writing was strongly biased with the intellectual currents of the times and the notion of the savage and beastly other is strongly reflected in their works. They expected to find a cannibalistic savage other (Obeyesekere 2005), one that would, by seeing the world in binary opposites, confirmed their view of themselves as civilised and rational.

An example of this is shown by Geschiere (2000[1997]) in his book *The modernity of Witchcraft: Politics and the occult in postcolonial Africa* about the Maka people living in Cameroon. In the early period of the colonisation of Cameroon by the Germans a young German merchant was killed by the Maka and was reported to have been eaten. These reports were easily accepted in Germany and spread fast, as there was and as there is now, a great fascination with crimes involving cannibalism. It was easy for German people to believe this tale as they were already convinced that outside of their supposedly civilized world cannibals were lurking in every jungle and on every island. This caused a great uproar in Germany and, with a description of the horrible details of the killing and with a mention of the benefits to the rubber trade, the German government sent an expedition to conquer the Maka (Geschiere 2000[1997]: 30). Cannibalism was used by the German troops to interrogate the local people, but it also became the foundation for establishing the Maka as primitive savages by the Europeans (Geschiere 2000[1997]: 32).

Accounts of cannibalism were quickly accepted as authentic as it validates and cements the image that people already have of a brutal and savage people. It then becomes the excuse for conquest and for taking over the control of local natural resources from the supposed irresponsible and childlike natives. The colonisers needed access to the rubber rich region of the Maka, and portraying them as the most primitive of all primitives would give a moral excuse for the conquest. In labelling the Maka as ferocious cannibals it was easy to construct an image of them as savages. This is not to say that cannibalism was not practised by the Maka before the Germans came (Geschiere 2000[1997]: 33). What the German colonisers did was to use a small aspect of Maka cultural tradition of sometimes engaging in cannibalism to translate the Maka people into cannibals and therefore savages.

Writing about remote places and about far away peoples allows a writer to write without incurring the danger of being examined or contradicted (Avramescu 2009: 13). Travel writing is an important source in the descriptions of cannibalism and most of the accounts about this subject were written by sailors, missionaries and adventurers (Arens 1998). These travellers' accounts are central data in both contemporary and later anthropological writing on cannibalism. Avramescu (2009: 13) argues however that travel writing and moral science are linked because any travel literature describing difference will lead to reflections on moral norms. This is a problem in anthropology too, because making people and places anonymous, or doing research that is impossible to retest, means that there is little or no way of verifying the data that have been produced (May 2010). This becomes an increasingly important critique when ethnographic data are used to justify and conceal structural violence.

At the end of the 19th century, through Marx and others, the image of the cannibal is turned on its head and used in social resistance (Avramescu 2009: 254). While it takes more than half a century for it to become dominant in the academic discourse, the cannibal becomes the colonialist and capitalist systems that used to push the category on and define others, and rather than to critique primitivism and savagery it is utilised in the critique of the brutality of the modern world. It is the exploiters and conquerors, the rulers of the civilised world that are devouring masses of people. Anthropology is also influenced by and takes up this critique, and the ethnographer is now seen as a colonialist collaborator and of misrepresenting the people they have researched (Asad 1975; Mafeje 1976). It is in this vein that I begin to conceptualise the anthropologist as a sort of symbolic cannibal, consuming the dynamic nature of human practice and social experience and turning it into a static object in the written accounts. As I will elaborate on below the anthropologist removes the humanity of the 'subject' until there is no agentic power or specificity of culture and all that is left a shell the former self.

The paradox of modernity and of the Enlightenment is that it was the advent of a modern humanism in European thought, but at the same time also the period in which Europe exerted its most brutal conquest upon the rest of the world. It is in this paradox that the image of the savage cannibal and the mission to civilise is concocted. Only by painting the colonialist venture in the light of the humanist cause could the paradox of modernity be solved. Being tied in with the humanistic science of the Enlightenment, and as unwilling accomplices to colonialism, anthropology struggles with a similar paradox. Anthropology is torn between the academia as a product of modernism, and therefore having to produce texts about what they observe, and between the dynamic and changing ways in which they know people actually behave, which could be written down with difficulty.

The ethnography of cannibalism: representing the other

To further get a sense of how academic debates can consume research subjects I wish to examine the debates about cannibalism and its existence which has been going on for the last 40 years. In 1979 the controversial book *The man-eating myth: Anthropology and Anthropophagy* was written by William Arens. Arens (1979) argued that there had never been any society that had practised ritual cannibalism over a sustained period of time; cannibalism was only the result of the practical and material need for food. Gananath Obeyesekere (1992) wrote the book *The Apotheosis of Captain Cook* which disputes the claim that James Cook was ever worshipped as a god on Hawaii. Both arguments are directed towards and challenged by Marshall Sahlins (1983), and belong to a larger argument about the way in which people in ethnographic writing are represented and anthropology as creating an exotic other. For Sahlins (1983) culture becomes the motivation and drive for human action, and in his writing it seems, perhaps in a misguided devotion to cultural relativism, almost as if it is only the exotic subject of anthropological studies that are guided by culture. Obeyesekere (1992), on the other hand, argues that everyone is guided by a sense of practical rationality, and that this was also what guided the Hawaiian people's attitudes towards James Cook.

In exploring the way that cannibalism has been written about, it becomes fruitful to enter via the following discussion. I will focus on two different sets of essays that separately make up two different whole ethnographies. The first, *The Ethnography of Cannibalism* (Tuzin and Brown 1983) is a collection of essays in the defence of the perspective that cannibalism is and has been a cultural practice in many places of the world. The other *Cannibalism and the Colonial World* (Barker, Hulme and Iversen 1998) is, on the other hand, an ethnographic account of how cannibalism has been written about. Both books show different ways of writing and doing anthropology and are widely opposed on the question of how cannibalism should be seen in academia. By critiquing and engaging with these two works I wish to go further into the analysis of the concept of cannibalism being a way of translating people into savages.

The Ethnography of Cannibalism (Tuzin and Brown 1983) is a collection of essays, each describing the cultural background of cannibalism in different parts of the world. Whether actual or symbolic cannibalism, the authors focus on the cultural specificities and contexts that underpin cannibalistic practices. The various authors try to move the notion of cannibalism away from what it meant in the colonial discourse on local peoples, while still maintaining the notion that some people are in fact cannibals. In a sense the effort was to destigmatise the concept of cannibalism while keeping the concept strictly within its traditional framework of something which belongs to the non-western other. It is written as a counter argument to William Arens's (1979) *The Man-Eating Myth: Anthropology and Anthropophagy* and his claim that cannibalism has never been a sustained cultural or ritual practice but it does, at the same time, accommodate some of the critique that Arens (1979) makes. It shows how attempts to move past the creation of the savage in anthropology are hampered by anthropologists in an effort to dialogue away the issues of representation, instead of the radical alteration of the discipline which is needed.

Each chapter of *The Ethnography of Cannibalism* (Tuzin and Brown 1983) conveys a different setting in which cannibalism is examined. Two of the essays are built on first-hand accounts, but the rest are substantiated by texts gathered by adventurers, sailors and missionaries. The reason for this is that cannibalistic practice seemed to disappear as soon as a place was colonised, so therefore there are few ethnographic studies to be done on this subject (Tuzin and Brown 1983: 2). There is little reflection by the authors of how using these sources reproduce the colonialist image of primitive and cannibalistic natives. There is a sincere object in the book to truly see the people practising cannibalism as actual people. They are no longer the childlike beasts of the colonial discourse. There is definitely a presence of the post-modern critique in Lindenbaum's (1983) argument of how anthropology can transcend the dichotomy of myth and reality. Yet there are still present the boundaries that are inherent in the anthropological writing of the time. The need to create a field or 'a people' that can be studied is still an issue for anthropological research (Ferguson 2005) and a location which is always in far-away places from the writers and the intended readers. This becomes the same boundary that separates the primitive from the civilised in the enlightenment binary thinking.

The editors of *The Ethnography of Cannibalism*' book recognise the controversy of writing about cannibalism and that cannibalism can become a device for one group to create moral superiority over another (Tuzin and Brown 1983: 3). Despite this recognition the essays that follow reproduce an image of the people studied as stuck in a time of cannibalistic practice and some use highly problematic sources. While cultural relativism might give the appearance of no moral discourse being present, it is in fact present by the way that people are written about. Arens (1998) argues that Tuzin and Brown (1983) make a moral judgement on cannibalism by cementing the relationship between the sickness, kuru, and cannibalistic funeral practices without necessarily having any sound evidence for it.

Sahlins's (1983) essay 'Raw women, cooked men' is mainly built on the observations of missionaries, explorers and on the book

'Cannibal Jack'. 'Cannibal Jack' is written by a sailor, under either the name William Diapea or John Jackson, who travelled around Fiji in the late 18th to early 19th century. In the book he describes his own adventures, which include vivid descriptions of several cannibal feasts, which were a popular literary subject of the colonial era. While the book is supposed to be a form of shipboard journalism, it is more fictional than anything else and certainly not ethnographic (Obeyesekere 1998: 79).

Another author that Sahlins (1983) draws on is W. Endicott, another shipboard journalist. Again this account is more fiction than ethnography or journalism. Using these sources Sahlins (1983) begins to describe in detail the brutality of cannibalism on Fiji. On the basis of these sources the people are transformed into cannibals and the Fijian society into a cannibalistic one. Like most ethnographic work of those days Sahlins (1983) writes in the present tense, which in turn freezes the people that he writes about in time. He brings in historical sources, but these sources are not critiqued for their involvement in creating a colonialist discourse of the cannibal savage. Sahlins (1983) argues that there are distinct cultures which imply a clear boundary around it. Because of this timeless and insular perspective the text hides the historical and political context of colonialism that devastated Fijian and other colonised peoples in the period when most of his sources were written. All the essays in the collection follow this pattern of excluding the significance that colonialism might have had. There is little mention of the presence of colonialism despite the time written about being the height of the colonialist expansion.

Sahlins and the other authors of *The Ethnography of Cannibalism* are all trying to show that cannibalism emerges in a particular reference and in a particular cultural orbit (Lindenbaum 1983: 95). With the recognition of this there is still no reflection upon the cultural orbit that affects the authors themselves and other observers of cannibalistic practices. This combined with writing in the ethnographic present about 'a people', reproduces the notion of the exotic other being cultural and timeless creatures while the anthropologists themselves are the rational opposite. The people that they speak of are also marked as cannibals or as cannibalistic societies, which, intentional or not, will always invoke a set of images and moral judgements.

The book *Cannibalism and the Colonial World* ((Barker, Hulme and Iversen 1998) is also a collection of essays, but rather than focus on societies that practise cannibalism, they focus on how cannibalism has been written about. The authors of the book seek in different ways to answer the questions: 'Why were Europeans so desirous of finding confirmation of their suspicions of cannibalism? And why does cannibalism feature so insistently as a contemporary trope in different forms of writing?' (Hulme 1998: 4). The authors of the ethnography analyse why western intellectuals and especially anthropologists are so fascinated with cannibalism. Hulme (1998) argues that for western thinkers cannibalism is the greatest imaginable cultural difference and therefore the most difficult for our understanding. This in turn makes it the greatest tool for creating a primitive other, even if it is unintentional. Huggan (1998) argues in the same volume that cannibalism becomes an excuse for racial oppression and that we therefore need to challenge and critique claims to cannibalism. This is done to unearth the racism or oppression that is hidden by certain kinds of knowledge.

Kuru is an illness in Papua New Guinea that has by some researchers been connected with the practice of eating one's dead. The way that the disease, kuru, has been written about is an example of the continued myth making by anthropologists around cannibalism. Arens (1998) argues that with very little evidence and despite being contradicted by other specialists in the field, some anthropologists continued to reproduce stories of the connections between contracting kuru and the consumption of human brains. This is then part of again creating myths about cannibalistic practices, and also creates a myth that stigmatises the people affected with kuru as cannibals. Tuzin and Brown (1983) not only reproduce this fact, but cement it by stating as a set fact that kuru is caused by the eating of human flesh. The anthropologist in the writing of ethnography is in this case part of bringing new life into the myths around cannibalism.

Anthropologists have a dual role in the creation of the cannibal, by first to focus on and create an image of the cannibal through ethnography and then to claim through cultural relativism that the cannibal is not to be considered morally inferior (Arens 1998: 55). This is the exact reason why *The Ethnography of Cannibalism* (Tuzin and Brown 1983) can be seen as problematic. It reproduces very troubling notions that certain people are cannibals and guided by culture and while others are not. The people written about are made into static actors whose actions are controlled by culture, frozen in writing and forced into the category of a cannibal. In light of the space that the cannibal has had and the imagery that he has invoked in the western intellectual history, is it possible to translate a people into cannibals and expect the reader not to make any moral judgements?

Obeyesekere (1998) argues that the moment of meeting between the colonial adventurers, such as James Cook, and the local people who were soon to be colonised was too complex to be simply written into an ethnographic category (1998: 63). In the meeting between coloniser and local people both brought a series of discourses which all played a part in shaping their interaction. This meeting is extremely well described by Comaroff and Comaroff (1991), in where the missionaries and local people both come with a multiplicity of ideas and discourses and how in their meeting they affect and are affected by each other. This is similar to what happened when James Cook and other adventurers met with local people across the world – there were fluid interactions and both sides reacted to each other. The creation of the cannibal savage was in order to create a clear boundary between the civilised and the primitive: classical ethnography was about creating similar boundaries and ignoring the fluidity outside of them.

The ethnography *The Modernity of Witchcraft: Politics and the Occult in Postcolonial Africa* by Peter Geschiere (2000[1997]) is more conscious of the complexities of the colonial meeting. His ethnography is anthropological research done amongst the Maka people in Cameroon. Geschiere's (2000[1997]) account is a contrast to that of Sahlins (1983) in that it shows the way that cannibalism is constructed both by the discourses of colonial regime and how it used the local people, and in doing this also accounts for how the ability of people to react to and try and alter their circumstances. It is different from the other texts that I have chosen in the sense that it conveys more how notions such as cannibalism and modernity are experienced and conceptualised by a people that was the victim of colonialism. The ethnography is critically engaged with the many different discourses that were in play in the colonial meeting between the colonised and the colonisers. Geschiere (2000[1997]) focuses on how modernity and politics are understood in relation to local notions of witchcraft and sorcery. The author describes how to frighten Europeans the Maka would sometimes make statements like: 'Did you know that we eat whites?' (Geschiere 2000[1997]: 28). By making themselves out to be cannibals they show a concerted effort in making themselves seem more ferocious. This shows cannibalism can be written about in a way that does not simply reproduce the notion of the helpless native of the colonial era.

Both colonialism and anthropology turn(ed) people into objects – by making them quantifiable and measurable, set in a certain time and a certain place, turned into units. The colonial conquest and the western science that came with it was a process of '*thing-ification*' argues Aimé Césaire (2000[1955]). It turned people into tonnages of cocoa, tobacco or rubber, or in some cases into savage cannibals, rather than human beings. Anthropology, in the colonial and post-colonial eras, has been guilty of turning peoples into objects, usually through creating a cultural boundary to define 'a people'. No clearer is this boundary made than by invoking the cannibal. This is not to say whether cannibalism, symbolic or not, is a reality for many people. Cannibalism is certainly invoked by many people and is used metaphorically or symbolically all over the world. Inspecting how ethnographers have written about cannibalism is rather a critique of the field of anthropology and recognition of the violence present in the translation of cultures and people. To understand and solve the problems of anthropology, as Van Maanen argues, is to create a story about the makers and takers of anthropological research and not about subjects (1995: 13).

So far in this essay, I have focused on how ethnography and western academics and explorers have described and talked about cannibalism in previous times. Cannibalism remains a hot topic, and in some ways the discourse about cannibalism has completely changed. In other ways, it is the same as ever. I will now look at how the notion of cannibalism is treated in contemporary instances. There is no doubt that forms of cannibalism exist all around us. It has for some people in North America and Europe become popular for women to eat the placenta after giving birth to a child (Lindenbaum 2004). Tourism has also become popular, and this has spawned a new kind of explorer, in the likes of James Cook, who is looking for and creating an exotic other.

To illuminate the mainstream view of cannibalism, one can look at the movie *Cannibal Tours* by Dennis O'Rourke (1987). The movie illuminates the point about using cannibalism in the post-colonial era to construct an image of a people as savage. It shows how translating people into primitives still hides the historical structural violence and exploitation of colonialism. While the filmmaker himself has stated that it is not an ethnographic film, it holds great ethnographic value. The film has many layers. It is about western tourists who visit a place based on its peoples' reputation for having been cannibals. The tourists are essentialising the local people as hopeless primitives, and at the same time the filmmaker is showing the tourists in an equally essentialised way.

Cannibal Tours (O'Rourke 1987) is a documentary about a group of tourists who travel to Papua New Guinea on holiday. In the beginning of the film there is a German tourist who was very excited and wished to know more about the old cannibal practices of the local people. Lindenbaum (2004: 491) argues that the notion of the cannibal is still used to label people as primitive and that it retains much of its ideological force. The tourists in the film reproduce the enlightenment way of thinking about the other, the local people are seen as quiet and peaceful, a people of nature. This is set as a binary opposite to the busy lives of Europeans. A bit later in the film three Italian tourists are talking about the bartering and buying of souvenirs from the local people. It becomes clear from the conversation that they believe that it is the primitivism of the local people that keep them poor, but they hope that development from the western world can come and save them from their poverty. Again boundaries are erected between binary opposites. Only now the new categories are first and third world, and the development discourse has taken over some of the rhetoric from the colonial one (Escobar 1995; Ferguson 2005). The legacy of colonialism is covered up by a discourse about primitives not being able to develop themselves, and in line with Farmer's (2004) argument the structural violence of colonialism and exploitative capitalism is historically erased. The cannibal is again one of the markers for the boundary around primitivism.

The people that go on the trip have a clear view of cannibalism and the local people as something primitive and exotic. The continued usage of the cannibal as a tool for showing the development perspective of the primitive into a superior civilised (Arens 1979). Cannibalism has again resurged as a marker for the primitives. Cannibalism is however also used by people themselves to seem strong in the face of oppression or as exotic to attract tourism (Lindenbaum 2004: 493). This is seen amongst the Maka, for example, when they remind the researcher that they eat white people (Geschiere 2000[1997]: 28). The tourists, on the other hand, long to see the world that colonialism destroyed, the primitive other, much like the world that colonialists and anthropologists were once searching for (Bruner 1989: 440). All three seek to create a static image of a primitive native, exotic for the tourist, culturally bound for the anthropologist and an irrational savage for the colonialists. For all three the previously colonised peoples of the world are seen as non-agentic and irrational, controlled by traditions and cultures, a creature only acted upon.

An interesting aspect and common critique (Bruner 1989) of *Cannibal Tours* (O'Rourke 1987) is that Dennis O'Rourke is not himself very present in the movie. He remains detached and behind the camera, with little reflexiveness about his role in the data that are being created. This is a position that is reminiscent of the early anthropologists' aim of being an objective observer, unnoticed and without disturbing the field – not really reflecting on their connections with colonialism and the way that anthropology could be an exploitative pursuit. There is still an exploitative element to anthropology. Ethnographic research is based on the extraction of knowledge from people, knowledge from which we profit by getting academic salaries or degrees. The anthropologist becomes the symbolic vampire or cannibal feeding on other people's lives as the elixir or food of their own academic life.

Ethnography and the violence of making a text from data

A large part of anthropology's consumption of people has to do with attempting to put into text an ever-changing living and breathing world. This requires freezing that world despite knowing that it is always in flux. Mosse (2006) argues that ethnographic writing breaks the relations created in the field and erects boundaries between researchers and researched. Publication of ethnographic writing is in danger of breaking the social relationships created by the fieldwork (Mosse 2006: 936). Further, the specific dynamic of any locality could in a sense be destroyed as it is turned into text and people thus become static representations of themselves – life is after all never static but always changing.[1] Ethnographic research can thus be violent. Anthropologists insert themselves into the field and create social relations, friendships and sometimes co-dependants. This causes ripples in the local community. Even more violent effects may come about when the anthropologists attempt to put their research field into a text. To limit the size of any text to something readable involves creating boundaries that did not necessarily exist in the field (i.e. talking separately about health and school and water when people may experience these as part of a continuum). As evidence of this Mosse (2006) shows how influential informants resist this boundary making and reject the ethnographic account of them. Writing can alter relations made in the field and also benefit the writer(s) who thus profit from the people written about. This could be seen as a form of exploitation. The anthropologists further their careers, while the participants in the research are often left with little in return.[2]

Discussing violence and translation in anthropology seems appropriate, given that anthropology has over a long period of time been referred to as cultural translation (Asad 1986: 142), and as such anthropology is about translating people into consumable knowledge. Ethnographic research takes language, customs, social relations and culture and translates them into an academic discourse. In the concept of cultural translation lies a notion of the anthropologist trying '... to reproduce one social space in the discourse of another' (Hastrup 1995: 22). Inherent in this translation is an asymmetrical power relation between the ethnographer with academic authority and, what is often known as, the research participant whose life is being turned into data. The ethnographer has the final say and is the editor of the final knowledge that is produced and disseminated. This has been for several decades a huge headache for the anthropologists all over the world and much discussion has been had around this subject. Most recent have been the attempts to include the voice and agency of research participants into ethnographic accounts. The disproportionate power relations between researcher and researched cannot be written or dialogued away, this would only serve to obscure and hide this power relation (Mosse 2006: 937). It is therefore only by being aware of this asymmetrical power relation and making a critique of it part of the anthropological research method that we can have a more egalitarian academic discipline.

The notion that scientific anthropology would create an account of 'a people' or 'a culture' was what gave rise to the concept of ethnography as an account of a whole people or a whole culture ethnically defined (Ferguson 2005: 143). The origins of ethnographic research and participant observation have caused anthropologists to appropriate a moment in people's lives and freeze the moment and the people through writing in the ethnographic present tense. The ethnographic present is the literary device by which ethnographic research is transferred into text. It is a point of view in which peoples and societies are described as bounded in both time and space and does, in effect, remove people from a historical context. One can neither see them as the result of a certain history and they do not have the agency to move forward; it is a people and a society that does not change. In line with this, according to Hastrup (1995: 23), that to translate a culture the anthropologist will inevitably destroy the specificity of the culture which is being translated. There are therefore several levels of violence inherent in the anthropological pursuit of knowing and writing about people. There is violence in turning data into writing because it erects boundaries around a people which break social relations, but also because the ethnographic

119

account freezes a people in a static notion of space and time. Another violent aspect of anthropology is the destruction of specificity and the dynamic and ever-changing quality of culture that is entailed in translating a culture and a people.

The method that Malinowski described was essentially about how data could be extracted from the informant (Van Maanen 1995). Fieldwork in ethnographic research is in its essence about drawing out the human experience and translating it into a part of a body of literature. This is not necessarily wrong, and there is plenty of literature about how it could be done in an ethical fashion, but the similarities between the process of creating ethnography and the consumption of a human being are striking. Like the Maka (Geschiere 2000[1997]: 28), we anthropologists use the essence of other people to create notions of personhood for ourselves. For the Maka, it is for establishing ferociousness and for the anthropologist it establishes us as academic intellectuals who create science. If one follows the argument of Obeyesekere (2005) that most of the ethnography on cannibalism in Fiji, Hawaii and amongst the Maori is nothing but a dangerous fantasy, then the translation of culture takes on yet another violent form. It is not just consuming the essence of 'a people' but violently altering it in the way that it is represented.

Cannibalism: beyond the modern world and towards a new anthropology

Cannibalism continues to conjure up a host of different images. The colonialist discourse of cannibalism being the mark of a primitive savage is still alive and well. Yet people who were under the yoke of colonialism have themselves started to use the notion of cannibalism as descriptive of their own practices. The symbolic or literal consumption of other people is part of many people's lives and cannot be ignored. Symbolic consumption of people could be attributed to Catholics in Holy Communion, to capitalism and consumerism as it exploits those who toil under it, or as I suggest, to anthropologists in our professional capacity. If cannibalism will continue to be written about in the post-modern era then it becomes important to ask the question: How do we write about it?

120

If the anthropologist is a cannibal, then the debates between Sahlins (1995) and Obeyesekere (1992), about the deification of James Cook in Hawaii are a cannibal feast. The argument, which was in its essence about whether Hawaiians were compelled by culture to deify and kill Cook or whether their acts were guided by a practical rationality, completely destroyed the notion that Hawaiians are the creators of their own history (Geertz 1995). They, and their history, were either the puppets of European manipulation or bound by culture to believe that Cook was actually a god. No matter which side one chooses their history is the result of European trickery. Local history and belief is destroyed in the process of academic discussion, and left is nothing of their self-representation and agency – they are indeed left as empty shells. The historical Hawaiians have effectively been consumed by the two anthropologists. The translation of Hawaiians into academic writing and debate has, as Hastrup (1995) argues, destroyed the specificity of Hawaiian culture.

The discipline of anthropology has however moved forward since then. The focus on local representations and knowledge as more prominent in ethnographic writing has changed the way that anthropologists relate to the participants of their research. The issue of exploitation and violence in anthropological research has spawned many different ways of writing ethnographies. In the last two decades there has been much work done in attempting to create a less extractive approach to anthropology, and focus on ways in which the research can be beneficial to all parties involved. There is still a problem, however, of whether anthropology can truly become an egalitarian discipline, which erases the difference of power between researchers and researched. This has in the last few years been problematised by many scholars, and different solutions have appeared. David Graeber (2004), on the one hand, suggests that anthropologists need to develop anarchist anthropology, one that truly incorporates the diversity of lived human thought and practice into practical solutions for new ways of organising the world we live in. Although this might also reproduce the exotic other, he argues that anthropologists should not be afraid to be seen as romantics. It is in the continued questioning of and constant reflection on the role of the anthropologist and the writing of ethnographies, in which we

121

can formulate ways to ethically engage with people through research.

Francis Nyamnjoh (2012) argues that anthropologists need to move away from the classical anthropology of studying downwards and of studying the other, and rather focus on studying the powerful and 'at home'. This is becoming more of a common occurrence in the anthropology of today. This would mean that anthropologists would no longer seek seemingly exotic and new places where they can find flesh-eating cannibals, but rather to interrogate the cannibalism in their midst as well as their own cannibalistic practices. Perhaps the consumption of people is unavoidable in any forms of writing and telling stories about people. As this book argues we are all cannibals of sorts. Yet we can devour people as a product which we consume thoughtlessly or we can eat human flesh with the care and compassion which Conklin (2001: xv) describes in Wari' funeral rites.

Endnotes

[1] This is not applicable to anthropologists alone. All those who write about people attempt to translate them into the particular discourses of their discipline and intended audience. Journalists are probably the most ferocious in their devouring of subjects as they have little time for nuance and considerations as peoples' lives become news stories. Journalism has a crisis in its civic responsibilities as much of news media propagate stereotypes and misrepresentations of people (Blumler 2010: 243).

[2] It is possible to be a cannibal who consumes people with care rather than violence (Conklin 2001: xv). We see in recent years many examples of non-extractive ways of doing anthropology. As they consume people for nurturing their own essence they are cannibals, but cannibals of care and respect for the people they devour.

References

Arens, W. (1979) *The Man-Eating Myth: Anthropology and Anthropophagy*, New York: Oxford University Press.

Arens, W. (1998) 'Rethinking anthropophagy' in Francis Baker, Peter Hulme and Margaret Iversen (eds): *Cannibalism and the Colonial World*, Cambridge University Press.

Asad, Talal (ed.) (1973) *Anthropology and the colonial encounter*, Ithaca Press.

Asad, Talal (1986) 'The Concept of Cultural Translation in British Social Anthropology' in Clifford and Marcus (eds): *Writing Culture*. University of California Press.

Avramescu, C. (2009) *An Intellectual History of Cannibalism*, Princeton: Princeton University Press.

Banivanua-Mar, Tracey (2010) 'Cannibalism and Colonialism: Charting Colonies and Frontiers in Nineteenth-Century Fiji', *Comparative Studies in Society and History*, Vol. 52(2): 255–281.

Blumler, Jay G. (2010) 'Foreword', *Journalism Practice*, Vol. 4(3): 243–245.

Burley, Mikel (2016) 'Eating Human Beings: Varieties of Cannibalism and the Heterogeneity of Human Life', Philosophy, Vol. 91, Issue 4, October 2016. pp. 483-501

Bruner, Edward M. (1989) 'Of Cannibals, Tourists and Ethnographers' in Cultural Anthropology 4: 438–445.

Césaire, A. (2000 [1955]) 'Discourse on colonialism', NYU Press, pp 1–31.

Comaroff, Jean and Comaroff, John L. (1991) *Of Revelation and Revolution, Volume 1: Christianity, Colonialims, and Consciousness in South Africa*, The University of Chicago Press.

Conklin, Beth (2001) *Consuming Grief: Compassionate Cannibalism in an Amazonian Society*, Austin, Texas: University of Texas Press.

Escobar, Arturo (1995) *Encountering Development: The Making and the Unmaking of the Third World*, New Jersey: Princeton University Press.

Farmer, Paul (2004) 'An Anthropology of Structural Violence', *Current Anthropology*, Vol. 45(3): 305–325.

Ferguson, James (2005) 'Anthropology and Its Evil Twin:

"Development" in the Constitution of a discipline' in M. Edelman and A. Huagerud (eds): *The Anthropology of Development and Globalization: From Classical Political Economy to Contemporary Neoliberalism*. Blackwell Publishing. pp. 140-155.

Galtung, Johan (1990) 'Cultural Violence' in *Journal of Peace Research*, Vol 27(3): 291–305.

Geertz, Clifford (1995) 'Culture War' in *N.Y. Rev. Books Nov. 30*, pp. 4–6

Geschiere, Peter (2000[1997]) *The Modernity of Witchcraft: Politics and the Occult in Postcolonial Africa,*.University of Virginia Press.

Graeber, David (2004) *Fragments of an anarchist anthropology*, Chicago: Prickley Paradigm Press.

Hastrup, Kirsten (1995) *A passage to anthropology: Between experience and theory*, London and New York: Routledge.

Huggan, Graham (1998) 'Ghost stories, bone flutes, cannibal countermemory' in Francis Barker, Peter Hulme and Margaret Iversen (eds): *Cannibalism and the Colonial World*, Cambridge University Press.

Hulme, Peter (1998) 'Introduction: The cannibal scene' in Francis Barker, Peter Hulme and Margaret Iversen (eds): *Cannibalism and the Colonial World*, Cambridge University Press.

Kilgour, Maggie (1998) 'The function of cannibalism at the present time' in Francis Barker, Peter Hulme and Margaret Iversen (eds): *Cannibalism and the Colonial World*, Cambridge University Press.

Lindenbaum, Shirley (1983) 'Cannibalism: Symbolic Production and Consumption' in Paula Brown and Donald Tuzin (eds): *The Ethnography of Cannibalism* Society of Psychological Anthropology. pp. 94-106.

Lindenbaum, Shirley (2004) 'Thinking about Cannibalism', *Annual Review of Anthropology*, Vol. 33, pp. 475-498.

Mafeje, Archie (1976) 'The problem of anthropology in historical perspective: An inquiry into the growth of the social sciences', *Canadian Journal of African Studies/Revue canadienne des études africaines*, Vol. 10, Iss. 2, pp. 307-333.

May, Shannon (2010) 'Rethinking anonymity in anthropology: a question of ethics', *Anthropology News*, April 2010. pp. 10-11.

Mosse, David (2006) 'Anti-social anthropology? Objectivity,

objection, and the ethnography of public policy and professional communities', *Journal of the Royal Anthropological Institute (N.S.)*, Vol. 12: 935–956.

Nyamnjoh, Francis B (2012) 'Blinded by Sight: Divining the Future of Anthropology in Africa', *Africa Spectrum*, Vol. 47(2–3): 63-92.

Obeyesekere, Gananath (1992) *The Apotheosis of Captain Cook: European Mythmaking in the Pacific*, Princeton University Press.

Obeyesekere, Gananath (1998) 'Cannibal Feasts in nineteenth-century Fiji: seamen's yarns and the ethnographic imagination' in Francis Barker, Peter Hulme and Margaret Iversen (eds): *Cannibalism and the Colonial World*, Cambridge University Press pp. 63-87.

Obeyesekere, Gananath (2005) *The Man-Eating Myth and Human Sacrifice in the South Sea*, University of California Press.

O'Rourke, Dennis (1987) *Cannibal Tours*, Canberra: O'Rourke and Associates.

Phillips, Jerry (1998) 'Cannibalism qua capitalism: the metaphorics of accumulation in Marx, Conrad, Shakespeare and Marlowe' in Francis Barker, Peter Hulme and Margaret Iversen (eds): *Cannibalism and the Colonial World*, Cambridge University Press pp. 183-204.

Rosman, Abraham and Rubel, Paula (2003) 'Introduction: Translation and Anthropology' in Rosman, Abraham and Rubel, Paula (eds): *Translating Cultures: Perspectives on Translation and Anthroplogy*,. Berg Publishing: Oxford, New York.

Sahlins, Marshall (1983) 'Raw women, cooked men and Other "Great Things"' in Paula Brown and Donald Tuzin (eds): *The Ethnography of Cannibalism*, Society of Psychological Anthropology pp. 72-83.

Sahlins, Marshall (1995) *How 'Natives' Think, About Captain Cook, for Example*, University of Chicago Press.

Tuzin, Donald and Brown, Paula (1983) 'Editor's Preface' in Paula Brown and Donald Tuzin (eds): *The Ethnography of Cannibalism*, Society of Psychological Anthropology pp. 1-5.

Van Maanen, John (1995) 'An End to Innocence: The Ethnography of Ethnography' in John Van Maanen (ed.): *Representation in Ethnography*, Saga Publications pp. 1-35.

Chapter 3

Incorporated or Cannibalised by Posthuman Others? Sanctions and Witchcraft in Contemporary Zimbabwe

Artwell Nhemachena & Maria Kaundjua

Next to cannibalism as a ceremony/praxis, it is also an embodied figure in that it is constructed through how it relates to other bodies. It takes other bodies in itself, making it a body of monstrosity ... to become a nomad, one must be constantly on the move, never really settling somewhere. Cannibalism is the nomad that is insatiable, and consequently, is constantly looking for nourishment and nutritious others. It is moving out of a desire to encounter other material bodies, eating and incorporating all that it encounters during its errantries ... Derrida and Spinoza think the ethical through digesting, devouring and desiring the other, and consequently, how this digesting will either lead to greater compositions or is, an acknowledgement of the other's alterity ... For Derrida, ethics is thus also an ethics of cannibalism and consuming the other/otherness ... Spinoza's ethics is an ethic of appetite and desire in which no natural , moral imperative of 'good' and 'evil' exists; there are only ethical implications of 'good' and 'bad', which are wholly contextual, relative and thus ever-changing and differing. Morality is thus non-existent, in that morality presupposes some sort of common ground, an agreement between individuals on what should or should not do

(Wijnants 2016: 33–4).

Did you ever see a chameleon catch a fly? The chameleon gets behind the fly and remains motionless for some time, then he advances very slowly and gently, first putting forward one leg and then another. At last, when well within reach, he darts out his tongue and the fly disappears. England is the chameleon and I am that fly – Ndebele King Lobengula to the London Missionary Society Hope Fountain based missionary Reverend C. D. Helm (The Sunday News, 3 January 2016)

Thus the game of seduction is essentially mimetic; the one seduced finds herself in the person of the seducer, whom she is therefore compelled to embrace mimetically. However – and this is the key point – for the seducer to succeed, he is not supposed to create a truthful image of how his victim sees herself but instead an ideal representation of or a fantasy image of what she could become. This, in turn, causes the seduced to desire this image and to do everything possible to obtain it. In other words, the seducer has to act as an ideal reflection of the seduced, that is, as an incomplete copy of her, and practices of mimetic empathy ... provide him with this ability to be like, yet also different from, his victim ... The dances of the modern Yukaghir represent ... movements mimicking animals ... Sometimes interrupted by a guttural rattle and by other sounds in imitation of the cries of various animals ...

(Willerselv 2007: 108).

Introduction

Drawing on ways in which Zimbabwe has been cannibalised and incorporated into the (neo-) imperial world since the colonial era, this chapter examines the figures and figments of the cannibal in colonial historical perspective. The chapter also draws on contemporary discourses of posthumanism (see for instance Braidotti 2016) and the attendant contemporary discourses on ethics to map out the terrain of cannibalism in the envisaged and emergent posthuman world. Thus, with insights from colonial history in which the African humanistic ethics of *hunhu/unhu* (Nhemachena. 2017; Muzvidziwa et al. 2012; Nyamnjoh 2015; Mogobe 1999) were destroyed in favour of colonial cannibalism, this chapter spells out the implications of the envisaged and emergent posthuman ethics, including 'ethics of care' and 'ethics of vulnerability'. Underscoring ways in which (posthumanistic) transnational corporations, institutions and some foreign governments cannibalise Africa, and Zimbabwe in particular, the chapter sheds light on the duplicities of 'ethics of care' and 'ethics of vulnerability' that are foregrounded within Western academies even as Africa is being cannibalised in a world that has since deposed and disposed of African humanistic ethics. In the light of associations of cannibalism with witchcraft in Zimbabwean epistemologies and ontologies (Lan 1987), this chapter holds that (neo-)imperial contrivances at incorporating Africa constitute logics of cannibalistic witchcraft, however cloaked, in discourses of 'ethics of vulnerability' and 'ethics of care'.

Erroneously premised on the presuppositions that the cannibalised colonised others had no variants of their own ethics, colonial logics of 'ethics of care' and 'ethics of vulnerability' served to hide the nefarious ambitions of the colonisers of Zimbabwe and Africa more generally. It is argued in this chapter that portrayals of the colonised people as savage cannibals, as animals without taboos and ethics against eating the flesh of human beings, as incapable of separating human beings from animals (Watson 2010), served to create images of the colonised people as in urgent need of an imperial 'ethics of care' and 'ethics of vulnerability' (Pettersen 2011; Held 2005) – but such ethics, sadly, served to legitimise the establishing of exploitative imperial relations within Zimbabwe.

Portrayed as savage cannibals eating the flesh of their own, the colonised people supposedly suffered unique forms of precariousness and vulnerability in the midst of their own kind – they impliedly needed an imperial 'ethics of vulnerability' that called for 'ethical' responses and 'moral agency' from outside their African societies. In other words, they did not necessarily bring to Africans the ideals of self-sufficiency, autonomy, willpower or agency (Cortina et al. 2016). Rather, Westerners created forms of vulnerability for the colonised peoples who thereby suffered the cannibalistic vagaries of empire. Also, imperial images of the colonised as chaotic and utterly vulnerable to their own societies' cannibalistic tendencies served to undergird supposed weaknesses, powerlessness, dependency, deficiency and negativity of the colonised (Gilson 2014). Because the savage act of cannibalism was held by Westerners to represent the inability to control the body (Watson 2010), colonial logics of 'ethics of vulnerability' were used to legitimise imperial cannibalistic incorporation of the supposed (African) savages. While the logic of 'ethics of vulnerability' is that (neo-)imperial intervention is solicited by the images of the distant suffering and abjection of Africans (see for instance Butler 2012), it is necessary to note that the distant suffering of Africans is also a result of (neo-)imperial cannibalistic machinations including exploitation and dispossession.

As in other parts of the colonised world where Europeans were deemed to be (neo-)colonial bloodthirsty cannibals (Watson 2010), the incorporation of Zimbabwe into the imperial world was similarly understood by the Ndebele King Lobengula using the metaphor of the imperial chameleon catching African 'flies'. Lobengula's metaphor of the chameleon and the fly aptly underscores the import of posthumanism and the attendant posthuman ethics in so far as it uses the image of the chameleon and the fly wherein humanist ethics have disappeared. Furthermore, Lobengula's metaphor indicates the shortcomings of posthumanism and the attendant 'posthuman ethics' in so far as the relations between the chameleon and the fly are not governed by moral and ethical imperatives of good and bad, but rather, of animistic Darwinian survival of the fittest and of zero-sum games. The colonial cannibalisation of Africa, and Zimbabwe in particular, dispensed with the truly inclusive humanistic moral imperatives between good and bad. Lobengula's metaphor of the chameleon catching a fly underscores the unpredictable and undependable nature of the chameleon that keeps on changing its colour (and principles by implication) to disguise and camouflage itself in the different environments in which it finds itself – such was also the nature of imperial cannibalism. Thus, the imperial pretences to help 'civilise', 'develop' and 'save' Africans were – to use Lobengula's metaphor – part of the chameleon's camouflaging of itself in the African environment being afflicted by imperial plunder and cannibalisation. In this regard, colonial cannibalism was not merely about marooning Africans on a 'shipwrecked' continent – it was also about 'ambiguating' and disguising the colonial cannibals as saviours with good and godly intentions. Via the resilient imperial and capitalist logics of accumulation and incorporation (Quan 2012), Africans continue to be cannibalised under the misapprehension that capital and empire exercise 'ethics of caring' for and of encountering the vulnerable African others. Also, via (neo-)imperial cultural and institutional ideologies, Africans are cannibalised through processes of imperial institutional and cultural incorporation.

Since the colonial era, Zimbabwean cultures have been placed on imperial chopping boards for purposes of cannibalisation. African identities have been rendered fractious with divisions, for purposes of divide and rule, being created along gender, age, 'ethnicity', and so on. The divisions and the attendant cannibalisation of otherwise African collective identities are pivotal in explaining the acute political divisions that have afflicted Zimbabwe for decades since the year 2000. The African *Ubuntu/unhu/hunhu* collectivist ethics marked by respect for other people have been cannibalised together with the African collectivist identities. Rendered fractious and fragmented, African men and women are made to feel more comfortable in the hands and even in the bellies of foreigners than in the midst of their own African people, who are often still conveniently portrayed, metaphorically and literally, in global media as savage cannibals. Much as during the early colonial era when African Kings and Chiefs were portrayed (for purposes of petrifying their African subjects) as archaic despots, contemporary African leaders are also subjected to imperial, including ideological, chopping boards for purposes of (neo-)imperial cannibalisation. In this sense, the imperial divide and rule tactics can be understood as part of rituals of chopping off Africans into smaller chunks of delicacies for purposes of (neo-)imperial cannibalism – 'choppies' are best served in small chunks that make them easy to bite and swallow.

The processes of cannibalistic incorporation (Estok 2013) have been central to the colonisation processes on the African continent where to eat an African has for long been a delicacy for (neo-)imperialists. Important to note in this respect is Janes's (2015) observation that eating has for long been a metaphor for the cannibalistic nature of (French) imperialism in Africa. Thus, Janes (2015: 176–183) writes:

> The physical and metaphorical consumption of the colonized African other was featured dramatically in the French dessert tête de negre, which presented a representation of an African head for French consumption, ritualizing and taming the violent incorporation into the French empire ... The representation of the cannibalistic act itself – the failure to perceive the boundaries of edibility and the hierarchy of

species – defines insiders and outsiders by separating those who know how and what to eat from those who do not … Furthermore, the metaphoric consumption of the colonized African is demonstrated in the French dessert tête de negre, which presented a stylized representation of an African head for French ingestion. This dish, which ritualized and domesticated the violent incorporation of African bodies into the French empire continues to exist in France in the name tête de negre long into the postcolonial period … The use of the black head as the model for food is in some ways just as dehumanizing as the reoccurring image of the black cannibal. Here the African is far enough from human to be considered edible. As the black head sits on the table without the body, tête de negre portrays black Africans as dehumanized and rendered edible through metaphoric decapitation … The name continues to ritually connect the pastry to the French consumption of Africa and destruction of African lives.

Thus, the colonial era decapitation of African heads – Kings and Queens – including the deposition of the Ndebele King Lobengula, the fragmentation of Africans into colonially invented menus or categories – tribes, ethnicities, gender and races – all amounted to imperial decapitation and cannibalisation of Africans served as meals of various courses. The colonial assumptions that Africans were savages next to animals can be understood as attempts to legitimise the cannibalisation of Africans, including the Zimbabweans, from the time of Cecil John Rhodes and his Rhodesian banquets organised to lure young, able-bodied ambitious Britons to his treasure-hunting paradise, where the indigenous populations were as much fair game as their resources and wildlife. In fact, Lobengula's protestations that the British were chameleons seeking to catch Africans – supposedly considered by the chameleons to be flies (Mungazi 1999) – can be understood as complaints against British cannibalistic imperialism that thrives on consuming African heads of (precolonial) states as part of their trophy hunting expeditions on the continent. Also, Lobengula's protestations can be conceived as complaints against British imperial assumptions that Africans were not human beings. In fact, Lobengula's utterance can also be understood as a complaint against the British who, in spite of their pretences to be civilised and to be seized with godly missions, including morals and ethics, nomadically went about as chameleons catching and feeding off other people in the world. This made of these other humans, whatever their pretentions of humanity, nothing more than wild game to be stalked, captured, harnessed and consumed with little compunction, but with all the delightful display of superiority that one could muster.

The Capture and Cannibalisation of Zimbabwe: on the Imperial Leviathan

The British imperialist Cecil John Rhodes was assisted, in colonising Zimbabwe, by some missionaries such as Robert Moffat and C. D. Helms who negotiated with the Ndebele King Lobengula with whom the missionaries, as precursors of colonists, initially pretended to establish friendships and a false sense of a common humanity with the Africans they encountered and were committed to converting into Christianity. Like nomadic tribes, the missionaries, carrying the Bibles, marauded the entire African continent establishing missions which were initially resisted by Africans who were targeted for conversion. While the missionaries sought to cannibalise Africans by preying on their precolonial religions, converting and incorporating them into the (neo-)imperial religions that were being proselytised, Cecil John Rhodes and his ilk coaxed African kings, chiefs and queens (including Lobengula) into treaties that were deceptively addressed as 'protection treaties'. Notwithstanding the promises of 'protection', African kings and queens were in fact ensnared, deposed and cannibalised by the British imperialists whose promise of 'protection' was nothing but a ploy to render the Africans vulnerable to imperial cannibalistic machinations.

After deceptively securing the Rudd Concession with King Lobengula, Cecil John Rhodes moved to colonise Zimbabwe in the 1890s. The initial attempt to colonise Zimbabwe was resisted by the Shona and Ndebele people who waged wars of the First Chimurenga in the 1890s. The second resistance to colonisation was marked by the Second Chimurenga war in the 1960s and 1970s, which culminated in the political independence of Zimbabwe in 1980.

During the negotiations for independence at Lancaster House in Britain, the Lancaster House Constitution was drawn up for the governance of post-independent Zimbabwe. The Constitution seemed keen, all of a sudden, to recognise and provide for a common humanity, now that there was a serious prospect of those to whom the colonialists had denied all humanity in reality, taking over political power and controlling economic resources. Even then, while the Lancaster House Constitution granted political independence to Zimbabwe, it did not grant economic independence – it also did not grant the land back to indigenous Zimbabweans who had, for close to a century, fought for the restitution of their land which had been stolen from them (eaten up) by British colonists during the colonial era. In fact, the Lancaster House Constitution protected the 5,000 white farmers (treasure-hunters who 'owned' and controlled about 75 per cent of the land) via outlawing majoritarian compulsory acquisition of the land by the post-independence government.

Although, at the Lancaster House negotiations, the British government agreed to fund the post-independence land redistribution designed to ensure that the land was ultimately returned to its original black indigenous Zimbabweans, Tony Blair's British government reneged on the payments in 1997 (Moyo and Chambati 2013; Gono 2008). During the 1990s the Zimbabwean government was also afflicted by the cannibalistic and debilitating World Bank and International Monetary Fund neo-liberal economic reforms that made it impossible for the impecunious government to put together funds for the purchase of land for purposes of redistribution. Meanwhile pressure on communal lands continued to build up until in the year 2000, the government of Zimbabwe decided to compulsorily acquire the cannibalised land for purposes of redistribution to the land hungry peasants who had been in uncomfortable crammed positions on overcrowded, infertile and poorly watered communal areas since the colonial era, while a handful of whites, in the manner of boa constrictors, swallowed up the bulk of their choicest and most productive land.

Former President Robert Mugabe told the British that the Zimbabweans would go ahead and repossess their land even without compensation to the white farmers. From the year 2000 onwards,

Zimbabwean war veterans and peasants took over the farms from white farmers around the country. Britain, America and the rest of the European Union responded by imposing sanctions on Zimbabwe – the USA's Zimbabwe Democracy and Economic Recovery Act (ZIDERA) which was passed in the early 2000s urged international institutions not to provide funding to Zimbabwe, Zimbabwe's voting rights in some international institutions were suspended and the International Monetary Fund and the World Bank stopped support to Zimbabwe. In spite of the fact that it sought to inclusively democratise ownership of land and other resources in Zimbabwe, the Zimbabwean government was alleged to have violated human rights, democracy and good governance. In fact, the then sitting Zimbabwe African National Union (Patriotic Front) government was alleged to have breached democracy because the ruling party consistently trounced the ramshackle opposition Movement for Democratic Change (MDC) Party – this opposition party had been hurriedly formed in 1999, two years after the British government of Tony Blair had undiplomatically and unceremoniously reneged on its obligation to pay for orderly land redistribution in Zimbabwe. Morgan Tsvangirai, the then president of the opposition party shamelessly called for sanctions to be imposed on Zimbabwe.

Having heard the calls, for the imposition of sanctions on Zimbabwe, by their darling in the name of the late president of the opposition party – the Movement for Democratic Change – Morgen Tsvangirai, Euro-American states slammed Zimbabwe with cannibalistic sanctions. The United States of America (USA), Britain and some other countries even tried to sponsor a United Nations Resolution for sanctions on Zimbabwe but the Resolution was vetoed by Russia and China. USA and Britain then supplied huge amounts of funding for, their darling, the opposition political party, the Movement for Democratic Change, as well as to some 'civil society organisations', including NGOs and media organisations that were supposed to effect regime change in Zimbabwe. A huge number of reports have since been issued by the different organisations often summarily and singularly castigating, demonising and cannibalising the Zimbabwean government in various ways. In other words, the funding from the Euro-American governments was provided to organisations that not only demonised but also cannibalised the Zimbabwean government which was thereby erroneously singularly blamed for the crises within the country. Thus, the sanctions were meant to generate intense vulnerability of Zimbabweans while at the same time condemning and cannibalising the Zimbabwean government that was put on the global media, NGOs and civil society organisations' chopping boards – the Zimbabwean government and the ruling Zimbabwe African National Union Patriotic Front (ZANU PF) (as indeed African people more generally) became (neo-)imperial choppies. Also, the Zimbabwean currency became a delicate choppy of the sanctioning institutions as evident in the devaluation and hyperinflation that afflicted the country during the eras of neoliberalism and sanctions.

Faced with hardships cascading to the local spaces, Zimbabweans were acutely divided along political party lines, gender, 'ethnicity' and age – along these lines the citizens have also cannibalised one another. During elections, members of opposing political parties have had their properties looted and their physical integrity violated in ensuing conflicts; persons including of different genders have fought to succeed the aging former President – in this regard, the most salient incident has been between the former first lady Grace Mugabe and the former Vice President of Zimbabwe, Emmerson Mnangagwa – both of who vied to succeed the aging former President of the country. The poisoned ice cream incident (News24 25 November 2017), wherein Mnangagwa alleged that he consumed poisoned ice cream from a dairy owned by the first family, amply showed ways in which struggles for succession culminated in attempts to cannibalise one another both literally and metaphorically. The culmination of these struggles for succession was the 'cannibalisation' of the former President Robert Mugabe who was deposed through a coup that replaced him with his former Vice President.

While historically the Euro-Americans held that cannibalism (in their societies) was a symbol of total confusion, a lack of morality, law and structure (*Independent* 4 August 2017; *Pambazuka* 28 July 2016; Ford 2013), they deliberately chose to be blind to the ways in which they cannibalised Africans. Zimbabweans were for instance robbed of their land, cattle, minerals and their labour – they were forced into cheap labour in imperial mines, farms and factories. The loot committee that was established by the British South African Company looted livestock, land and minerals belonging to indigenous Zimbabweans (Palmer 1977). Zimbabwean land was apportioned in terms of race, 'ethnicity', class, gender and 'tribes'. The indigenous Zimbabweans were pushed into infertile and poorly watered reserves from which they were drawn, from time to time, as cheap labour for the colonialists. Such cannibalisation of Zimbabweans required the colonialists to consider the indigenous Africans as 'animals' rather than human beings. For this reason, Africans who were pushed into reserves were considered to live in 'kraals' much like cattle stay in kraals, and with 'kraal heads' also addressed as village heads. Since the colonial era, Africans' villages are alternatively addressed as African 'kraals' – implying that Africans were/are animals reserved to labour in colonial factories, mines and farms. For this reason, arguments that Mugabe's government created unemployment erroneously presume that (neo-)colonial employment is liberating – such arguments ignore the (neo-)colonial history of forced and cheap African labour wherein African life forces are sapped and cannibalised by nomadic transnational corporations that also sponsor organisations (including academies) opposed to African sovereignty and autonomy.

For the above reason, while Westerners held themselves as upright, superior and civilised, Africans have historically considered the Euro-Americans to be bloodsucking cannibalistic witches who exhumed corpses from graves and undertook savage hunts for African children that they kidnapped and cannibalised (Biersack 2017; Stevens 1991). Thus, considered to be lustful for human flesh and blood and for 'eating' the life-force of victims in ways that caused debilitation, cannibals are associated with witchcraft and with colonialism in so far as they sap the life-forces of the colonised people, whose cultures, institutions, originality and essences are replaced with counterfeit identities. Furthermore, the fact that the slave trade that preceded colonialism involved the capture, death and disappearance of enslaved Africans explains the apprehensions that the nomadic imperialists were cannibalistic witches and satanists that devoured African life-forces. Thus, witchcraft and (contemporary global) satanism are considered as bloodthirsty, devouring or cannibalising the others' life-forces during witches' invisible and nightly global orgiastic sabbaths (Barker 2014; De Blecourt et al. 1999; Ross 1995). With respect to Zimbabwe, the Euro-American sanctions were designed to sap the life-forces of the Zimbabwean economy, polity and society – the sanctions were in other words cannibalistic and predatory even though the Euro-American media conveniently presented the sanctions as legitimate and as furthering the ends of 'democracy'.

Although globalisation, including the invisible forces it unleashes, is often celebrated, it is necessary to note its connections with cannibalistic (neo-)imperialism that, like a chameleon, has over time merely changed its colours but not its cannibalistic essence – the global cannibalisation of the (neo-)colonised peripheries in Africa. The sapping of the African life-forces including the sapping of African labour power, the (neo-)imperial looting of African resources, the (neo-)imperial plunder of African cultures, religions and epistemologies in order to feed the invisible global hierarchies of cannibalism all speak to the global consumption of Africans. Though in countries like Uganda, cannibals are exorcised, made to confess and induced to vomit (Behrend 2009), unfortunately Zimbabweans could not force global cannibalistic entities to confess, to be exorcised and to vomit the essence of (neo-)imperial cannibalism. In fact Zimbabweans and other Africans who refuse to be cannibalised by the invisible global forces are often subjected to sanctions, wars and other forms of depredations designed to force them back into the insatiable invisible global and imperial networks of cannibalism. As will be explained below, Zimbabwe suffered sanctions, imposed by Euro-America, when it challenged the resilient (neo-)colonial land ownership patterns within the country – the (neo-)imperial cannibalistic decoy was 'human rights abuses' and absence of 'democracy' in Zimbabwe.

Whereas cannibal witches are known to be borne by invisible evil spiritual forces (Chavunduka 1980; Behrend 2009; Niehaus 2012) that explain their cannibalism, globalisation has also managed to cascade powerful virtualities that often overbear on sanctioned

138

individuals and organisations within the local African spaces. With respect to Zimbabwe, the powerful and overbearing forces of the World Bank, the International Monetary Fund and other institutions that often dictate to Africa induce destabilising global cannibalistic shocks in African societies and political economies. Thus, post-independent Zimbabwe was subjected by the World Bank and the International Monetary Fund to neo-liberal shocks – the shocks cannibalised, demobilised and deindustrialised the post-independence Zimbabwean economy with ravaging domino effects in various sectors of the society. While in African cosmologies cannibalistic witches are deemed to raise, keep and use invisible familiars such as snakes, hyenas, owls and baboons (Gelfand 1959; Lan 1987), in the cannibalistic global/imperial dispensation, there is the constitution and deployment of corporeal and incorporeal agents including invisible institutions such as the Bretton-woods institutions, transnational corporations and other entities that, under veils, visit global/imperial voodoo-inspired depredations on African societies.

Although transnational corporations are often celebrated as indispensable 'investors' for Africa, it is necessary to note that Zimbabwe was colonised through cannibalistic imperial companies such as the British South African Company which sponsored the colonisation process. African precolonial industries in Zimbabwe were also cannibalised and destroyed by colonial era administrations that were keen to stem competition from the African industries (Posselt 1935; Ellert 1984). Similarly, Zimbabwean artefacts were cannibalised when the colonial administration resorted to looting the artefacts and even exhuming corpses which they stripped of jewellery and other valuables with which they were buried (Posselt 1935; Ellert 1984). As hinted above, the colonialists (via the colonising British South African Company) established what they called the 'loot committee' which was tasked with cannibalising Zimbabwean resources including minerals, livestock, land, artefacts and so on. To legitimise cannibalism, colonialists had to assume that there were no laws, no polities, no states, no economies, no morals, no ethics and, more broadly, no civilisation in precolonial Africa. In other words, the cannibalistic colonialists assumed that Africans were mere flies –

without economies, polities, states, religions, morals, ethics, laws and societies.

The upshot of the above is that colonialists relied on logics of 'ethics of vulnerability' and 'ethics of care' to legitimise their colonial projects in Zimbabwe and the rest of Africa. Africans were assumed to be vulnerable to their supposedly harmful cultures, traditions, polities, states, barbarity, savagery, backwardness and more broadly, stasis. The Africans were deemed by colonialists to be vulnerable to witchdoctors among themselves, as well as to the irrationalities of beliefs in cannibalistic witchcraft. In this vein, the colonialists conveniently ignored their own imperial sorcerous conjurations which infected and afflicted the dispossessed, exploited and famished Africans. In spite of the presence of cannibalistic Satanism and cannibalistic spiritual and virtual forces emanating from the global north (*Independent* 4 August 2017; *The Telegraph* 26 July 2010; Gelfand 1959; Noble 2011; Lindenbaum 2004; *Independent* 10 May 1993; Sugg 2016; Au 2017), colonial anthropology erroneously assumed that it was Africa that was predominated by cannibalistic witchcraft.

Under the pretext of archaeology, colonists dug up corpses of precolonial Zimbabweans – in fact they enlisted (forced) Africans to exhume the corpses of their relatives for purposes of colonial cannibalism. At Great Zimbabwe and other monuments, corpses, including skulls, were exhumed and cannibalised by the colonialists. Also, Africans' skulls (including of Africans who were hanged or executed during the colonial era) were shipped to Europe (Shigwedha 2017). While the exhumation and shipment of corpses to Europe was explained in terms of war trophies, we contend herein that the real purpose was for cannibalism which existed in Europe – in fact cannibalism still exists in the global north where some restaurants and traders are noted as serving human flesh and medical establishments rely on trafficking human body parts (News24 26 July 2017; *Al Jazeera* 25 August 2003; *Express* 17 April 2013; *Independent* 28 January 2013; *News Europe* 18 December 2002; Scheper-Hughes 2001; Ross 1995; *Mirror* 17 August 2015).

Apart from literal cannibalism, Africans have also been cannibalised in metaphoric senses particularly when the global north coerces Africans into a supposedly inclusive world system that paradoxically eats up the Africans. Via economic and other forms of sanctions, Africans are cannibalised by the global north (African Union Report 28 October 2015; *Express* 17 April 2013; *Independent* 28 January 2013; *The Sun* 30 December 2016). In so far as sanctions are meant to enforce incorporation or inclusion in a supposedly international system, the sanctions – as modalities of inclusion – are in effect apparatuses of cannibalism designed to eat up African others, to get them mixed up, to make them disappear as autonomous and sovereign entities (Nunes 2008).

In so far as Zimbabwe is concerned, the Euro-American regimes of sanctions including virtual power and global vitalities can be understood as instantiating modalities of cannibalistic incorporation or assimilation. The virtual 'global' inorganic spirit that is considered to grip the world, to render the world acentred and rhizomatic and to render African human beings indistinct from animals (Pearson 2001), is a cannibalistic one – including in the sense that such 'global' inorganic spirit or vitality is considered to render the African human bodies anarchic, demonic – and it renders the human body traversed by the powerful nonorganic and imperceptible force from outside (Albert 2001; Poxon 2001). In Africa, and Zimbabwe in particular, powerful 'global' forces including sanctions regimes permeate local scenes and as they do so, they reduce afflicted and affected indigenous Africans to the level of animals; they decentre Africa and render it rhizomatic. In other words outside 'global' imperceptible vitalities and virtualities unhinge ethics and morality by reducing African human beings to scavenging animals. In this regard, the xenophobic and Afrophobic violence against Zimbabwean immigrants can be understood not merely in terms of anti-immigrant sentiments but in terms of sentiments against sanctions-animalised Zimbabwean immigrants – more accurately turned into global scavengers and not merely into immigrants. For this reason, what cannibalistic, Afrophobic and xenophobic individuals saw was not necessarily human immigrants but animalised scavengers entering their territories. Thus, xenophobia and Afrophobia are in fact cannibalistic actions and reactions on fellow Africans that have unfortunately already suffered cannibalistic (neo-)imperial sanctions including dispossession and exploitation which are inspired at the global level.

Drawing from Dale (2001) we can argue that sanctioning imperceptible global forces and vitalities cause the afflicted and affected Africans to begin to 'dance for incorporation inside out as in the delirium of accordion dances and that inside out is their true side out'. The violence and cruelty of sanctions, which are sanitised through spurious discourses on democracy, human rights, good governance and humanitarianism, are in essence the violence of cannibalistic incorporation into a global order that is itself unequal, hegemonic and oppressive. As a technique of incorporation, the powerful global virtual forces, which are beyond the control of individual African states, visit violence and cruelty on the African bodies causing them to plunge into the virtual or spiritual depth which, to use Goddard's (2001) terms, exceed them and their localities. The point here is that a world that treats others as delicacies in order to incorporate, assimilate and include them is a cannibalistic world founded on the Derridean 'ethics' of cannibalism and consumption of the other. Thus, the 'ethics' of sanctioning the African others are in fact ethics of cannibalising or consuming Africa in the sense that they are, at their core, ethics of appetite, ethics of incorporation and assimilation of Africa into the predatory global (neo-)imperial leviathan. But the 'ethics' of cannibalism also involve subtle animistic techniques of mimesis and seduction of the African targets of (neo-)imperial cannibalism.

Luring and Incorporating 'Delicious' Africa in a Cannibalistic World: Zimbabwe and Sanctions

Rane Willerslev's (2004: 629) work is important in examining the contemporary logics of mimetic cannibalism and sanctions in Zimbabwe. While he observes that in Siberia, humans and animals can turn into each other by temporarily taking on one another's bodies, he holds that this is dangerous for a hunter because he may thus lose sight of his original species' identity and undergo an irreversible metamorphosis. Much like in global human rights and democracy discourses where the cannibalistic global north often

142

mimics the viewpoint and even the pain of the African others, Willerslev (2004: 629) notes that the hunter has to assume the viewpoint of his prey but not in an absolute sense. For Willerslev, 'mimetic practice allows the hunter to be similar to the animal being impersonated, yet also different, giving him a double perspective by which he can seduce and kill his prey'. The logics of mimesis, animism and cannibalism explicated by Willerslev can be used to understand the logics of cannibalistic incorporation or assimilation in the world. In much the same way as animals are seduced by hunters' mimesis, nations and peoples are seduced through Euro-American mimesis for purposes of assimilation into the global world. In seduction through mimesis, the seduced find themselves in the persons of the seducers and for the seducer to succeed he/she is not supposed to create a truthful image but instead an ideal representation of or fantasy image of what she/he should become (Willerslev 2007). Such mimesis and seduction raise questions as to ways in which those who impose sanctions on others mimic the pain and suffering of the targets of seduction, they raise questions about the truthfulness of their empathy, sympathy and apparent ethics of care that are implied in the impositions of cannibalistic sanctions against regimes that are often summarily and conveniently portrayed as rogue, authoritarian, abusive of human rights, absconders of democracy and good governance. In fact, Zimbabweans upon whom sanctions were imposed were also seduced into the global order via images of economic recovery with aid and reconnection to the Euro-American establishment. In other words, Euro-American states imposed sanctions on Zimbabweans while at the same time conveniently and fortuitously mimicking the pain and suffering of ordinary Zimbabweans.

As Willerslev (2007) argues, in mimesis, the seducer has to act as an ideal reflection of the seduced, that is, as an incomplete copy of her, and practices of mimetic empathy provide the seducer with the ability to be like yet also different from the victim of seduction. With respect to Zimbabwe, the cannibalistic West through the global media, civil society organisations and non-governmental organisations, frontloaded empathy, sympathy and 'ethics of care' for the supposed African victims of dictatorships. NGOs and other civil society organisations carried out researches that made it possible for the West to practice mimetic empathy – to mimic the cries of the suffering Africans. In fact, the 'prefabricated' NGOs and civil society organisations helped create jobs for Westerners who headed such organisations – Africans being employed mainly in precarious contract positions within most of the organisations. So, much like hunters who mimic movements of animals, imitate the cries of animals (Willerslev 2004, 2007: 108) so as to draw the targeted animals closer before spearing them, logics of global cannibalistic incorporation drew Zimbabwean victims of sanctions closer to Euro-America via mimesis and seduction, as modalities of global incorporation and assimilation. Many statistics were generated to evidence the cries and levels of suffering from the supposed Zimbabwean cannibalistic 'dictatorship' in the figure of Robert Mugabe. Such logic of mimesis and seduction require hunters and researchers to be carefully observant of the 'animals" behaviour patterns, the hunters have to cultivate good listening and mimicry skills which are used to great effect to call animals to them, make fake animal calls to lure them within range and view so that they can shoot or spear them (Willersev 2007; Lewis 2009: 5).

Thus, in Zimbabwe, NGOs have generated a lot of reports detailing how much they have 'cared for' and assisted the 'vulnerable' supposed Zimbabwean victims of 'dictatorship'. Reports about (phantom) food donations, projects to help orphans, the elderly, the homeless, the poor and so on have been churned out together with calls for regime change in the country – that is, NGOs and Euro-American states called for eating the African (Zimbabwean) head of state in the ways that the French dessert noted above enjoins the consumption of African heads. In other words, it is never the heads of cannibalistic and colonial transnational corporations, or heads of the cannibalistic foreign states that imposed the sanctions that were supposed to be eaten – it was rather the African heads that were, within the discourses, up for consumption in the regime change agenda. In the discourses, it was surprisingly not the cannibalistic (neo-)imperial regimes that were supposed to be changed but rather the African nationalistic regimes were to be cannibalised and changed.

In order to sufficiently examine global cannibalism that is catalysed by regimes of sanctions on the global south, we draw on the logics of mimesis and seduction to show that for Africa, and Zimbabwe in particular, pretexts of human rights abuses, authoritarianism, abstentions from democracy and good governance are (neo-)imperial techniques of mimesis and seduction. These are techniques of mimesis in the sense that they allow the (neo-)empire to pretend to sympathise with Africans even as the same empire is cannibalising and devouring them (Barker et al 1998). It can be argued that discourses of human rights, democracy, good governance and authoritarianism are convenient apparatuses for imperial mimesis because they are themselves not grounded in the original, deep history of Africans who have suffered dehumanisation, dispossession and exploitation at the hands of the same empire – including some contemporary states in the global north that currently paradoxically claim 'humanitarian' stewardship and guardianship over Africans. We contend that if claims of human rights, democracy, good governance and authoritarianism that are used as pretexts to unleash sanctions on Africans and the global south are genuine and not mere mimetic techniques, the overdue centuries-old redress of (neo-)colonial and enslavement wrongs would logically be the first to be addressed.

While some scholars like Grebe (2010) argue that the Euro-American imposed sanctions (on some government officials, banks and other companies) were meant to help Zimbabwe in democratic transition and to revitalise the collapsed economy, it is imperative to note that the sanctions were meant principally to (re-)incorporate and cannibalise Zimbabwe into the world system that is undemocratically controlled by the same Euro-American countries which imposed the sanctions. It is necessary to also note that genuine democratic transition cannot possibly take place in Africa if democracy is defined in ways that exclude democratisation of ownership and control of material resources by Africans (Nhemachena et al, 2017a; Nhemachena et al, 2017b; Nhemachena 2015). If the Euro-American countries that claim to have democracy also own resources within and outside their territories then why would they expect countries of the global south to have democracy without ownership and control of their resources? Why must democracy in Africa be merely political and electoral and not be restorative, restitutive and premised on African ownership and control of African resources? Do African countries need sanctions in order to transition to democracy or do they need restitution and restoration of ownership and control of their material resources in order for such transition to democracy to be realised? Are the sanctions not merely Euro-American mimetic tools for taming, whipping up and cannibalising Africa that has for centuries already been a delicacy for Euro-America?

In a world in which Africans and other indigenous people are waking up and claiming restitution and restoration of their material resources looted during the (neo-)colonial eras, the fundamental question that underlies their claims is how democracy can be broadened to include restitution, restoration and return of ownership and control over resources? In other words, they are challenging Euro-American parochial and predatory definition of democracy that is meant to operate as a tool for mimesis and seduction, without restoration or restitution. The point here is that narrow political/electoral democracy without material restitution and restoration amounts to a cannibalistic form of democracy that is merely meant to serve the purposes of imperial incorporation and assimilation. Such a narrow form of democracy shies away from incorporating or assimilating multiplicities of varieties of democracy, even as it claims to embrace and incorporate diversity of peoples. To the extent that such democracy shuts out other variants of democracy including democracy premised on ownership and control of materialities (Nhemachena et al, 2017a), it is a form of democracy that is already a form of sanctioning and cannibalising the other. The point here is that Euro-American democracy is already a form of sanctioning the African peoples who are, *a priori*, not allowed to develop and proffer their own variants and forms of democracy. In this sense, while the West purports to clearly separate and distinguish sanctions from democracy, and autocracy from democracy, the Western democracy is already a form of sanctioning and cannibalisation – it is already a form of autocracy and authoritarianism in the sense of it originating from one source and denying epistemic visas and hearings from other peoples' seeking to

146

articulate their variants of democracy. For this reason, it is a form of democracy that denies varieties and diversity because it *a priori* shuts out variants of democracy – it is thus a form of democracy that is predatory in the sense of being cannibalistic, designed principally as a tool for mimetic and seductive incorporation into the predatory global or imperial leviathan.

The upshot of the above is that though the United Nations failed to impose sanctions on contemporary Zimbabwe because of the vetoes by Russia and China (Chinese Embassy 25 June 2009; United Nations 11 July 2008; *The Guardian* 11 July 2008; *The Guardian* 9 November 2011, Alao 2012; Allison 2013), Africa is yet to get assistance within the United Nations system to veto the centuries old sanctions that date back to enslavement and colonial era cannibalisation of the continent. In other words, while the United States of America, Britain, Belgium, Costa Rica, Italy, Panama, Burkina Faso and France supported the United Nations Resolution for sanctions against Zimbabwe (United Nations 11 July 2008), the unfortunate thing is that they failed to notice that Zimbabwe like all other African countries has already been under centuries-old sanctions since the dawn of colonial era cannibalism. The point here is that while some African countries may be afraid of the kind of Euro-American sanctions which were imposed on Zimbabwe, the sad fact is that Africa as a whole is already reeling under sanctions which it has had to endure since the enslavement and colonial era depredations and cannibalism. The unfortunate thing is that many Africans also fail to notice that they are already under cannibalistic sanctions. Africa is a delicacy, to Euro-America, that is devoured whether out of mimetic love or out of hatred/vengeance – cannibalism can be borne out of both love and hatred.

Thus, whether Africa does good or bad things in the eyes of Euro-America, Africa is set to be sanctioned and cannibalised, nonetheless, because Euro-America cannot survive without the African delicacies. The point then is that Africa is sanctioned not necessarily because Africa is full of devils, criminal leaders or cannibals but because Euro-America needs Africa as a delicacy for imperial cannibalistic rituals. Colonial and enslavement era cannibalism shows that one does not have to be a deviant to be sanctioned and cannibalised – whether or not Africa is ruled by autocrats, dictators, absconders of democracy and human rights, Africa will suffer cannibalistic sanctions of incorporation, dispossession and exploitation. Superficial discourses of human rights, democracy, and good governance are simply apparatuses for imperial mimesis and seduction that are meant to subtly generate wide African consent to be cannibalised and devoured. Therefore, underlying the discourses on human rights, democracy and good governance are the logics of colonial era 'ethics of care' and 'ethics of vulnerability' wherein the other is (neo-)imperially 'cared for' for purposes of present and future ritual cannibalisation.

Conclusion

In the light of the above, it is cause for wonder why discourses on sanctions have revolved merely around trade restrictions, trade embargoes, travel bans and so on without also including colonial forms of depredation and cannibalism that date to centuries ago. Sanctions and the attendant cannibalism of Africa cannot merely and narrowly be defined in terms of trade restrictions, travel bans, trade embargoes and so on. Sanctions can feature in the guise of missions for 'civilisation' and 'development' such as during the colonial era when imperial cannibalisation of Africa was hidden in discourses of 'civilisation' and 'development' of Africans. Like other forms of cannibalism that involve opening up graves and exhuming corpses, the cannibalism of imperial incorporation thrives on discourses of opening up targeted societies – and then devouring them. Cannibalistic democracy and human rights thrive on discourses of opening up Africa much as other forms of cannibalism depend on opening up graves and exhuming corpses. Targeted societies that close up (as sovereign and autonomous) would be inviting vengeful imperial cannibalistic sanctions. Yet opening up the African societies creates vulnerability to cannibalisation. Cannibals often appear with predatory promises of 'ethics of care' and 'ethics of vulnerability' that motivate the opening up to the devouring other.

References

African Union Report (28 October 2015) Commission of Inquiry on South Sudan, http://www.peaceu.org/en/article/abc. Accessed 20 February 2018.

Al Jazeera (25 August 2003) 'Man-Eating Sorcerer Detained in Cameroon, http://www.aljazeera.com/archive/2003/08/200841012332719 608.html. Accessed 20 February 2018.

Alao, A. (2012) *Mugabe and Politics of Security in Zimbabwe*, McGill-Queens Press.

Albert, E. (2001) 'Deleuze's Impersonal, Hylozoic Cosmology' in M. Bryden (ed.) *Deleuze and Religion*, London: Routledge. pp: 184-195.

Allison, R. (2013) *Russia, the West and Military Intervention*, Oxford University Press.

Au, S. (2017) Cutting the Flesh: Surgery, Autopsy and Cannibalism in the Belgian Congo, in *Medical History* vol 61 (2): 295-312. Accessed 9 May 2018.

Barker, F. (1998) *Cannibalism and the Colonial World*, Cambridge University Press.

Barker, K. R. (2014) *Cannibalism, Blood Drinking & High-Adept Satanism*, Createspace Independent Publishing Platform.

Behrend, H. (2009) 'The Rise of Occult Powers, AIDS and the Roman Catholic Church in Western Uganda' in F. Becker et al. (eds) *Aids and Religious Practice in Africa*, BRILL.pp: 27 – 47.

Biersack, A. (2017) *Afterword: From Witchcraft to the Pentecostal-Witchcraft Nexus*, Springer.

Braidotti, R. (2016) 'Posthuman Critical Theory' in D. Banerji et al. (eds): *Critical Posthumanism and Planetary Futures*, Springer: 13-32.

Butler, J. (2012) 'Precarious Life, Vulnerability, and the Ethics of Cohabitation', *The Journal of Speculative Philosophy*, Vol. 26(2): 134–151.

Chavunduka, L. (1980) Witchcraft and the Law in Zimbabwe, *Zambezia* Vol. VIII(2): 129–148.

Chinese Embassy (25 June 2009) 'China Justifies Veto of Zimbabwe Sanctions', https://www.chinese-embassy.org.za.eng/zfgx/t569372.htm. Accessed 20 February 2018.

Cortina, A. & Conill, J. (2016) *Ethics of Vulnerability*, Springer.

Dale, C. (2001) 'Knowing One's Enemy: Deleuze, Artaud and the Problem of Judgement' in M. Bryden (ed): *Deleuze and Religion*, London: Routledge: 126-137.

De Blecourt, W, Hutton, R. and LaFontein, J. (1999) *Witchcraft and Magic in Europe: The Twentieth Century*. London: Bloomsbury.

Ellert, H. (1984) *The Material Culture of Zimbabwe*, Harare: Longman Zimbabwe Ltd.

Estok, S. C. (2013) 'Cannibals, Ecocriticism and Portraying the Journey', *Comparative Literature and Culture*, Vol. 14, Issue 5 in https://docs.lib.purdue.edu/clcweb. Accessed 20 February 2018.

Eves, R. (1995) 'Shamanism, Sorcery and Cannibalism: The Incorporation of Power in the Magical Cult of Buai', *Oceama*, Vol. 65(3): 212–233.

Express (17 April 2013) 'North Korean Reveals Cannibalism is Common after Escaping Starving State', https://www.express.co.uk/news/world/392610/North-korean-reveals-cannibalism-is-common-after-escaping-starving-state. Accessed 21 February 2018.

Ford, J. (2013) 'Vampiric Enterprise: Metaphors of Economic Exploitation in the Literature and Culture of the Fin de Siede', PhD Thesis, University of Portsmouth.

Gelfand, M. (1959) *Shona Ritual with Special Reference to the Chaminuka Cult*, Cape Town: Juta and Co Ltd.

Gilson, E. (2014) *The Ethics of Vulnerability: A Feminist Analysis of Social Life and Practice*, Routledge.

Goddard, M. (2001) 'The Scattering of Time Crystals: Deleuze, Mysticism and Cinema', in M. Bryden (ed): *Deleuze and Religion*, London: Routledge: 53-64.

Gono, G. (2008) *Zimbabwe's Casino Economy: Extraordinary Measures for Extraordinary Challenges*, Harare: ZPH.

Grebe, J. (2010) 'And They Are Still Targeting: Assessing the Effectiveness of Targeted Sanctions against Zimbabwe', *Africa Spectrum*, Vol. 45(1): 3–29.

Held, V. (2005) *The Ethics of Care: Personal, Political, and Global*, University Press.

Helm, C. D. (3 January 2016) 'The Chameleon Nursery in Town', in The Sunday News http://www.sundaynews.co.zw/the-chameleon-nursery-in-town/. Accessed 20 February 2018.

Independent (4 August 2017) 'Even Cannibals Observe Manners and Etiquette When Eating Human Flesh', http://www.independent.co.uk/life-style/food-and-drink-even-cannibals-observed-table-manners-when-eating-human-flesh-97852416.html. Accessed 20 February 2018.

Independent (10 May 1993) 'History the Common Cannibal: It's Not Everyone's Idea', http://www.independent.co.uk/life-style/health-and-families/health-news/history-of-the-common-cannibal-its-not-everyone's-idea-of-a-wholesome. Accessed 20 February 2018.

Independent (28 January 2013) 'North Korean Cannibalism Fears amid Claims Starving People Forced to Desperate Measures', http://www.independent.co.uk/news/world/asis/north-korea-cannibalism-fears-amid-claims-starving-people-forced-to-desperate-meaures-8468781.Accessed 20 February 2018.

Janes, L. (2015) 'Writing about Cannibal, Diets and Consuming Black Africans in France During the First Half of the Twentieth Century', *French Cultural Studies*, Vol. 26(2): 176–185.

Lan, D. (1987) *Guns and Rain: Guerrillas and Spirit Mediums in Zimbabwe*, Berkeley and Los Angeles: University of California Press.

Lewis, J. (2009) 'As Well As Words: Congo Pygmy Hunting, Mimicry and Play' in R. Botha, & C. Knight (eds) *The Cradle of Language*, Vol. 2: African Perspectives.

Lindenbaum, S. (2004) 'Thinking about Cannibalism', *Annual Review of Anthropology* Vol. 33: 475–498.

Mirror (17 August 2015) 'Killer Cannibal Reveals He Cooked Women in Stews and Pies and Says It's the Same as Eating Beef', http://www.mirror.co.uk/news/world-news/killer-cannibal-reveals-cooked-women-6263586. Accessed 20 February 2018.

Mogobe, R. (1999) *African Philosophy through Ubuntu*, Mond Books.

151

Moyo, S., & Chambati, W. (2013) *Land and Agrarian Reform in Zimbabwe*, African Books Collective.

Mungazi, D. A. (1999) *The Last British Liberals in Africa: Michael Blundell and Garfield Todd*, Greenwood Publishing Group.

Muzvidziwa, V. N. & Muzvidziwa, I. (2012) 'Hunhu (Ubuntu) and School Discipline in Africa', *Journal of Dharma* Vol. 37(1): 27–42.

News24 (25 November 2017) 'Mugabe's Successor and the "Poisoned Ice Cream" Plot', https://www.news24.com/Africa/Zimbabwe/mugabe's-successor-and-the-poisoned-ice-cream-plot-20171125. Accessed 20 February 2018.

News24 (26 July 2017) 'Five in Court for Grave Digging', https://www.news24.com/southafrica/local/express-news/five-in-court-for-grave-digging-20170725. Accessed 20 February 2018.

News Europe (18 December 2002) 'Cannibal "was influenced by Death Spell Witch"', https://www.independent.ie/world-news/europe/cannibal-was-influeced-by-death-spell-witch-26024577.html. Accessed 20 February 2018.

News24 (25 November 2017) 'Mugabe's Successor and the "Poisoned Ice Cream Plot"', http://humanitariannews.org/20171125/news24.com-mugabes-successor-poisoned-ice-cream-plot. Accessed 20 February 2018.

Nhemachena, A. (2015) 'Indigenous Knowledge, Conflation and Postcolonial Translation: Lessons from Fieldwork in Contemporary Rural Zimbabwe', in M. Mawere, & Awuah-Nyamekye, S. (eds) *Between Rhetoric and Reality: The State and Use of Indigenous Knowledge in Postcolonial Africa*, Bamenda: Langaa RPCIG: 59-108.

Nhemachena, A. (2017). *Relationality and Resilience in a Not So Relational World? Knowledge, Chivanhu and (De-)Coloniality in 21ˢᵗ Century Conflict-Torn Zimbabwe*, Bamenda: Langaa RPCIG.

Nhemachena, A., Kangira, J. & Mlambo, N. (2017a) *Decolonisation of Materialities or Materialisation of (Re-Colonisation? Symbolisms, Languages, Ecocriticism and (Non)Representationalism in 21ˢᵗ Century Africa*, Bamenda: Langaa RPCIG: 1-54.

Nhemachena, A., Warikandwa, T. V. & Mtapuri, O. (2017b) 'Transnational Corporations Land Grabs and the Ongoing Second Mad Scramble for Africa: an Introduction', in T. V. Warikandwa, A. Nhemachena, and O. Mtapuri, (eds) *Transnational Land Grabs and Restitution in an Age of the (De-)Militarized New Scramble for Africa: A Pan Africanist Socio-Legal Perspective*, Bamenda: Langaa RPCIG: 1-50..

Niehaus, I. (2012) 'Witchcraft and the South African Bantustans: Evidence from Bushbuckridge', *South African Historical Journal*, Vol. 64(1): 41–58.

Noble, L. C. (2011) *Medicinal Cannibalism in Early Modern English Literature and Culture: Early Modern Cultural Studies 1500-1700*, New York: Palgrave MacMillan.

Nunes, Z. (2008) *Cannibals Democracy: Race and Representation in the Literature of the Americas*, University of Minnesota Press.

Nyamnjoh, F. B. (2015) *C'est l'homme Qui Fait l'homme: Cul de Sac Ubuntu-ism in Cote d'Ivoire*, Bamenda: Langaa RPCIG.

Palmer, R. (1977) *Land and Racial Domination in Rhodesia*, Berkeley: University of California Press.

Pambazuka News (28 July 2016) 'White Supremacy as Cultural Cannibalism', https://www.pambazuka.org/pan-africanism/white-supremacy-cultural-cannibalism. Accessed 21 February 2018.

Pearson, K. A. (2001) 'Pure Reserve: Deleuze, Philosophy and Immanence', in M. Bryden (ed) *Deleuze and Religion*, London: Routledge: 141-156.

Pettersen, T. (2011) 'The Ethics of Care: Normative Structures and Empirical Implication', *Health Care Anal*, Vol. 19(1): 51–64.

Posselt, F. W. T. (1935) *Fact and Fiction*, Salisbury: Government House.

Poxon, J. (2001) 'Embodied Anti-Theology: The Body without Organs and the Judgement of God', in M. Bryden (ed) *Deleuze and Religion*, London: Routledge: 42-51.

Quan, H. L. T. (2012) *Growth against Democracy: Savage Developmentalismi n the Modern World*, Lexington Books.

Ross, C. A. (1995) *Satanic Ritual Abuse: Principles of Treatment*, University of Toronto Press.

Scheper-Hughes, N. (2001) 'Commodity Fetishism in Organ Trafficking', *Body and Society*, Vol. 17(2–3): 31–62.

Shigwedha, V. A. (2017) 'The Return of Herero and Nama Bones from Germany: The Victims' Struggle for Recognition and Recurring Genocide Memories in Namibia', in D. Jean-Marc, & Anstett, E. (eds) *Human Remains in Society: Curation and Exhibition in the Aftermath of Genocide and Mass Violence*, Manchester University Press: 197-219.

Stevens, P. (1991) 'The Demonology of Satanism: An Anthropological View', in Bromley. D. G., Best, J. & Richardson, J. T . (eds) *The Satanism Scare*, New York: Aldine de Gruyter: 21-40.

Sugg, R. (2016) *Munumes, Cannibals and Vampires: The History of Corpse Medicine from the Renaissance to the Victorians*, Routledge Second Edition London.

The Guardian (9 November 2011) 'Russia Rejects Further Sanctions of Iran over Nuclear Programme', https://www.theguardian.com/world/2011/nov/09/russia-rejects-iran-sanctions-nuclear. Accessed 20 February 2018.

The Guardian (11 July 2008) 'China and Russia Veto Zimbabwe Sanctions', https://www.thegurdian.com/world/2008/jul/11/unitednations.zimbabwe. Accessed 20 February 2018.

The Sun (30 December 2016) 'Desperate Measures', https://www.thesun.co.uk/news/2501517/pictures-human-body-parts-cannibals-russian-famine-1921-1922. Accessed 20 February 2018.

The Sunday New (3 January 2016) 'The Chameleon Nursery in Town', http://www.sundaynews.co.zw/the-chameleon-nursery-in-town/.

The Telegraph (26 July 2010) 'Russian Satanist Jailed for "Ritual Sacrifice" Teen Killings', https://www.telegraph.co.uk/news/worldnews/europe/russia/7910893/russian-satanists-jailed-for-ritual-sacrifice-teen-killings-html.Accessed 20 February 2018.

United Nations (11 July 2008) 'Security Council Fails to Adopt Sanctions against Zimbabwe Leadership as Two Permanent Members Cast Negative Votes', https://www.un.org/press/en/2008/sc96396.doc.htm. Accessed 20 February 2018.

Watson, K. L. (2010) 'I Laid My Hands on a Gorgeous Cannibal Women: Anthropophagy in the Imperial Imagination 1492-1796', PhD Thesis, Bowling Green State University.

Wijnants, R. (2016) 'Consu/Me: Posthumanist Cannibal Ethics and Subjectivities in the Literary Imagination', M A Thesis. Utrecht University https://dspace.library.uu.nl/handle/1874/338229. Accessed 9 May 2018.

Willerslev, R. (2004). 'Not Animals, Not Not- Animal: Hunting, Imitation and Empathetic Knowledge among the Siberian Yukaghurs', *JRAI Journal of the Royal Anthropological Institute,* Vol. 10(3): 629–652.

Willerslev, R. (2007) *Soul Hunters: Hunting, Animism and Personhood among the Siberian Yukaghurs,* University of California Press.

Chapter 4

'The Body of Christ? Amen': Christianity and the Cannibalisation of the Bamenda Grassfielders (Cameroon)

Walter Gam Nkwi

Introduction

The Bamenda Grassfields is located in the Northwest of Cameroon. It has a land surface of 6,680 sq. miles, almost the size of Belgium. Following the 2010 census its population stood at 1,828,953 people at a density of 100/km². It has more than thirty ethnic groups and languages and was administered as part of the British Southern Cameroons from the end of the First World War between 1916 and 1961 (Fanso 1989; Ngoh 1987). In 1903, the Basel Mission introduced Western Christianity to the region and after a slow and steady growth other Christian churches like the Catholic and Baptist followed and became the strongest and most important institutions in the Grassfields. Christianity since then has become the central life feature of most of the people. Even traditional rulers who before this period were custodians of traditional religions suddenly became identified with Christianity (Jindra 2005), through the delegitimisation of their authorities by the European colonisers and missionaries.

On 1 January 1932, the Basel missionary in the Bamenda Grassfields of Cameroon, Wilhem Zürcher, took a photograph with the indigenous people which he captioned 'sharing a drink with cannibals, a sign of friendship'. The picture below shows Wilhem in a white hat and his supposedly human eaters.

Figure 1: Basel missionary in the Bamenda Grassfields of Cameroon, Wilhem Zürcher, (in white hat) with 'cannibals'
Source: Mission21 Archives, Missionstrasse, Basel, Switzerland

On 31 December 1945 he took another photograph which he captioned 'Has everyone got his Bible? The new pupils of the catechist course are asked'. The photograph below shows the pupils of the catechist school raising their Bibles for inspection by the African superior.

Figure 2: The new pupils of the catechist course displaying their Bibles
(licensed weapons to cannibalise the Grassfielders
Source: Mission21 Archives, Missionstrasse, Basel, Switzerland

The two pictures are a German (Western) representation of the
Bamenda Grassfields, Cameroon. V.Y. Mudimbe (1979) has referred
to such a micro form of representation as the 'colonial library' of
contested knowledge created by the coloniser, the European
anthropologist and Western missionary to define and redefine,
recreate and reformulate Africa; invent and re-invent Africans and
African ways of life in the image of the West and according to their
whims and caprices.

In the perspective of Wilhem Zürcher and his evangelising zeal,
photograph one shows how 'paganic, primitive, backward and
diffident' the Bamenda Grassfields people were purportedly living
before Christianity ('civilisation'), allegedly by eating human flesh and
drinking palm wine, a cuisine which the Basel missionary mockingly
(or is it playfully?) partakes in. While the second photograph shows a
level of 'civilisation' because the people are proudly holding up their
copies of the Bible and dressed in clothes which the Western

159

missionaries can identify and appreciate. As it will be demonstrated in this essay, the Bible became the instrument of co-optation, a licence, authorisation, legitimation and certification to attract Africans as converts and in turn to enable them to cannibalise fellow Africans in the name of the Whiteman's God and the civilisational pretensions of the European colonisers and missionaries. Ngugi (1986: 76) argues that, 'An African, particularly one who had gone through a colonial school, would more readily relate to the Bible with its fantastic explanation of the origins of the universe, its divine revelations about the second coming and its horrifying pictures of hell and damnation for sinning against the imperialist order' in other areas of Africa. Africans and African-American intellectuals like Africanus Horton, Samuel Ajayi Crowther, Edward Blyden and Pierre Boilat, all products of a kind of African renaissance, weaponised the Bible to rival the growth of Islamism as a cultural force in Africa (Vaughan 2006).

Christianity was introduced in the Bamenda Grassfields in the early years of the 20th century. There exists a plethora of literature on the subject. Whether anthropologists (Jindra 2005; Nkwi 1976) or historians (Ndi 2005; De Vries 1998; Nkwi 2011, 2012, 2015) or missionaries (Booth 1973, they have all suggested that Christianity transformed the people and region tremendously, as well as it was, in turn, transformed by the region. Awoh (2012) studied Christian enclaves in British Southern Cameroons and maintains that traditional as well as colonial authorities provided grounds on which the church compounds and missionary activities flourished, yet the paradox became clear when royal wives started running away from royal compounds to seek refuge in church compounds, and as a result, threatened the power base of traditional authorities. Awoh concludes that by offering a safe haven to the runaway wives and welcoming women who were outside the traditional male authority in a 'tribal' setup, the missionaries had, in earnest begun sowing within Christian communities the seeds of their own destruction. Consequently, through Christianity and/or colonialism the people of the Bamenda Grassfields were despoiled, brainwashed and sullied. Thus, they were actually consumed by the missionaries/Christianity and colonisers and have remained dependent on the mission/

Christian/ideologies. Such dependence, however, was not entirely passive, as, eventually, the Christians of the region would deploy their creativity and improvisation to renegotiate and insinuate the reintroduction into their lives as Christians the vital components of their cultural traditions, customs and values which had been summarily dismissed or suspended as 'pagan' beliefs and practices by the colonising missionaries and their overly zealous first generation African converts.

In writing this essay, inspiration has been drawn first from my previous work in which I touched on Christianity to show that it was a technology and also that it was responsible for social change and geographical mobility of the Kom people between 1800 and 1998 (Nkwi 2015). Like Ndi (2005) and De Vries (1998), I wish to re-interpret the data and write against the grain of what has been handled so far in the history of Christianity in the Bamenda Grassfields. The essay is also predicated and positioned on the work of scholars who have argued that humans, regardless of geography, ethnicity, race or degree of civilisation are all cannibals, and have always been cannibals, from time immemorial (Lévi-Straus 2016; Travis-Henikoff 2008).

In his seminal work, *Orientalism*, Edward Said has argued that Western knowledge about the Orient in the post Enlightenment period has been 'a systematic discourse by which Europe was able to manage even-produce-the Orient politically, socially, militarily, ideologically, scientifically and imaginatively' (Said 1979: 175). He further opines that Euro-American views of the Orient created a reality in which the Oriental was forced to live. Although this work deals primarily with discourse about the Arab world, much of his views hold true with most regions of the world, Africa included. Following Said's Orientalist line of thought, this essay positions and focuses on Christianity as a form of cannibalism amongst the Bamenda Grassfielders. From the outset, the Europeans set out to control Africans and Africa in all facets of life, defining and redefining them and their realities in the image of their vision of the world and their expectations of those they encountered with ambitions of dominance. The Europeans introduced their own jargon and contested representations of Africa and Africans.

The introduction of the colonial/Western church and Christianity in Africa in the 19th century brought about tremendous changes. Ajayi (1980 & 1965), writing on Eastern Nigeria contends that the Christian church eventually produced new men and social change in the form of new social groups and new forms of social status in indigenous circles of African societies. Markowitz (1973) studied the Congo and reached the same conclusion. Fields (1982) undertook studies in Zambia and concluded that the efforts by the Western church and missionaries to abolish 'paganism' failed. According to Fields, the intention of Christianity to convert Africans to the new beliefs did not completely transform the Africans targeted. Even if it did in some quarters, it was temporary because the indigenes later more or less returned to their traditional mores completely, or sought to bring those mores into conversation with their newly acquired Christian beliefs, norms and practices. Fields concludes that Christianity provided Africans with principled grounds for denying customary obligations such as arranged marriages and communal labour, even if this did not necessarily result in Africans rejecting such practices wholly. Often, when Africans acted, they tended to be caught betwixt and between the prescriptions of their new found Christianity and the weight of expectations of their age-old indigenous traditions and cultures. Ndi (2005) studied the Mill Hill Missionaries in the British Southern Cameroon, and concluded that the church did a lot in the formation of the educated elites who were ready to take up positions in the British colonial administration. But even the elites did not completely abandon their cultural traditions and belief systems, pagan though these were purported to be by the Christianity that they had imbibed. Although these authors have not focused on cannibalism as such, their work provides insights that are relevant to an understanding of Christianity as cannibalisation, as this chapter attempts to demonstrate.

The act of humans eating humans has long been known by the West as cannibalism, even if the tendency by the West has for long been to confine its existence and practice to the 'heathen' peoples in Africa and other parts of the non-Western world (Stephen 2009; Bernault 2008; Ivanov 2002; Mintz and Du Bois 2002; Fernadez-

162

Jalvo et al. 1999; Price 1978). It was based on such acts that 19th century Europe in defence of colonialism took up the civilising mission as its 'holy grail' to convert, inter alia, the people of Africa.

According to European missionaries, somebody in Africa with two or more wives was bad. Polygamy was unpardonable in God's eyes. Yet the very same Europeans who condemned polygamy were practising serial monogamy, which allows for marriage and divorce as many times as one wished. This essay therefore moves away from the conventional usage as well as from the European social/conceptual gerrymandering of and around cannibalism. It moves away from accounts that have tended to limit cannibalism only to the eating of human flesh. Considered as cannibalism in this chapter are issues that range from the curbing of the powers of traditional rulers, to new romantics of love and sex through the conversion of people by baptism and other sacraments.

Missionaries and colonisers saw whatever could not be understood as paganic or fetishes. Sometimes they took photographs and displayed the objects in order to show proof of the veracity of the event. Behrend (2011) has shown that in Tooro of Western Uganda these photographs were circulated in the albums of the missionaries and also shown to visitors as trophies of power and success. Some of these objects which were branded as fetishes were burnt. Missionaries and colonial authorities therefore acted as dissident, heretic and iconoclasts towards 'pagan' religious objects called 'fetishes'. A closer look at this iconoclasm was part of the process of cleansing and renovating public space in African settings but the Western missionaries set out to destroy the fetishes and even invented what they called witchcraft.

Etymologically, Pietz (1988) maintains that the terms *'feitico'*, *'feiticeiro'* and *'feiatcara'* were actually used in 15th and 16th century Portugal to mean witchcraft and idolatry. Yet Western discourses about fetish and any other derogatory terminologies in Africa can also be read and understood as a debate on the Christian and Christianity, especially Catholic sacraments like the Eucharist and other relics of the Catholic Church that has been the subject of controversy since the Reformation of 1517. For instance, for many

163

Protestants, African fetishes and Catholic sacramental objects were equated with fetishes as well as false sacraments.

In what follows in this essay, I will start by first sketching the projection and delegitimisation of traditional rulers in the Bamenda Grassfields by the missionaries and colonial administration through which they were eaten up. The second part will focus on consumption of the Bamenda Grassfields by the 'holy men' who will include priests, catechists and pastors and the tools which were used to kill and consume these people, namely sacraments and the Bible. The rest of the paper focuses on the Bamenda Grassfielders as people who refused to be completely eaten up by Western Christianity. In turn they cannibalised the Western Christianity. The chapter ends with the conclusion.

Eating up Traditional Rulers: the Projection and Delegitimisation Argument

Socio-politically, the Bamenda Grassfields is organised around Fondoms and ruled and administered by Fons. Fons prior to the introduction of Western Christianity and colonial rule exercised unquestionable power over their people. They were semi-divine, sacrosanct and performed quasi-religious functions. Their palaces were filled with harems of women with some palaces having up to 100 royal wives. In the prism of Western Christianity and colonialism, traditional rulers who were custodians of their people and traditions were projected and beamed to have many wives, which was in the eyes of the colonial officers and missionaries very bad and unacceptable. For instance, writing in 1924, in the Annual Report for the League of Nations, D.O. Hunt for the Bamenda Division said:

> The root causes that urge pagans here to become Christians have given food for thought. They cannot be purely religious causes, any more than the mass movement of the Untouchables in Madras towards Christianity is religious in the full sense of the term. In India, it is a revolt against the social tyranny of the castes, but here it is difficult to diagnose. Perhaps it is in part the emancipation of youth, or it may be a revolt against the social tyranny of polygamy.[1]

164

Social tyranny of polygamy does not leave the reader in doubt as to what the inner mind of the colonial writer insinuates. Missionaries took to pen and paper to report back in Europe that there were Fons with 700 wives such as in Kom (Reyer 1953; Ritzenthaler 1960). They were practising polygamy which was bad. Western Christianity failed to recognise that polygamy as a custom was found all over Africa and fitted well into the social structure of traditional life; they failed to understand that polygamy was well fitted into the thinking of the people, and served many useful functions. Mbiti argues that:

> ... if the philosophical or theological attitude towards marriage and procreation is that these are an aid towards the partial recapture or attainment of the lost immortality, the more wives a man has the more children he is likely to have, and the more children, the stronger the power of immortality in that family. He who has many descendants has the strongest possible manifestation of immortality, he is reborn in the multitude of his descendants, and there are many more who remember him after he has died physically and has entered his personal immortality' Mbiti (1990: 138–139).

Without spending any time to understand such a custom, Western missionaries branded it as 'social tyranny'. Initially, the Fons put up stiff resistance against the introduction of Christianity as they felt that their powers were to be curbed by such doctrines. One of the Fondoms in the Grassfields, which resisted Western Christianity to its teeth, was Kom under the rule of Fon Ngam (1912–1926).

As an 'unremitting opponent' of Christianity, Fon Ngam died in 1926, leaving unresolved the situation of the Christians at Njinikom (a village in Kom in which the Catholic Church settled in the 1920s), where Christians already numbered 3,000 out of a Kom population of 18,000.[2] He stood his ground and refused to be easily consumed by Christianity. The royal throne of Kom Fondom passed to Fon Ndi, who started his reign by legitimising Christianity, a thing which his predecessor had refused to do and something which in the final analysis ate him up and his subjects. The literature suggests that Fon Ndi was a reformer. Nkwi (1976: 163, 1977) claims that Fon Ndi was very conciliatory to the church and the Christians of Njinikom.

Immediately after his enthronement, Fon Ndi announced that he would allow the establishment of Christian churches in the three other populated areas of Kom – Njinikom, Fundong and Belo – for a probationary period of six months. Nkwi further says he did so because the British colonial administration appointed Captain Coley to install him. De Vries (1998: 80) also maintains that 'the leadership of the mission had changed hands from Kom ex-nchinda, to the European priests. For Fon Ndi, this change of leadership meant that conflicts with the church could largely be fought out by the colonial government, which had a clear interest in re-establishing and maintaining traditional authority in Njinikom'. Further archival reports portrayed Fon Ndi as the Fon who was the antithesis of Fon Ngam and therefore ready to carry out meaningful reforms in Kom.[3]

One example of Fon Ndi as a reformer was reported by M.C. Denton, the acting Divisional Officer (D.O.) for Bamenda. Among other things he claimed:

> Endima (sic) a brother of the late chief of Bikom has succeeded the deceased, and has been to Bamenda for official recognition by the Divisional Officer. Although not possessed of the dominating personality of his predecessor, he has from the first evinced his desire first not to repeat the errors of the past and secondly to govern the whole of his subjects, Christians and pagans alike. ...[4]

This at first appeared like a new dawn compared with the perennial antagonism between Fon Ngam and the Njinikom Christians. Denton's comment also refers to Fon Ndi's official recognition. He also claimed that from the beginning Fon Ndi had shown signs that he was not to repeat the errors of his elder brother, Fon Ngam. The official recognition of Fon Ndi by the British showed that his loyalty was with the British and therefore the Fon had started losing grip over his Fondom. Visiting Bamenda for official recognition by the British colonial administration and recognising Christianity meant that the fon was consumed from both ends. The picture below shows Fon Ndi with his consuming missionaries, who had eaten their way confidently into the heart of his Fondom, thanks to his conciliatory attitude.

166

Figure: 3: Fon Ndi with the missionaries in the church compound at Njinikom

Source: Fr. Leo Onderwater's album, Osterbeek, Holland

Assuming that Fon Ndi was an example of a Fon who appeared to transform, indeed, it is little wonder whether he knew that he was consciously changing the basis of his power and by the same token being consumed by Christianity. With new social hierarchies like the Christian converts set in motion, the gradual erosion of the Fon's powers lasted into the 1960s and 1970s. By legitimating the church and its ancillary, the school, there was an unintended trimming of his own royal powers. The legitimating of Christianity led to the waning and the delegitimation of the Fon's power. The League of Nations Report for 1937 was unequivocal in portraying the decline of traditional authority in Kom and the Bamenda Grassfields in general. It read:

> They (people of the Grasslands) are not prepared to give unquestioning obedience to the commands (sic) of one man, and the autocrat must seek advice and get the weight of public opinion on his side if his orders are to be enforced. Other factors are the spread of

Christianity with its demand for a loyalty that may clash with customs of paganism and of education; the detribalisation of those who leave their homes for long periods of time in search of work and knowledge and the gradual abolition of rights and services once accorded by customs to the chiefs but now exacted only with difficulty or else forbidden. ...[5]

Clearly, the Fon's power was challenged not only by Christians. Those who migrated from home and spent a long time in search for jobs in the plantations and for schooling were a threat to the status quo. Hence, apart from Christianity which was already causing considerable rupture with the traditional authority of Fon Ndi, there was also the geographical and social mobility of the Kom people that led them to discover other ways of being and relating in the course of their travels. The coastal plantations and the introduction of colonial taxation led to the spatial mobility of many people, especially from the Bamenda Grassfields, who came to work in the plantations. The D.O.'s report makes clear that many people went and stayed for 'long periods', and 'the plantations were already causing some discontent' in their villages of origin. Below is a picture of a traditional ruler who seems to have been completely consumed and delegitimised until he had given up his son and had nothing except his walking stick. A parallel of such happenings has been captured by Chinua Achebe in his fourth novel, *Arrow of God*. At the advent of missionaries entering into Umuaro, Ezulu, the chief priest decided to send one of his sons, Oduche, who would act as his 'eyes' and 'ears' in the Whiteman religion (Christianity). By doing so he had placed in motion a chain of events that would erode and rupture the power base of the society. After the missionaries had thoroughly chewed and digested the son, the son turned around to see no cultural values in things that existed before Western Christianity and ended up locking the sacred python in a footlocker box, an aberration which the people had hitherto not known in their society (Achebe 1964).

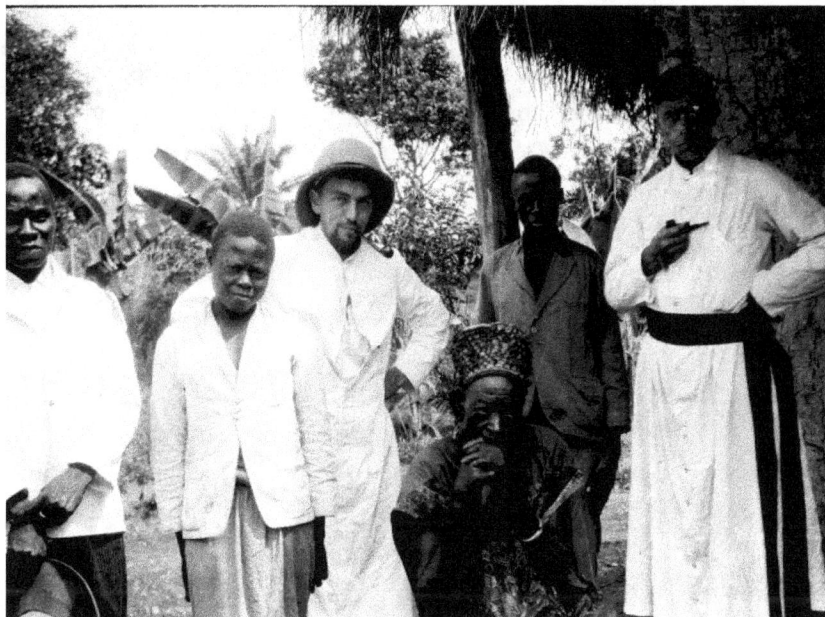

Figure 4: A traditional ruler visiting the son who has become the missionary's house boy

Source: Rev. Fr. Leo's Onderwater album, Mill House, Osterbeek, Holland

The greatest headache which confronted Fon Ndi was provided by Anyway Ndichia Timti who sued the Fon in court, a situation that was unheard of before then. Born in 1912, Anyway Ndichia Timti served in the palace and in frustration because he was never given two wives as the custom demanded, left for the colonial plantations of coastal Cameroon. While at the coast he acquired farmlands and cultivated cash crops like cocoa and coffee.[6] Back in Kom in 1948, he sued the Fon, claiming that he had served the Fon for 18 years without pay. The Fon responded that Anyway Ndichia Timti had not been compensated because he was stubborn. The chief judge had to rule in the favour of the Fon, fearing that if Anyway Ndichia Timti won then most of the NativeAuthority and principles of indirect rule would lose credibility.[7]

But what is significant here is that the Fon was even taken to court, a court of which until quite recently the Fon had been the president. The judges, as well as the defendants, were really shocked

169

and many more called the incident *ghu-i-wo-fyi*, a new happening. Still, important was the fact that Anyway Ndichia Timti represented the tension which existed between some of the new men and the traditional elites. Dike (1956) has shown how the new elites in the Niger Delta of Nigeria who were formerly under the tutelage of slave masters challenged the old hierarchy under which they had been during the slave trade. They did so during the period of legitimate trade. The case of Kom as represented by Anyway Ndichia Timti was similar.

That notwithstanding, it indicated that the power of the Fon had waned tremendously. The legitimisation of Christianity and colonial structures undermined and consumed the power of the Fon. Some mobile people had acquired modernity both in doing and thinking and so could not respect traditional mores and authority in the same way they used to do prior to their travels. One of these changes was embedded in the power position of the Fon who legitimated Christianity. However, such legitimation is not to imply that the Fon was a blind collaborator with the church and Christianity. He had accepted to 'ride the tiger' as much as he knew that his people needed progress and the church and Christianity were relevant in achieving that goal. This situation was similar to what Roberts (1962) experienced in other parts of the African continent such as in Uganda, where the Kabaka of the Buganda negotiated his position along similar lines.

Those who widely threatened the existing power structure of the Fondom were the youths. The local hierarchies which were re-enforced by the colonial church and administration, as argued by Gupta and Ferguson (1992: 6–23) and Mamdani (1996: 37–62) had little place for the Bamenda Grassfielders' youths. The local hierarchies had even contributed to some migrating from home. But the youths were anxious to be recognised. The church appeared to be the only place for them. The youths appropriated Christianity and became a social hierarchy in their own right while paying little or no respect to the traditional authority and helping the Western missionaries in the eating of their kith and kin. These youths were mostly returnees from Fernando Po who had followed the Germans defeated during the First World War and interned on the island.

Ex-soldiers or 'Fernando Po Repartees' and the Licence to Consume Grassfielders

Although the introduction of Christianity in this region predates 1918, the German missionaries who were responsible for introducing and maintaining it had vacated the territory as a result of Germany losing the First World War. Many young soldiers who had fought on the side of the Germans were interned with the remnants of German forces at Fernando Po. While in Fernando Po they were converted to Christianity, given Bibles and asked to spread Christianity in their regions of origin. They were the first to be consumed. Hence, the ex-soldiers who were scattered throughout the Bamenda Grassfields took upon themselves the responsibility of spreading the 'glad tidings' amongst their own people against all odds even against their semi-divine Fons. Every village with a Catholic community of any size had its own story of the repartees to recount. These men were obstinate, overbearing and even condescending to the traditional rulers, although sometimes they were not submissive to their own priests (Ndi 2005: 55). This was largely because of their German Military formation and the very stringent religious instruction which they had received from the German military chaplains both at the warfront and in the concentration camps at Fernando Po. Consequently, they constituted a new powerful elite, and at the same time wielded influence totally out of proportion to their small numbers in their particular communities (Ndi 2005: 55; De Vries 1998: 84; Nkwi 1976: 158–168).

The repartees also embarked on opening church buildings which represented nodal zones of conversion or consumption of their kin, for instance, churches were in their villages even if this was against the wishes of the traditional rulers. They also introduced entertainment dances. In Nkwen, a neighbouring village to the Bamenda station, the repartees opened a church at Futru, much against the wishes of Fon Azefor. They eventually scored a success by taking the *jujus* (masquerades) which persecuted them to the administration for redress. But following the death of one of the *jujus* in detention, they were reluctantly permitted by the traditional authorities to practise their religion without further headache. In

Tabenken, an outreach of the Kumbo Mission which had flourished during the German missionary epoch, some of the ex-servicemen from Fernando Po led by John Kibu, Damian Nginyu, John Chifu and Anthony Nchiring from Mbot, introduced the *Mbaya* dance which was a means to attract (mostly youthful, energetic) or lure converts into the abattoir (church compound) for slaughtering. Whatever change they introduced, the overall complaint was that these men whose knowledge of the Christian faith was by no means really profound, while proving recalcitrant both to traditional and British colonial authorities, often did not accept the advice of their religious authorities, especially if this was conciliatory towards the traditional religion and practice (Ndi 2005: 55). In doing all these, they were consuming their kith and kin as well as being consumed by Christianity, which they, in turn, were consuming by their selective attention to the instances of legitimation within the churches of their subscription.

Amongst all the areas in the Bamenda Grassfields where the First World War repartees and their Christianity received stiff resistance from the traditional administration, Kom appeared to have been the superlative. It has been maintained in both oral and written documents that the introduction of Christianity in Kom, as already said, predates the 1920s, going back to 1912 when the Catholic Fathers of the Sacred Heart of Jesus started their work at Fujua, near Laikom, the traditional capital of Kom. The missionaries had barely settled in Kom when the First World War broke out in Europe, and later in Cameroon which led to their expulsion from Cameroon and Kom. Everything they had started to construct, such as their mission compound, fell into ruins. The Germans demanded from Fon Ngam (The 8th ruler of the Fondom), that he should provide people who could help fight the war against the French and British. Fon Ngam condescended and decided to provide troops from Kom. Little did he foresee the boomerang which his decision was to cause him and the entire Fondom. Amongst the soldiers was one of the most stubborn palace guards, Timneng, whom the Fon offered to be recruited into the German army in the hope that he would be killed at the warfront. That was never the case. Paradoxically, Timneng returned and challenged the traditional mores including Fon Ngam himself, thereby eating up the Kom people and the Fon's powers. He had been licensed to carry out such acts by the Christian missionaries who gave him a Bible as a weapon to use in luring his kin away from their traditional religion and ways of life.

The war and subsequent internment at Fernando Po had a striking impact on Timneng, his compatriots and the cannibalisation of their people. While at Fernando Po concentration camp, Rev. Fr. Baumeiester who had worked at Fujua shortly before the outbreak of the war is said to have recognised Timneng and convinced him to become a believer and to swear on the day of his baptism that he would carry the faith back home and spread it widely. Timneng adopted a new baptismal name, 'Michael', was happy with his new identity, and felt that he could use it as a counterweight to threaten the authority of the Fon with whom he had been at loggerheads since before he was sent to join the German army (De Vries, 1998: 37–39). Here was a case of a stubborn palace guard apparently fed to the wolves of colonialism and its wars, only for him to turn around and feast on the very same traditional authority and normative order that thought they had seen the back of him for good.

Michael Timneng (his new identity following his incorporation of Christianity) kept to his word. Back in Kom, he erected a chapel at Wombong, a quarter in Njinikom, where he conducted daily prayers with his new converts, evidence that he was determinedly eating into the Fondom with his radically innovative beliefs and practices. He had also learnt to read and write, a magic which gave him added respect in a context where the majority of people were often mesmerised by the Whiteman and his scripts. As early as 1921, Njinikom was already grappling with astronomical numbers of catechumens waiting anxiously to be converted at a new church under Timneng's leadership as vicar. The ex-soldiers and Timneng stood up to and defied the traditional hierarchy of the Fon and his executive council, the *nkwifoyn*. As a matter of fact, 'many of the repatriated men were enthusiasts, uncompromisingly contemptuous for traditional mores' (Chilver 1963: 119). While in Njinikom, Timneng also searched for and found another apostle, Andreas Ngongbi. The two combined to devour the new converts and by extension, the old established order of authority and value system which they were encouraging the converts to violate with impunity in the name of Christianity. The picture below shows Timneng and Ngogbi.

Figure 5: Michael Timneng in a black suit and his acolyte, Andreas Ngongbi, standing in bare feet
Source: Mill Hill Archives, Oosterbeek, Holland

The resistance to traditional mores by the people of Timneng's category led to a protracted tug of war between them, the new converts and the Fon of Kom. One of Timneng's earliest followers was Thecla Neng, who was born around 1908. She had to trek about 140 km to Shisong, Nso with other Christians for doctrine classes and was finally baptised there. She told me that the war of words (*i-wong-a-wo*) between the ex-soldiers (*ghu-ghelli-wong*) under Timneng, and the Fon on the other hand, led to the humiliation of the Fon, who was commanded by the colonial administration that was acting under the auspices of the colonial officer to open the chapel that had been locked in Njinikom on the Fon's orders. Timneng's mobility, both geographical and social and that of his colleagues did not only create a new social order but attempted to offset the previous one. Their mobility had instilled in them new ways of thinking and doing things and by extension he was really eating up the people and the Fondom in its configuration prior to contact with European colonialism and Christianity. The novelty of what they had learnt meant they could stand up against the traditional norms, protected by the powerful intruders who urged them on. The church in the hands of new converts became the governing structure and started to criticise the authority of the Fon, which he clearly did not like. Timneng and a host of returned ex-soldiers represented the cynosure that attracted the royal women to the church at Njinikom, and with this came critical attitudes towards polygamy and the genesis and/or proliferation of romantic ideas of love under the canopy of monogamy or love and marriage with the blessings of Western Christianity. What is more relevant here is that these ex-soldiers attracted women by the way they dressed, talked and behaved and above all, because they were from Fernando Po. They preached and sought to convince their converts that the Fon was not all that divine as he appeared and this led the royal wives to realise that they too could disobey the Fon and escape to an area with a liberal doctrine. The people who champion this in Kom were again Michael Timneng and his apostles (Nkwi 2012: 70).

The Ex-servicemen and Cannibalism

The greatest weapon which the returned soldiers held in their hands to kill and consume the Grassfielders was the Bible.

Missionaries formulated and re-formulated the Bible in the best way to suit their purpose so they could easily eat the Grassfielders. Christianity appealed to women and the main centres where church compounds sprouted became the cynosure which attracted royal women. The doctrine taught 'one man, one wife' or better still monogamy. It also taught the sacrament of matrimony where one wife and one husband are bound forever in poverty or in riches, in sickness or in health till death do them part. Marriage did not only have only a spiritual dimension but it also had a material dimension. The couple were married in new outfits: suit for men and a wedding gown with a white veil for the woman. The Christian doctrine couple, with its material indicators, acted as an incentive for women to escape their different palaces from marital structures which they found constricting (Ndi 2005: 54–56). The church also stressed the doctrine of one transcendental and omnipotent God. This God was all powerful and all seeing, and there was no other God above this God. The Ten Commandments were also evoked. The royal women had lived with the understanding that the Fons were their spiritual leaders, since they performed quasi-spiritual functions and were seen as the only God in the eyes of the women. The Christian theology of one God was thus more attractive to the women and also challenged their former view that the Fon was all powerful as they had thought. So, if old beliefs had enabled the Fon to eat them up and to accumulate as many women as possible to cater to his royal appetites, Christianity and its new doctrines of individual freedom empowered the women to keep their distance from the Fon and, in turn, to treat and relate to the Fon and Fondom as predators – determined to eat traditional beliefs and values into oblivion, all with the encouragement of Michael Timneng.

In these palaces the women numbered 500 and above and in Kom they were more than 700 following the hypothetical statistics of a Roman Catholic nun, Sr. Loreto in the *Times Magazine*. She claimed that these women were living under inhuman conditions, having been coerced into the palace for the carnal enjoyment of the Fon. Even if her hypothetical assumptions had an element of truth, the Christian doctrine ran counter to such pre-colonial practices.

Through conversion royal women underwent profound changes and were spiced for biblical consumption in the entire Bamenda Grassfields. In Kom again, unlike other women in the political and social set-up of the Fondom, the royal women belonged to the palace. According to the oral traditions of Kom and other Fondoms of the Bamenda Grassfields, these types of women constituted the privileged and belonged to the Fon. Unlike other women who were wooed by prospective suitors, the royal women were those considered to be beautiful and who should be reserved for the Fon. They were selected by the palace guards, *nchisentoh*, and once chosen, camwood was sprinkled on their door posts and a royal spear pinned in front of their houses at night (Nkwi 2012: 70). The girls' fathers had to take them to the palace with some palm wine. The girls wore royal bangles around their necks and on their right wrists to indicate that no man should set eyes on them, let alone make love to them. This was not the best way of contracting marriage, although some of the women loved the idea. Gradually, the Fon had a harem of women, maybe not for conjugal pleasures but for practical necessity, the pride of being polygamous and the need for clans and families to have their eyes and ears present and representing their interests in the royal corridors of power and privilege. The ex-servicemen from Fernando Po with their new doctrine and new outfits acted as subversive liberators and better still consumers of these women who were claimed almost to have been living in 'bondage,' although it is contestable whether they were ever living in bondage, or if they situation necessarily evolved as a result of their conversion to Christianity.

These ex-servicemen became extensions of Western missionary cannibals. Their role was to fish the people through baptism and other sacraments before they were finally consumed when they were eaten in the process of enactment of Christianity. Church compounds also became abattoirs and kitchens where Bamenda Grassfielders were symbolically slaughtered, cooked and consumed.

Consuming and being Consumed: 'Love' and 'Sex' in the Church Compounds

From the foregoing it could be speculated from the missionary and colonial administration perspectives that most of these royal women were sexually starved. Having women numbering up to between 500 and 700 was indicative that they were seen more in economic, political and cultural than in emotional terms. In Kom for instance, the women ploughed the Fon's farms and prepared food for the palace guests, as well as served as the representatives for their clans, lineages and families in the palace. They were prompted to protest and move out of the palace because the returned ex-soldiers were alluring and charming. Colonial reports support this view and, writing about the returnees who brought Christianity, the D.O. for Bamenda, Hunt, claimed that the return of Christianity in the Bamenda Grassfields and especially in Kom, with its emotional appeal attracted many young women, the wives of the Fons among them. Writing about the flight of royal women, he claimed that:

> In particular this has been the case with the chief of Bikom, a man between 60 and 70 with over a hundred wives of whom some are 20. Some of these , mostly young, have left him to attend the mission church and refused to return to him unless he gives them facilities for conversion, of which he will not hear. The result is a bitter estrangement between him and the Christian congregation, of whom some have harboured and more than harboured the runaways, so that he has practically cut off communication with the Njinikom quarter where the church is. Seduction of the wives of their people has also helped to set the chiefs of Banso and Kom against the mission.[8]

The Fernando Po returned migrants not only represented Christianity but also something deeper in their eyes, namely, a different romantic aspect, which the women had never had at the palace. The returnees and Christianity symbolised 'romantic love' which was not only new but attractive to the royal women: they introduced a 'love of newness'. Cole and Thomas (2009: 4–10), writing about love in Africa between the wars maintain that 'we cannot understand sex or intimacy without understanding ideologies of emotional attachment ... and that claims to love were also claims to modernity'. This appeared to be linked to what was going on between the Fon's wives and the new arrivals in Kom and to a lesser extent Nso and other parts of the Bamenda Grassfields. In making love and sex with these women the Fernando Po returnees were doing nothing short of eating the women up in more senses than one, in light of the cultural and political tensions engendered by the advent of prescriptive Christianity as a zero-sum religion.

The issue of making love with a royal woman was scandalous and aberrational with consequences largely unforeseen. The D.O. for Bamenda further provides us with some illuminating evidence as he said:

> There were about twenty-five of these women in Njinikom, four of whom had children by unknown persons, while several more were pregnant. The Administration was certain that the mission people were responsible for this brazen act of defiance against a very sacred aspect of tradition. This they maintained was committed with impunity under the sanctuary provided by the Mission grounds. Together with the women, were a large number of Kom ex-servicemen, who had been repatriated from Fernando Po. These constituted the Fon's greatest headache and threatened his over-lordship of the Fondom, which under the circumstances was also a direct challenge to the British Colonial policy of Indirect Rule in the Territory.[9]

After the de-legitimisation of the Fon, his wives started to flee from the palace, looking for refuge in the church compounds where they were consumed by the ex-service men. The converted ex-servicemen like Timneng used their 'holy phallus' to bring forth children whom the colonial administrator says 'was committed with impunity under the sanctuary provided by the Mission grounds'. The picture below shows the church compound in Njinikom, one of the typical compounds in Bamenda Grassfields.

Figure 6: The church compound in Njinikom in 1956
Source: Mill Hill Archives, Oosterbeek, Holland

Ndi (2005: 54) arguably maintains that the issue of the Fon's wives generally was a complex question, which neither the missionaries nor the administrative officers could fully comprehend at the time since to a large extent both were just coming into the territory. It was only a decade later when British anthropologists had carried out rigorous intelligence and assessment reports detailing how these Bamenda societies were structured, that these intricate aspects of Bamenda tradition became better understood. Since the Fons were regarded as sacrosanct, semi-divine and highly revered human beings, their wives by proxy were actually accorded extraordinary deference as well. Following the traditional pedigree of the Bamenda Grassfields, eloping with a Fon's wife was an incomprehensible abomination and adultery, both of which were inexcusable offences. Men suspected of having an affair with a Fon's wife either underwent trial by ordeal or were banished from society, while those who were caught 'with their pants on their knees' (if they had pants) were summarily executed by the *ngwerong* in the case of Nso; *nkwifoyn* in Kom or *ngumba* in Bali, Mankon and Bafut. These were hooded *jujus* or masquerades which acted as the traditional police. The ex-soldiers instilled braveness and courage in people who consequently, with the ex-servicemen, violated and trivialised traditional laws and customs with ever-increasing disregard all over the sub-region (De Vries 1998: 84; Nkwi 1976: 158–168;).

Whether it was in love and sex making or in the new religious theological appeal, the Fernando Po returnees were cannibalising the new converts, especially women, as well as being cannibalised in turn. Whichever way one looks at it, these young men had been licensed by giving them those Bibles to go and consume humanity and traditional worldviews and belief systems of their stock in the name of Christ seen and presented through the prism of colonising Europeans. The sacraments of Baptism and First Holy Communion gave their followers the right and empowered them to even eat the body of Christ and drink his blood in order to remember Him who had been sent by His father to save humanity from eternal damnation – free humanity from the fangs of the preying Devil, so to speak (Lévis-Strauss 2016; Noble 2011; McGowan 1994). Through such sacraments they also had the authority which empowered them to teach others how to read the Bible, such as in figure 7.

Figure 7: A reading drama in Njinikom, or a consumption exercise of early catechist by the Bibles in hand, while people in the background looked on with longing 'admiration' and 'awe'
Source: Rev. Fr. Leo Onderwater album

The eating of a communion wafer which is presented as the body of Christ and the drinking of wine insinuated as the blood of Christ bring to the fore the contradictions of interculturality and the power of the missionaries and colonialism in attempting to silence the same thing which Africans were doing prior to contact with a colonising and Christianising Europe. Behrend (2011) did an excellent job amongst the people of Tooro in Western Uganda in relation to Christianity and cannibalism as portrayed by the missionaries. According to him in Tooro, the inversion of Christian themes such as resurrection and the holy supper and their integration into the local witchcraft discourse have to be seen in the context of intense power struggle between missionaries, African Christians and 'pagan' religious experts that took its beginnings at the end of the 19th century. Cannibalistic occasions became very subversive and paganic, and even satanic, and missionaries produced counter images to the dominant Christian discourses that turned the African cannibal into some sort of Antichrist. The historical dynamics which began in Africa with slave trade, legitimate trade, colonial conquest and colonisation and Christianisation were conceived and perceived as forms of power by the colonial world and by extension missionaries who were and could really be understood in terms of eating, digesting, cannibalisation and witchcraft (Behrend 2011). By the same token external powers – encapsulated in explorers, missionaries and colonial administrators who sought in their own ways to make and remake the world of Tooro and to free it from cannibals, because they thought that it was malevolent, awful, pagan and primitive, were conceived by the indigenous populations of Tooro as bringing new and newer forms of witchcraft. To ram home the point of the communion and holy supper being extradited from cannibalism by the missionaries, Comaroff and Comaroff (1991) maintain that the cannibal and/or cannibalism emerged and congealed at interfaces with historically constructed Others who themselves were engaged in simultaneous processes of formation and reproduction. That notwithstanding, the Bamenda Grassfielders were not passive recipients of western cannibalism. On the other hand they also cannibalised Western Christianity and missionaries.

Domestication of Western Christianity by the Bamenda Grassfielders

The Bamenda Grassfielders were not passive victims of being cannibalised by the Western missionaries. They did not allow themselves to be eaten flesh and bone willy-nilly. They therefore, even when they were baptised and confirmed into Christianity, selected what was good for their anatomy and domesticated Western Christianity. The majority of the population has been converted to Western Christianity, although pockets of traditional/indigenous population still exist, yet the new religion did not seem in practice to have a widely unifying effect, although their doctrines sometimes proclaim the appearance of a prophet sent by God expressly to be a saviour of all Africans (Jibrin 1991). Broadly speaking, some Africans expressed disillusionment with Christianity as it has been presented by missionaries. From the missionary perspectives Christianity was a religion which promised to all the children of God but to the disillusioned Africans, in practice, Christianity appeared to be no more than the supernatural source of Western domination. Consequently, African churches, each with its own Messiah, cropped up in many places. A case in point was Kimbanguisme, which arose among the Bakongo in the twin towns of Brazzaville and Leopoldville (Kalu 2005; Mair 1960).

Christianity did not mirror the Grassfielders' religions in many ways. As Mbiti (1990:3) has demonstrated, 'It is not enough to learn and embrace a faith which is active once a week, either on Sunday or a Friday, while the rest of the week is virtually empty. It is not enough to embrace a faith which is confined to a church building or a mosque, which is locked up six days and opened only once or twice a week'. It has been ignored or forgotten by the Western crusaders that Africans were deeply religious prior to contact with Christianity And that African religions were not guided by creed or orthodoxy. Africans had the creeds written all over in their hearts and each one, himself or herself, a living creed of his own religion. Consequently, 'where the individual is there is his religion, for he was a religious being' (Mbiti 1990:3).

Bamenda Grassfielders selected what they saw as relevant in the Western Christianity and blended it with their own and left the irrelevant. Consequently, they could attend church service on Sunday and after that visit their soothsayers, something that was abhorred by the Western missionaries. Just like the python episode in Achebe's *Arrow of God,* which symbolises the old gods in the conflict between Western Christianity and Umuaro's religion and the religious python which is the religious icon, many of the local Christians are not prepared to violate the sacred python even though they have embraced the new religion. The Bamenda Grassfielders embraced both the aspects of their indigenous religions and Western Christianity. As a matter of fact, African religions have suffered and even been ignored by the Western missionaries on simplistic grounds that Africans never had a religion just as it never had a history. Such apologetics have so far created a theology which made Africans wholly dependent on Western religious thought (Lafon 2001). In the case of the Grassfielders, they selected and even imposed some of

184

their cultural traits on the Western missionaries themselves. The photograph below shows a missionary putting on a traditional hat which shows that the Western missionaries were also consumed by the Grassfielders or actively domesticated through making them wear local dress and partake in related cultural practices. The traditional hat as well as the language of a people was very instrumental for their evangelisation. As far as this was concerned, Pope Paul VI, in his Apostolic Exhortation, *Evangelii Nuntiandi* of 8 December 1975 said amongst other things:

> Evangelization loses much of its force and effectiveness if it does not take into consideration the actual people to whom it is addressed, if it does not use their language, their signs and symbols, if it does not answer the questions they ask, and if it does not have an impact on their concrete life (Mbi 2004: 2).

Figure 8: A Mill Hill missionary putting on the traditional hat

185

The papal exhortation emphasising such indigenous values meant that African values were also licensed to enter the church and by extension consume the Western missionaries and their protracted dominance on the continent's religious landscape. In 2000 the papal encyclical, *Ecclesia in Africa* was very clear on integrating African values into the church. Amongst other things the pope appealed:

> I put before you today a challenge: a challenge to reject a way of living which does not correspond to the best of your traditions and your Christian faith. ...Today I urge you to look inside yourself. Look to the riches of your own traditions, look to your faith. Here you will find genuine freedom; here you will find Christ who will lead you to the truth (EA 48).

Long before the papal statement on *Ecclesia in Africa,* the Bamenda Grassfielders had learnt to select what was relevant to their bodily systems rather than to give up themselves to be swallowed whole by Western Christianity/missionaries. They had translated the Christian names from Standard English names into their traditional indigenous languages as well as made more meanings in the liturgical doctrines of Western Christianity. Missionaries had to consciously or unconsciously join in the ways of the Grassfielders. Thus, the aphorism of Wilhem Zürcher, in the beginning of this chapter, who took a photograph with the indigenous people and captioned it as 'sharing a drink with cannibals, a sign of friendship' might not in reality be far from the truth, but rather that he used cannibals in the pejorative. Of course, if he did not share a meal with the cannibals his evangelisation adventure would not have been a great success. Missionaries therefore had to see reason in engaging with the cultural norms of the Grassfielders who, in turn, were involved in consuming them. The picture below shows a missionary in a white cassock while those surrounding him are clad in traditional regalia and Dane guns, sharing a common commitment to celebrate an event.

Figure 8: Rev. Fr. Leo Onderwater with a men's social group during a celebration

Traditional musical instruments were appropriated and used in the church during the liturgy. Songs were translated into the vernacular and into Pidgin English, a language that underpins the negotiated outcome of contact and a desire to communicate intelligibly between Europe and Africa in the region. What the missionaries had hitherto regarded as fetishes were now part of the celebration and are increasingly being re-appraised in light of the serious demand of the idea of a world championed by creative diversity in culture and encounters in belief systems. According to Pietz (1988: 106 cited in Pels and Salemink 1999:11) the fetish was a Christian category, conceived 'as the worship of haphazardly chosen material objects believed to be endowed with purpose and a direct power over the material life of both human beings and the natural world'. To some Western anthropologists killing rituals were likened to fetishes and West Africa became an area where such killings were rampant, with South-eastern Nigeria taking the lead (Bascom 1969).

European missionaries became vulnerable and could be easily eaten up by the Africans when they faced challenges and difficulties on the ground during evangelisation. To a greater degree the

187

missionaries were narrowly out to spread what they saw through their own lenses to be good, even as they often failed to see anything that was good from the Grassfielders' perspective beyond a soul consumed by paganism desperately seeking salvation, even when unbeknown to itself. Yet they could not carry out the evangelisation without mastering certain aspects of the indigenous cultures such as language, drumming, traditional vestments and biblical translation. Language which was both a means of communication and a vehicle of culture (Ngugi 1986:13) was initially Latin and sparingly English. In the second layer, indigenous languages entered the services. A few converts were trained to manage the local church and through them much of the eating of missionaries was done. The photograph below shows the Fon and a European missionary watching an event.

Figure 9: Rev. Fr. John Haak and Fon Jinabo II (Michael Mbain) in 1977 during the Golden Jubilee marking the introduction of Western Christianity in Njinikom

Whether cannibalism is read and understood from a missionary perspective or an African perspective, the red lines in the Bamenda Grassfields and amongst the Bamenda Grassfielders suggest that it was invented and reinvented at particular moments in time to justify

188

purposes in context. At first, the Western missionaries employed the term to dismiss all Grassfields practices which they could not understand and in line with post-Enlightenment Europe, all Grassfields civilisations were primitive, backward and cannibalistic. Rather than understanding the logic through which such customary practices were carried out, the Western missionaries were instead frightened and tended to frighten the locals off their own cultures. On the backdrop of this 'scaring away' the Grassfielders, they in turn had to re-insert and reassert themselves. In the process of being consumed by a hungry and thirsty Christianity, the Grassfielders in turn consumed Western missionaries by gradually opening them up, whatever the hurdles, into appreciating the fact that there was a lot more to them, their cultures, ways and indigenous beliefs than just disgusting paganism.

Put in proper context, cannibalism appeared in two layers. In the first layer, which was predominantly, the nascent period of evangelisation, the missionaries hungrily consumed the Grassfielders through their sacraments, language, dress codes, naming and renaming, and taboos surrounding love and sex. And all the Grassfields' customs were swept aside and under the table or carpets of European Christianity and its evangelical crusades against religious and cultural difference. In the second layer, the missionaries found that it was too challenging and difficult to completely chew and digest the Grassfielders because they could not understand completely the ways of the people. The Grassfielders, even under the weight of the screaming prescriptiveness of Western Christianity, selected what was good and continued with their normal ways of life. By taking up a select number of items of Christianity they imposed some of their cherished customs on the missionaries. At this point, while the missionaries consumed the Grassfielders, the Grassfielders in turn consumed the missionaries, each in their own way. Cannibalism became a two-ended endeavour of eating and being eaten.

The invention and reinvention of cannibalism to suit particular purposes and situations in the colonial period has been replicated in the post and contemporary period by Pentecostal missionaries, both local and foreign. Mainstream missionaries invented cannibals and witches since to a large extent, missionaries had become rivals of witches (Schumaker 2001:200). Today, most of the churches have invented ways of delivering people whom they claimed have been possessed by evil spirits but also doing so for financial gain.

Conclusion

Cannibalism over the years and centuries has been narrowed in most quarters to simply mean the eating of human flesh by human beings. Scholars of Eurocentric backgrounds did groundbreaking work to prove that it was done mostly by primitive heathen peoples of Africa and other parts of underdeveloped Asia and ancient Latin Americas. However right they were, it is time to start re-reading and reconfiguring the meaning of cannibalism in line with the complex, nuanced and lived realities of people the world over. Through this method, narrow definitions are no more fashionable in the social sciences. Thus, thinking out of the box enriches and fundamentally gives new meanings and invokes more and wider contexts.

The attempt in this essay has been to re-interpret and re-examine Western Christianity in the nascent years of its introduction in the Bamenda Grassfields of North West Cameroon as a way in which many Christians were metaphorically eaten up through its dogma and practices. This was to juxtapose with the so much trumpeted Western reading of cannibalism and to show that what Christianity and colonialism downplayed and saw as paganism while, at the same time, practising it. Beginning from delegitimisation of the powers of traditional authorities and the return of the ex-soldiers to the introduction of holy sacraments, the essay upholds the view that Christianity cannibalised their Christians, something which has not been hitherto systematically thought and presented as such. Seen through these lenses it becomes clearer and enriches our understanding of concepts such as cannibalism, rather than staying frozen within the 'divine' definitions supplied down to us by northern lexicographers. On the other hand, cannibalised as they were, the Christians of the Bamenda Grassfields were not passive victims. As their Christianity confronted and challenged their cultural values and ways of life, they in turn developed ways of cannibalising Christianity and its missionaries through efforts at domesticating them to fit their

African ways of life. In this way their Christianity ended up as a hybrid or a composite of its Western variant and their local, indigenous African cultural and religious values. The chapter therefore concludes that cannibalism exists in all societies and is practised by everybody in all walks of life, in developed as well as underdeveloped worlds, by poor and rich people alike, in Africa, Asia, America and Europe. The case study of the Bamenda Grassfields has hopefully shed light on the fact that cannibalism is mutual and not one way directional and that African Christianity could not be an exact mirror of Western Christianity. Cannibalism is a daily occurrence which scholars should not avoid for if it is taken to belong only to certain societies and practised by a certain people then it blurs the very scholarship which we set out to achieve.

Endnotes

[1] File Cb/1924/3 Annual Report Bamenda Division, 1923.

[2] File Cb (1937)1 Bamenda Division Annual League of Nations Report (NAB). The colonial files on this census are not reliable. One file in mission 21 archives gave me the total population of 13,454. Another one found in NAB put the total at 1,800. The number of Christians in Njinikom and Fuanantui too vary from 2,969 to 3,000. The only compromise here is that the population was quite large at least. We can only take these statistics with a pinch of salt. Fon Ngam had opposed Christianity from its nascent introduction to Kom since 1919 till his death in 1926. He saw with Christianity that his power would be affected if he accepted it in Kom.

[3] File Cb (1924)3, Annual Report on the Bamenda Division, Cameroons Province for 1926 by Captain M.C. Denton, Acting Divisional Officer, Bamenda (NAB).

[4] Ibid.

[5] File Cb (1937)1 Bamenda Division: Annual League of Nations Report, 1937 (NAB).

[6] Interview with Ivo Nkwain, Fuanantui, Kom, 1 August 2008. He was the only surviving brother of Anyway Ndichia Timti.

[7] For the full proceedings of that judgment see File Md/e (1956)1 Kom Native Court Area Complaints, 1956 (NAB).

[8] File No. Cb/1929/2, Annual Report Bamenda Division for 1929 (NAB).
[9] File Ba (1922)1 Annual Report for Bamenda Division, (NAB).

References

Achebe, Chinua (1964) *Arrow of God*, Heinemann: London.

Ajayi, Jacob Francis Ade, (1965) *Christian Missions in Nigeria: The Making of New Elites*, London: Longman.

Ajayi, Jacob Francis Ade (1980), "A critique of themes preferred by Nigerian historians" *Journal of the Historical Society of Nigeria*, Vol.10, No. 3:33-40.

Awoh, Peter Acho (2012) *The Residue of the Western Missionary in the British Southern Cameroons: The Christian Village: A Sad Tale of Strife and Dissension*, Mankon, Bamenda: Langaa RPCIG.

Bascom, William (1969) *The Yoruba of Southwestern Nigeria*, New York: Holt, Rinehart and Winston.

Behrrend, Heike (2011) *Resurrecting Cannibals: The Catholic Church, Witch-Hunts and the Production of Pagans in Western Uganda*, London: James Currey.

Bernault, Florence (2008) 'Body Power and Sacrifice in Equatorial Africa', *Journal of African History*, Vol. 47: 207–39.

Booth, B. F. (1973) *Mill Hill Fathers in West Cameroon: Education health and development, 1884-1970*, Bethesda: International Scholars Publication.

Chilver, E. M.(1963), "Native Administration in West Central Cameroons, 1902-1954", pp100-108. In Kenneth Robinson and Frederick Madden.eds. *Essays in Imperial Government*. Oxford: Basil Blackwell.

Cole, J. & Thomas, L.M. (eds) (2009) *Love in Africa*, Chicago and London: The University of Chicago Press.

Comaroff, John and Comaroff, Jean (1991) *Of Revelation and Revolution: Christianity, Colonialism and Consciousness in South Africa*, Vol. 1, Chicago and London: University of Chicago Press.

De Vries, Jacqueline (1998) *Catholic Missions: Colonial Government and Indigenous Response in Kom (Cameroon)*, Leiden: ASC.

Dike, Kenneth Onwuka (1956) *Trade and Politics in the Niger Delta, 1830-1885: An Introduction to the Economic and Political History of Nigeria.* Oxford: Oxford University Press.

Elango, Lovett (1985) 'The Anglo-French "Condominium" in Cameroon, 1914–1916: The "Myth and the Reality"', *The International Journal of African Historical Studies,* Vol. 18(4): 656–673.

Fanso, V.G. (1989) *Cameroon History for Secondary Schools and Colleges Vol. 11: Colonial and Post-Colonial Times.* London: Macmillan.

Fernadez-Jalvo, Yolanda, Carlos Dietz, J., Caceres Isabel, Rosell, Jordi (1999) *Human Cannibalism in the Early Pleistocene of Europe,* Spain, Gran Dolina: Sierra de Atapuerca Burges.

Fields, Karen E. (1982) 'Christian Missionaries as Anti-Colonial Militants', *Theory and Society,* Vol. 2: 95–108.

Gupta, Akhil & James Ferguson (1992) 'Beyond "Culture": Identity, and the Politics of Difference' *Cultural Anthropology,* Vol. 7(1): 6–23.

Ivanov, Paola (2002) 'Cannibals, Warriors and Colonisers: Western Perceptions and Azande Historiography', *History in Africa,* Vol. 29: 99–119.

Jibrin, Ibrahim (1991) 'Religion and Political Turbulence in Nigeria', *Journal of Modern African Studies,* Vol. 29(1): 115–136.

Jindra, Michael (2005) 'Christianity and Proliferation of Ancestors: Changes in Hierarchy and Mortuary Ritual in Cameroon Grassfields', *Africa: Journal of the International African Institute,* Vol. 75(3): 356–377.

Kalu, Ogbu U. (ed.) (2005) *African Christianity: An African Story,* Pretoria: Pretoria University Press.

Lafon, Patrick (2001) 'African Traditional Religion and Us', *Cameroon Panorama.*

Lévi-Strauss, Claude (2016) *We are All Cannibals: And Other Essays,* Columbia: Columbia University Press.

Mair, L. P. (1960) 'Social Change in Africa' *International Affairs,* Vol. 36(4): 447–456.

Mamdani, Mahmood (1996) *Citizen and Subject: Contemporary Africa and the Legacy of Late Colonialism,* London: James Currey.

193

Markowitz, Marvin D. (1973) *Cross and Sword: The political Role of Christian Missions in the Belgian Congo, 1908–1960*, Stanford: Stanford University Press.

Mbi, Jude Thaddeus (2004) *Ecclesia in Africa is us: An Attempt at Liturgical Inculturation for the Ecclesiastical Province of Bamenda*, Yaounde, Cameroon: AMA-CENC.

Mbiti, John S. (1990) *African Religions and Philosophy*, 2nd Edition, London: Heinemann.

Mbuy, Tatah Humphrey (1994) *African Traditional Religion as Anonymous Christianity: The Case of the Tikars of the Bamenda Grassfields*, Virginia: Virginia University Press.

McGowan, Andrew (1994) 'Eating People: Accusations of Cannibalism against Christians in the Second Century', *Journal of Early Christian Studies*, Vol. 2(4): 413–442.

Mintz, Sidney W. & Christine M. Du Bois (2002) 'The Anthropology of Food and Eating', *Annual Review of Anthropology*, Vol. 31: 99–110.

Mudimbe, V. Y. (1979) *The Invention of Africa: Gnosis, Philosophy and the Order of Knowledge*, Bloomington and Indianapolis: Indiana University Press.

Ndi, Anthony M. (2005) *Mill Hill Missionaries in Southern West Cameroon 1922–1972: Prime Partners in Nation Building*, Nairobi: Paul's Publications Africa.

Ngoh, Victor Julius (1987) *Cameroon 1884–1985: A Hundred Years of History*, Yaounde Cameroon: Navi-Group Publications.

Ngugi, wa Thiong'o (1986) *Decolonising the Mind: The Politics of Language in African Literature*, Heinemann: London.

Nkwi, Paul Nchoji (1976) *Traditional Government and Social Change: a Study of the Political Institutions among the Kom of the Cameroon Grassfields*, Fribourg: the University of Press, Fribourg.

Nkwi, Paul Nchoji (1977) *The Catholic Church in Kom: Its Foundation and Growth, 1913–1977* (mimeograph).

Nkwi, Walter Gam (2015) *African Modernities and Mobilities: An Ethnographic History of Kom, Cameroon, c.1800-2008*, Mankon, Bamenda: Langaa RPCIG.

Nkwi, Walter Gam (2012) "Patriarchy Turned Upside Down: The Flight of Royal Women of Kom, Cameroon from 1920 to the

1960s"pp.65-80, In Mirjam de Bruijn & Rijk van Dijk (Eds) *The Social Life of Connectivity in Africa,* London: Palgrave.

Nkwi, Walter Gam (2011). *Kfaang with its Technologies: Towards a social history of mobility in Kom, Cameroon, 1928-1998.* Leiden: ASC Publication.

Noble, Louis (2011) *Medicinal Cannibalism in Early Modern English Literature and Culture,* London: Palgrave.

Pels, Peter and Salemink, Oscar (1999*) Colonial Subjects: Essays on the Practical History of Anthropology,* Ann Arbor: University of Michigan Press.

Pietz, William (1988) 'The Problem of the Fetish II: The Origin of the Fetish', *RES: Journal of Anthropology and Aesthetics,* Vol. 13: 23–45.

Price, Barbara J. (1978) 'Demystification, Enriddlement and Aztec Cannibalism: A materialist rejoinder to Harner', *American Ethnologist,* Vol. 5(1): 98–115.

Reyer, Rebecca (1953) *The Fon and His 100 Wives,* London: Victor Gollancz.

Ritzenthaler, Robert (1960) '*Anlu*: A Women Uprising in British Cameroon', *African Studies,* Vol. 19(3): 460–475.

Roberts, Andrew (1962), "The Sub-imperialism of the Baganda" *Journal of African History,* Vol.3, No.3 435-450.Said, Edward (1979) *Orientalism.* New York: Vintage Books.

Schumaker, Lyn (2001) *Africanizing Anthropology: Fieldwork, Networks and the Making of Cultural Knowledge in Central Africa,* Durham & London: Duke University Press.

Stephen, Daniel Mark (2009) "'The White Man's Grave": British West Africa and the British Empire Exhibition of 1924–1025', *Journal of British Studies,* Vol. 48(1): 102–128.

Travis-Henikoff, Carol A. (2008) *Dinner with a Cannibal: The Complete History of Mankind's Oldest Taboo,* With a foreword by G. Turner II Christy, Santa Monica, CA: Santa Monica Press.

Vaughan, Megan (2006) 'Africa and the Birth of the Modern World', *Transactions of the Royal Historical Society,* Vol. 16: 143–162.

Chapter 5

Researching Cannibalising Obligations in Post-apartheid South Africa

Ayanda Manqoyi

Introduction

This paper examines cannibalism through the prism of the language of 'black tax' to describe tensions with home and host communities among black middle-class men and women living in post-apartheid South Africa. Through liberal logic, to be black and middle class in post-apartheid South Africa invites the sacrifice or cannibalisation of fellow South Africans in the biblical sense of where 'many are called but few are chosen' (Nyamnjoh 2002), regardless of solidarities cultivated and a collective experience of victimhood – dispossession and debasement under colonialism and apartheid. To be inclusive and black middle class is constructed by social research and media as an anathema. To be black and middle class is to be an individual to its liberal extreme. It is to cultivate insensitivity to the lives of fellow South Africans wasting away in neglected villages, townships and informal settlements. It is, in other words, to make a meal of the humanity of others by blaming them for not being creative, innovative or hardworking enough to make it in life. Despite the asphyxiating dominant one-dimensionalism of the liberal logic, upwardly mobile black South Africans in post-apartheid South Africa use their own encounters and experiences to argue against a constrictive idea of success narrowly confined to a purported rights-bearing autonomous individual as a unit of analysis. Notwithstanding the challenges of obligation confronting them, upwardly mobile black South Africans insist on inclusive success, taking along with them kin and kith or those who may not have made it in life, not always through any particular or personal fault of theirs, especially when extractive colonialism and apartheid are factored into the equation. Such upwardly mobile post-apartheid black South Africans

197

tend to insist more on flexible, negotiated, relational and realistic ideas of belonging based more on conviviality and a shared humanity than on the essence of class, geography and biology. In other words, the problem in prescribing reductionist indicators to constitute black middle class is that it misrepresents – cannibalises, so to speak – philosophies of collective success.

Background on Black Middle Class in South Africa

South Africa, since the inception of unequal encounters between the territory's indigenous populations with treasure hunters from Europe in the 17th century, is founded on discriminatory philosophies and laws that transformed the black population from active market competitors in industries such as farming into cheap labour, dispossessed and debased human beings. The fundamentals on which the society, economy and industry were established relied on a stratified workforce following racial hierarchies. Land dispossessions that crystallised and were institutionalised under the Native Land Act of 1913 foreclosed many opportunities for black people to compete in business and contribute to the South African economy as producers and industry leaders. Many black South Africans lost productivity due to the laws that forced them into Bantu reserves characterised by diminished opportunities and stability. The vision of white South Africa was taken up and refined by the National Party. Under a revised apartheid system, exclusionary structures continued the vision for a new South Africa that involved an ambitious effort to transform the large Afrikaner population into a middle class (Teppo 2004), while at the same time actively producing working classes and those beneath any sensible classificatory system among the non-white mostly black African majority population. In a limited number of cases (often when it served its interests to divide and rule), the apartheid government reluctantly afforded a separate development plan that succeeded to create a stable environment and opportunities for a few black people who became producers, industry experts and specialists in certain occupational fields but for most black South Africans instability and diminished opportunities cannibalised future

198

prospects. The initial plans by the colonial government to transform the black population into wage-labour heightened under the apartheid government.

The political history of the Southern African region reflects racial exclusion where the formal distribution of cash as a safety net was reserved for white South Africans in the form of various grants and insurances by the state. Exclusion of black people from distributive payments was justified by the existence of extended family relations which provided the necessary support to prevent any misfortunes such as ill health, job loss, etc. (Seekings and Nattrass 2005; Posel 2010; Ferguson 2015). Since post-1994 increasingly black South Africans have been included in all institutionalised forms of redistribution. The contentious and still highly limited expansion of access to education, job occupation and high income has enabled mobility from townships and rural villages to residences previously reserved for white South African in cities such as Johannesburg, Cape Town and Durban. A combination of income, occupation and material consumption has created the much-celebrated black middle class South African (and African). Not without a combination of mockery, envy and unease, this black middle class in the making is sometimes derogatorily and discouragingly referred to by white South Africans as 'black diamonds', from their perceived flashy lifestyles of consumerism gone wild.

The sociological focus on indicators that improve life chances for social economic mobility has privileged the individual as the unit of analysis, a disturbingly inadequate option in a context where black South Africans were systematically until 1994 discriminated against as a collective and not as individuals only. From a household perspective of married couples, survey methods often carried out in suburbs to account for the expansion of the new black middle class constructed images of nuclear families. Such research influenced market surveys focused on income bands of Living Standard Measures (LSMs) to define what it means to be the black middle class (Southall 2016). Over the years the LSM index was refined by the South African Audience Research Foundation (SAARFF). The LSM index was widely used to inform private corporations seeking to expand their markets to the new category. Articles that circulated and contributed to an understanding of the black middle class as a profitable market (termed 'black diamonds' by 2004) have been supported by the Unilever Institute's studies. For example, the one entitled *Booming black middle class represents R400 billion spend* argued that, even in the recession, this category continues to grow and/or spend (UCT website, 13 June 2013). Along with its growth in size and characteristics, the researchers found drastic changes in its members' consumer behaviour over the previous eight years, partly as a response to the post-2008 recession and continuing economic decline. These factors, the Institute's John Simpson states 'have led to a new financial conservatism, with respondents reporting that it is no longer "bling" at all costs' (UCT website 13 June 2013).

The prescription on what defines the black middle class in post-apartheid continues the early cannibalistic visions of the Union of South Africa to create upward mobility only through wage-labour, however high the salaries. Another aspect that is worth illuminating is that of turning the category into consumers – and passive consumer zombies at that! The combination of excluding black South Africans from achieving upward mobility as producers and confining them to the material consumption industries to which they are refused entry as equal players characterises the modern form of cannibalising domination.

However, the construction of a salaried black middle class based on the major elements (education, wage labour and material consumption) creates an incomplete understanding of the social connectivity of the individual (Nyamnjoh 2002). The effort to construct a category of black middle class dominantly consists of drawing on theories that are limited in context and Eurocentric in view, and all too eager to reproduce than to critically interrogate and expand conventional wisdom and practices in knowledge production (Goodhew 2000; Seekings and Nattrass 2005; Veblen and Banta 2009; Weber in Seekings 2009). Informed by university curricula nationwide, social sciences' almost schizophrenic celebration and criticism of the black middle class is often set by 'critical' accounts of neoliberalism of South Africa's post-apartheid transition and economic change. The narrative on South Africa's adoption of neoliberal policies during the negotiations fails to connect the establishing of the economy and industries to global financial networks from mainly Britain, Europe and USA as the foundation of the Union in 1910. Also, distorted is that South African industry along with the same global networks disagreed only with those aspects of apartheid that affected labour costs from colour-bar policies, along with the expansion of merchant industries such as the chain stores into racially segregated reserves and townships (Kaplan & Robertson 1986; Ngcukaitobi 2018). The partial inclusion of the black middle class in a democratic South Africa as expendable high salaried labour and a market for luxury material consumption would also serve a political function. The black middle class would be a buffer between global capital and white upper middle class, and the majority of working-class and under-class South Africans (Aristotle in Bendix & Lipset 1966; Lipton 1986). Yet, some contemporary scholars lead us to believe that the black middle class is largely constituted in the politics of the liberation struggle (Southall 2016).

According to this cannibalistic version of history the liberation struggle of the apartheid South Africa is shaped by the black middle class involvement in the political organisation. By foreclosing Bantu reserves areas as illegitimate locations that can in part be understood as creatively negotiated in the face of two untamed cannibals (imperial merchant industry expansion and the transition to an apartheid Afrikaner government), stability and opportunity for prestige and status for the black middle class is only achieved by links to the ANC (Southall 2016). When the ANC takes over the government after the 1994 transition the organisation abandons its commitment to socialist economic transformation. Instead the ANC adopts neoliberal and 'free-market' policies in the hope of making the new South Africa an attractive destination for international capital investment (Seekings and Nattrass 2005; Seekings 2008; Posel 2010). Democracy enables political rights but is also the sheepskin that covers the same imperial cannibalism that was kept at bay long enough to produce the most successful landowning and industry-specialised black middle class to date. Given this 'compromise' (Msimang 2016), it becomes easy to blame neoliberalism, and cannibalism under the ANC for: the inability of graduates to find work and transform into middle-class entrepreneurs and salary earners; the retrenchments of black middle class; their debt trap; conspicuous consumption; and even the now popular raw deal of high salaried black middle class to respond to calls for distribution by social relatives in what is called 'black tax' and subsequently 'black guilt' (Ratlebjane 2015; Sefalafala 2015; Seid 2016). The liberal template of freedom in South Africa ignores continuities directly related to imperialism's cannibalistic expansions aimed at transforming even the upwardly mobile black business owners into high salaried employees. Any means of understanding post-apartheid lived experiences is 'captured' (State Capture Report 2016) by the narrative to outsource guilt within the liberal template between the apartheid cannibalism and the cannibalism under the ANC.

Cannibalising Black Middle Class

Cannibalism provides us with a useful metaphor to understand the ideological relations of individuals and societies to development and modernity. This entry into modernity is positively described as a society of 'free' wage labour as opposed to bonded 'family' labour. In a 'free' society characterised by democracy citizens, in principle at least, participate as equals. More recently, 'free' trade and the unsurpassed Internet images and messages have created a density of global interaction that has enabled intimate interaction between those afar and those nearer. Yet Western modernity in Africa, even when professing equality and 'free' autonomous individuals, is better understood as a continued feeding frenzy to nourish the gut of superiority and supremacy (Devisch 1996). In reality, it is about plunder, cannibalising the non-Western Other. Cannibalism gobbles up without shame and reduces a person, a people to naked dependency, diminished self-confidence and self-worth, left with barely any respectability, personhood and agency. In a cannibalistic post-apartheid South Africa black middle classes are expected to emerge as vanguards of only occupational and consumerist forms of success, without an underpinning system of values over and above the market and its consumerist fixations. Participation in freedoms framed by neoliberal logic and globalised consumerism is not optional. Everyone is supposedly tethered to it willy-nilly. To attain visibility, one is required to be consumed by the prejudices and expectations of modernity and its technologies of authentication (Ferguson 1999), the lack of which has justified social exclusion rendering invisible any attempts and aspirations to restore humanity, personhood and dignity (Povinelli 2011). Through an engagement with cannibalism as expressed by the language of 'black tax' to describe obligations to relations and kin, this paper begins a conversation that complicates who is eating whom, how and why, and the power relations that render such eating or being eaten visible and invisible in particular ways and contexts.

In constructing South Africa as a place of hope indexed by the rising black middle class, what is left out is the co-existence and intersection of the new and the old; the modern and traditional; the neoliberal and the social; individual economic accumulation and collective success (or social distribution). The underlying decision to leave out such parts and rationalise the dismemberment of collectivities, in the manner a butcher dismembers a cow for supermarket shelves, is reminiscent of the social engineering techniques initiated by British industrialists and fine-tuned by apartheid planners. The aim was to violently transform African populations from independent economic players driven by an ethics of inclusivity and collectivity in success and in failure into labour, and a market for the expansion of white ambitions of dominance through resource accumulation and the devaluation of the humanity of those encountered in the process (Lipton 1986; Redding 1992; Posel 2010; Magubane 2004; Nyamnjoh 2012). The plan for constructing the black middle class has largely been twofold: as a political buffer between the global economy and much of the working class and unemployed South Africans, on the one hand; on the other hand, to expand the market while foreclosing the participation of the emerging black middle class as producers and industry leaders. Such stability enables economic expansion of luxury goods, produces profits for global companies and enriches South African white business owners.

To realise these systems of cannibalism, the post-apartheid transformation created opportunities through private corporations to earn high salaries for black people accompanied by mobility to suburbs, estate communities and enclave urban development areas (Chevalier 2011; Kaus 2013). However, the realities of increasing unemployment as a function of the industry's inability to absorb surplus labour have been outsourced from both private industry and state to the individuals. In liberal terms, the 'free' individual is said to achieve black middle-class status by working hard to gain a university degree, secure a job in a private company and earn a good salary. What is less emphasised and debated is the retrenchment of the black middle class in high paying jobs. Also, the mistreatment of the black middle-class professional by their white counterparts in the workplace is often brushed over as an exceptional event. Sometimes working in such abusive conditions leads to mental illness that is often followed by being fired. Just as the cannibalistic system prescribes personal success exclusively, free individuals are to blame for failure. To critically engage with precarious lived experiences risks further cannibalistic economic and social exclusions by industry and by fellow black middle-class South Africans.

Given the unspoken precarity and cannibalistic forms of exclusion experienced by the black middle class, family and societal relationships are important. The uncertainty of work and earnings, along with the responsibility to remit, affects black people regardless of class, gender, ethnicity and geography. It is particularly such uncertainty that makes 'staying in touch with home' and 'going home' central, not only as a home to return to, but one where you are welcome to return to (Mhlungu 2015). Even with sufficient policy covers and insurances, the black middle class often return home during times of vulnerability and need. In between leaving home and returning home, they stay in touch with home in myriad ways, often appropriating new information and communication technologies to assist in this regard (Nyamnjoh and Brudvig 2016). This makes it important to attend to the needs of relatives faced with various struggles, past and present. Focusing on the question of distribution through compassionate obligations creates fertile ground for new possibilities for the analysis of the black middle class through concepts of personhood, respectability, interdependence, embodied labour, livelihoods, markets and money (Nyamnjoh 2002; Salo 2003;

Ferguson 2015). However, it has been from the construction and dissemination by intellectuals and media of the singular concept of a black middle class as an autonomous 'free' consuming individual that the cannibalising obligation with kin and the extended network relations emerged. One cannot be critical enough, especially in a South African context where doctrines of white supremacy and racialisation have meant the systematic and collective debasement and dispossession of non-white people not only and not primarily as individuals, but as racialised and inferiorised collectivities.

Cannibalising Obligations

The concept of Black Tax as a metaphor to describe the cannibalising obligations in relation to family and extended networks faced by middle-class black South Africans is quickly becoming common knowledge. The obligations to the family are often described by black graduates in corporate jobs as burdensome and at times coupled with perpetual demands by relatives for money. It is the young black South Africans freshly graduating from university in their first paying jobs who often face these struggles. Social scientists and the media at large have demonstrated less interest in historicising these obligations, even as they uncritically paint such obligations and solidarities as exploitative, to be condemned and abandoned as a relic of outmoded solidarities of primitive and traditional Africa. Specifically, how to socially constitute a black middle class through human connections with relatives is treated as a contradiction in terms among social scientists and the media. What is often taken as a complete picture and discussed as a moral assessment, albeit in perfect abstraction, is an emphasis on an autonomous individual and the 'freedom' of choice.

The narratives about the obligation to various relations, particularly kin, under the term 'black tax' have been the main focus in the media – radio interviews, television shows, newspaper articles, blogposts and social media. Drawing from various local newspapers in South Africa, stories on the burdens, whether demanded by relatives or a sense of responsibility and obligation, describe the relationships across different geographies. Mobile black people take up work in major cities such as Durban, Cape Town and Johannesburg after leaving places of birth in smaller towns, villages and the countryside. Such mobility also occurs with closer relations often marked by new and established black graduates moving from townships to the suburbs and increasingly gated estate communities.

Yet, my research on black middle-class mobility during the Christmas festivities depicts another reality. Even though many upwardly mobile black South Africans have a 'choice' to remain in the areas of work, they often make the historical journey of obligation to reconnect from cities to the region (village or town) of origin – such as from Johannesburg and Cape Town to the relatively less industrialised Eastern Cape Province (where I conducted fieldwork for my Hons and MA degrees at the University of Cape Town). A few days are often spent in equally modern cities, though much smaller in scale in comparison, such as East London, before Christmas Day. On Christmas Day, the upwardly mobile leave the city for the various places of birth, which include townships and rural villages. Some of the upwardly mobile black South Africans growing up in second generation prosperous families might be at holiday homes. At the secluded holiday homes nested in upmarket suburbs the use of family labour (instead of hired labour) and the unpacking and moving of luxury goods reaffirm 'traditional style' obligations, which intersect age and gender. For such families to occupy the top ranks economically is domesticated by family obligations that emphasise collective success without rejecting individual accumulation. Emphasis is on recognising and providing for the reality of interconnections, inclusivity and interdependency in success and failure, not only because of lessons learnt from the collective dispossession and disenfranchisement experienced under apartheid, but, even more importantly, because it is a more humbling and fulfilling philosophy of life.

For the most part, discussions in media about obligations to the family have been framed in broader economic terms as being a hindrance to the country's economic growth. This outlook takes on from a neoliberal reinvention within global capitalism, which suggests with the dubious logic that the reduction of inequality and economic growth is better achieved through the expansion of a consuming middle class and a middle class that consumes its relations and interconnections with the lesser classes. It is this logic of the death of sociality through the projection of shadows fronting as success that could be said to transform almost miraculously the African continent from a place of economic disaster to one of hope and on the rise. It is the reported rise of the continent that makes cannibalistic obligations to the economy and state through consumption as a zero-sum game. For the middle-class black South Africans cannibalising obligations to the economy and the state compete with obligations to various relations including those of kin. Research and discussions on the black middle class have tended to ignore these obligations to the economy.

At a conference I attended in Switzerland, for example, largely dedicated to researching Black Middle Class in Africa, the presentations and keynotes had nothing to say about the demands of the global economy on Africa. At discussion groups, I was discouraged by leading scholars to engage in the history of the economy and the cannibalising obligations it established. Given the colonial and imperial history of cannibalism in establishing industry and the state, such obligations are better understood as the outsourcing of guilt and indebtedness (Graeber 2014). The South African industry and its intellectual institutions persist on outsourcing taxing obligations which create precarious conditions even for the upwardly mobile black professionals. Another dimension less covered is the arguments that Black Tax can be used as a particular manifestation of dominant neoliberal ideologies against taxation of all kinds. Ultimately, the very reality that Black Tax highlights – historical disadvantage, inequality between 'middle classes' so to speak, precarity and lack of a safety net – is employed ideologically by the system to undermine the building of a solid welfare state that would provide a safety net to all. In the book *Give a Man a Fish*, James Ferguson (2015) argues that the relations of distribution that are rooted in practices of sharing dependence continue to be crucial. Hence fundamentally stabilising middle class lives, as it is the case in other welfare states. The following stories on the obligation by the black middle class to family relations are exemplified and summarise the discussion in various media outlets.

Media on Cannibalising Black Tax

One newspaper article on 'black tax' included the story of a young black educated professional and the obligations to her siblings.[1] Mbali Nhlapo (25) and her mother are the only people working and contributing to a family of up to 14 dependants. 'I might be forgetting someone', she says. This includes her unemployed brother, his two children and his girlfriend's two children; three unemployed cousins with three children; an unemployed aunt and her three children; and her grandmother, who receives a government pension. Travelling to work is a continuous struggle. 'I live in Daveyton and have had to find a job in Randburg because there aren't many opportunities where I live', this business consultant says. 'It's either I'm overqualified or I'm demanding too much money, so I don't have a say in how much I earn. I mean, you're black! You're not allowed to have a voice.' She describes her life as a constant sacrifice of not only luxuries but also necessities such as insurance. 'If I should get medical aid, I would have to cover me and my daughter only. And that's R2 000. With that money, I could do so much more. It's an unnecessary expense.' By mid-month Nhlapo's pockets are empty and shame sets in, as she finds herself unable to provide any more for her family.

A similar narrative regarding obligations to family relations can begin while a student at the university earns stipends from various scholarship and student financial programmes. Kgomotso Mauguwane (22) always has his mother, older sister and four nieces and nephews in the back of his mind. And he is likely in the back of theirs, as they wait for his monthly contribution to their basic necessities. 'My mother was a domestic worker and tried to put my sister through nursing school, but that did not work out and my sister had to settle into a job due to lack of funds', he says. For this third-year BCom Law student who also holds down a job, more than half his salary goes back home every month. 'So, what usually happens [is] when I get paid, I will get my sister to buy whatever groceries [are] needed in the house. And I will give them money for electricity, give them the money to pay for their burial societies. I basically fill in the gaps of whatever they want and give my mother money as well.' Mauguwane says at times he feels stuck in a vicious cycle of poverty that will never end unless he wins the lottery. 'I think that my kids will probably have to provide for me when I'm old.' At just 22, he is an old hand at paying it forward – and backward. To the one side is his older sister and her two children, to the other side, are his late sister's two children. On each end, he sees an opportunity to improve their lives. 'We had to move out of rural Limpopo and … so I contribute at least R1,500 a month to renovate the new family home in Mpumalanga.' Mauguwane has opened a savings account to try to break the cycle. 'I know that it won't pay [university] tuition fees for my nieces and nephews, but it will go towards paying for their registration at least.' The most recent story being that of the University of Johannesburg civil engineering student forced to live in a shack after losing his bursary and forced to leave the student residence. Framed as a narrative about determination for education rather than the continued cannibalising racialised and global capitalist injustice, the student can attend class and survive by selling recycled plastics. From the money he makes recycling plastics, the student remits to his impoverished family located in a different province.[2] While these three examples of obligation to the family are about the black middle class and the responsibility to those that helped get them to university and lead to finding well-paying jobs, stories of cannibalistic obligations are common. In the paper titled 'Images of Nyongo', Nyamnjoh's (2005a) ethnographic work explains similar obligations to family in Cameroon. To work endlessly in faraway places imagined as characterised by endless opportunity and wealth for family in places of birth is described as witchcraft. 'Nyongo', like 'black tax', refers to a world of abundance, but such abundance comes at a price: the humanity of those sacrificed to slave away as zombies, and the risk of disharmony with the home village. Double exploitation – by 'home of origin' and 'home of refuge' generates critical discourse of complaint of helplessness and to wish for more flexible ideas of what it means to feel at home (Nyamnjoh 2005a). Some of the newly working black middle class expressed stories of relatives often guilt-tripping them into sending money on a continuous basis. Along gender categories, black women with children taken care of by relatives 'back home' often experience gruelling demands. Relatives often use the children as bait to extend unrealistic demands for money using every reason possible. Since cellular phones and free communication social media such as WhatsApp and Facebook have become accessible, the relatives are able to make demands for money without empathy. Manicured and curated images often depicting successful (real or imagined) lifestyles do little in helping distant relatives understand the struggles related to living in the city. The young men are not spared either. The example of world famous Togolese international footballer Emmanuel Adebayor's Facebook post complaining about the cannibalistic obligatory demands endured by the ingratitude of his family despite extraordinary generosity reveals these struggles beyond South Africa.[3] Emmanuel Adebayor played football for international soccer teams, Manchester City and Tottenham Hotspurs, and won prestigious awards. On many occasions Adebayor made frequent trips to Togo attending to various obligations; whether driven by a sense of responsibility, guilt or altruism. In the process spending a fair share of the fortune he built up attending to the insatiable cannibalistic demands by his family (Nyamnjoh 2015). Young black fathers also have children staying with relatives while working to establish themselves as fresh graduates in new jobs. Distant relatives often calling or sending messages asking for financial assistance adds to obligations to immediate kin and extended networks.

Such obligations to family and extended relations are not exclusive to young graduates in their first jobs. For instance, in *Run Racist Run* Eusebius McKaiser (2015) describes the untimely obligations known as 'black tax' at moments as one is about to bite on a delicious steak at an expensive restaurant. These intimate moments are rudely disturbed when a text message arrives from a relative asking for money to buy a school uniform for young cousins at the beginning of the school year. Even when one is established financially as black middle-class, obligations to relatives can be manipulative and often difficult to assess whether one is not taken advantage of. Some black middle-class South Africans have expressed that these obligations are a choice and depend on whether one is able to send money home. They express to family and extended relations that to remit and help often depends on the financial ability. However, those who are 'black taxed' as financial providers at times internalise the glorification by family and relatives. The black middle class can be controlling of family affairs sometimes to a point of arrogance and disrespect. In this way, the 'black taxed' have the capacity to cannibalise obligations towards the family. The ones rising up from the shackles of the cannibalised (i.e. poverty/disadvantage) are now pushed into cannibalising others (i.e. reduce/rescind obligations to increase/maintain their privilege).

All this time while the cannibalising system of neoliberalism goes on and favours differentially diverse groups, in particularly well-established upper middle classes and the very rich. Ultimately, 'black tax' becomes a mechanism in this systemic cannibalism, deployed by big capital and the upper middle class to avoid a uniform progressive system of taxation that would make them pay for their privileges, thus ensuring better conditions and lives for all – including the cannibalising/cannibalised middle classes. A good example is the recent ideological propaganda deployed at all levels to sink free higher education as 'unsustainable' – because a sustainable plan can only be financed by higher taxes for the rich. This means of course that some of the not-so-established middle classes will also have to pay at some points in their lives (when they are at peak so to speak) more taxes. But because of their obligations and general structural disadvantage *vis-à-vis* well-established upper/middle classes, a state that provides top quality free education, free health and other key services, including a substantial welfare state in terms of unemployment benefits, child grants etc. would be much more convenient and stabilise their lives. But the ideological pressure makes people adopt beliefs and political views that go against their basic interests. The ideological pressures and the version of the mutually constituting obligations are often not heard of. The enthusiasm of newspaper articles, television shows and even publications houses to reproduce the narrative of the individual is astonishing. But there seems to be less of an emphasis on how to research the lived realities of black middle class and to compare this to empirically informed knowledge on the white middle class in South Africa and elsewhere. Managing the individual through better financial planning, discerning the extent of kin, desisting pressures by social media, especially Instagram are common solutions at talk shows.[4] The government settled on providing fee-free tertiary education for poor South Africans. In the 2018 budget speech the finance minister Malusi Gigaba stated that 'Starting this year, free higher education and training will be available to first-year students from households with a gross combined annual income of up to R350,000'.[5] The programme will be financed by increasing the value added tax (VAT) by a percentage point to 15 per cent from 1 April 2018.[6]

Citizenship and Cannibalism

In a context where the state is not obligated to citizens and the reality that industry is increasingly not able to absorb waged labour, the burdens experienced through cannibalising obligations to relatives on the black middle class is understandable. In such situations, not only is the successful urbanite expected to fill in for the state and its obligations to 'give a man a fish' (Ferguson 2015), he or she runs the risk of becoming the fish themselves. What is emphasised in training and the work produced by scholars researching the area is an autonomous 'free' individual that is removed from the social. However, the solution is also not solved by increasing consumption by the black middle class. Henning Melber (2013) casts doubt on the silver bullet that is middle class to resolve matters of inequality by drawing on an insightful metaphor. He writes that 'Pinning hopes for social advancement on the emerging middle classes is like trusting those who row the galley to decide its course. Meanwhile, the captain and his adjuncts are navigating from the commanding bridge, and not rowing at all. The rowers keep the galley moving, but the course coordinates are defined, decided upon and followed by a handful of others – unless – or until there is a mutiny' (Melber 2013: 118). The black middle class at any point of the climb toward stability are at the receiving end of any possible distribution that might lead to an upliftment of many impoverished Africans.

Yet, like Seekings and Nattrass (2005) and Alexander (2013), Melber (2016) suggests that 'middle class' is a better signifier or analytical concept than 'race' because it 'is the desired self-signifier'

212

(Melber 2016: 7). Why are scholars of class, even when they are sympathetic to the historic injustices suffered by blacks as victims of racialised encounters, so keen to cannibalise and to make invisible the salience of race as an analytical category? Does factoring race in necessarily imply denying the importance of class? Whatever happened to the importance of intersectionality in contrast to single factor analysis? As Milazzo rightly cautions, 'In the colorblind talk, individualization is deployed to obfuscate the causes of white advantage and to portray Black disadvantage as unrelated to racism' (Milazzo 2015: 15). A documentary such as Peter Alexander's *Phakathi* locates the causes of black poverty in the homes constructing a narrative that pathologises the black family. Such arguments delegitimise racial stratification and experiences of explicit and implicit forms of racism where the focus becomes 'the culture of the natives' (Zuberi and Bonilla-Silva 2008).

Where corporate cannibalism meets race, for instance, the allegations of racism at Old Mutual initiated by several black women are a testament to the realities of post-apartheid life even for those occupying senior managerial positions. Such stories are not uncommon where abusive treatment as the norm for black middle class reduces one to suffer nervous breakdowns. As disposable labour, the black middle class depleted of humanity by corporate cannibalism are 'taken to a hospital and then fired' from work (*IOL* November 2017). Even at the most upmarket bars and restaurants where the most affluent of the black middle-class wine and dine are not exempt from the reality of race cannibalism. Taking to social media to share her story, in December 2015, Tumi Mpofu had an unpleasant experience along with her family at the upmarket restaurant in Camps Bay called Twelve Apostles. Even though black, a woman and middle class, she was denied a telephonic booking reservation after the person on the other side of the line heard an African name. This must have followed a brief conversation exchange with an accent that could pass for a white person. For Mpofu states that 'Everything was going well until I told them my name and then suddenly there wasn't a table available for me'. Suspecting that there was more to the sudden change in attitude she got her friend who is white, to make the same booking using her name. It was her friend and not Mpofu that got the booking (*IOL* 2015). The uncertainty of being black middle class strongly suggests the importance of social investment through negotiated obligations and collective success. As a cannibalistic system, an unchecked Western modernity and global consumerism eats its own glory and gain in practice while upholding ideology of 'free' individuals as the criteria for 'inclusion' as a good and normal citizen and person (Nyamnjoh 2002).

Cannibalising Systemic Obligations

Western modernity along with global consumerism is a cannibalistic system of fallacies and contradictions. Ideologically many black people in South Africa are called to serve the roles as political protective buffers of 'free' middle-class individuals located between the unemployed majority and global capitalism along with white-owned businesses. However, in reality, even the chosen ones are excluded in certain spaces on the basis of race which intersects with gender, sexuality, ethnicity and geography. Such a cannibalistic system outsources guilt for the pressures to participate in abstract ideas of freedom where consuming and being consumed is not an option. To attain visibility, one is required to be consumed by the prejudices and expectations of modernity at all cost. The fiction of merit prescribed by a cannibalistic system in the form of shifting standards of university education, excellence and trendsetters suggest that to whiten up the black middle class must accept a debt or tax repayable but never complete. This is achieved by a denial of a cannibalistic colonial and imperial history that stripped agency and personhood. Even when race, class, and gender intersect, the fiction of merit dictates and outsources guilt to those in the same middle class to berate one another. The systemic outsourcing of guilt to the black middle class today is reminiscent of Helen Zille's instruction to musician Simphiwe Dana after tweeting that Cape Town was racist. Dana, along with Lindiwe Suttle (also a black musician living in Cape Town), expressed via the social network, how they feel Cape Town is racist regardless of wealth, status and class. Directly responding to Dana, Zille tweeted that 'You're a highly respected black professional. Don't try to be a professional black. It demeans you' (*IOL*, 2011). In other words, in a cannibalistic system of professional whites and global whiteness, one must further reduce, degrade and acclaim dependency by succumbing to the entitlement of power, white privilege, and globalised consumerism as a 'free' black professional individual.

The insidious highjacking of 'black tax' discourse by Western modernity, neoliberal and global consumerism continues its cannibalistic quest for superiority and supremacy by further dividing and ruling by outsourcing debt. As a cannibalising system neoliberalism and global consumerism require those seeking respect as Zille's black professionals to profess individual entitlement to sacrifice social relations and their society. Yet, the black professional is denied at many turns the respect as educated, consuming class at upmarket restaurants and boardrooms in private companies. This leads to a cycle of a cannibalistic system of whitening tax obligations. It is this form of taxing obligations that have far-reaching consequences of social exclusion. What is rendered invisible by scholars, industry, media and government are any attempts by mobile black people in post-apartheid South Africa to restore humanity, personhood and dignity (Povinelli 2011).

Conclusion

The paper has argued for a systemic approach to cannibalising forms of neoliberalism and global consumerism by taking seriously debates and scholarly work on the black middle class. I have argued for analytical tools that are inclusive of the intersections of race, class, gender and geography in lived experiences of black people in post-apartheid South Africa. The paper demonstrates doubt at the efforts to underplay and delegitimise race and elevating 'middle class' by well-intended studies seeking to depict the lived experiences broadly in Africa. Even the selected black professionals exceeding the fictitious merits that should institutionalise them as respectable are no exception to a cannibalising neoliberal system dictating differential treatment based on race more so than class at spaces of global consumption. The unequal encounters and experiences

215

through 'black tax', on the one hand, argue for more flexible, negotiated, relational and realistic ideas of belonging based less on the essence of class, geography and biology than on conviviality and a shared humanity. On the other hand, there is mounting pressure through the process of outsourcing guilt to pay endless white tax by calling on 'black tax' and subsequently black guilt as a reason to cut valuable social safety nets. It is the contested family relations that protect from the precarity of a cannibalistic system – a cannibalistic system that is inherently fictitious and contradictory excluding even those chosen as respectable black professionals in professionally white establishments and cities.

Endnotes

[1] M. Ratlebjane, 2015. 'How 'Black Tax' cripples our youth's aspirations' HTML http://mg.co.za/article/2015-10-29-how-black-tax-cripples-our-youths-aspirations.

[2] SABC Digital News February 2018: https://www.youtube.com/watch?v=foQTbCCxzkU&feature=youtu.be.

[3] F. B. Nyamnjoh, 2015, *C est l homme qui fait l homme: Cul-de-Sac Ubuntu-ism in Côte d'Ivoire*, Bamenda: Langaa RPCIG.

[4] *Daily Thetha*, 14 June 2017, on youtube https://www.youtube.com/watch?v=hpti3oftsGQ.

[5] *Times Live*, February 2018: https://www.timeslive.co.za/politics/2018-02-16-gigaba-to-provide-details-of-financing-of-free-education-next-week/.

[6] Fin24, February 2018: https://www.fin24.com/Budget/live-all-eyes-on-malusi-gigaba-for-budget2018-20180221.

References

Printed Publications

Alexander, P. (2013) 'Conclusion.' In: P. Alexander, C. Ceruti, K. Motseke and M. Phadi, K. Wale, in *Class in Soweto*, KwaZulu Natal Press, Scottsville.

Bendix, R., and Lipset, S. M. (1966) *Class, status, and power: social stratification in comparative perspective*, New York: The Free Press.

Bezuidenhout, A., and Fakier, K. (2006) 'Maria's Burden: Contract Cleaning and the Crisis of Social Reproduction in Post-Apartheid South Africa', *Antipode*, Vol. 38(3): 462–485.

Bonilla-Silva, E. (2006) *Racism without racists: Color-blind racism and the persistence of racial inequality in the United States*, Maryland: Rowman & Littlefield Publishers.

Chevalier, S. (2011) 'The Black Diamonds: a South African Phantasmagoria', *Economic and Social Research Council*.

Connell, R. (2007) *Southern theory*, Crows Nest, NSW: Allen & Unwin.

Devisch, R., and Nyamnjoh, F. B. (eds) (2011) *The Postcolonial Turn: Re-Imagining Anthropology and Africa*, Bamenda/Leiden: Langaa RPCIG/African Studies Centre, Leiden.

Devisch, R. (1996) '"Pillaging Jesus": healing churches and the villagisation of Kinshasa', *Africa*, Vol. 66(4): 555–586.

Dolamo, R. T. (2014) 'Botho/Ubuntu: perspectives of black consciousness and black theology', *Studia Historiae Ecclesiasticae*, Vol. 40: 215–229.

Goffman, E. (2002) *The presentation of self in everyday life 1959*, New York: Garden City.

Goodhew, D. (2000) 'Working-class Respectability: The example of the western areas of Johannesburg, 1930–55', *Journal of African History*, Vol. 41(2): 241–266.

Graeber, D. (2014) *Debt-Updated and Expanded: The First 5,000 Years*, New York and London: Melville House.

Graeber, D. (2001) *Toward an anthropological theory of value: The false coin of our own dreams*, New York: Palgrave Macmillan.

Ferguson, J. (2015) *Give a man a fish: reflections on the new politics of distribution*, Durham, NC: Duke University Press.

Ferguson, J. (2006) *Global Shadows: Africa in the neoliberal world order*, Durham and London: Duke University Press.

Ferguson, J. (1999) *Expectations of Modernity: Myths and meanings of urban life on the Zambian Copperbelt*, Berkeley: University of California Press.

Ferguson, J. (1985) 'The bovine mystique: power, property, and livestock in rural Lesotho', *Man*, (N.S) Vol. 20 (4): 647–674.

Innes, D., and O'Meara, D. (1976) 'Class Formation and Ideology: The Transkei Region', *Review of African Political Economy*, Vol. 3(7): 69–86.

Kaplan, M. and Robertson, M., (1986) *Jewish roots in the South African economy*, Cape Town: Struik.

Kaus, W. (2013) 'Conspicuous consumption and 'race': Evidence from South Africa', *Journal of Development Economics*, Vol. 100(1): 63–73.

Laden, S. (2003) 'Who's Afraid of a Black Bourgeoisie?: Consumer Magazines for Black South Africans as an Apparatus of Change', *Journal Consumer Culture*, Vol. 3(2): 191–216.

Letseka, M. (2012) 'In defence of Ubuntu', *Studies in philosophy and education*, Vol. 31(1): 47–60.

Lipton, M. (1986) *Capitalism & Apartheid: South Africa, 1910–1986*, Cape Town: David Phillip.

Mabandla, N. (2015) 'Rethinking Bundy: Land and the black middle class–accumulate on beyond the peasantry', *Development Southern Africa*, Vol. 32(1): 76–89.

Mabovula, N .N., (2011) 'The erosion of African communal values: a reappraisal of the African Ubuntu philosophy. Inkanyiso', *Journal of Humanities and Social Sciences*, Vol. 3(1): 38–47.

Magubane, Z. (2004) *Bringing the empire home: Race, class, and gender in Britain and colonial South Africa*, Chicago: University of Chicago Press.

McAllister, P.A. (2009) 'Ubuntu-Beyond Belief in Southern Africa', *Sites: a journal of social anthropology and cultural studies*, Vol. 6(1): 48–57.

McKaiser, E. (2015) *Run Racist Run: Journeys into the heart of racism*, Northcliff: Bookstorm.

Melber, H. (ed.) (2016) *The rise of Africa's middle class: myths, realities, and critical engagements*, London: Zed Books Ltd.

Melber, H. (2013) 'Africa and the Middle Class (es)', *Africa Spectrum*, Vol. 43(3): 111–120.

Milazzo, M. (2015) 'The rhetorics of racial power: Enforcing colorblindness in post-apartheid scholarship on race', *Journal of International and Intercultural Communication*, Vol. 8(1): 7-26.

Ngcukaitobi, T. (2018) *The Land Is Ours: South Africa's First Black Lawyers and the Birth of Constitutionalism*, Penguin Book: South Africa.

Ngwane, Z. (2003) "'Christmastime" and the struggles for the household in the countryside: Rethinking the geography of migrant labour in South Africa', *Journal of Southern Africa Studies*, Vol. 29(3): 681–699.

Ngwane, Z. (2001) "'Real Men Reawaken Their Fathers' Homesteads, the Educated Leave Them in Ruins": The Politics of Domestic Reproduction in Post-Apartheid Rural South Africa', *Journal of religion in Africa*, Vol. 31(4): 402–426.

Nyamnjoh, F. B. (2016) *#RhodesMustFall: Nibbling at Resilient Colonialism in South Africa*, Bamenda: Langaa RPCIG.

Nyamnjoh, F. B. (2015) *C'est l'homme qui fait l'homme: Cul-de-Sac Ubuntu-ism in Côte d'Ivoire*, Bamenda: Langaa RPCIG.

Nyamnjoh, F. B. and Brudvig, I., (eds) (2016) *Mobilities, ICTs and Marginality in Africa: Comparative Perspectives*, Cape Town: HSRC Press.

Nyamnjoh, F. B. and Brudvig, I., (2014) 'Conviviality and negotiations with belonging in urban Africa', *Routledge Handbook of Global Citizenship Studies*. New York: Routledge, pp. 217–229.

Nyamnjoh, F.B. (2012) "Potted plants in greenhouses': A critical reflection on the resilience of colonial education in Africa' *Journal of Asian and African Studies*, Vol. 47(2): 129-154.

Nyamnjoh, F. B. (2000) "'For Many Are Called but Few Are Chosen": Globalisation and Popular Disenchantment in Africa', *African Sociological Review/Revue Africaine de Sociologie*, Vol. 4(2): 1–45.

Nyamnjoh, F. B. and Page, B. (2002) 'Whiteman Kontri and the enduring allure of modernity among Cameroonian youth', *African Affairs*, Vol. 101(405): 607–634.

Nyamnjoh, F. B. (2005a) 'Images of Nyongo amongst Bamenda Grassfielders in Whiteman Kontri', *Citizenship Studies*, Vol. 9(3): 241–269.

Nyamnjoh, F. B. (2005b) 'Fishing in troubled waters: disquettes and thiofs in Dakar', *Africa*, Vol. 75(3): 295–324.

Nyamnjoh, F. B. (2002) '"A Child is One Person's Only in the Womb": Domestication, Agency, and Subjectivity in the Cameroonian Grassfields' in R. Werbner (ed.) *Postcolonial Subjectivity*, London and New York: Zed Books, pp. 111–138.Posel, D. (2010) 'Races to consume: revisiting South Africa's history of race, consumption and the struggle for freedom', *Ethnic and Racial Studies*, Vol. 33(2): 157–175.

Povinelli, E.A. (2011) *Economies of abandonment: Social belonging and endurance in late liberalism*, Duke University Press.

Praeg, L. and Magadla, S. (eds) (2014) *Ubuntu: Curating the archive*, University of KwaZulu-Natal Press.

Qunta, Y. (2016) *Writing what we like: A new generation speaks*, Cape Town: Tafelberg.

Ricard, M. (2015) *Altruism: the power of compassion to change yourself and the world*, New York, Boston and London: Back Bay Books.

Salo, E. (2003) 'Negotiating gender and personhood in the New South Africa adolescent women and gangsters in Manenberg Township on the Cape Flats', *European Journal of Cultural Studies*, Vol. 6(3): 345–365.

Sandel, M. J. (2012) *What money can't buy: the moral limits of markets*, London: Penguin Books.

Seekings, J. (2008) 'The continuing salience of race: Discrimination and diversity in South Africa', *Journal of Contemporary Studies*, Vol. 26(1): 1–25.

Seekings, J. (2009) 'The rise and fall of the Weberian analysis of class in South Africa between 1949 and the early 1970s', *Journal of Southern African Studies*, Vol. 35(4): 865-881.

Seekings, J. and Nattrass, N. (2005) *Class, race and inequality in South Africa*, New Haven: Yale University.

Southall, R. (2016) *The new black middle class in South Africa*, Auckland Park: Jacana Media.

Spronk, R. (2012) *Ambiguous pleasures: Sexuality and middle-class self-perceptions in Nairobi*, New York and Oxford: Berghahn Books.

Redding, S. (1992) 'Beer Brewing in Umtata: Women, Migrant Labour, and Social Control in a rural town' in *Liquor and Labor in Southern Africa* (eds). J. Crush and C. Ambler Athens, Ohio University Press pp 235 – 251.

Teppo, A. (2004) *The making of a good white: A historical ethnography of the rehabilitation of poor whites in a suburb of Cape Town*, Research Series in Anthropology, Helsinki: University of Helsinki.

Tilley, C., Keane, W., Küchler, S., Rowlands, M., and Spyer, P. (eds) (2006) *Handbook of material culture*, London, California, and Singapore: Sage.

Veblen, T. and Banta, M. (2009) *The theory of the leisure class* Oxford University Press.

Zuberi, T. and Bonilla-Silva, E. eds., (2008) *White logic, white methods: Racism and methodology* Rowman & Littlefield Publishers.

Online Articles

IOL online (2011) 'Zille sparks new twitter war with "professional black jibe"'
https://www.iol.co.za/capetimes/zille-sparks-new-twitter-war-with-professional-black-jibe-1205626

IOL online (2017) 'More Allegations of racism at Old Mutual', https://www.iol.co.za/capetimes/news/more-allegations-of-racism-at-old-mutual-11899247.

IOL online (2015) 'Elite Cape Town restaurant denies racism', https://www.iol.co.za/news/south-africa/western-cape/elite-cape-town-restaurant-denies-racism-1801645.

Laterza, V. and Manqoyi, A. (2016) 'What Future for South African Democracy?', http://bostonreview.net/world/vito-laterza-ayanda-manqoyi-future-south-african-democracy.

Laterza, V. and Manqoyi, A. (2015) 'Looking for leaders: Student protest and the future of South Africa democracy', http://www.dailymaverick.co.za/article/2015-11-06-looking-for-leaders-student-protests-and-the-future-of-south-african-democracy/.

Mhlungu, G. (2015) 'Black Tax is not real', http://city-press.news24.com/Voices/Black-tax-is-not-real-20150508 (5 October 2016).

Msimang, S. (2016) 'Shutdown – on the death of compromise in South Africa'
https://africasacountry.com/2016/10/shutdown-on-the-death-of-compromise-in-south-africa

News24 online (2018) 'All you need to know about #Budget2018 – AS IT HAPPENED', https://www.fin24.com/Budget/live-all-eyes-on-malusi-gigaba-for-budget2018-20180221.

Ratlebjane, M. (2015) 'How "Black Tax" cripples our youth's aspirations', http://mg.co.za/article/2015-10-29-how-black-tax-cripples-our-youths-aspirations (5 October 2016).

Sefalafala, T. (2015) 'History has poisoned the fruits of the black middle class', http://mg.co.za/article/2015-08-27-history-has-poisoned-the-fruits-of-the-black-middle-class (30 October 2016).

Shelly Seid, S. (2016) 'Black Tax blocks roads to success for many employed South Africans', http://www.timeslive.co.za/thetimes/2016/09/29/Black-tax-blocks-road-to-success-for-many-employed-South-Africans (5 October 2016).

Times Live online (2018) 'Budget speech to reveal details of affording free education', https://www.timeslive.co.za/politics/2018-02-16-gigaba-to-provide-details-of-financing-of-free-education-next-week/.

Unilever Institute (2013) 'Booming black middle class represents R400 billion spend', http://www.uct.ac.za/dad/news/archives/?id=73. 'http://www.uct.ac.za/dad/news/archives/?id=73&t=int'& 'http://www.uct.ac.za/dad/news/archives/?id=73&t=int't=int (13 June 2013).

Chapter 6

Lehu la gago le ya mphidisha
'Your death nourishes me'

Veronica Dimakatso Masenya

'*Lehu la gago le ya mphidisha*' is a Sepedi[1] proverb colloquially used in everyday conversations in African communities in South Africa to express different scenarios that depict the consumption of death. Proverbs are propositions that are passed down through the generational lines based on the lived experiences of the forefathers and -mothers 'affirming clearly or metaphorically popular indisputable truths' (Sibanda 2015: 2). Proverbs form part of the African oral literature[2] and they comprise short, popular witty belief statements that act as a storehouse of indigenous wisdom, ethical regulation and code of conduct (Gogoi 2017: 52; Alimi 2012: 122). Consequently, proverbs serve an important role in human activities and relations to assist in guidance, teaching, reflection, criticising and praising (Sibanda 2015: 3: Ukoma, Egwu and Ogechukwu 2016: 326). David (cited in Alimi 2012: 122) argues that 'the effectiveness of a proverb lies largely in its brevity and directedness. The syntax is simple, the image is vivid and thus easy to understand. Memorability is aided through the use of alliteration, rhyme and rhythm'. Chinua Achebe[3] echoes the relevance and importance of proverbs as they function to 'enable the speaker to give universal status to a special and particular incident and they are used to soften the harshness of words and make them more palatable' (cited in Ihueze and Umeasiegbu 2015: 30). Thus, proverbs are significant to life and language as they provide 'flesh' to the skeleton and a 'soul' to the body that is life and language (Ihueze and Umeasiegbu 2015: 30). Case in point, '*Lehu la gago le ya mphidisha*' proverb which bring to light the prevalence of recipients benefiting from the demise of an individual, either from death or other forms of defeat – with the recipient 'eating' and the benefactor getting 'eaten'. The '*Lehu la gago le ya mphidisha* proverb highlights the multifaceted aspects of cannibalism, where the meaning is either literal or metaphorical. The literal meaning is conveyed in the orthodox definition of cannibalism (anthropophagy), the practice of human beings physically consuming, ingesting or eating human flesh (Henderson 2013: 831). Conklin (2001; 1995) argues that human beings eat human flesh for various reasons, such as *hunger cannibalism* to curb starvation and for nutritional purposes. *Mortuary cannibalism*[4] is 'an institutionalised form of cannibalism' that was prevalent in the Lowland South America, stretching out from the coastal Venezuela to the Caribbean islands. By the early 20th century, mortuary cannibalism was predominant in the Western Amazonian region, amongst groupings such as the Wari' from the western Brazilian rain forest, Panoan speaking people, Chapakuran of Rondonia and Bolivia, Melanesian and the ache-Guayaki of Paraguay (Conklin 1995: 95; Fausto 2007: 510). Mortuary cannibalism is an indigenous and specific method of disposing of dead bodies by eating the boiled and/or roasted flesh, certain organs and on occasion bones from the corpse. Distinction is made between those who can take part in the eating ritual and those who cannot be involved, and these rules follow the kinship relations, even though the sequence may differ from each group. In some cases, distant kin members such as affines and extended family are expected to consume the flesh, while close family members consume the bones and control how the bones are distributed. This differentiating system is complex, with some groups consuming either the flesh or the bones and other groups consuming both (Fausto 2007: 510. Conklin 2001).

According to Conklin (2001; 1995) the flesh consumption tradition was symbolic in nature, a sign of respect to both the deceased and the deceased's family and a grief and mourning mechanism to lessen the sorrow and to emotionally and physically disconnect from the memories[5] of the deceased. As a result, eating voraciously, equating the corpse to animal meat or refusal to participate in the flesh-eating ritual was considered as an ultimate insult. The eaters were also compelled to eat decayed flesh and, in most cases, they would excuse themselves from the gathering to vomit elsewhere and return to consume more flesh. Therefore, the ritual of eating human flesh is perceived differently from eating animal meat even though they are described to have similar taste and texture. But eating human flesh is an act of compassion for the deceased and their families, opposed to the burial which is cruel and disrespectful to leave a spirit being to rot in cold and wet ground (Conklin 2001: 89–97; Conklin 1995: 82).

These cultural groupings also engaged in *warfare cannibalism (exocannibalism)*, which is the ritual of eating the flesh of the members of social circles and enemies outside one's own social group. This form of eating human flesh was distinct as it was 'expressed in the language of food desire and revenge' (Fausto 2007: 508). In this case, the human meat was perceived as appetising and sweet and those who participated wanted to inflict pain and revenge on their enemies. The human flesh was reduced to an object and the eating was done with hostility, disrespect and contempt to demonstrate defeat and disrespect towards the enemies (Conklin 2001: 95-96). The process of eating strengthened bonds between those who ate together and alienated those who were potential food, with the 'eaters' as predators and the 'eaten' as prey (Fausto 2007: 508). The cannibal way of life of the Lowland South Americans (and other parts of the world) was frowned upon and extinct by the westerners (Jooma 1997: 61; Conklin 2001: xvii), who, despite their own cannibalism and cannibalistic incursions into other territories and cultures (see Nyamnjoh, this volume) regard(ed) these practices as cruel and forcefully introduced burials as an improved and civilised method (Conklin 2001: xvii).

The western explorers and thinkers, while oblivious of the histories and practices of cannibalism in their societies of origin, were keener to expose the customs of the 'other' consuming human flesh in the fifteenth century (Carrasco 1995: 429) and this practice was condemned and criticised by the 'modern' societies, reducing the cannibals to an animal status and also being perceived as selfish and antisocial (Barley 1995: 199). Christopher Columbus reported that he had come across islands that were 'inhabited by people who were regarded in all the islands as fierce and who ate human flesh'

(Carrasco 1995: 429). Explorers such as Americo Vespucci claimed to have encountered a cannibal that proclaimed to have eaten over two hundred corpses. More 'incidences' of cannibalism were documented such as: the cannibal feast of the Indians of Mesoamerica, the banquet of Moctezuma with the menu that included human flesh and organs (Carrasco 1995: 430-432) and the Aztech human sacrifice where war prisoners were ritually slaughtered and their hearts were eaten by the Aztec gods and the flesh was shared amongst the priests, nobles, warriors and their relatives and friends (Carrasco 1995: 432: Conklin 2001: 88).

The Biafra war warriors from Southern Nigeria consumed human flesh and organs to increase their strength and mercilessly conquer their opponents (Barley 1995: 199). Similar ritual sacrifices (warfare cannibalism) are recorded in Sierra Leone with enemies captured in battle are cut up into pieces and their flesh is ether smoked and cooked to be served with rice. The Mane community was proclaimed as cannibal by the Portuguese and other explores after their arrival on the Sierra Leone coast. However, the indigenous groups along the African Atlantic coast turned the tables, accusing the European slave traders of consuming the flesh of African slaves on the ships (Shaw 2001: 51–54). The Americans and Europeans also engage(d) in cannibalistic customs such as placentophagy, the eating of the placenta by the woman after giving birth, and the 'bone-ash cannibalism' with relatives eating the cremated ashes of the deceased mixed with honey. But the Western countries justified their ways of cannibalism as decent and respectful, while critiquing the ways of others as barbaric (Harvey 2004: 259). The negative attitude towards other's ways of cannibalism is accurately captured by an anonymous writer, who echoed the practice as a 'cursed practice, for they eat more gladly man's flesh than any other flesh […] thither go merchants and bring with them children to sell them in the country and then buy and they say that it is the best flesh and the sweetest in the world' (Carrasco 1995: 430). Consequently, cannibalism (of the non-western societies) is still considered one of the greatest taboos regarding food consumption and it is also a distasteful topic that is not comprehendible to the 'modern' human mindset (Henderson 2013: 831).

The mystery surrounding cannibalism has not prevented the national (South African) and international media platforms from reporting incidences occurring globally. The well-reported form of cannibalism that plagues South Africa (and other parts of the African continent) is the ritual murders where corpses are found with missing body parts and organs. This phenomenon is pre-dominantly known as '*muti* killings' and they are on the rise in the rural and peri-urban areas of Southern Africa. The driving force behind these '*muti* killings' is generally the 'promise' of monetary wealth, good proceeds for entrepreneurs and immoral ritualistic purposes to fuel the wicked economy (Niehaus 2013: 3; Shaw 2001: 51: Barley 1995: 198). Niehaus (2013: 3) describes these killings as a 'brutal forms of extraction, involving the destruction of others, but have the allure of making profit without ordinary production costs'.

The *muti*-making procedures in most cases are facilitated by individuals (traditional healers and/or spiritual leaders) with the supernatural ability to tap into the spiritual realm and manipulate forces/energies to 'unlawfully' enrich the recipients at the expense of life and anguish of the bereaved families and their communities. These ritualistic killings are also believed to be interlinked (even though there are not necessarily similar) to the satanic cults with harmful magic, where people's lives are literally taken as 'sacrificial lamb' in order to nourish others – this so called 'nourishment' ranges from healing of illnesses and diseases, removal of misfortune, cultivating financial prosperity to hurting of enemies. The rituals require the recipients to either ingest, smear the *muti* on their bodies or place the *muti* in various places to make sure the victim comes into contact with the *muti* (Swart 2012: 69–70; Petrus 2011: 5; Labuschagne 2004: 193).

'*Muti* killings' are motivated by strong cultural beliefs and practices that certain body parts[6] and organs possesses supernatural properties, making these body parts and organs essential ingredients for *muti*,[7] used for the medicinal and ritualistic purposes. The common belief is that *muti* made from the human body parts and organs is stronger and more powerful compared to the normal herbal medicine. The targeted body parts and organs are 'genitals, breasts, hearts, fingers, tongues, ears, eyes, hands, legs, lungs, guts, skin, arms, jaws and lips'[8] (Swart 2012: 70; Petrus 2011: 5). The practice of '*muti*-killings', can be compared to the medicinal cannibalism that originates from Europe, as early as the 16th century, which involves the extraction and ingestion of 'human flesh, blood, heart, skull, bone marrow and other body parts' (Gordon-Grube 1988: 406), typically 'referred to as mummy,[9] for healing purposes' (Noble 2003: 678). The human body in both situations (traditional and biomedical) is perceived and used as a source of power with healing and 'enriching' properties, making the human body somewhat 'sacred' and in demand, giving rise to the industry of medical tourism (Scheper-Hughes 2001c: 81).

There is a global market[10] that is unregulated and worth multi-million dollars of trading human body parts and organs in particular for biomedical and surgical procedures and traditional 'healing' purposes. The third-world countries tend to exchange human tissue with the first-world countries for funding, medical technology and expertise. As in the case of a South African medical centre director, who traded human heart valves taken without consent from paupers at the police mortuaries to medical centres in Germany and Austria (Scheper-Hughes 2001c: 82) . The human body within the 'capitalised economic exchanges' transition into an object, a 'highly fetishised one, and a commodity' (Scheper-Hughes 2001a: 1, 3) with economic, spiritual and social value that is bartered, sold and stolen (Scheper-Hughes 2001a: 1; Scheper-Hughes 2001c: 82–83). As a result, the commodification of the human body renders it as more than an object but also a 'semi-magical and symbolic representation' (Scheper-Hughes 2001a: 2). These developments bring forth the emergence of the black market where the human body parts and organs are stolen and trafficked, as in the case of '*muti* killings' where some people are murdered and others are butchered alive to 'acquire' the relevant tissues for those who are in 'desperate' need (Scheper-Hughes 2001c: 83).

The syndicate of trafficking human body parts and organs is a global predicament that wears different faces in different geographical and social spaces. In the biomedical fraternity, this illegal practice is endorsed by 'certain' physicians, surgeons and bioethics practitioners, proclaiming the end act as unselfish and serving the good of those in need, in both ends. This viewpoint stirred up debates and friction between the principles of human rights of not hurting others versus the beneficence argument of moral obligations to perform good acts. This precarious debate was 'settled' on the principles of 'libertarian sense of fairness' that suggests that those who with financial means must be permitted to purchase these organs, regardless of how they were acquired. This 'solution' is seen as a 'win win' for the involved parties (Scheper-Hughes 2001b: 31–32). Thus, this form of medicinal cannibalism is guised as 'life saving' and it is applauded, accepted and celebrated as opposed to the '*muti* killings' that are condemned and deemed as evil and savage (Himmelman 1997: 185). For this reason, the biomedical practitioners have attempted to distance the fact that the trafficking of human body parts and organs is unlawful and also wrapped with negative repercussions, especially for those who are 'forced' to give up parts of their bodies (Scheper-Hughes 2001b: 32).

The Human Sciences Research Council (HSRC) (2010: 8) differentiates between the criminal acts of killing for the purpose of removing body parts and organs from a cadaver, at the killing site, the mortuary or from the grave. There are also cases where the body parts and organs are removed and the victims survive to live with the consequences of 'forced' mutilation which ranges from severe disability, psychological disorder to mental instability. On an international scale, the target victims are generally from the marginalised population groups such as women, children, people living with disability, the brain dead and in African context it includespeople living with albinism. The chain of the traffic circuit usually comprises buyers, sellers, brokers and surgeons and in Africa this circuit is made up of murders and/or gravediggers, buyers and traditional practitioners. This essay acknowledges the distinctions made by the HSRC regarding forms of harvesting the human body parts and organs but argues for the similarity in the manner of which recipients 'gain' or 'profit' at the expense of others. The perpetrators violate the basic human rights of life and privacy for self-preserving reasons without remorse of their victims, families and the community. The loss of life and body parts/organs of others seems to weigh less than their own enrichment and prosperity (Scheper-Hughes 2004: 31–33).

However, there are some instances where the guilty consciences seem to have the upper hand, and perpetrators confront their deeds seeking atonement. Nino Mbatha a South African traditional healer, who walked into the police station[11] (in Estcourt in KwaZulu-Natal in August 2017) holding a reeking bag containing human body parts and told the police that he was 'tired of eating human flesh and wanted out' (Olifants 2017; Stone 2017; Pieterse 2017). Mr Mbatha ousted his associates as well; this news left the community terrified to the extent of fearing to walk at night, in case they fall victim to '*muti* killings'. Some families might get their closure as the police continue with the investigation and they have asked the community of Estcourt to report to the station if they have missing family members, especially those who did not report the matter immediately it occurred.

The opposers of cannibalism have always been aware that this custom is not exclusive to human flesh consumption, but is also underlined with symbolic and ceremonial connotations (Jooma 1997: 61). This position is echoed in the introductory chapter (Nyamnjoh, this volume), indicating the broad spectrum entangled in the meaning of cannibalism that reaches beyond the literal ingestion to figurative, symbolic, metaphorical and fantasy 'realities', to name a few. Peggy Reeves Sanday (an anthropologist) describes cannibalism as a 'primordial metaphor for relations of domination and submission and for creating self- and social consciousness; it is an ontological system consisting of the myths, symbols, and rituals by which a people explore their relationship to the world, to other beings and to being itself' (Jooma 1997: 62). Guest (2001: 1) points out that classifying others as cannibals is the means of justifying their oppression based on the 'eat or be eaten rule'. The word 'cannibalism' is rooted in the colonial discourse to undermine the 'political, social and economic power' of the other, using labels such as savage and uncivilised. This conception metaphorically emphasises the power dynamics between the eaters 'recipient' and the eaten 'benefactors'. The proverb '*Lehu la gago le ya mphidisha*' emphasises the figurative connotations where the 'eating' is not necessarily the physical ingestion of the flesh, but rather symbolic in nature. In this case, the proverb highlights the metaphorical cannibalism where individuals exhaust other people's opportunities, reducing them to be 'lifeless', meaning they are left depleted – relative to the situation. This consumption, translates into self-fulfilment, demonstrated in terms of money, food, material properties, book collection and social status. This essay aims to explore and discusses the metaphorical meaning embedded in some social context in which this proverb operates, highlighting the nuanced manifestation of this proverb in the consumer capitalist society.

Examples of case studies undertoned with metaphorical cannibalism are vividly portrayed in Zakes Mda's book '*ways of dying*' with the main character, Toloki, who relocated from his rural village to a city in search of a better life. Toloki struggled to get this better life because the urban areas were under white domination, and as such there were few opportunities for black[12] people. The story takes place during the transitional period in South Africa between 1990 and 1994, with the leaders of the liberation movements tied up in constant negotiations for change with the apartheid regime leaders. The confrontations between these forces (state and the excluded masses), often ended in violence, bloodshed and killings – with the apartheid government resisting change and liberation movements insisting on change of equal opportunities, in particular the inclusion of the black population into the mainstream resources of the country. Toloki found a niche of earning an income as a *professional mourner*, since death had become prevalent due to the uproars in the country 'today, as you know, there are funerals every day, because if the bereaved had to wait until the weekend then the mortuaries would overflow' (Mda 1995: 145).

Toloki wore a black costume and a hat as his 'work' attire to attend funerals, where his job description was to weep and make grief-ridden sounds during the procession. This space allowed him to cry out his own frustrations that haunted his childhood, from his father's disapproval of his existence to the constant mockery from the villagers. Funerals became his own therapeutical platforms, as not only did they permit him to mourn for his own life pains but also comfort the bereaved families and communities by sharing their grief of losing their loved ones (fellow comrade) and of the systematic oppression that limited their livelihood. Funerals 'nourished' Toloki with tangible remuneration in forms of either money, food, objects and materials, which he exchanged for money to sustain his survival. And also intangible the remuneration of healing his past and present scars – as he also re-connected with his childhood 'nemesis', Noria, at her son's funeral. Toloki 'hated' Noria because the villagers admired and applauded her beauty, especially Toloki's father who held Noria in high regard compared to his own son. Toloki's detestation of Noria transformed into desire and love after he saw the pain in her eyes during the burial and initiated a 'friendship' that turned to bring healing to both parties.

Mortuary rites (burial preparations, funerals, after-tears parties/celebrations and tombstone unveiling) especially within the black communities of South Africa tend to be a 'safety net' for the bereaved families and those in attendance, gathered to mourn with the bereaved. This distressing period evokes the spirit of solidarity, as death is inevitable to everyone, so it renders a collective effort to cope and manage with the anguish. The family and community elders avail themselves to assist with the prescribed rituals that are expected to be conducted before and after the burial, ensuring that proper protocol is adhered to for the deceased and the family. The mourners come to assist the family with the burial preparations. This assistance is multifaceted as it can be in the form of money, prayers, groceries, accommodation for the distant travellers and equipment ranging from chairs, pots, plates, gas stoves, utensils, etc. This assembly requires no invitation and, as such, it is open for any individual who wants to show compassion to the family. The open nature of these ceremonies is beneficial to those in attendance, as families are expected to provide food, beverages and prayer sessions, and the communal nature ensures social conversations – as means of showing their gratitude. Therefore, the proverb '*Lehu la gago le ya mphidisha*' is applicable in a sense that: those in need of food, especially the poverty stricken will be fed and sometimes three meals a day, the distressed from their personal problems get to attend daily prayer sessions and those who have not seen each other are given the space to re-connect. This forum allows estranged family members and neighbours to reunite in pain of their loss. As a result, mortuary rites are social spaces encompassed with varying forms of 'nourishments' for the involved parties. The phenomenon of tombstone unveiling and 'after tears parties' are therapeutic as people 'celebrate' the life of the deceased and also given the platform to show off their material possessions, re-emphasising their social and economic statuses (Jindra and Noret 2011:1).

Another case study is portrayed in the inheritance dynamics within some cultural groupings, and in most cases leading to family disputes. Asiimwe (2011: 236) conceptualises inheritance as a system of wealth accumulation, based on culturally and legally prescribed distribution. This wealth varies from possessions such as money, businesses, cars, houses, book or music collections, jewellery and clothing items. Bourdieu and Goody cited in Hann (2008: 150) share similar sentiments of inheritance being the procedure of 'maintaining status and power and reproducing symbolic capital'. South Africa, like other formerly colonised countries subscribe to the complex indigenous customary and western frameworks of inheritance and both these systems are underlined by unequal distribution. The indigenous customary practice is dictated by the cultural regulations which generally promote patriarchal ideologies, with predominantly male descendants preferred to inherit their father's possessions. The oldest son inherits the leadership responsibilities[13] and the youngest son inherits the father's house to continue with the livelihood with his own family. There are some exceptions, where women are allowed to inherit, in cases where the family only has female children

233

and in within communities that follow the matrilineal descent line (Asiimwe 2011: 237).

The western framework of inheritance is determined by the legislative laws that encourage individuals to choose beneficiaries to take over their possessions. This procedure orders people to document their last wishes in a will and testament to be read after their death, revealing who gets which possessions. Both these systems have a high risk of causing rifts between the survivors, depending on who gets which possessions because of the unequal distribution outline – while some survivors are left out completely and this is the greatest cause of disputes and fighting. The customary and legal laws are consulted to facilitate the resolution of disagreements such as where the family members disapprove of the elected beneficiaries and when they suspect foul play. The dynamics can range from children out of wedlock claiming a share from the estate to widows being 'stripped' of their belongings after the death of their spouses, especially if the husbands did not leave wills specifying their wives as the main benefactors (Gordon 2005: 2–3: Asiimwe 2011: 238). The politics around the distribution can go as far as family members becoming enemies and, in worse cases, killing each other to access the deceased's possessions. Therefore, the systems of inheritance in South Africa function on the basis of people 'gaining' after the death of the 'owner', enriching only the exclusive survivors.

There are many more incidences in everyday interactions that highlight different shades of the subtle consuming and cannibalistic relationships, but this essay concentrates on two particular themes that emerged when I was conversing with different people for my doctorate research. The first case study is the insurance policy scams where people take out life and funeral insurances in the name of the individuals, and they receive pay-outs after those individuals are deceased but they do not use the money for funeral arrangements. Instead they take the money for their own purposes, thus using the death of those individuals to enrich their lives. The second theme is the rising suspicion of 'Nyaope boys' as they are known smoking human cremated ashes. This phenomenon became known (to me at

234

least) in South Africa when the late South African music icon, Brenda Fassie (who was known as the Madonna of Soweto), who was also struggling with drug addiction was rumoured to have smoked her mother's cremated ashes.

The investment of 'life'

The end of the apartheid dispensation in South Africa was synonymous with hope and promise of a better life for all, especially for the previously disadvantaged and marginalised groupings. These previously disadvantaged groupings were eligible to contribute to the landscapes that they were formerly denied such as political, spiritual, economic, legislative and educational sectors of the country. They were officially recognised as citizens which means they could be part of practices such as voting for the government leadership, occupy employment positions that were only for the selected[14] and build a 'credit-worth' life to be able to take out loans and invest their money to improve their standard of being and living. The upward mobility saw the rapid growth and the emergence of the new black middle class which opened up opportunities to be exploited and catered for within the micro lending and micro insurance businesses. The 'new' consumers welcomed the prospects of borrowing and investing their money as means of securing a better life but this came at a cost of credit starting to be commercialised. This credit goes beyond 'material consumerism but to satisfy the desire for what felt necessary' (James 2014: 20). The satisfaction of this desire for some people translates into providing a memorable end-of-life gathering in the name of the deceased, by hosting an honourable and 'dignified' farewell occasion.

The 'dignity' underlining this event is relative as different groupings have subjective meanings and construction of this notion. The *Concise Oxford Dictionary* defines dignity as 'the state or quality of being worthy of honour or respect'. Some people quantify 'dignity' to a good and decent funeral, where the proceedings go as planned with minimum disruptions. The success of the occasion relies on the fulfilment of the social obligations of: informing 'relevant' people about the death, producing necessary documentation, ensuring that rituals are correctly observed, making arrangements with the mortuary or funeral undertakers in time, preparing catering services (burial societies), arranging transportation and overseeing that mourners are dressed according to the cultural protocol. Thus, making sure that everybody in attendance is well looked after and the deceased is sent off in a respectful manner (Ranger 2004: 119; Golomski 2015: 360; Lee and Vaughan 2008: 346). The burial location constitutes a 'dignified' funeral amongst many African societies, as it symbolises the completion of the cycle of life for the deceased – the conclusion of their life journey with their physical bodies returned to the soil that observed their birth, to re-unite with their ancestors. The migrants are repatriated to their place of origin 'home' for eternal rest (Nunez and Wheeler 2012: 211–212). Geschiere and Nyamnjoh (2000: 434) resonate this sentiment of the significance of burial place, 'where one is buried is the crucial criterion of where one belongs'.

Other people measure 'dignity' based on monetary value which is attached to the 'honour' bestowed on the deceased. The sentiments of respect and honour are common in both these conceptions; however this grouping particularly expresses them in financial terms. Van der Geest (1997: 541) said 'funeral celebrations are unthinkable without the ingredient of money'. The deceased is sent off in a 'dignified' funeral conducted by classy undertakers that provide luxurious products and services. The deceased is placed in a coffin (bearing a heavy price tag) that is displayed to the mourners as a sign of 'respect and love' that the family has for the deceased. These expensive coffins are covered in concrete once in a grave to avoid theft. Thus, funerals have evolved into spaces characterised by 'power, wealth and status' (Kotze et al. 2012: 760). Therefore, 'dignified' funerals reflect more on the survivors than the deceased, as one elderly community member echoes this sentiment – 'as I am sitting here now, if I die and my people don't give me a fitting funeral, it will be a disgrace to them' (Van der Geest 1995: 35).

The insurance and advertising industry has 'cashed' in on this notion of 'dignity' turning this *desire* into a commodity. The South

African Broadcasting Corporation (SABC) runs frequent commercials encouraging customers to 'purchase' from the wide-ranging funeral cover packages of different insurance companies, suitable to their 'pockets' and needs. The customers are reminded that death is inevitable and as such they need to at least be financially prepared for this unavoidable anguish and be in a better position to provide a 'dignified' funeral for themselves and their loved ones. Insurance companies make use of the prominent South African celebrities such as the late Hugh Masekela (who was affectionately known as 'Bra Hugh' by his supporters) as their brand ambassadors; to attract customers, increase the sales and to allure people to join a company that is 'certified' by the renowned member of the society. Assupol utilises Bra Hugh's status to appeal to the potential and loyal customers as this brand personifies a South African music legend, who was respected and his association with the company translates to high quality services, even more so now that he has passed as his legacy will live on within the Assupol ranks, attracting even more customers.

The importance attached to 'dignified' funerals, in particular within the middle and low classes of the black community, results in the majority of them seeking refuge in both the formal and informal microinsurance sectors. This movement comes with financial implications and also the liberty of being involved in the preparation of their own and family members' decent funerals, at least assist in the alleviation of the monetary constrains during the distressful time. Informal microinsurance is termed 'burial societies' in South Africa and it functions as an informal insurance scheme or collaboration institution that absorbs some cultural requirements as means of showing support to the bereaved families. The membership of these burial societies is on a voluntary basis as they are self-governed and they have survived decades of structural discrimination because of the trust and self-reliance of the community (Dandala and Moraka 1990: 2; Semenya 2013: 698–699; Bester et al. 2005:1).

There are different types of burial societies with the common goal of reducing burial pressure and membership is fluid. '*Aretsebaneng*' translates into 'let us know each other' and consist only of family members, and assistance reaches to other events such as weddings and parties. Block societies consist only of members living within the same residential block and the street society with members from the same street. These mutual-assistance-based institutions provide resources such as funds, groceries, domestic work and attendance of daily prayers (and if applicable night vigils) to assist the family to provide a 'dignified' burial. They also strive to provide services that are accessible and reliable like their counterparts within the formal insurance sector, even though this informal sector is not regulated (Dandala and Moraka 1990: 2; Semenya 2013: 698–699).

Ramsay and Arcila (2013: 64–65) argue that life insurance and funeral (burial) insurance are the most common products 'sold/bought' in the formal insurance sector in developing countries and South Africa is not different. These formal insurance policies serve as a protection veil against threats such as death, illness and property loss, in exchange for monthly premium payments. The life insurance (loan protection insurance) is compulsory for the consumers who are in search of a loan. This policy has two general functions of covering the 'loss that the lender may incur upon the death of a borrower and it relieves the borrower's family of the burden of repaying the remaining loan, thus ensuring that the debt dies with the debtor' (Ramsay and Arcila 2013: 64). Funeral insurance[15] is a 'stand alone' policy aimed to primarily cover the expenses of funeral arrangements. The formal insurer is not the only enterprise offering funeral policies but also undertakers/funeral parlours, soccer teams and retail shops. The policy offers different packages depending on the affordability power of the policy holder. However the policy holder gets a cash payment when they claim and they are not dictated to on how to use their investment. The flexibility and widespread nature of funeral insurance poses a challenge to regulate[16] and police this sector, and people have identified and taken advantage of this loophole by committing different forms of fraudulent acts to 'invest and access' the money (Ramsay and Arcila 2013: 64; Bester, et al. 2005:1).

The following themes emerged during my conversations describing different forms of fraudulent practices concerning life and funeral insurance and the proverb '*Lehu la gago le ya mphidisha*' was used explicitly to describe this phenomenon. However there is dearth[17] in literature on these behaviours. Firstly, the policy holders[18] would include dependants[19] that are on the verge of death (either through illness or aging) and also those who are exposed to 'risky' behaviours such as regular drinking in nightclubs/taverns? where they are often involved in quarrels that manifest into physical contact (fighting). The outcome of their lifestyles has landed them in emergency rooms with stab wounds, gunshots and broken legs/arms. Therefore, these individuals are in the face of death and one can expect such news at any moment. Some policy holders have decided to 'benefit' from these individuals because their death converts into an income or rather 'pay back' from their investment.

Secondly, policy holders are not obligated to disclose the amount which they have 'invested on the lives' of the dependants to the family members, so after the claim payout, they only contribute a portion towards the funeral arrangements – in most cases they will offer to buy the livestock to be slaughtered and groceries such as vegetables, mealie meal, flour, sugar, tea and spices. The remainder of the money goes into their pockets to pursue their own purposes. These actions have the potential to cause disputes within the family (siblings because burial of a parent should be handled equally), especially if they are aware that some people only contributed a fraction of their budget. Lastly, some funeral policies do not limit the number of dependants nor question their relations to the policy holders, so some people include their extended family members, friends and neighbours to increase their 'investment' and when these dependants pass away, the policy holders claim the money and contribute minimally towards the burial preparations. There are cases where the policy holders do not contribute at all towards the funeral and come up with excuses to get the relevant documentation to be able to claim from the insurer. People have taken advantage of the commercialisation of death by enhancing their own standard of living.

In situations where the policy holder passes away, the money goes out to the beneficiary, who would have been indicated when the policy holder first signed up. Allocation of the beneficiary is a compulsory act and policy holders are expected to alert these companies when their beneficiaries are incapacitated through either being committed to a facility, death, injury and other means of being out of action. In such cases, the policy holders are encouraged to allocate new beneficiaries. It becomes a challenge if a policy holder passes away and the beneficiary issue is not sorted because the companies find it difficult to release that money, so usually the state will intervene to assist in allocation of suitable people based on the dynamics of the family.

One person narrated a story of a mother who passed away and made her five children the beneficiaries; however the siblings kicked out the brother who stayed with the mother in the house because of the system of inheritance and decided to rent the house and equally distribute the rentals. The brother that was kicked out was not pleased with the decision but 'culture' was not on his side. He secured well-remunerated employment that afforded him a house and a car. The insurer summoned the siblings to alert them about their mother's money but five signatures were needed to release the funds, so the kicked out brother refused to sign as means of revenge for the actions and decisions taken against him. This issue was critical because the siblings were in need of the money but their brother stood as a stumbling block and he had 'divorced' the siblings. This matter could escalate the conflict that already existed to the point of murder because that is what the brother told them 'you will receive the money over my dead body'. So his death could be one way of ensuring the release of the money.

The saga of human ashes

Substance (drug) abuse is a worldwide catastrophe that is on the increase and the most commonly used drugs in South Africa are mandrax, white pipe (mixture of cannabis and mandrax), heroin, tik (methamphetamine), Nyaope and prescription/over-the-counter medication (National Drug Master Plan 2006–2011). The Nyaope[20] drug stands out because of the devastating impact caused in the townships across South Africa. This specific drug is well documented in the media publications: newspapers, television programmes, documentaries and various platforms of the internet. The reports indicate that it first emerged in the early 2000s in the Pretoria townships of Mamelodi and Shosanguve. The demographic popularity of Nyaope is what makes it unique from other drugs because it is almost exclusively used by the black community, in particular the youth with boys being great in numbers (Mokwena 2016: 138; National Drug Master Plan 2006–2011).

The popularity is due to the impact on social conditions within townships of high rate of unemployment, lack of recreational facilities and opportunities, poverty and crime. Nyaope is easily accessible because it is relatively cheap compared to other drugs and the difficulty involved in monitoring and policing the dealers, as it was classified an illegal drug in 2014. The Nyaope users tend to have poor personal hygiene, slow movements and confused appearances. They are notorious for committing criminal activities to maintain their habit, earning themselves the title 'Nyaope boys'. Their addiction does not only affect them but also their families and neighbours as they steal objects from electrical appliances, jewellery, clothes, blankets, plates to cutlery – basically if it has an economic value, it becomes target for the 'Nyaope boys' (Mokwena 2016: 138; National Drug Master Plan 2006–2011).

There are uncertainties regarding the ingredients contained in the Nyaope drug because they are constantly changing but the Department of Social Development cited heroine and cannabis as the main constituents which are mixed with lethal cutting agents. Cutting agents or adulterants are the substances that are diluted with the main ingredients and they tend to be less expensive. Rat poison, soap powder and the Anti-Retro Virals (ARVs) have been recorded as part of the 'ever-changing' cutting agents. The ARVs are targeted because they contain ingredients that possess 'hallucinogenic effects', especially Efivarenz.[21] The side effect of hallucinating attracts the 'Nyaope boys' because it assists with the 'getting high'[22] process by re-designing the concoction of the drug. ARVs are easily accessible because of the high number of people who receive the treatment for free from the health-care facilities across the country. As a result, ARVs are commodified with some people selling their pills (as they know that the health care will replace the pills) and in some cases the patients are robbed. Patients are required to report the matter to the South African Police Service to acquire a case number before they are given another prescription. Some users are rumoured to contract HIV deliberately to access this treatment. This matter is a national crisis, more intense in some areas such as Tshwane/Pretoria, Ethekwini/Durban and Emalahleni/Witbank (Chinouya et al. 2014: 114–120)

The Nyaope drug is highly addictive because of its uncertain nature as the content is constantly altered. There are rumours circulating in my home town, Emalahleni in Mpumalanga province, of the 'latest' cutting agent being an old sock which is burned and the remains are added into the concoction of Nyaope. This old sock is 'believed' to possess certain elements that, after burning, can help users to get 'high'. The withdrawal symptoms are intense and the users experience great difficulties (manifesting into physical pains) when attempting to quit smoking. There is a lack of drug rehabilitation facilities and services in the public sector, so the majority of families struggle to afford the services within the private sector because of the escalating unemployment rates. Because of the severity of the drug, it can at least take up to a year to be rehabilitated as such there are high rates of relapses. Family plays an important role in successfully rehabilitating a Nyaope addict, so this process requires support from the social networks of the addict – that is if they have not burnt those bridges by stealing or hurting them. Some 'Nyaope boys' resort to alternative rehabilitation methods such as locking themselves up as means of isolation from the social environment which encourages the smoking (Mokwena 2016: 138).

The latest trend circulating in the media and communities of the cutting agent added into the concoction of Nyaope are cremated human ashes. The walls of remembrance in most cemeteries across the country have been vandalised and emptied for criminal purposes, such as theft of jewellery and other accessories families 'bury' with their beloved deceased. The state of the cemeteries has deteriorated

242

with some walls completely emptied. The Nyaope users are infamous for their reckless actions such as physically injecting a 'high' person's blood into their own bloodstream[23] but this latest trend has left many shocked at using human cremated ashes to 'spice' up their Nyaope (Venter and Lotriet 2017). One person I was conversing with about the state of the cemeteries across the country narrated their shock when they realised the criminal purposes have reached to actual human remains. In the past, the walls would be vandalised and the ashes left behind but lately the walls are left completely empty – leaving behind letters and/or documents the family 'buried' along with the deceased. At first they suspected 'dark arts or Satanism rituals' but now rumours have emerged of the 'Nyaope boys' stealing these cremated ashes to smoke them.

The phenomenon of 'utilising' human cremated ashes is not new, as it was also traced amongst the loyal followers of Wally Hope, a founder of the 'Stonehenge people's free festival' in Britain who died in 1975. His followers against all odds (the state interference) continued with Wally's legacy and commemorating his death by hosting the festivals in his honour. These festivals took on spiritual and cultural significance with his memory being animated, and seen as an ancestor who was present in these gatherings. The festival of 1975 was organised for his cremated ashes to be scattered by his fans in Stonehenge – with each taking a handful and dispersing them on the ground. A child dipped his fingers in the box containing the cremated ashes and licked, some people followed this trend and also consumed Wally's ashes (Harvey 2004: 255–257). This 'unintended' ritual consumption gained meaning because it reinstated Wally's presence to his loyalists, who contextualised his presence as 'metaphysical' and his scattered ashes in Stonehenge as a 'charter of the festival and solstice celebration' (Harvey 2004: 258).

Therefore, human ashes serve different purposes in various spaces but the smoking of cremated ashes is not comprehendible to many people, making it a sensitive subject. The person, whom I was conversing with regarding the state of the cemeteries in South Africa, continued to narrate about how it was unthinkable to imagine the remains of loved ones being an ingredient of a drug. The effects are similar to those of the '*muti* killings' (discussed in the introduction of this essay) where the organs and body parts are reduced to ingredients in a supernatural concoction. The person continued to wonder if families are alerted or if the families report these missing ashes to the South African Police Service. I took advantage of my home town as it is drug infested and spoke to neighbours and some community members and they all are aware of the 'rumour' but they have never physically seen these users smoking the human cremated ashes. Another person further explained their concerns of this matter sympathising with those affected families but at the same time did not see this as a problem for black families as cremation is still a foreign practice. Another person discredited the Nyaope users as they will say anything (to the extent of lying) and demand incentives in return to feed their addiction, so the rumour remains a mystery. The majority wondered where these 'Nyaope boys' got this idea and whether cremated human ashes really can get one 'high'.

A young male painted a scenario for me in an attempt to solve the mystery of why these 'Nyaope boys' resorted to smoking human cremated ashes. He asked me if I was familiar with a movie, *How High*, that came out in 2001 and he continued to tell me story line. It features two United States of America Hip Hop Legends known as Method Man and Redman who are still in high school and they are both addicted to marijuana (cannabis). Method Man grew the plant and he mistakenly used the cremated ashes of their friend as a fertiliser in one batch. When they smoked that particular batch, they were visited by the ghost of the friend only visible to them, when they were in a 'high' state. The ghost friend would talk to them and give them guidance to the extent of giving them answers during the test/examination sessions. This man wondered if the 'Nyaope boys' got the idea from this movie, with similar aspirations in seeking existential answers for their deteriorating lives.

Luhanga (2017) reiterates the ambiguity of this phenomenon (which seems to be a national crisis) being registered or known by the authorities – Captain Lesibana Molokomme from the Norkem Park police station confirmed that cases of vandalism had been reported in Mooifontein cemetery but could not confirm if those ashes were stolen by the 'Nyaope boys'. Jenny Moodley from Johannesburg City Parks said no cases were reported regarding stolen human ashes. Eileen du Toit reported her mother's missing ashes that were allegedly stolen from the bedroom closet in her house. This incident traumatised her and the family to the extent of their placing the house on the market, as they could not continue staying 'without' her mother. Eileen continued to say 'You don't feel safe anymore, you feel violated. My mother lived with us in this very house, it's very difficult' (Lotriet 2017).

It is evident that cremated human ashes are in demand and it does not matter where they are stored (cemeteries, churches or homes) as they are a current target, even though the reasons are not quite clearly supported by empirical research but that does not expel the existence of this form of crisis which has been widely reported in newspaper outlets such as the *Daily Sun*, *Sowetan*, *Citizen* and *Krugersdorp News*. This 'rumoured' trend leaves question marks of whether this form of metaphorical cannibalism really nourishes an individual or moves them closer to their own graves. There are spiritual and psychological implications involved in these incidences and they are bound to take their cause up on the perpetrators, turning them into victims of their own actions. If the reports and the conversations (I had with numerous people) have base then the 'Nyaope boys' do benefit from these ashes as they fuel up their addiction, which is their primary concern at that particular moment. However, their addiction comes at a cost, leaving the deceased's remains extinct and the families in anguish as the remains of their loved ones have vanished.

Conclusion

Cannibalism is still part of everyday life as it continues to be practised worldwide regardless of the different forms in which it manifests. The modern society tends to shy away from the practice of cannibalism regarding it as 'savage and uncivilised' but this denial does not eliminate its existence. The introductory chapter (Nyamnjoh, this volume) mentions Lévi-Strauss's argument that 'cannibalism is cannibalism, symbolic or real, direct or indirect, virtual or otherwise'. This essay echoes Lévi-Strauss's argument of cannibalism's continual existence in different societies, 'wearing' various faces. The practice and understanding of cannibalism remain tainted with negative implications, especially in the light of the consumer capitalist societies, where life and death are commodified for personal profit and sustenance. This behaviour is demonstrated by the Sepedi proverb '*Lehu la gago le ya mphidisha*' which is the basis of the argument of this essay. This proverb demonstrates literal and metaphorical meanings of different situations where people 'nourish' themselves from the demise or death of others. These people 'ingest' the benefits that came at a cost of others. It can be physical ingesting such as the ever rising phenomenon of 'muti-killings' or medicinal cannibalism with modern medicine – to the figurative ingestion such as the 'Nyaope boys' mixing the human cremated ashes with other ingredients in the smoking concoction and insurance policy holders' deceitful actions of taking out funeral policies for dependants and 'cash' in after their death, seeing their lives as a form of economic and financial investment.

Endnotes

[1] Is referred to as Northern Sotho and forms part of the Sesotho (South Sotho, Tswana and Sepedi/North Sotho) group languages. Sepedi is also one of the Official languages in South Africa (Brenzinger 2017: 39).

[2] 'myths, legends, anecdotes, songs, riddles, sayings etc.'(Gogoi 2017: 52-53).

[3] Nigerian novelist and a founder of 'school of Achebe' who defined and established the 'Nigerian tradition in the novel, a tradition that takes its roots from folk culture and creatively make use of proverbs, legends, folktales and local myths'. Thus giving the expression to the Nigerian and by extension to the African culture. Achebe's life work was to rehabilitate the image of African dignity (by incorporating oral art into literary art) that was 'bruised and damaged by the colonial master' (Nnolim 2011: 30).

[4] Used interchangeably with funerary cannibalism, funerary anthropophagy, compassion cannibalism and endocannibalism, where the eating ritual takes place within the same social group (Conklin 2001: xxiv).

[5] The process of disconnection is literal with relatives burning all the belongings of the deceased including the house, the neighbours modifying their houses by eradicating old doors to make new ones a different side of the house and old walking paths being abandoned, and new paths being created (Conklin 2001:84).

[6] Different body parts from different individuals are used for different purposes and occasions. The usage of these body parts is contextual, meaning the purpose/reasons are specific to each individual's specific needs at that particular time.

[7] The concept 'muti' (which can also be spelled 'Muthi') is derived from the Nguni languages (Zulu, Ndebele, Swati and Xhosa) in South Africa referring to the concoction (liquid or ointment) made from herbs and/or plants containing healing properties. This definition is recognised by the World Health Organisation (WHO), however the usage of human body parts and organs to make muti is a harmful practice which is considered as witchcraft and/or satanic (Swart 2012:70; the Human Science Research Council 2010).

[8] They also have economic value and they are sold to interested parties in the black market, where different people buy these parts and organs for a variety of reasons, but muti making being the most common. It is also believed that body parts and organs of people of lighter skin complexion (white people and people with albinism) possess special supernatural or magical properties of attracting money. Their fat is more effective and another way of accessing this fat is to have a relationship with medical practitioners especially those who work in the surgery facilities (Phatoli, Bila and Ross 2015: 2).

[9] '[M]edicinal preparation of the remains of an embalmed, dried, or otherwise "prepared" human body that had ideally met with sudden, preferably violent death' (Gordon-Grube 1988: 406).

[10] Harvey (2004: 259) reports the existence of evidence indicating the United States of America and Europe's involvement in the trade of human body parts and organs for medicinal purposes in the 20th century.

[11] The print and visual media have widely reported these cannibalism incidences usually linked to muti sagas across the country. These reports indicated that these muti killings have been a national crisis since the mid-1990s, with each province having its share of these experiences (Petrus

2011: 2). Grave mutilation of corpses is also a well-reported issue at the police stations and media houses, with television programmes (such as Leihlo la Sechaba on SABC 2) documenting the community speaking out on how the dead are still tormented as their lifeless bodies have now transitioned into being potent and attractive to those who use unorthodox mechanisms to obtain power. These communities fear for themselves and their dead it as none of them are safe from these practices and their perpetrators.

[12] Socially constructed racial categories of 'Black' and 'white' that are entrenched in the South African society from the era of apartheid which promoted racial segregation. 'Black' roughly refers to the groupings that were disadvantaged during the apartheid regime, including the so-called 'Coloureds' and 'Indians'. This essay loosely uses the term 'Black' to address both the Black Africans and Coloured communities, especially those residing in the urban and peri-urban areas.

[13] These responsibilities range from decision making for the entire family (usually their siblings and children, such as electing a delegate to represent the family during *lobola/magadi* negotiations to managing livestock – in cases where the family has a rural homestead.

[14] The selected refers to the white South Africans and they were the only group deemed to enjoy the resources of the country, they received quality education, health care, employment, housing and other materials during the apartheid regime.

[15] For the purpose of this essay, funeral insurance and funeral policy(cies) are used interchangeably.

[16] Laws are regulated in order to curb or address these problems but people still find ways of working around these laws. In the past, death certificates and identity documents of both the policy holder and the deceased were requested upon release of the funds. But today companies also want the notification of death document obtained from either the hospital or mortuary.

[17] This incident is briefly mentioned in the article 'Introduction: Themes in the Study of Death and Loss in Africa' authored by Lee and Vaughan 2012.

[18] The individuals who are responsible for the payment on the insurance cover are usually the breadwinners or have some sort of monthly income to be able to pay the instalments.

[19] The people whom the policy holders include in the insurance cover packages and they pay accordingly on a monthly basis.

[20] In KwaZulu-Natal province it is known as 'Whoonga'. It is purchased or bought in a powder form that is white in colour.

[21] 'Is a non-nucleoside reverse transcriptase inhibitor (NNRTI), which works by blocking the progression of HIV and AIDS' (Chinouya et al. 2014: 118–119).

[22] 'Drowsiness and relaxation which are similar to effects of the heroin drug. Continued use is associated with the development of tolerance, and addicts therefore resort to using increasingly greater and more frequent amounts of the drug to achieve the same 'high' (Mokwena 2016: 138).

[23] This phenomenon is known as 'Bluetooth' and it was reported to have first emerged in the Tshwane region.

References

Alimi, S. A. (2012) 'A Study of the Use of Proverbs as a literary Device in Achebe's Things Fall Apart and Arrow of God', *International Journal of Academic Research in Business and Social Sciences* Vol. 2(3): 121–127.

Asiimwe, F. A. (2011) 'Gender, Inheritance laws and Practice: Experience of Urban Windows in Uganda', in M. S. Mapadimeng, and S. Khan (eds) *Contemporary Social Issues in Africa: Cases in Gaborone, Kampala and Durban*, Pretoria: Africa Institute of South Africa, pp. 236–253.

Barley, N. (1995) *Dancing on the Grave: Encounters with Death*, London: Abacus.

Bester, H. Chamberlain, D. Short, R., and Walker, R. (2005) *A Regulatory Review of Formal and Informal Funeral Insurance Markets in South Africa*, Genesis Analytics Research Paper Prepared for the FinMark Trust.

Brenzinger, M. (2017) 'Eleven Official Languages and more: Legislation and Language Policies in South Africa', *Journal of Language and Law* 67, pp. 38–54.

Carrasco, D. (1995) 'Cosmic Jaws: We Eat the Gods and the Gods Eat Us', *Journal of the American Academy of Religion*, Vol. 63(3): 429–463.

Chinouya, M., Rikhotso, S. R., Ngunyulu, R. N., Peu, M. D. Mataboge, M. L. S., Mulaudzi, F. M., and Jiyane, P. M. (2014) '"Some Mix it with Other Things to Smoke": Perceived Use and Misuse of ARV by Street Thugs in Tshwane District, South Africa', *African Journal for Physical, Health Education, Recreation and Dance*, Vol. 1(1): 113–126.

Conklin, B. A.(1995) '"Thus Are Our Bodies, Thus was Our Customs": Mortuary Cannibalism in an Amazonian Society', *American Ethnologist*, Vol. 22(1): 75–101.

Conklin, B. A. (2001) *Consuming Grief: Compassionate Cannibalism in an Amazonian Society*, Austin: University of Texas Press.

Dandala, H. M., and Moraka, K. (1990) *Masicwabisane/A re Bolokaneng*, Braamfontein: Stokaville.

Fausto, C. (2007) 'Feasting on People Eating Animals and Humans in the Amazonia', *Current Anthropology*, Vol. 48(4): 497–530.

Geschiere, P. and Nyamnjoh, F. (2000) "Capitalism and Autochthony: The Seesaw of Mobility and Belonging" *Public Culture* Vol.12(2):423-452.

Gogoi, G. A. (2017) 'A Study on Chinua Achebe's Use of Proverbs in Things Fall Apart and No Longer at Ease', *Journal of Humanities and Social Science*, Vol. 22(12): 52–56.

Golomski, C. (2015) 'Urban Cemeteries in Swaziland: Materialising Dignity', *Anthropology Southern Africa*, Vol. 38: 360–371.

Gordon, R. (2005) 'Introduction: On the Perniciousness of Inheritance Problems', in *Gender and Advocacy Project: The Meanings of Inheritance: Perspectives on Namibian Inheritance Practices*, Windhoek: Legal Assistant Centre.

Gordon-Grube, K. (1988) 'Anthropology in Post-Renaissance Europe: The Tradition of Medicinal Cannibalism', *American Anthropologist*, Vol. 90: 405–409.

Guest, K. (2001) 'Introduction: Cannibalism and the Boundaries of Identity', in K. Guest (ed) *Eating Their Words: Cannibalism and the Boundaries of Cultural Identity*, New York: State University of New York Press, pp. 1–9.

Hann, C. (2008) 'Reproduction and Inheritance: Goody Revisited', *Annual Review of Anthropology*, Vol. 37: 145–158.

Harvey, G. (2004) 'Endo-cannibalism in the Making of a Recent British Ancestor', *Mortality* Vol. 9(3): 255–267.

Henderson, H. (2013) 'Cannibalistic Delight: Human Consumption in Contemporary German Literature', *The Journal of Popular Culture*, Vol. 46(4): 831–846.

Himmelman, P. K. (1997) 'The Medicinal Body: An Analysis of Medicinal Cannibalism in Europe, 1300–1700', *Dialectical Anthropology*, Vol. 22(2): 183–203.

Human Science Research Council (2010) 'Tsiriledzani: Understanding the Dimension of Human Trafficking in Southern Africa', *Research Report*, available from: <http://www.hsrc.ac.za/Document-3562phtml>.

Ihueze, A. O., and Umeasiegbu, R. (2015) 'Proverb Usage in African Literature', *International Journal of Humanities and Social Science Invention*, Vol. 4(3): 30–35.

James, D. (2014) 'Deeper into a Hole? Borrowing and Lending in South Africa', *Current Anthropology*, Vol. 55(9): 17–29.

Jindra, M., and Noret, J. (2011) 'Funerals in Africa: An Introduction', in: M. Jindra, and J. Noret (eds) *Funerals in Africa: Explorations of a Social Phenomenon*, New York: Berghahn, pp. 1–15.

Jooma, M. (1997) 'Robinson Crusoe Inc. (Corporates): Domestic economy, Incest and the Trope of Cannibalism', *Lit: Literature Interpretation Theory*, Vol. 8(1): 61–81.

Kotze, E., Els, L. and Rajuili-Masilo, N. (2012) ""Women ... Mourn and Men Carry on": African Women Storying Mourning Practices: A South African Example', *Death Studies*, Vol. 36(8): 742–766.

Labuschagne, G. (2004) 'Features and Investigative implications of Muti Murder in South Africa', *Journal of Investigative Psychology and Offender Profiling*, Vol. 1: 191–206.

Lee, R., and Vaughan, M. (2008) 'Death and Dying in the History of Africa since 1800', *Journal of African History*, Vol. 49: 341–359.

Lee, R., and Vaughan, M. (2012) 'Introduction: Themes in the Study of Death and Loss in Africa', *African Studies*, Vol. 71(2): 163–173.

Lotriet, A. (2017) 'Nyaope Addicts Smoking Cremated People's Ashes?', *Krugersdorp News*, 20 June, viewed 29 January 2018, <https://krugersdorpnews.co.za/328873/nyaope-addicts-smoking-cremated-peoples-ashes/>.

Luhanga, E. (2017) 'Addicts Smoke Human Ashes', *Daily Sun newspaper*, 22 May 2017.

Mda, Z. (1995) *Ways of Dying*, Cape Town: Oxford University Press Southern Africa.

Mokwena, K. (2016) '"Consider our Plight": A Cry for Help from Nyaope Users', *Health SA Gesondheid*, Vol. 2: 137–142.

National Drug Master Plan 2006–2011, Department of Social Development.

Niehaus, I. (2013) *Witchcraft and a New Life in the New South Africa*, New York: Cambridge University Press.

Nnolim, C. E. (2011) 'Chinua Achebe: A Re-Assessment', *Tydskrif Vir Letterkunde*, Vol. 48(1): 39–50.

Noble, L. (2003) '"And Make Two Pasties of Your Shameful Heads": Medicinal Cannibalism and Healing the Body Politics in "Titus Andronicus"', *ELH*, Vol. 70(3): 677–708.

Nunez, L., and Wheeler, B. (2012) 'Chronicles of Death Out of Place: Management of Migrant Death in Johannesburg', *African Studies*, Vol. 71(2): 212–233.

Olifants, N. (2017) 'Dark Secret of Poor Villagers "Tired of Eating Human Flesh": Local Inyanga Blows Whistle on Gruesome Practice in KZN Town', *Sunday Times*, 27 August, viewed 10 December 2017, <https://www.timeslive.co.za/sunday-times/news/2017-08-26-dark-secrets-of-poor-villagers--tired-of--eating-human--flesh/>.

Petrus, T. (2011) 'Defining Witchcraft-related Crime in the Eastern Cape Province of South Africa', *International Journal of Sociology and Anthropology*, Vol. 3(1): 1–8.

Phatoli, R., Bila, N., & Ross, E. (2015) 'Being black in a white skin: Beliefs and stereotypes around albinism at a South African university', *African Journal of Disability*, Vol. 4(1): 1–10.

Pieterse, C. (2017) 'Hundreds Confess to Eating Human Flesh', *News 24*, 22 August, viewed 10 December 2017, <https://www.news24.com/SouthAfrica/News/hundreds-confess-to-eating-humans-20170821>.

Ramsay, C. M., and Arcila, L. D. (2013) 'Pricing Funeral (Burial) Insurance in a Micro insurance World with Emphasis on Africa', *North American Actuarial Journal*, Vol. 17(1): 63–83.

Ranger, T. (2004) 'Dignifying Death: The Politics of Burial in Bulawayo', *Journal of Religion in Africa*, Vol. 34(1–2): 110–144.

Scheper-Hughes, N. (2001a) 'Bodies for Sale – Whole or in Parts', *Body & Society*, Vol. 7(2-3): 1–8.

Scheper-Hughes, N. (2001b) 'Commodity Fetishism in Organs Trafficking', *Body & Society*, Vol. 7(2–3): 31–62.

Scheper-Hughes, N. (2001c) 'Neo-Cannibalism: The Global Trade in Human Organs: Special Issue on the Body and Being Human', *Hedgehog Review*, Vol. 3(2): 79–99.

Scheper-Hughes, N. (2004) 'Parts unknown: Undercover Ethnography of the Organs-trafficking Underworld', *Ethnography*, Vol. 5(1): 29–73.

Semenya, D. K. (2013) 'Burial Society versus the Church in the Black Society of South Africa: A Pastoral Response', *Verbum et Ecclesia*, Vol. 34(1): 698–707.

Shaw, R. (2001) 'Cannibal Transformation: Colonial and Commodification in the Sierra Leone Hinterland', in H. L. Moore, and T. Sanders (eds): *Magical Interpretations, MaterialRealities: Modernity, Witchcraft and the Occult in Postcolonial Africa*, London: Routledge, 50–70.

Sibanda, N. (2015) 'An Analysis of the Significance of Myths and Proverbs as African Philosophies of Peace and Justice: A Case of the Ndebele, Shona and Tonga Tribes from Zimbabwe and the Igbo from Nigeria', *Journal of the Humanities and Social Sciences*, Vol. 20(4): 1–6.

Stone, J. (2017) 'KZN Seems to Have a Bit of a Cannibal Problem', *Ocean Vibes*, 22 August, viewed 10 December 2017, <http://www.2oceansvibe.com/2017/08/21/kzn-seems-to-have-a-bit-of-a-cannibal-problem/>.

Swart, D. N. (2012) 'Human Trafficking and the Exploitation of Women and Children in a Southern and South African Context', *Child Abuse Research: A Southern African Journal*, Vol.13(1): 62–70.

Ukoma, A. N., Egwu, R. O. U., and Ogechukwu, C. I. E. (2016) 'African Traditional Religious Philosophy and Life Problems: Use of Proverbs, Idioms, Wise Saying and Folklores/Myths', *World Applied Science Journal*, Vol. 34(3): 323–329.

Van der Geest, S. (1995) 'Old People and Funerals in a Rural Ghanaian Community: Ambiguities in Family Care', *Southern African Journal of Gerontology*, Vol. 4(2): 33–40.

Van der Geest, S. (1997) 'Money and Respect: The Changing Value of Old Age in Rural Ghana', *Africa*, Vol. 67: 534–559.

Venter, J., and Lotriet, A. (2017) 'Are Drug Users Smoking Dead People's Ashes?', *Citizen*, 26 June viewed 29 January 2018, <https://citizen.co.za/news/1555609/doseofdeath-drug-users-smoking-dead-peoples-ashes/>.

Chapter 7

Rainbow Nation of the Flesh

Dominique Santos

'Food is food – be it for the belly, the mind and the soul or for the senses of the body, and be it solid, liquid, virtual or intangible' (Nyamnjoh, p. 33 in this volume)

The spectacular sexified cannibalisation of human bodies as a feature of the voracious consumer appetites of late capitalism is explored here through the lens of social life in Paradise, a lap dancing club in the province of Gauteng, South Africa in the early 21st century. The lap dancer is a form of exotic dancer, defined by Bernard et al. as 'one who removes all or most of her clothing in a sexually suggestive fashion to a paying audience' (2003: 2). That such a dance should be defined as 'exotic' is more telling of the normative moral and physical values of a narrowly defined euro-centric and heteronormative gaze, which veers between moral revulsion, desire for flesh and desire to extract wealth from the commodification of the bodies of others, from Saartjie Baartman to Josephine Baker. It is, as Berger would put it, a way of seeing that establishes the order of the world, unknowingly, without reflexivity (Berger 1972). The lap dancer comes on the heels of five centuries worth of industrial–consumer capitalism's development as cannibalistic practice, extracting energy and wealth literally from the bodies of others.

Practices of cannibalism which consume other bodies as a form of social dominance are currently being exposed and highlighted as the #metoo movement gathers momentum, exposing the extent to which bodies of mostly, though not always, women, have been commanded to satisfy the appetites of mostly, though not always, men in positions to grant favours or assert domination. Focusing in on the preparation for, and delivery of, exchanges that take place between female dancers and male customers, I explore the charged terrain of commodified sexualities as practices of eating in the highly ritualised, gendered and competitive environment of the lap-dancing club. A sense of new opportunities to consume and be consumed are heightened by the historical moment in which the club is located as the policy of Black Economic Empowerment is being introduced with a shift in perception by the club's management as to who might hold the keys to wealth and power, and which bodies are desirable. This is a microcosm of the negotiation of power sharing, through the practice of consuming lap dances, between emergent black elites and unchallenged white male privilege as a practice of feasting. The descriptions are drawn from participant observation in the club during a two-month period working as one of two resident DJ's, playing a continuous musical soundtrack during opening hours and calling girls on stage to dance.

Lap dancing clubs are features of cities and resorts around the world (Bott 2006), enjoying a surge of popularity in the early 21st century as an accessible, acceptable and glamorous adjunct of the sex trade. Lap dancing quickly became mainstream, losing its association with seedy strip clubs and attaining a reputation as a job where young women with the right look could make obscene amounts of money. The reality of guaranteed high earnings frequently fall apart in what is, in truth, a precarious profession, located in regimes of neo-liberal employment practices (Hardy & Sanders 2014; Bott 2006; Deshotels et al. 2012). The paying of house fees to work, a cut of each dance going to the club and unstable wages can result in being caught in cycles of debt. After slow nights, dancers can find that they *owe* money to the club in house fees. The self-employed status of dancers means no access to employee benefits such as sick pay, maternity leave, pensions or insurance. Thus, the owners of clubs maximise their own feasting on the fruits of dancer's bodies (Hardy & Sanders 2014:121). Despite these risks, there is still opportunity to make money for those who perfect the game, leaving another avenue of risk open which is the issue of feeling 'trapped' by lap-dancing work (Barton 2006; Colosi 2010; Maticka-Tyndale et al. 2000). As one efficient and professional dancer at Paradise in her fourth year working at the club remarked, 'I'd love to leave but the money is too good'.

To join the feasting of late consumer capitalism is to enter a realm of unlimited appetites. Like an enchanted banquet in a fairy tale that will never satisfy, bringing with it, 'Eternal cycles of indebtedness, manipulation, zombification and the never-ending search for fulfilment' (Nyamnjoh 2005:38). Nyamnjoh draws these allegories in the context of other forms of sexualised cannibalism. In Senegal, the figures of *diriyankes*, *disquettes* and *thiofs* jostle to maximise their potential to eat and be eaten. *Diriyankes* are older, generously built women who favour opulent traditional dress and the bought and paid for attentions of younger men. Younger, slimmer *disquettes* are the westernised girls who play the field for favours, both material and social. While these figures may seem in opposition, both emphasise the charms of women as commodity – whether the feast comes as virginity (both genuine and performed), the possession of bodies or skills as housekeepers.

The playing of patron *thiofs* offers to the girl cooking herself into the succulent *disquette* the opportunity of mobility in circumstances that might otherwise be severely limited by consuming poverty or limited opportunities (Nyamnjoh 2005: 305). This resonates with Bott's (2006) exploration of the world of British women who migrate to Tenerife to take up lap dancing. With all its risks and exploitations, stripping still appears as a glamorous and lucrative alternative to the drabness of council estate life or limitations of working class opportunities back in the UK. The metaphor of eating, in some shape or form, is never far from the scene. Examining the relationship between *disquettes* and *thiofs*, Nyamnjoh describes young, pretty girls from modest backgrounds literally fishing for the biggest catch, a man who can sexually transmit property or other kinds of social capital such as the marks needed to obtain university degrees (2005:305). Roberts et al., in the context of lap dancing, have discussed the 'sexual economy of Higher Education' (2010:14), drawing a direct correlation between the privatisation of education and rising participation in sexual commerce. That some lap dancers are using these jobs to fund their studies is documented by Lantz (2005), Duval-Smith (2006) and Roberts (2010). It is something that is considered appealing in the trade, used to market girls as more wholesome, removing some of the guilt from transactions – as Ward the owner of Paradise emphasises when he holds weekly meetings with the dancers – dancers are not trapped in degrading sex work, they are motivated young businesswomen simply paying their way through school.

Disquettes fish for and eat *thiofs*, while *thiofs* will feast on multiple *disquettes*. The game of mutual eating (though rarely from positions of social equality) is varied and complicated. Triangles of *disquettes*, *thiofs* and *diriyankes*, in which the boundaries of who is eating, by whom and how, are constantly being reassembled, abound. The rise of HIV as another consequence of sexual transmission attends to the risks of the socio-sexual cannibal network (Nunes 2008). There are many sacrifices to be made to appetites gone wild. However, conversely, the alternative responses to unbridled consumerism in the form of religious fundamentalisms and social conservatisms of all kinds attest to alternative mechanisms for coping with the excessive desires of the current moment, though arguably the appetites of these paradigms are just as demanding.

Like the social worlds of Senegalese socio-sexual cannibalism, the lap-dancing club is an eating landscape. No human flesh is chewed and digested. Nevertheless, it is flesh, which is revealed and consumed in a number of ways, all of which feature ritualistic elements of preparation and display that are key to the eating, and counter-eating that takes place – eating the money of customers in exchange for the feasting on young female nakedness. In this sense, the exchange is entirely congruent with Lévi-Strauss's definition of cannibalism, '... intentionally introducing into the bodies of human beings parts of substances from other human beings' (Lévi-Strauss 2016(2013): 88). The lap dancer's form, and the manipulation of that form to achieve an aesthetic with value in this setting, exemplifies the rise of the body in consumer culture as a bearer of symbolic value. This is, as Shilling would put it, the body as 'a phenomenon of options and choices'. The practices of the dressing room kitchen that I describe in the following paragraphs are part of an advancement in 'the potential many people have to control their own bodies, and to have them controlled by others' (Shilling 1993: ix).

The Kitchen

There are four kitchens at the Paradise. The first is a cavernous space with a half a dozen workers, cooking on industrial catering equipment, producing steaks, chops, chips, hamburgers and chicken wings. The second is an open view sushi bar in the smaller part of the club, staffed by a Chinese South African called Jason who looks in the low lighting as if he might be from Tokyo as he rolls fresh salmon and tuna into seaweed and rice rolls alongside slivers of sashimi. The third is an open-air BBQ area, with a spit roast, where on a Sunday huge chunks of meat turn provocatively, dripping fat into the fire pit below. The fourth is the dressing room, located behind the DJ booth in the main area of this upmarket lap-dancing club in Sandton, Gauteng, Africa's richest square mile. The food that this kitchen produces, supported by a veritable micro-economy of goods and services, ingredients and tools are the girls who are employed by Paradise to dance. In this kitchen, they are chefs preparing their bodies for metaphoric consumption.

Following Bourdieu (1986), the bodies of dancers here are absolutely forms of capital, and sites for improvement. Intense self-regulation, regulation by the club and expectations of clients ensure that girls are cooked to make them as irresistible and edible as possible, sweet and juicy treats that cannot be refused. And they are always girls, never women (too raw and natural) or ladies (too genteel and domestic). Girls imply sweetness, malleability, a state of transition. We are reminded of this at the weekly meetings held by club owner, Ward, where he tells us that this work can only ever be temporary, a two-year career that will pay for the girls to take university degrees. Alternatively, maybe find wealthy husbands, though he does not say this. Ward's wife is a former dancer – slim, white and pretty, long blonde hair flicked away from her face as she sneaks cigarettes by the DJ booth where I am newly employed as a novelty female DJ, 'Ward will kill me if he sees this', she whispers, pointing down to her heavily pregnant belly. She tells me she misses dancing, this kind of eating can provide an adrenaline rush not available in more domesticated settings.

The glittering skyscrapers that make up the centre of Sandton rose rapidly in the decade following the first democratic elections in 1994, as a rival to the skyline of Johannesburg's CBD. The municipality here capitalised on its location in a wealthy, protected enclave of the greater Witwatersrand area to draw many businesses and organisations eager to relocate from what was perceived as the lost cause of the CBD. The final cementing of its status as a counter financial super power came with the relocation of the Johannesburg Stock Exchange from its downtown Jozi headquarters in Diagonal Street to new facilities in the heart of Sandton. This is where you can visit Louis Vuitton shops and Gucci outlets or buy any luxury goods you may desire, if you can afford them. The only indication that this is still South Africa is the taxi rank, which carries working class commuters to and from their homes in the African townships, particularly Alexandria, Sandton's shadow twin sister. Around the towers, a maze of dead ends and strange small roads house low-rise business parks and gated luxury communities for their workers off the main highways. It is in one of these cul-de-sacs that Paradise is located, like a large suburban house with its own car park. Unlike a suburban house, the entrance is guarded by two enormous bouncers and a narrow turnstile must be passed through under a sign stating 'strictly no jeans, casual or sportswear', after a fee of R350 has been paid, a not insubstantial amount. It is a status affirming entrance ritual, to come into Paradise; one must have the resources to eat well in all regards.

The DJ booth, adorned with flashing neon lights and overlooking the stage where a succession of girls will take turns to dance from when the club opens at 1pm until it closes at 3am, similarly, is divided from the dressing room by the thinnest of walls. Extending into a narrow passageway, it marks a boundary point between the dressing room as kitchen and the club as consumption space. The consumption side is painted black, to minimise the appearance of the wall so that it seems hardly to exist at all. The other side, facing the dressing room, is dominated by an enormous pin board. On this, a variety of services advertise themselves to the dancers. They are all aimed at providing ingredients to aid the process of preparation that takes place in the dressing room. From masseuses to yoga classes. Make up tutorials, makers of exotic, flimsy costumes. Purveyors of outlandishly high Perspex 'stripper' shoes available in all the colours of the rainbow. Plastic surgeons. Mobile hairdressers, pedicurists, manicurists, colourists, fake tan units that can be brought through the back door and set up discreetly in a corner to provide a temporary spray booth to turn pale skin burnished bronze, weave specialists who will come on site and replace Bantu knots with glossy Brazilian manes.

Following strict guidelines from the club displayed in printouts, with fraying edges, attached to the wall, bodies are plucked and shaved, waxed and smoothed, lathered with honeyed lotions and adorned with dressings that accentuate smooth, naked *flesh*, and its availability, above all else. The rules stipulate no underarm, leg or facial hair. The pubic mound must be fully waxed or feature a neat and narrow 'landing strip'. The bodies of dancers are highly commodified, and commodifiable – a girl whose looks may not fit the mould can, with attention to diet and investment in hairpieces, surgical enhancements, clothing and make up, spectacularly enhance her participation in the space to maximise her appeal. Bodies are personal resources and business resources, social symbols whose message are actively worked on at the level of the body, and the environment the body is presented in, to enhance the transactions that will take place. One night, a dancer came off stage and verbally attacked me in the DJ booth, screaming that I had not turned off the back lighting, leaving her flesh over-cooked in the eyes of potential customers. The right lighting is crucial for masking imperfections, and my mistake had left this dancer vulnerable, her transactional value diminished.

The wise dancer will ensure that income she makes from her body is re-invested into the regimes of self-care and ornamentation required to renew the body's appeal and capacity to be consumed repeatedly. The symbolic value of the dancer lies in her capacity to perform as a commodity sign. She makes herself consumable, an edible body. Those with the financial capacity to do so can eat that body, within the limits prescribed by the club. There is a hierarchical system of meaning involved in the practice of this consumption, which confers more or less prestige on the consuming client depending on the level and extent of how, and

261

how much, he can eat.

The transaction is symbolic, 'feasting with the eyes', and there are strict rules forbidding actual touching of the dancer's body. However, these rules are enforced haphazardly, and only as far as is required to ensure the establishment does not lose its licence, or the quasi-respectability Ward claims for his 'girls'. It is particularly in higher-value transactions that take place in private booths or in secluded corners of the club where these rules are flouted. Here, bodily fluids might be exchanged through kissing and friction contact with genitals resulting in ejaculation. The flouting of rules is directly proportional to the amount of money transacted, or (for some) the potential for further nourishing transactions to take place outside the club space.

Whether rules are flouted or not, there are dangers in offering up one's body for consumption. As Zita Nunes puts it, eating (and being eaten) has its risks, 'It is not always possible to keep what is perceived to be harmful outside of the body' (2008: 37). The risk is to both the dancers and the customers. It is on this point that Ward's insistence that the girls in Paradise are 'clean' comes into play. He is specific in marking their distinction from the prostitutes plying their trade on nearby Oxford Road. This is a safe space to innocently indulge in the consumption of women without risk to health, mitigating what Nunes describes as 'the danger of inadvertently taking into the body, through contagion for example, that could lead to the destruction of the body' (2008: 37). For the dancers' protection, bouncers are always ready to eject customers who flout the rules of no touching. However, the risks for the girls are as much emotional as they are physical. One night, a new dancer started her first shift tottering on pink spiked heels, but after being called on stage for her first display dance, during which two dances are performed for the length of two songs, the first wearing clothing (if scanty), the second disrobed to nakedness, she burst into tears and left, never to return. For those who are prepared to toughen up to the vulnerability of being naked in front of strangers, the dressing room economy offers the seclusion to prepare one's body in such a way as to separate the self from the performer. This is key to mitigating emotional risks, as well as maximising the potential for making money. Dancers must cook themselves in order to change their relationship with what they do. As Bott relays when quoting an interview with a British migrant lap dancer on the Spanish island of Tenerife, 'The first night I went home and cried, now I don't mind it and I'm quite good and earn enough money to rent a flat with my boyfriend. I usually make about 100 euros a night doing a few hours exercise. Can't be bad can it?' (2006: 29).

It is not the spaces themselves, but the intention that goes into them, that make them work. These are the 'intention displays' as described by Goffman in relation to the ways in which the individual makes him- or herself into something that others can read and predict from (1990:11). Goffman talks about this in relation to public spaces – streets, subways and the like. The nightclub, with its exaggerated sense of entry and active pursuit of being a site of liminality and transformation, occupies a space somewhere between the public and private. Goffman turns his discussion of these intention displays to this kind of space when he talks about the 'structured scanning' that goes on in some social settings. He uses the example of the 70s phenomenon of singles bars in American cities (1990: 21), but it can be extended to a variety of other settings which are neither public nor private and need to be negotiated between individuals positioned in a variety of ways within.

In contexts of liminality and transformative performances (Turner 1969), the importance of entrance, of creating the conditions for a performance, is vital. There is the time prior to the performance, where preparation and expectation are the primary features that make it possible for the performance to occur. The performance itself transforms all participants, even if only temporarily. Then the time after the performance, when senses and possibilities are heightened that, '... confer on the actors, by nonverbal as well as verbal means, the experiential understanding that social life is a series of movements in space and time, a series of changes of activity, and a series of transitions in status for individuals. They also inscribe in them the knowledge that such movements, changes and transitions are not merely marked by, but also effected by, ritual' (1969: 78). In the club, these transactions and transitions mark shifts in status as the mutual cannibalism between dancers and customers takes place.

The social forms generated by the carefully constructed and regulated social world of the club and the bodies in it reiterate Shilling's assertion that the body is not only a location for social classifications but is generative of social relations and human knowledge (1993: ix). Shilling's expansion on the limitations of naturalistic versus social constructionist approaches (The body just is! No! The body is socially constructed!) helps us to think beyond the dichotomies of nature versus culture, 'outlining a view of the body as a material phenomenon which shaped, as well as being shaped by, it's social environment' (1993: ix). Hertz's assertion that 'man is double' is followed Durkheim in making the distinction between the universal physical body and the morally imbued socialised body (Hertz 1973; Durkheim 1995). Shilling takes this distinction and elaborates it further to highlight the tension and socially generative energy of the interplay between the body as physical form, and the body as social text, following Mauss (1973) in locating the body as a powerful classificatory tool that is generative of the social order.

The body is thus a source of social form that is dynamic, though these forms ossify. The performances of lap dancer's bodies, the bodies of customers and the bodies of other workers in the club are performances of gendered social divisions that form the basis for subsequent social relationships. The bodily practices and adornment adopted by the various actors in the club enact what Terence Turner described as a 'powerfully generative symbolic language'.

When Butler (1993) invites an evaluation of the sex of materiality, rather than the materiality of sex, it offers a framework to examine how different kinds of sexed bodies move through the club, eating in different ways. I return to the figure of the club owners' pregnant wife looking to all intents and purposes like a lap dancer ready for her shift in a short and sexy dress, high-heeled sandals and blonde extensions, cleavage displayed. But her obvious pregnancy moves her body into another category which is too obviously in the realm of the reproductive, rather than being a virgin canvas on which projections and fantasies of reproductive power – the power to create, to conquer, to transform – can be projected. The discourse of the virgin, the presentation of the dancer's body as a sexualised figure available as commodity resonate with the conquering and possession of virgin territory – or the conquering of fertile territory and people – exemplified by colonial expansion come together in the lap dance. This is fruitfulness directed in cannibalistic fashion to being eaten and eating in a pure commodity exchange, without any of the complications of care or social obligation.

Appetisers

The club was almost empty, Monday night of course. Dancers of various skin tones sat around in groups wearing evening gowns or lingerie, looking bored. A thin white girl with shortish blonde hair, small breasts and an expression that read a kind of blank haughtiness danced on the main stage in the centre of the room, swinging between the three poles, which stood at each corner. Emmanuel, her performance name, is a working-class Afrikaans girl from the southern suburbs of Johannesburg. She has a reputation as a bitch amongst the other dancers, some of whom refer to her as 'white trash'. They are probably motivated by jealousy. Emmanuel is a skilled dancer, extremely proficient in the acrobatic feats of turning her body upside down on the pole, supporting her weight with hands gripping the base, sliding her legs effortlessly down into a knee bend then flipping her body back the right way up. She is also extremely popular, often on lucrative 'exclusives' whereby a girl was paid to spend an entire hour or evening with a client who does not want to share her company with anyone but his party. On this quiet Monday, she was the only girl I saw performing a lap dance, the basic unit in which a dancer makes her money, being paid to strip and dance on the lap of a customer for the length of two songs. Emmanuel had figured out the game. She was here to eat, to extract as much money as possible from customers through her mastery of the pole dance and willingness to go dirty in the private booth, allowing touching and friction if the client had paid sufficiently for privacy and time. Eventually, she would invest some of her not insubstantial earnings in long blonde hair extensions and a pair of pneumatic chest implants, carefully cultivating the image of a desirable doll-like stripper to maximise her potential to be eaten and to eat. Emmanuel understood the value of the presentation of her body in this space, and she was never resistant to her turn coming to dance on the stage and make the necessary display to attract the customers who would maximise her potential to extract wealth from each night.

The appetiser at Paradise, and many other lap-dancing clubs like it, is the stage dance. A method for structuring time and presenting the body in the club, its purpose was twofold. On the one hand, it provided a non-stop musical soundtrack, and ensured that even on a slow night, there would always be a girl dancing on the stage, providing a continuous floorshow. The unit of time was two songs per girl per dance. The first song would be danced to while clothed – and this could vary from a clinging evening gown to a bikini; during the second song these clothes would be removed leaving the dancer fully naked. I would move between the DJ booth and the club floor, playing a continuous soundtrack, armed with a microphone and list of names of all the dancers who were working that night so that every two songs I could call another girl to take to the stage, ensuring that floor show kept rolling. It was like reading out the descriptions in the top of a chocolate box: Candy, Ginger, Midnight, Velvet, Angel, Destiny, Venus.

At my trial gig to become Paradise's new DJ, I was interviewed by Sean, a partner in the business and floor manager. He made it very clear that as the DJ, my job lay primarily in reading the crowd and ensuring that a cross section of girls based on phenotype was presented, so that all the potential tastes of customers could be satisfied. It was a bit like reading out a menu to a party of diners whose tastes one could not be sure of. We sat down on plush sofas in the VIP section, next to the Supper Club, which was due to open shortly. It was decorated in an opulent Afro-chic style – lots of leather, deep fabric cushions, earthy colours and reed woven trimmings. It reminded me of the décor at other clubs in the city aimed at the BEE and Y crowd, only even more sumptuous. I was brought a latte to drink by one of the waitresses. Sean was extremely tall and well-built with translucently pale skin and very white blonde hair. He was of Scottish descent, but described Scotland as a hellhole: 'It's full of council estate teenage mothers and rough as fuck guys with stunted growth and too much aggression.' His parents came here when he was a young child to open a hotel in Amanzimtoti on the KwaZulu-Natal coast, so he has been around the hospitality trade all his life. He has no problem with frequently referencing stereotypes of race in his dissections of the world as he sees it, making sweeping statements about the correlation between crime and blackness, stating that 'local swarties' are not responsible, but foreign 'blacks' are. He questioned me in a direct and fairly confrontational way about what I do in the day, where I've DJed before, the realities of working in a strip club. I answered him straightforwardly, explaining that I was working towards a PhD in Anthropology exploring music and mixed communities in South Africa, and how, as well as furthering my DJing career, playing here would be an opportunity to see the interface of performer/dancer and music in a unique way. He told me that this club was his PhD, and that what he wanted for his club was a female DJ to be playing the kind of urban music that would broaden the appeal of the club to its non-white customers, 'The colour of money is changing in this place' he stated flatly. He emphasised the importance of reading the floor, how at places in London like Stringfellows and Spearmint Rhino, the DJ controlled the place, working out what 'flavour' girl customers wanted. Sean framed the flavours available at Paradise in the language of the apartheid population groups that retain descriptive currency in contemporary South Africa, 'So you bring on more black girls or whites or coloureds if that's what the guy is after'.

In Paradise, new social formations and conceptions of the location of power in South Africa are the locus for approaches to running the club, attracting a new clientele, and a point around which conflict is articulated. This is framed in discourse which alludes strongly to metaphors of eating, both in the attraction of a new clientele representing the BEE elite and the presentation of girls. Sean's use of the word 'flavours' to describe the skin shades of dancers and how this might correspond with their attraction to customers and how their body would be read in the space is indicative of this.

The majority of dancers were white, though not all South African. A substantial number was recruited through agencies abroad and came from former eastern bloc countries like Bulgaria, Romania, Russia and Poland. They were provided with accommodation by Paradise and were taken home after their shifts in a minibus provided by the club. There was one Chinese dancer, who had been recruited under a similar arrangement. In addition, there was a growing number of Black dancers, all of whom were South African, as well as several coloured and Indian dancers, all South African. The clientele were mostly male and affluent. The majority was South African and white but there were also substantial numbers of black, coloured and Indian men. 'Mixed' groups of businessmen entering to celebrate or make deals were common sights. Some customers were regulars who visited frequently and had built client relationships with particular dancers. Male customers came in groups, pairs and alone. Women customers did come into the club, though this was infrequent and they never came alone or in large single sex groups, as many of the male customers did. There were also customers from abroad, brought in with calling cards left at nearby luxury hotels. During my time there, these came from Europe and other parts of Africa. Additionally, on nights when there were big rugby matches at Ellis Park, dancers would go out dressed in sexy business suits, accompanied by a senior manager, to hand out calling cards for the club. They did not do this for Premiership soccer matches. Sean explained this to me as, 'The rugby supporters have got money to spend. Those township guys don't'. Rugby is a sport traditionally associated with the white population in South Africa, while soccer is associated with the black working class.

Main Course

While the primary unit of consumption at Paradise is the lap dance, this is preceded, and also surrounded, by the display of what can be consumed in close contact, and eaten with the eyes from afar. Lap dancers can be consumed in a number of ways: straight up in the club, in full view; in discreet corners of the room; or the most expensive option in private booths.

Things start getting busy towards the end of the week at Paradise. The slowness of Monday builds over the next few days until Thursday becomes the new Friday. It was on a Thursday that a group of five men came in. They were playing by the rule book of white South African masculinity and casual affluence with their private school accents and uniforms of Ralph Lauren polo shirts, the prototype for Paradise's main client base, even as there were moves to attract the money associated with the emerging black middle class. They moved and spoke with the easy confidence of those who are utterly secure in their social position at the top of the hierarchy and in the prime of life. These were regulars, greeted by name by those dancers with whom they had frequent contact, who walked over to their table to sit alongside the men and make small talk while beers were delivered. The method of approaching customers by sitting and chatting with them is frequently deployed and becomes part of the social repertoire to maintain bonds with regular clients, and initiate contact with new ones. One of these, a dancer named Jess who went by the moniker of 'Candy', walked over to the table. Wearing a pink and white striped bra and pants set, she was soon invited to perform a lap dance. On the second song, now stripped naked, she turned her back to her client, moving forward to touch her toes, thus displaying her completely hairless vagina, whose labia she held apart with her fingers. Her customer, laughing, reached in and placed his hand over her exposed genitals. Jess coquettishly moved away, wagging her finger in a mock-serious telling-off manner, then climbing back on to his lap to simulate a sexual act. She walked off at the end, fully nude, back to the dressing room, blowing a kiss as she went. Once she was out of sight, her face screwed up in rage and she hissed, 'Fucking cunts' to no one in particular.

Jess's youthful appearance and small frame made her look much younger than her 25 years, and made her look 'fresh' though she had worked in the club for two years. Though highly accomplished at fronting like she was having fun, Jess was increasingly jaded by the transactions that took place, and the intrusions into her body that these entailed. Conklin's (2001) ethnography on compassionate cannibalism among Wari' interprets cannibalism as the removal of the person being consumed from the category of the human. The encounter between Jess and her client alludes to how in this very different context, the eating of girls saw them being removed from the categories of humanness operating in the wider culture which would not tolerate this kind of invasive contact. Unlike the Wari', in this context, those being removed from the category of human are alive and participating in their objectification as sexualised fodder in order to eat too. After washing in the dressing room, applying more makeup and a fresh outfit of a short lavender negligee, Jess would return to the floor and the men she had called 'fucking cunts' moments earlier to laugh, do expensive tequila shots and take her clothes off again.

The dancers at Paradise are located in a lineage of consumable bodies across time and space, operating between discourses of sentimentalism and exploitation, to ensure that as they are eaten, so they must eat too. The success of this balancing act comes with varying results, some self-inflicted, others the inevitable consequence of structural limitations, though it is difficult to discern where one begins and the other ends. Carter's (1985) telling of the story of Jeanne Duval, Baudelaire's mistress, locates the status of the prostitute as both 'seller and commodity in one, a whore is her own investment in the world and so she must take care of herself' (1985:20). Holmes (2007) re-iterates the necessity and inevitability of this position for Saartjie Baartman, the 'Hottentot Venus', who, to the surprise of the abolitionist Clapham Sect who had brought a highly publicised case against her managers to free her from exploitation, would not testify to ill treatment that might break the fetters of her body as exhibition. Instead, she used the case to obtain a contract, warmer clothes, passage home and written security of profit sharing in the enormously successful show she was the star of. The performance of her body, presented as the ultimate 'exotic other' in Georgian London, was the primary attraction, 'The white whigs might argue over whether she was slave or free woman, but Saartjie knew that she was seller and commodity in one, and must take care of herself ... Business at 225 Piccadilly continued as usual' (2007:107). Saartjie's pragmatic acceptance of, and working with, the limits of her position would ultimately not protect her. When management of the spectacle shifted to other hands and the locale of Paris, the protection afforded by these concessions unravelled. The exploitation of her body that followed, both in life and death, was a true act of cannibalism by the voracious appetites of 19th Century rationalists like Cuvier. Their preoccupation with the validity of her humanity, and eroticised obsession with her form, saw her literally stripped bare and dissected, feeding the development of the scientific racism which would justify the oppressive extraction of wealth from the land and bodies of lesser nations. This cannibalism would, in acts of bitter irony, feed itself on stories of the cannibalism of the Other.

Dessert

Sometimes there is a sweetness in the transactions that take place on the club floor of Paradise. A moderately busy weekday night, and a voluptuous dancer who works under the name, Glory, is getting cosy with a client. With long curly black hair and an ample body shape, her appearance speaks to a Mediterranean background, though she hails from Bulgaria, one of about a dozen dancers from the eastern regions of Europe, and one from China, who are recruited by agencies to dance in clubs around the world. South African visa rules permit these dancers to enter on three-month 'visitor' permits. In this time, they make money in the club, and for the club, paying a cut of their earnings for room, board and transport in a Paradise-branded minivan that ferries them to and from the club-owned flat they stay in. Once her three-month stint here is up, Glory will head to her next job with the agency. She has danced in Spain, Greece, Italy and Belgium. Her ultimate aim is to dance in the United States, where the most money can be made.

Glory is sitting on the lap of a man around the same age as her, with a similar southern European appearance, and a body type verging on chubby. They are gazing at each other with a look that resembles genuine affection. One could be forgiven for thinking that this was an intensely intimate moment between deeply familiar lovers. Except that Glory is topless, and this moment of intense intimacy, where she and her companion are wrapping their arms around each other as she sits on his lap, is being witnessed by a room full of other people. She gets up and dances her signature style to a popular Shakira number, incorporating belly dancing moves as he smiles up at her. When the song is done, she returns to straddle his lap while his hands reach for her breasts. This is a flagrant contravention of the 'no touch' rule, but Glory does not object, and the bouncers do not intervene. She rests her head on his shoulder in a posture of rest.

Gluttony

'Hope you girls are waxed. No hairy legs here', Clint, the other resident DJ at Paradise, shouts out on the mic to a half empty room, as he calls another dancer on stage for her two-song offering. Jackie, a dancer from the nearby township of Alexandria, rolls her eyes and fixes me with a knowing look. She is eating a McChicken burger, wearing jeans and a sports top, just out of sight of the main club. She and I have arrived for the evening shift where I will take over from Clint on the decks, and she will dance under the name 'Midnight', a play on her ebony skin tone and the 'flavour' she offers.

Jackie heads into the dressing room to change into a tiny tropical print bikini, her first outfit for the night. She likes to rotate them, keep things fresh. The night starts slowly, and she comes to hang out with me in the DJ booth. We are talking about a bachelor party held the night before, when a large all-white group of stags booked a private room in the club, and enjoyed a complimentary stage show from a selection of the dancers on shift, including Jackie. After the group dance on stage, the girls had circulated amongst the men, chatting and flirting, keen to score the lucrative lap dances that usually flow with groups of this kind. Jackie, the only dancer of colour in the group, had found that none of the men wanted to pay her for a dance; some had been outright hostile. Giving up, she had come to find me in the main room where I was playing out to the usual crowd. Visibly angry, she swore at the management who had made her go into the room to dance, and the men who had rejected her, 'Those fucking pigs are racist', she spat, humiliated and mad that a sizable chunk of her time at the club had been taken up that night giving the free show.

Dancers at Paradise are not paid a wage. Like lap dancing venues in Europe and the US, the dancer is responsible for generating her own income by attracting customers who want to pay her on a sliding scale for services. The entry-level service is a two-song lap dance at a public table; taking this experience into a private booth doubles the price. The most lucrative transaction is a 'special', whereby she is paid by the hour or for the whole night to spend time exclusively with that customer. During 'specials' multiple lap dances occur in both secluded and visible spaces in the club, on request from the customer or suggestion of the dancer who benefit from showing the client a 'good time' when they have paid so expansively to have exclusive access. When appetites are skilfully built by dancers it is a lucrative business. A single lap dance (R200) can turn into a private booth dance (R400) can turn into a 'special' (R1,000 per hour). Popular girls adept at working the room can make up to R4,000 a night, a reason cited by many for staying in the trade beyond what they would like. The club provides a facilitating space for this exchange, and takes a fee from dancers for the privilege of being there. Tokens purchased at the entrance are used in lieu of payment, and these are cashed in by dancers at the end of their shift, minus the club's commission.

Jackie is thus understandably annoyed that her capacity to eat was jeopardised the night before in order to provide some 'flavour' in a space that once the show was over, was interested only in paying for close contact with white bodies. As we gear up for this shift, she complains about the advantages white girls have in the club for generating income, 'White guys are racist. They don't want black girls to dance for them. If a white guy comes in, I won't even bother going to talk to him because I know he's not going to want to get a dance from me. I'll only go and talk to black guys, but even then, sometimes they don't want to know because they want to have a white girl dance for them too because it's something different for them'.

As Clint, a white South African guy in his late 30s, moves into the final part of his set, she complains about him too, highlighting what is at stake in the relationship between DJ and dancer in terms of self-management and the potential to generate income, 'He plays for the white girls. He's so rude to us. He knows I like to dance to Sean Paul (a popular mainstream Jamaican dancehall artist) but if he plays it he won't call me up even if I ask. He makes us dance to that 80s shit'.

Clint's selections are dominated by 80s pop music, mixed with a smattering of current hits. Where more non-mainstream music genres, like dancehall, are played by him it is because those particular songs and artists have had a breakthrough into the mainstream. Clint uses a pre-mixed computer program, never using the available decks to mix songs together live. He is authoritative towards the dancers and the dance floor as 'his space', preferring to play what he wants to, and calling girls up to dance regardless of whether they like the music or not. He cultivates 'special' relationships with some girls (his current girlfriend is a dancer), for whom he will play requested tracks if they have developed a routine that goes with them. When we talk, Clint paints a picture of himself as very close to the owners, one of 'the guys', though I notice that Sean the co-owner repeatedly gets his name wrong when addressing him. Clint emphasises the extra cash he makes through girls tipping him to play songs they want. He also makes a commission like the 'group of ou's' (South African slang for men, usually white) he'd convinced to have their bachelor party at Paradise instead of Teasers, a rival club down the road, therefore taking a cut of their entrance fee – 'Bang. 1500 bucks in my pocket'. He too is maximising his potential to eat in the club, both in earnings and in access to potential physical connections to attractive dancers. Our style of playing and interacting with the girls is very different. My method is entirely based on live mixing, and friendlier interactions with the girls, emphasising a more egalitarian relationship where I let it be known that I will play what a girl wants to hear when she's dancing. However much I feel that I am different from Clint

274

though, I too am embroiled in the cannibalism that takes place here. Though I don't stay long enough to start making the kind of money on commissions that Clint makes, I will eat the stories and observations of life here to write part of a PhD, and this article.

Once Jackie has finished eating, we get to work. It is early in the evening, and there aren't many customers in. The show must go on though. I have to keep playing songs like there is a fantastic party going on, I have to keep girls coming on the stage and dancing like there is a room full of people to watch them. Dancers are not always co-operative on this front. When the club is packed and the money is flowing, they will line up to dance, ask me to call them up next. When it's lacklustre, with dancers outnumbering customers, it's more of an effort to muster up enthusiasm and willingness. I play some of my favourite music and ask girls who I know enjoy dancing just for the sake of it to get up on stage. It's an attempt to get an atmosphere going so that when more customers do arrive, the club doesn't feel dead. Jackie dances for two songs, followed by some other girls with whom I also have a good relationship. I feel like it's going as well as can be, making the best of a bad situation. As I play, a white dancer called Mel comes into the DJ booth to talk to me. I've already called Mel up to dance on stage that night. We have a pretty good relationship, though I don't know her very well. She is always willing to dance during quiet times, or will volunteer to, making my job easier. I am surprised then when she sits down next to me and says, 'Listen. A lot of the girls don't want to say this to your face but I'm going to'. I ask her what the problem is. 'Basically, a lot of us think that the music you're playing is too black, and it's not fair'. I reply, 'What do you mean too black?' She quickly backtracks, I think my response has made her fear an accusation of being racist, a particularly sore point for many white South Africans, 'No, it's not like that, I just mean that a lot of the girls here think you play too much of that kind of music'. Now my method in the club is to get to know girls and play music that I know they like to dance to when I call them up on stage. It creates a better atmosphere, and allows girls to maximise their earnings. When they look and feel good, they make more money. When the money flows, the atmosphere in the club is electric and creates a reputation that keeps customers coming back. I point this out to Mel, and tell her to let these other girls know that if they want me to play anything in particular for them I'm always happy to accommodate requests. I suspected that the main source of the complaints were two white girls, who had just been sitting with Mel, with whom I did not get on very well. They did not enjoy dancing on stage, and had a general agreement with DJs that they would only be called to dance if absolutely necessary. Their method of attracting customers was based more on sitting and talking, rather than their rhythmic abilities. As the club was nearly empty and the atmosphere cold as a result, my 'heating it up' with specific music aimed at generating a particular atmosphere, which did them no favours, had focused their discontent on me.

These two incidents, one in which Jackie complained about white racism, the other where Mel accused me of black favouritism, brings up several issues. Conflicts in the club between dancers are invariably around the potential to eat from customers. As the primary way in which this is done is through girls' bodies, the complaints expressed by Jackie and Mel were indicative of a perceived bias which favours one body over another, giving an advantage in access to this money. The unit in which the body is displayed, whether this is on-stage dancing or doing a lap dance at a table or in private booth, is two songs. A girl dances for two songs at a time, and the musical soundtrack is continuous. Thus, rhythm and the relationship to this soundtrack are critical to the way in which a dancer creates her persona and interacts with the customers who are her exclusive source of income.

When conflict at Paradise over resources became racialised, it was often around access to, and knowledge of, particular music genres. Rhythmic understanding, and relationships to songs, became avenues to express tensions that emphasised racial difference. The DJ, as gatekeeper of the sounds moving through the club, becomes a focal point for articulating discontent, as well as cultivating advantageous sound/body relationships.

The club's management/owners were not really concerned about any of this if it did not directly affect the running of the club, nor did they have an ideological interest in creating one environment over another. The ruling ideology here was money and ensuring that it flowed into the club. In this respect, the club's decision to employ me was one that reflected the changing perception of who money can flow from in elite spaces in contemporary South Africa, who controls capital – the tactic to appeal to an extended clientele beyond the traditional affluent white, male customer, namely the emergent black elite of South Africa. This mirrored a shift in Gauteng's social politics and occupation of affluent space. The *communitas* that my style of play helped to generate allowed a new power configuration to be imagined.

As the night heated up, the energy of a strong money flow rippled through the club, changing the energy of the space. A hedonistic vision of a New South Africa seemed to materialise. A procession of multi-coloured girls took to the stage, danced on laps and spontaneously in corners, to the delight of the tables of single white and Indian men and mixed parties of coloured, black and white businessmen, celebrating sealed deals. I couldn't help but think of the ghosts of apartheid leaders, Verwoerd and Strydom, as a party of 10 young black men occupied a corner booth to celebrate a stag night. The husband-to-be had the first lap dance of the night performed on him by a white girl, called Sandy, from Cape Town. She took his tie off and put it on, surely, I thought, the most unimaginable horror to those architects of apartheid. Was this the outcome of the struggle? Requesting that everyone in the club give a round of applause for Thabo's girlfriend Pule, who had allowed him to come here tonight and have ladies from the other side of the former colour bar dance naked on his lap. The sound of clapping hands and whooping cheers was thunderous. A dystopian social performance of the defeat of white supremacy in South Africa, distracting from the reality that fundamental transformation of the kind promised by the Freedom Charter is yet to take place.

Power continues to be concentrated in the hands of wealthy white men who have negotiated power-sharing agreements with an emergent black elite, who are also largely male. The negotiation process, which resulted in constitutional reform as well as changes to macro-economic policy, was guided by ideologies of gender and 'race' that served the interests of dominant groups in society. South

Africa's transition has been described as a pact between elites (Sparks 1995; Osaghae 2002). The club can be read as a spectacle celebrating this pact. Elite power sharing is celebrated in Paradise at management level as an opportunity to access the capital promises of Black Economic Empowerment, while anxieties about accessing the spoils of this concentration of power play out amongst dancers. Conflict over access to resources continues to be racialised, while the fundamental structures of late consumer capitalism remain intact. The colour bar to affluence and privilege has simply been lowered, and this masquerades as a genuine shift in the type of society South Africa is. Here in Paradise the spectacle of cannibalised bodies affirms the primacy of wealth and those who have access to it, and the continued salience of race, both as a tool of body commodification and a language that easily articulates discontent in times of limited access to resources.

In Lieu of a Conclusion: After Dinner Mint, Coffee & Brandy

Inside the lap dancing club the particularities of modern South African cosmopolitanism and its meeting with capital combined in the ways in which girls were selected to represent available 'flavours' for customers' consumption. Understandings of race continue to provide a nexus around which expressions of discontent by dancers around who is eating or not eating are structured, even as these ontologies have less salience in other interactions.

This is a sociality in which the cannibalism of spectacle thrives, feeding in various ways on the bodies positioned in the feasting chamber of the club. A brisk backroom social life adds flavour and spice to the meals consumed in the arena of commodified sexualities, whose sustenance is mainly, though not always, the bodies of young women, disciplined into shapes that adhere to the rules of what can be offered for sexified consumption. Cannibalism is not limited to the literal consumption of human flesh; the capacity to eat others comes also as voyeurism and consumption through other bodily senses. The eating of lap dancer's bodies as spectacle, and the counter cannibalism of the wallets of customers, is a form of enrichment validating hierarchies of power that re-

278

inscribe the frequently gendered relationships between the blesser and blessee. These eating relationships arise in the specific circumstances of consumer capitalism, where appetites for goods and services are voracious, and the means to satisfy them limited by all kind of classed, gendered and raced restrictions. Desires so constrained find ways to be satisfied, framed as they are in conditions of structural inequality that create illusions of free choice, empowerment and enrichment, generating complex and contradictory eating landscapes.

References

Barton, B. (2006) *Stripped: Inside the Lives of Exotic Dancers*, New York, NY: New York University Press.

Berger, J. (1972) *Ways of Seeing*, London: Penguin.

Bernard, C., De Gabrielle, C., Cartier, L., Monk-Turner, E., Phill, C., Sherwood, J., and Tyree, T. (2003) 'Exotic dancers: gender differences in societal reaction, subcultural ties, and conventional support', *Journal of Criminal Justice and Popular Culture*, Vol. 10(1): 1–11.

Bott, E. (2006) 'Pole Position: Migrant British women producing "selves" through lapdancing work', *Feminist Review*, Vol. 83(1): 23–41.

Bourdieu, P. (1984) *Distinction: A Social Critique of the Judgement of Taste*, London: Routledge.

Bourdieu P. (1986) 'The Forms of Capital' in J.E. Richardson (ed.): *Handbook of Theory and Research for the Sociology of Education*, New York, NY: Greenwood, 241–58.

Butler, J. (1993) *Bodies That Matter: On the Discursive Limits of Sex*, London & New York: Routledge.

Carter, A. (1985) *Black Venus*, London: Bloomsbury.

Colosi, R. (2010) *Dirty Dancing: An Ethnography of Lap Dancing*, Abingdon: Willan.

Conklin, B. (2001) *Consuming Grief: Compassionate Cannibalism in an Amazonian Society*, Austin: University of Texas Press.

Deshotels, T., Tinney, M., Forsyth, C. J. (2012) 'McSexy: exotic dancing and institutional power', *Deviant Behaviour*, Vol. 33(2): 140–48.

Durkheim, E. (1995[1912]) *The Elementary Forms of the Religious Life*, translated by Karen E. Fields. New York: Free Press.

Duval Smith, A (2006) 40,000 French students join sex trade to fund degrees. The Independent, 31 October. Available (consulted 9 October 2014) at:
http://www.independent.co.uk/news/world/europe/thousands-of-students-join-sex-trade-to-fund-degrees-422287.html.

Enck, G. E., and Preston, J. D. (1988) 'Counterfeit intimacy: a dramaturgical analysis of an erotic performance', *Deviant Behaviour: An Interdisciplinary Journal*, Vol. 9: 369–381.

Goffman, Erving (1990) *The Presentation of Self in Everyday Life*, Penguin Books.

Hardy, K., and Sanders, T. (2014) 'The political economy of "lap dancing": contested careers and women's work in the stripping industry', *Work, Employment and Society*, Vol. 29(1): 119–136.

Hertz. R. (1973 [1909]) 'The Pre-eminence of the Right Hand', in R. Needham (ed): *Right and Left: Essays on Dual Symbolic Classification*, Chicago: University of Chicago Press, pp. 3–10, 13–14, 16–17, 19–21.

Holmes, R. (2007) *Hottentot Venus*, London: Bloomsbury.

Lantz, S (2005) 'Students working in the Melbourne sex industry: education, human capital and the changing patterns of the youth labour market'. *Journal of Youth Studies* Vol. 8(4): 385–401.

Lévi-Strauss, C. (2016) *We Are All Cannibals and Other Essays*, New York: Columbia University Press.

Maticka-Tyndale, E., Lewis, J., Clark, J. (2000) 'Exotic dancing and health', *Women and Health* Vol. 31(1): 87–108.

Mauss. M. (1973[1935]) 'Techniques of the Body', *Economy and Society*, 2: 70–88, reproduced by permission of Taylor and Francis Books Ltd.

Nunes, Z. (2008) *Cannibal Democracy: Race and Representation in the Literature of the Americas*, Minneapolis & London: University of Minnesota Press.

Nyamnjoh, F. (2005) 'Fishing in Troubled Waters: *Disquettes* and

Thiofs in Dakar', *Africa*, Vol. 75(3): 295–324.

Osaghae, E. (2002) 'What Democratisation Does to Minorities Displaced From Power: The Care of White Afrikaners in South Africa', *Forum for Development Studies*, Vol. 29 (2): 293–319.

Roberts, R., Bergstronm, S., La Rooy, D. (2007) 'Commentary: UK students and sex work: current knowledge and research issues', *Journal of Community and Applied Social Psychology*, Vol. 17(2): 141–6.

Roberts, R., Sanders, T., Myers, E., and Smith, D. (2010) 'Participation in sex work: students' views', *Sex Education*, Vol. 10(2): 145–56.

Shilling, C. (1993) *The Body and Social Theory*, London: Sage Publications.

Sparks, A. (1995) *Tomorrow is Another Country: The Inside Story of South Africa's Negotiated Revolution*, London: Heinemann.

Turner, Victor (1969) *The Ritual Process: Structure & Anti-Structure*, New York: Aldine.

Chapter 8

My African Heart: The Obscure Gourmandise of an Enlightened Man

Moshumee T. Dewoo

Introduction

Once but also twice and then for evermore upon a moment of unreserved moral myopia, it would appear, or perhaps it was a moment of vulgar, quixotic effrontery, just as it could also be fixed as a moment of critical weakness or hopeful abandon even ... Oh, well! I cannot quite hark back to which it was. But that is not important. Not right now. Not here. What is important is that once upon a moment and then for a very long time after, cannibalism would be imagined the thing of the tragically ill mind alone, especially of those non-people people, *quasi* persons, primitive humans, half-monkeys, barbarian pygmies, animals, charred skin demons, monsters, obviously, from the New World (Nunn & Qian 2010), those lands far, very far, away from the Enlightened Man (De Dijn 2012; Cassirer 2009), the *homo* twice *sapiens*, the *supercivilised* man (Novak 1963), a man of learning and means, who would at times be woman too, so enlightened in fact, that it should show through his skin so pale as well as the Enlightened, *supercivilised* Soil from which he would have grown, and by which I mean the soil of the Northern hemisphere, the Western world up there, modern-day Europe specifically ... soil much closer to the heavens, to divine light, wisdom and purity.

By now, however, it should stand clear that cannibalism would be the thing of the Enlightened Man *too*, if it ever were the thing of non-people people at all, and that it would occur in the present day, right from the Enlightened Soil from which the Enlightened Man would have grown. For the Enlightened Man may have spoken and still speaks of himself being a benevolent warrior, and it being his obvious 'white man's burden' (Hitchens 2004: 63–64; see also Yancy

2008) or his brotherly responsibility or moral duty to soothe and/or heal my body, bleeding, trying to save me, but if he is the one who would cut me open in the first place, and if he would be gorging away at my heart whilst trying to save me or, at least, claiming to do so, then would he not be a monster himself? And would it not be cannibalism that he would be, in the end, doubly guilty of?

For those who do not know of me, not yet at least, my name is Africa. And for those who may not be too well versed in the often much less magniloquent works that tell of it, this is my story. This is my true story. And it is about Extraction. It is about the extraction and export of the natural resources that I own including non-renewable ones as water, forestry and fisheries, and those of the oil, gas and mining sectors, by typically state-owned and/or private international extractive companies (Smith 2013), which I would refer to hereon as Extractors, from modern-day Europe specifically and quite blatantly, and involving the pale politician, policy maker or businessman (the Enlightened Man, in general) who would have grown from her Soil. It is about me being justifiably prey to an Enlightened Man in need of natural resources to sustain the ecosystem(s) that he would build around these. It is about the Enlightened Man gravitating to my natural resource-rich body, as would flesh-eating fly to open flesh. It is about the Enlightened Man as monster gorging away at my Heart, that vital part of my body,[1] in a manner mirroring the extractive policies, strategies and endeavours of the periods of enslavement and colonialism.

What is of interest here for me is the context within and from which Extraction would grow and persist. This would unfold along four themes, all finding root especially at the beginning of the periods of colonialism and slavery. The first would be on Extraction occurring and maintained under the guise of benefactor and politico-economic partnerships between Europe and me, which would serve quite well in hiding or muffling the destructive nature and potential thereof. The second would be about the clearly selfish drive for profit-making and surplus value accumulation by European monopoly-financial capital, which would really speak to a sort of frenetic competition at global level, a form of institutionalised and legitimised myopic greed in action that would leave no place for reciprocity, sympathy, friendship, altruism, co-operation, virtue and trust anywhere, and thus, would make way for the continued exploitation of African natural resources. The third, generously addressed in anti-colonial and post-colonial Third World scholarship, in particular, would be on the subject of the Enlightened Man justifying or continuing his exploitation of the Third World in general on the premise that this would be non-Enlightened. The fourth would be that pertaining to the mitigated success, if success at all, of attempts to stand against the Enlightened Man. It is this context that I build toward in this piece, hoping that it would serve lay bare the typically deceitful and terribly limited conversations and practices that would grow and have been allowed on and around the fact of cannibalism as this would occur in the world of Man.

The Pale Tale of Extraction

French President Emmanuel Macron (Viscusi & Gongo 2017) and German Chancellor Angela Merkel (Smith-Spark 2017), much like their predecessors and current peers of the Enlightened Soil, would have had the whole world hypnotised, almost, especially so at the time of the 5th Africa-EU Summit[2] held in Ivory Coast in 2017, with the promise of Extraction being couched on some sort of post-colonial brotherhood, development aid, a balanced economic partnership, a benefactor or benevolent friendship, a relationship of equals and fair exchange between Europe and me. In the manner of Daniel Defoe's *Robinson Crusoe* (Defoe 1994) who would seek to exert and implement rational control over the wild island that he would be stranded on (Birdsall 1985: 27), almost as this were eulogy of Enlightenment in the face of everything and anything else, the Enlightened Man would be to save me once again,[3] as he has had to and always had since he officially found me some hundreds of years ago (even as he is said to have hailed from my loins and cradle), positioning himself particularly in the form of Extractors putting into the global economic Market the resources that I own, where Extraction would imply the concurrent production of incredible amounts of monetary revenue, i.e. money (Ross 2012; Wenar 2008; Copley 2017), that should later be used toward helping me get out of

285

my demise, my poverty, inequality, underdevelopment, disease, terrorism, never-ending conflicts (Samuel & Squires 2017) ... the usual ... and so on and so forth.

Under this light (you would forgive me the choice of words here), the Enlightened Man should pass for Prince Charming. He certainly dresses like so. He acts like so. He speaks like so. He kisses like so. Sadly, he is not so. And he could not hypnotise everybody, not for very long at least, with many observers of the subject that I have never ceased to be taking to their pens or even microphones (Asiedu 2017) to speak against this fairy-tale, this enormously generous, idealistic story that the Enlightened Man would propose and promise unendingly, conceiving the relationship between Europe and me as one that is highly asymmetric, mistakenly optimistic and predatory instead, and calling Extraction a curse. This would be the Resource Curse (Collier 2000; Diamond 2004; Basedau & Lay 2009).

The Resource Curse, also known as the Paradox of Plenty, would imply the failure of natural-resource-rich bodies from fully benefitting from the natural resources that they own and should be gaining from as these are put into the Market by Extractors (Humphreys et al. 2007; Bauer & Quiroz 2013), showing by way of very little evidence of any sort of structural changes or advancement in high value-added activities and endeavours that grow from these bodies beyond their natural-resource sectors (Brunnschweiler & Bulte 2008; Van der Ploeg 2010; Caselli & Michaels 2013; Aghion et al. 2009). One of the strongest theoretical expansions on this Curse would be that which speaks to the limited capture of monetary revenue, entailing that only a fraction of the incredible amounts of money produced from the natural resources that are put into the Market by Extractors would be sent back to the bodies that own these resources. This would be typical of those bodies that permit Extraction at low tax rates and expect equally low royalties, quite likely without a clear understanding of the actual monetary value and/or true monetary revenue potential of the natural resources that they own. The Average Effective Tax Rate (AETR) for the mining sector in Peru as at 2017, for example, was set at less than 30% (Ernest & Young 2017), implying that the Extractors operating there would keep large amounts of the money made on the (extracted) natural resources that Peru owns.

This is my reality too, as a natural-resource-rich body. For, even if the (extracted) natural resources that I own produce billions of dollars in revenue annually, it is money that would flow back to me far too timidly (Copley 2017; Kabemba 2014; Honest Accounts 2017). In consequence, it is not money that would help me (Brunnschweiler & Bulte 2008; Dunning 2008). Proof thereof stands in the very fact that I still need to be saved. I still need to be helped out of my demise. In 2017, for example, oil-rich Equatorial Guinea, which is one of the smaller bodies that compose me, would hold an incredibly high annual Gross Domestic Product (GDP) per capita swaying at around $35,000 (Index Mundi 2018), and yet would stand at the lowest ranks of the United Nations Development Program's (UNDP) Human Development Index (HDI) in the same year, failing to provide even the most basic services to her citizens (Human Rights Watch 2018). There is not much benefit that Equatorial Guinea would gain from her high GDP as an oil-rich body. The 2010 report by the McKinsey Global Institute on the progress and potential of African economies would confirm this trend at continental scale only a decade ago: 'Natural resources directly accounted for just 24 per cent of Africa's GDP growth from 2000 and 2008' (McKinsey 2010). And their prediction for the decade after would not be any more hopeful.

The extraction of the natural resources that I own would then be Extraction for its own sake. It would be a case, again, very much à la Robinson Crusoe, who, stranded on an island, would obstinately engage with those things that would be useful and profitable to him, including the various tools, weapons, gunpowder and coins that he would, at some point, rescue from his ship, driven by his desire for self-aggrandisement beyond mere self-preservation, i.e. beyond survival (Birdsall 1985: 24–25). It would be a case of extractive neo-Imperialism (Acosta 2013; Kohnert 2008), the expression by European monopoly-financial capital today of a selfish and careless drive for profit making and surplus value accumulation. It would be a case of looting and plundering, benefitting my most fervent and loyal Extractors, i.e. Europe and her Enlightened Man (Kabemba

2014). It would be a case of the regulation, normalisation, legitimisation and institutionalisation of unscrupulous fiscal practice. It is a case of exploitation mirroring the extractive policies, strategies and endeavours of the periods of enslavement and colonialism and persisting today, where the Enlightened Man is as a monster gorging away at my Heart, my core, the resources I own, which ought to, or at least could, have sustained me instead. It would be Man eating Man, whether enlightened or blissfully cataleptic, of the heavens or from the darkest pits of Hell. It would be people feeding themselves on others, on me, on the most important parts of me. It is people eating people. It would be politico-economic cannibalism (Vassalo 2006). It would be human cannibalism. It would be Cannibalism, which is what I will refer to hereon, simply.

Having said that, and as appalling as it may or could have stood to be as the quintessential act of savagery, there would be not much in and about Cannibalism that should come as a shock. It is a fact of life on Earth. It is in fact defensible, not medically (Collinge et al. 2008; Levy 2013), and not always morally or ethically, but certainly in other ways, or at least one other way which I can really speak of. This is when Cannibalism is taken to be separate from the fact of people eating people, as if nonchalant Cannibalism instead, condoned rather than condemned. This is when Cannibalism is people eating people considered non-people, or people eating non-people people. This is when Cannibalism is no longer Cannibalism. 'It's only cannibalism if we're equals', as says Dr Lecter in Fuller's Television series 'Hannibal' (Hannibal 2015).

And I, Africa, would not be the Enlightened Man's equal. I have not been considered his equal at least since the beginning of the periods of enslavement and colonialism, which would see the entire world ordered and re-ordered from the Enlightened Man's vantage point, the 'white gaze' (Yancy 2008), by which would be fixed the 'the distance and difference between what is closer [to the Enlightened Man and the Soil from which he would have grown] ... and what is far away [from the latter]' (Said 1978), as this declared a certain Order of Things that would run the latitudes of Jorge Luis Borges's *Heavenly Emporium of Benevolent Knowledge,* by way of which I would be considered to be 'far away', and likely animal or at the very least, an animal-like person, or a non-person person:

> On those remote pages it is written that animals are divided into: (a) those that belong to the emperor; (b) embalmed ones; (c) those that are trained; (d) suckling pigs; (e) mermaids; (f) fabulous ones; (g) stray dogs; (h) those that are included in this classification; (i) those that tremble as if they were mad; (j) innumerable ones; (k) those drawn with a very fine camel's-hair brush; (l) *et cetera*; (m) those that have just broken the flower vase; (n) those that at a distance resemble flies (Foucault 2002: xv).

I would be less than the Enlightened Man, de-humanised, infantilised, feminised and eroticised for hundreds of years until today (Derrida 1978) as I were 'wilderness in human form' (Spurr 1993),[4] a primitive body, one without vision, capabilities, agency and intellect, to be helped, studied, displayed, disciplined and civilised, and shaped to be conquered (Ferguson 2006). There would not be much else to me but something along the following, which begins Binyavanga Wainana's satirical piece on '*How to Write about Africa*':

> Always use the word 'Africa' or 'Darkness' or 'Safari' in your title. Subtitles may include the words 'Zanzibar', 'Masai', 'Zulu', 'Zambezi', 'Congo', 'Nile', 'Big', 'Sky', 'Shadow', 'Drum', 'Sun' or 'Bygone'. Also useful are words such as 'Guerrillas', 'Timeless', 'Primordial' and 'Tribal'. Note that 'People' means Africans who are not black, while 'The People' means black Africans (Wainaina 2006).

There would be, within this context, no issue with the Enlightened Man, this Cannibal, gorging away at my Heart or any other part of me for that matter. I am fully exploitable. I am as eatable as a pig, purely pawn in a larger game of survival, or natural game to an enlightened predator. I am, justifiably, prey.

But there is no prey that should be particularly excited about being so. Let this be clear. There is no victim that would consent to being eaten. Well, not entirely. In 2002, Germany would see to trial one of her most gruesome cases of Cannibalism, with 42-year-old Arnim Meiwes admitting to having killed, dissected and consumed in March 2001, his 43-year-old lover, Bernd Brandes, whom he had met on the Internet after posting an advertisement which stated that he was looking for a body to eat (Connolly 2003). 'I didn't do anything against his will', Meiwes claimed in court, adding that Brandes 'knew that he could have turned back at any moment but he chose not to' (Harding 2003). This case stood defensible to a certain degree since Cannibalism was not then prohibited in Germany, by way of which Meiwes was able to plead mere assistance in Brandes's desire to die, and therefore eating the latter only on demand. But I am not Brandes. And I could not, in my right mind, have consented to the Enlightened Man gorging away at my Heart, especially in the manner that this has persisted since the beginning of the periods of enslavement and colonialism. I could not be excited about being prey to the Enlightened Man (or anybody else). I could not condone this Cannibal eating me into my demise.

But this is where things would become uncomfortable for me. For even saying that I could not condone the Enlightened Man gorging away at my Heart unendingly and doing so into my demise is in fact admitting to the failure to maintain and/or realise my Sovereignty. It is admitting to having no control over my own body. It is therefore turning against local Leadership, i.e. against such people as territorial chiefs and warriors, freedom fighters, self-proclaimed anti-colonial politicians, leaders of national movements, pro-independence intellectuals and resistance policy makers who would have grown from me, calling out their incapacity to keep me free and safe from Europe and her Enlightened Man, despite their vigorous attempts to this end, particularly those that came in between the 1890s and the 1960s (Anderson, 2005; Boahen 1987; Gerhart 1978; Wa Wamwere 2002; Landsberg & Kornegey 1998; Mboya 1963; Nkrumah 1965; Anderson 2006). It is also calling out some more members of local Leadership, some more sons of *my* Soil (Geschiere & Ceuppens 2005; Bayart, Geschiere & Nyamnjoh 2001), those of the (political) ruling class that came about through the attempts to achieving my Sovereignty, behaving as if agents of Extraction giving Extractors passage to my Heart seemingly without much official and/or tangible objection or retribution, i.e. without opposition, making them complicit at worst and incompetent at best re my demise (Pear 2014). Finally, it is pointing to the large uselessness and possible sightlessness of self-proclaimed Saviours, including the Enlightened Man in Politics[5] as well as non-governmental organisations (NGOs) (Matthews 2017) and development agencies including the International Monetary Fund (IMF) and the World Bank (Trabanco 2014; Chang 2007; Engdahl 2013), for example, trying, and claiming to try, to help me out of my demise by way of investing in and operating around local matters of health, education, food, poverty and so on and so forth (Amin 1990; Bond 2002; Vincent 1999; Drewry 2014). Their help would be merely seeing to the consequences rather than the cause of things. It would be bandaging my wounds, soothing my bleeding body, and ignoring the monster causing it all.

The path from here is natural and clear. It always was. My Heart would not be consumed to its death and, therefore, mine. I would not be eaten into my demise. But the question is, if so many and so much else have apparently failed at getting me there, what could possibly be left to work with, to this end? How would I now stand against the Enlightened Man? How would I go against Extractors? How would I get back control of the natural resources that I own? How would I save what is left of my core? How would I defend my interests in the face of this monster that has been gorging away at my Heart, unendingly, without opposition from those whom I thought and hoped would and should have protected me all the while? How could I not end up with a dead Heart? How could I stop this Cannibal who has, at some point in History, decided that his desire for my Heart, his taste for it, his greed for it, his need of it, would be more valuable than the life of it, more important than my survival? How should I navigate this relationship with Europe that turned lethal for me?

The Path of the Dying Heart

Prevention, we have all heard, at some point in our existence, would be much better than cure. Extraction, in all logic, if prevented, i.e. if I had had some sort of anti-predator mechanism up and running that would have served to keep Extractors from me, would not have had to be dealt with. The Enlightened Man eating away at my Heart would not have been my burden to carry. Cannibalism would not have been my issue to write on. But I am writing on it. It was not prevented. I ended up with a dying Heart. And the path of the dying Heart is simple. It could be allowed to die, or it could be fought for, enhancing the chances, the last bits of probability, of its survival in the face of predation. If the first choice were made, then there would be nothing left to write on. My Heart would die. I would be led straight to the depths of my demise and, eventually, to my own death. That would be the end of my story. If, instead, the choice was made to fight for my Heart and enhance its and, therefore my, chances to survive, it would be a choice that most likely would have to run the latitudes of the following: the dying Heart would have to go cold turkey. It would have to turn cold Heart. It would have to say, 'ENOUGH!' I would have to say, 'ENOUGH!', enough to being prey, and enough of the Enlightened Man eating away at my Heart, enough of his monstrosity, enough of his cannibalism!

Many have would have tried, as I mentioned earlier, toward the path of saying 'ENOUGH!'. Chiefs, warriors, scholars, poets, politicians, policy makers, wise, strong and loyal friends as I would like to think of them, men and women, sons of my Soil ... They would have tried in their own ways. But it would be quite the complicated path for them (this is of course not saying that there are many such paths that would be uncomplicated). Some would lose their tongues along the way – others, their wives and children, countless more, their lives. And a few, their drive, their hope that things would ever change, that the Enlightened Man would no longer eat me into my demise. It would, without doubt, stand foolish for anybody to even think of going, once more, along that same path of saying, 'ENOUGH!' And it would be! Now, saying, 'ENOUGH' is not the incorrect thing to do. Not at all! It is in fact what I would do. But what I am putting forward here is that the old path to this would just not be the one to take. This is not strictly because it would be complicated and eventually would not lead to the desired changes. It is also and mostly because it would run the latitudes of a series of unaligned, chaotic and unintelligible diagnoses by a multitude of Saviours, which would naturally not permit for a single adequate treatment. And the matter of saving a body implies getting to *a correct diagnosis* first and then following this up with *a correct treatment.*

I would propose here, as it were the beginning of a correct diagnosis, that I would be battling a Narcissistic Predator. For the Enlightened Man gorging away at my Heart would stand to display some of the strongest traits of this psychological or psycho-behavioural disorder, i.e. that of the narcissist (Russell 1985; DSM-IV & DSM-V 2012; Ronningstam 2016; DSM-V 2010; Ronningstam 2011), incapable of any amount of sympathy or affection for anybody beyond himself, absolutely oblivious to all the damage that he would be inflicting upon me through Extraction, and in constant denial, violently in denial, of this reality to the point of being delusional about it and turning, twisting or manipulating facts, i.e. the facts of his actions and of his very self, to suit his ego, his logic, his beliefs and lies. Emmanuel Macron, as if to add a cherry to the cake that is my point here, claimed loudly and clearly at the G20 summit in Hamburg in 2017, along the typically narcissistic line of reasoning, this narcissistic pattern of avoidance or this self-justificatory, self-effacing stance (which is that of not taking responsibility for anything at all), that Africa's demise, my demise, had not a bit to do with Europe and was, instead, a mere 'civilisational' issue (Tzouvala 2017).[6] This would be my opponent. This is who I would battle.

It is worth keeping in mind, to continue along the lines of a correct diagnosis for a correct treatment, that this would entail going to battle first and foremost, then, having the Narcissistic Predator as opponent, and, finally, having to handle both of these whilst being victim to the latter, i.e. the Narcissistic Predator, and trying to avoid being any more so specifically by battling him, and therefore, also having to avoid being victim to the former, i.e. the battle itself. It would be a battle fought that would have been lost partly, already, and this would happen in reverse, as it were a reverse battle, a battle done as it were for the opposite end game, where my desired finality would be to escape my opponent, only, twice.

By these dynamics, it would not be too far from the truth that going against the Narcissistic Predator would qualify, along the lines of the Just War theory (McMahan 2007), at least as a Just Battle, if I may call it so. It would not be a war[7] *per se* but more of a tenacious struggle and, therefore, a battle, and one that would be fought for a just cause, i.e. there would be justice presumed in the fact of having to resort to it in the manner of seeking to enhance the probability of my survival; the manner in which it would be fought would be expected to be just and fair, implying just conduct and, here, in particular, with the only finality being that of eroding the damage done by the Narcissistic Predator, and not actively seeking to cause damages; and, finally, other approaches to enhancing the probability of my survival would have been tried first, and none would have been successful (at least not in the desired manner), therefore prompting this battle.

But as close to a Just Battle this would be even when specifically explored in relation to the conduct and affairs of bodies such as mine, which would be political above and beyond anything else, it would still be closer to being that which experts in the laws of natural ecosystems would have deemed Threat-sensitive Predator Avoidance by way of escape (referred to as Predator Escape hereon) (Vamosi 2005; Roff 1992; Relvea 2002; Palleroni et al. 2005; Lev-Yadun et al. 2002). This would read here as the attempt toward the reduction in the probability of narcissistic prey consumption and/or narcissistic injury, and therefore the attempt to enhance the probability of prey survival after and despite detection (which would include detection, attack, capture and consumption) by the Narcissistic Predator. In other words, prey detection by the Narcissistic Predator would initiate a post-prey detection phase (Mobbs et al. 2015) that would in turn have developed, in the detected prey, a set of predictable anti-Narcissistic-Predator traits unfolding through stages or chronological components including attack deterrence, capture deterrence,and consumption deterrence.

I would put emphasis here on the fact of such stages being predictable, in the way of being predictable response, or predictable defence mechanism, having set off through such persons as Ghanaian President Nana Akufo-Addo speaking, at a joint press conference (Butler 2017), with French Premier Macron in Accra, Ghana, right after the Africa-EU summit in 2017, to a Ghana 'beyond Aid', a Ghana that says, 'ENOUGH!', and an Africa that stands aware of the Narcissistic Predator gorging away at her African Heart under the guise of benefactor and other kinds of partnerships, a vast and fertile and resource-rich Africa fully capable of standing and fending for herself, for her rightful and righteous positionality in the world:

> We have to get away from this mindset of dependency. This mindset about 'what can France do for us?' France will do whatever it wants to do for its own sake, and when those coincide with ours, '*tant mieux*', as the French people say … Our concern should be what do we need to do in this 21st century to move Africa away from being cap in hand and begging for aid, for charity, for handouts.
>
> The African continent when you look at its resources, should be giving monies to other places … We need to have a mindset that says we can do it …and once we have that mindset we'll see there's a liberating factor for ourselves.[8]

Akufo-Addo would do it all, or at the very least warned of it all, with this message to Macron, and to the world: I, Africa, would take the path of attack deterrence, capture deterrence and consumption deterrence.

Attack deterrence would imply the unfolding of *deimatic* behaviour by the detected prey in the manner of Signalling (Lev-Yadun et al. 2002: 59-60) to the predator as well as to others that may be around them that said predator would have also been detected. In the strictly animal ecosystem, Signalling would come about as the adoption of a strong posture, a sort of stance of power by the detected prey, in the form of loud sound emission, the display of bright colours or colour and colour pattern flashes, or the even the ejection of bodily fluids, as it occurs in skunks and octopi, for example, when faced with the predator. There would also be the possibility for detected prey to decide on attack deterrence in the manner of Signalling by Mimicry. There would be two ways of going about this, the first being the Müllerian type of Mimicry (Mostler 1935; Müller 1879), which is common, for example, in some butterflies, wasps and bees. This would involve an *aposematic* prey, i.e. a species dangerous to the predator or a species that would have

295

proven to successful Signalling already, whose signals to honestly re-iterate, to re-produce, i.e. to mimic (Härlin & Härlin 2003). This type of Mimicry is particularly hopeful in that the predator would tend to avoid the model (*aposematic*) prey, and therefore, should, in all likelihood, avoid the detected prey that would be mimicking the latter. The other type of Signalling by Mimicry, which would be the Batesian (Mostler 1935), would in the same manner as the first type, push for the predator to avoid the detected prey, but only in so far as said prey, by its very nature, would assert itself *of a different nature*, which the predator would fail to recognise as prey (Jacob & Brown 2000; Holtcamp 1997), and therefore, would fail to prey on. Insects resembling dry leaves or twigs would be such an example.

Would it be wild, extravagant, mad, a thought that if I were to position myself as the USA, Australia or Israel, for example, do in contemporary Politics and the current political ecosystem, as they were Europe's equal in their Enlightenment, their humanism, or even their predatory stance, I would be much better off than not doing so, which is what I have been doing, and ended up prey, my Heart eaten away by the Enlightened Man? Would it be far-fetched that if I were considered non-prey, that if I Signalled to the Enlightened Man that I could be or were strong opponent, as pointed by Akufo-Addo last year, even if it meant Mimicking traits that I, in fact, did not have, or evolving to appear as I were non-prey, he (the Enlightened Man) would not be as comfortable as he usually has been, eating away at my Heart? What if I were to write over the Order of Things, for instance, and assert my stance as non-prey, whether as twig copy-cat or as the Enlightened Man's absolute equal? Would this not enhance the probability of my survival post-detection? Would the Enlightened Man still be gorging away at my Heart if he no longer recognised me as prey?

Imagining that he could not care, i.e. that the Enlightened Man did not recognise me as prey and still decided on gorging away at my Heart, capture deterrence could follow. Capture deterrence would be that stage with the prey attempting to reduce the probability of success of prey capture post-prey detection. Rapid retreat would be one sure way to go about this, where the prey would choose or would be able to take flight from, to flee, quite literally, the predator and/or the ecosystem within which it would have been held that is lethal for it, i.e. that from which the predator would have grown, and wherein it would be its prey.

Now, here is some food for thought: What if I chose to flee the ecosystem that was lethal for me? Instead of trying to fix it to my advantage, instead of seeking, as so many have tried before, to undo hundreds of years of predation, Cannibalism, Leadership and NGO failures, Extraction, predatory relationships, terrible financial accounting, equally terrible business contracts, twisted fiscal practice, corruption, greed, treason, falsehoods, carefree Narcissism, de-humanisation, domination, objectification and so on and so forth, what if I just left? Of course, the political ecosystem would suffer; a lot of people would suffer, especially with the Enlightened Man no longer being able to gorge away at my Heart and, therefore, having to look to other paths to feed itself, others to prey on. But that would not have to be my issue to handle, certainly! And so, what if I just left?

Or could I ever leave? Could I really not care enough about those that would be preyed on if I were to leave successfully? Could I lead others into their demise? Could I ever be as the Enlightened Man, cold to the pain of others, cause of the pain of others? No. Proof thereof is that this, this coldness, is exactly what so many sons of *my* Soil have tried to stand against especially since the beginning of the periods of enslavement and colonialism. But would there be much choice left, if all else failed, but for me to actually fight the Enlightened Man as I chose to remain within the ecosystem that would have made food of my Heart, so as to avoid the pain that would be thrown onto others if I did not? Would I not have to go toward active defence, toward a real battle to defend my body, and do the very thing that I would have wanted to avoid, i.e. go to another using force, and therefore risk causing damage to the latter, even if that other were a Cannibal, a Narcissistic Predator, a monster with no care for my life? If I were not to be successful in my manner of attack deterrence and capture deterrence, if I remained within that context, that ecosystem from which the Enlightened Man would have grown, and if I did not fight back, would he not eat me into my demise, to my death, quite simply? What other path could I possibly take so as not to die?

The choice, again, which is no choice at all, would be to die or to fight back and hurt another but stand a chance to survive. The latter would be the entire form of a Just Battle, would it not be? I would not actively seek to cause damage to another, but there would quite likely be damage in that Battle and that damage would be necessary evil. It would not be the most morally or ethically comforting or comfortable path to take, surely, but it would be worth it, for me at least. This would be consumption deterrence, a third possible stage toward attempting to enhance the probability of my survival. If I would be left with no other choice than having to fight on my Soil to defend myself from the Cannibal gorging away at my Heart, then that is exactly what I would have to do.

And so, by way of attack deterrence, capture deterrence and consumption deterrence, my Heart would in all likelihood not be completely eaten away and I would not be led straight to my death. This would be a correct treatment to the matter of Extraction, or the answer to the series of questions that I posed earlier in this piece re the manner in which I could navigate this relationship with Europe that turned lethal for me. It all begins, of course, with a correct diagnosis.

Conclusion

Cannibalism would be too savage, too barbaric, too beastly, too much of a thing of a monster to be entertained as behaviour or act or endeavour or practice that the Enlightened Man would ever sway toward on purpose, unless, of course, extraordinarily ill of mind. There is nothing more that I would want than for this to be true. There is nothing more that I would want than to exist in a world where this would be true. For then I would not be left with writing on the fact of this same Enlightened Man gorging away at my Heart for centuries until today. I would not have to think of the fact of him taking from me no less than the very things that could serve keep me alive. There is nothing more that I would want than for this to be true. There is nothing more that I would want than to exist in a world where this would be true. I would not have to face the possibility of the end of me by his doing, his hunger, his greed and selfishness. I would not be speaking of myself as victim. And prey. And food … The obscure gourmandise of an Enlightened Man.

Endnotes

[1] Not as a body in actual flesh and bone, but referring to place, continent.

[2]. Read more on the Africa-EU Summit 2017 at http://www.africa-eu-partnership.org/en/about-us/how-it-works/africa-eu-summit.

[3] I make reference here to the idea of 'the white man's burden', to read in such pieces as Hitchens (2004) *Blood, Class, and Empire*; Yancy (2008) *Black Bodies, White Gazes*.

[4] See more on this in stories such as that of the Hottentot Venus, for example, to read in Holmes (2006) *The Hottentot Venus*.

[5].This is including French President, Macron, who in 2017 promised to invest against slavery in Libya, for example. The following article speaks to this: http://www.telegraph.co.uk/news/2017/11/29/europe-promises-44bn-marshall-plan-africa-migrant-slavery-libya/.

[6] See others speaking to this at
https://www.washingtonpost.com/news/global-opinions/wp/2017/07/14/macron-blames-civilization-for-africas-problems-france-should-acknowledge-its-own-responsibility/?utm_term=.08e6d3a20bb8;
https://www.politico.eu/article/macron-g20-angry-reaction-to-emmanuel-macrons-remark-that-africa-has-a-civilizational-problem/;
http://foreignpolicy.com/2017/07/17/is-it-racist-to-say-africa-has-civilizational-problems/;
http://www.aljazeera.com/blogs/africa/2017/11/macron-tours-africa-reset-francafrique-relationship-171128070955254.html.

[7] In reference to 'organised violence'. Read in Metz & Cuccia (2010) *Defining War for the 21st Century*.

[8] See excerpts from his speech, for example, at
https://www.informationng.com/2017/12/ghanaian-presidents-speech-shocks-french-president-macron.html;

http://africasacountry.com/2017/12/ghanas-president-and-what-the-west-wants-to-hear/;

https://www.npr.org/sections/goatsandsoda/2017/12/12/570139770/la test-viral-video-ghanas-prez-throws-shade-at-foreign-aid.

References

Acosta, A. (2013) 'Extractivism and Neoextractivism: Two Sides of the Same Curse', in M. Lang and D. Mokrani (eds), *Beyond Development: Alternative Visions from Latin America*, Amsterdam: Transnational Institute and Rosa Luxemburg Foundation.

Aghion, P., Baccheta, P., Rancière, R. & Rogoff, K. (2009) 'Exchange Rate Volatility and Productivity Growth: The Role of Financial Development', *Journal of Monetary Economics*, Elsevier, Vol. 56(4): 494–513.

Amin, S. (1990) *Maldevelopment: Anatomy of a Global Failure*, London: Zed Books.

Anderson, B. (2006) *Imagined Communities: Reflections on the Origin and Spread of Nationalism*, London: Verso Books.

Anderson, D. (2005) *Histories of the Hanged: The Dirty War in Kenya and the End of Empire*, New York: W. W. Norton and Company.

Asiedu, K. G. (2017) 'A Speech by Ghana's President calling for Africa to end its Dependency on the West is a Viral Hit', in *Quartz Media*, available at https://qz.com/1145953/ghanas-president-akufo-addo-shocks-frances-macron-with-africa-non-dependent-speech/.

Basedau, M. and Lay, J. (2009) 'Resource Curse or Rentier Peace? The Ambiguous Effects of Oil Wealth and Oil Dependence on Violent Conflict', *Journal of Peace Research*, Vol. 46(6): 757–776.

Bauer, A. & Quiroz, J.C. (2013) 'Resource Governance', in A. Goldthau (ed.): *The Handbook of Global Energy Policy*, Wiley-Blackwell.

Bayart, J-F., Geschiere, P., & Nyamnjoh. (2001) 'J'étais là Avant: Problématiques de l'Autochthonie', *Critique Internationale*, Vol. 10(1).

Birdsall, V. O. (1985) *Defoe's Perpetual Seekers: A Study of the Major Fiction*, London: Associated University Presses, pp. 24-49.

Boahen, A. A. (1987) *African Perspectives on Colonialism*, Baltimore: John's Hopkins University Press.

Bond, P. (2002) *Fanon's Warning: a Civil Society Reader on the New Partnership for Africa's Development*, New Jersey: Africa World Press.

Brunnschweiler, C. N. & Bulte, E. H. (2008) 'Linking Natural Resources to Slow Growth and More Conflict', *Science*, Vol. 32(5876): 616–617.

Brunnschweiler, C. N. & Bulte, E. H. (May 2008) 'The Resource Curse Revisited and Revised: A Tale of Paradoxes and Red Herrings', *Journal of Environmental Economics and Management*, Elsevier, Vol. 55(3): 248–264.

Butler, N. (28/11/2017) 'Macron Tours Africa to 'Reset' Francafrique Relationship', *AlJazeera*, available at https://www.aljazeera.com/blogs/africa/2017/11/macron-tours-africa-reset-francafrique-relationship-171128070955254.html?xif=;%20https:/www.euractiv.de/sectio n/eu-aussenpolitik/news/ghanas-praesident-akufo-addo-ueberrascht-macron-mit-deutlicher-absage-an-die-entwicklungshilfe/.

Caselli, F. & Michaels, G. (January 2013) 'Do Oil Windfalls Improve Living Standard? Evidence from Brazil', *American Economic Journal*, Applied Economic Association, Vol. 5(1): 208–238.

Cassirer, E. (2009) *The Enlightenment*, Princeton: Princeton University Press.

Chang, H-J. (2007) *Bad Samaritans: The Myth of Free Trade and the Secret History of Capitalism*, Bloomsbury Press.

Collier, P. (2000) 'Doing Well Out of War: An Economic Perspective', in M. Berdal & D. Mallone (eds): *Greed and Grievance, Economic Agendas in Civil Wars*, Boulder, CO: Lynne Rienner.

Collinge, J., Whitfield, J., McKintosh, E., Frosh, A., Mead, S., Hill, A. F., Brandner, S., Thomas., D. & Alpers, M. P. (2008) 'A Clinical Study of Kuru Patients with Long Incubation Periods at the end of the Epidemic in Papua New Guinea', *Philosophical Transactions of the Royal Society B: Biological Sciences*, Vol. 363(1510): 3725–3739.

Connolly, K. (2003) 'Cannibal Filmed Himself Killing and Eating his "Willing Victim"', Copley, A. (2017) *Figure of the Week: Extractive Resource Governance in Africa*, Brookings.

De Dijn, A. (2012) 'The Politics of Enlightenment: From Peter Gay to Jonathan Israel', *The Historical Journal*, Vol. 55: 785–805.

Defoe, D. (1994) *Robinson Crusoe*, London: Penguin Books.

Derrida, J. (1978) *Writing and Difference*, London and New York: Routledge.

Diamond, J. (2004) *Collapse: How Societies Choose to Fail or Succeed*, New York: Viking.

Drewry, M. (2014) 'It's Time NGOs Admit that Aid isn't going to save Africa',

DSM-IV & DSM-V (2012) *DSM-IV and DSM-5 Criteria for the Personality Disorders*, American Psychiatric Association.

DSM-V (2010) *DSM-V: Proposed Revisions: Personality and Personality Disorders*, American Psychiatric Association.

Dunning, T. (2008) *Crude Democracy: Natural Resource Wealth and Political Regimes*, New York: Cambridge University Press.

Engdahl, F. W. (2013) *Myth, Lies and Oil Wars*, Edition Engdahl.

Ernst & Young Global Ltd. (2017) *Mining and Metals Tax Guide: Peru*, EYGM Limited: EYG No. 03269-174GBL.

Ferguson, J. (2006) *Global Shadows: Africa in the Neoliberal World Order*, Duke University Press.

Foucault, M. (2002) *The Order of Things: An Archaeology of the Human Sciences*, London & New York: Routledge, p. xv.

Gerhart, G. (1978) *Black Power in South Africa: The Evolution of an Ideology*, Berkeley: University of California Press.

Geschiere, P. & Ceuppens, B. (2005) 'Autochthony: Global or Local?', *Annual Review of Anthropology*, Vol. 34.

Hannibal (2015) Season 3 Episode 1: *Antipasto*.

Harding, L. (2003) 'Victim of Cannibal Agreed to be Eaten', *The Guardian*, available at https://amp.theguardian.com/world/2003/dec/04/germany.lu keharding.

Härlin, C. & Härlin, M. (2003) 'Towards a Historization of Aposematism', in *Evolutionary Ecology*, Vol. 17(2): 197-212.

Hitchens, C. (2004) *Blood, Class, and Empire: The Enduring Anglo–American Relationship*, New York: Nation Books.

Holmes, R. (2006) *The Hottentot Venus*, Bloomsbury: Random House.

Holtcamp, W. N. Grant, W. E., & Vinson, S. B. (1997) 'Patch Use under Predation Hazard: Effect of the Red Imported Fire Ant on Deer Mouse Foraging Behavior', *Ecology*, Vol. 78: 308–317.

Honest Accounts Report (2014 [2017]) *How the World Profits from Africa's Wealth*, Global Justice Now.

https://www.frontiersin.org/articles/10.3389/fnins.2015.00055/full.

https://www.telegraph.co.uk/news/worldnews/europe/germany/1448497/Cannibal-filmed-himself-killing-and-eating-his-willing-victim.html.

Human Rights Watch (2018) *Country Summary: Equatorial Guinea*, Human Rights Watch.

Humphreys, M., Sachs, J. D. & Stiglitz, J. (2007) 'Introduction', in *Escaping the Resource Curse*, Columbia University Press.

Index Mundi Report, *Economy: GDP – Per Capita (PPP): Equatorial Guinea*, Index Mundi.

Jacob, J. & Brown, J. S. (2000) 'Microhabitat Use, Giving-up Densities and Temporal Activity as Short- and Long-term Anti-predator Behaviors in Common Voles', *Oikos*, Vol. 91: 131–138.

Kabemba, C. (02/03/2014) *Undermining Africa's Wealth: A Critique of the British Government's and British Extractive Companies' Role in Africa from the Colonial Era to the Current Scramble for the Continent's Resources*, OSISA.

Kabemba, C. (2014) *Myths and Mining: The Reality of Resource Governance in Africa*, OSISA.

Kohnert, D. (07/2008) *EU-African Economic Relations: Continuing Dominance, Traded for Aid?* GIGA Research Programme: Transformation in the Process of Globalization, No. 82.

Landsberg, C., & Kornegey, F. (1998) 'The African Renaissance: A Quest for Pax Africana and Pan-Africanism', in *South Africa and Africa: Reflections on the African Renaissance*, Foundation for Global Dialogue, Occasional Paper No. 17.

Levy, P. (2013) *Dispelling Wetiko: Breaking the Curse of Evil*, North Atlantic Books.

Lev-Yadun, S., Dafni, A., Inbar, M., Izhaki, I. and Ne'eman, G. (2002) 'Colour Patterns in Vegetative Parts of Plants Deserve more Research Attention', *Trends in Plant Science*, Vol. 7(2): 59–60.

Matthews, S. (2017) 'The Role of NGOs in Africa: Are they a Force for Good?', *The Conversation*, available at http://theconversation.com/the-role-of-ngos-in-africa-are-they-a-force-for-good-76227.

Mboya, T. (1963) *Freedom and After*, London: Andre Deutsch.

McKinsey Global Institute (MGI) (2010) *Lions on the Move: The Progress and Potential of African Economies*, McKinsey & Company.

McMahan, J. (2007) 'The Sources and Status of Just War Principles', *Journal of Military Ethics*, Rutgers University, Vol. 6(2): 91–106.

Metz, S. & Cuccia, P. (2010) *Defining War for the 21st Century*, 2010 SSI Annual Strategy Report, Strategic Studies Institute.

Mobbs, D., Hagan, C. C., Dalgleish, T., Silston, B. & Prévost, C. (2015) 'The Ecology of Human Fear: Survival Optimisation and the Nervous System', in *Frontiers in Neuroscience, Social and Evolutionary Neuroscience*, available at

Mostler, G. (1935) 'Beobachtungen zur Frage der Wespenmimikry', *Zeitschrift für Morphologie und Ökologie der Tiere*, Vol. 29: 381–454.

Müller, F. (1879) *Ituna and Thyridia; A Remarkable Case of Mimicry in Butterflies*, Transactions of the Entomological Society of London: xx–xxix.

Nkrumah, K. (1965) *Neo-colonialism: The Last Stage of Imperialism*, London: Heinemann.

Novak, M. E. (1963) *Defoe and the Nature of Man*, Oxford: Oxford University Press, pp. 130–163.

Nunn, N. and Qian, N. (2010) 'The Columbian Exchange: A History of Disease, Food, and Ideas', *The Journal of Economic Perspectives*, Vol. 24(2): 163–188.

Palleroni A., Miller, C. T., Hauser, M. & Marler, P. (2005) 'Predation Prey Plumage adaptation against falcon attack', *Nature*, Vol. 434(7036): 973–974.

Pear, D. W. (27/01/2014) 'Africa: Incredible Wealth, Exploitation, Corruption and Poverty for its People', *The Real News Network*, available at http://therealnews.com/t2/component/content/article/170-more-blog-posts-from-david-william-pear/1944-africa-incredible-wealth-exploitation-corruption-and-poverty-for-its-people-.

Relvea, R.A. (2002) 'Local Population Differences in Phenotypic Plasticity: Predator-induced Changed in Wood Frog Tadpoles', *Ecological Monographs*, Vol. 72(1): 77–93.

Roff, D. A. (1992) *The Evolution of Life Histories: Theory and Analysis*, Chapman & Hall, New York.

Ronningstam, E. (2011) 'Narcissistic personality disorder: a clinical perspective',*Journal of Psychiatric Practice*, Vol. 17(2): 89–99.

Ronningstam, E. (2016) 'Pathological Narcissism and Narcissistic Personality Disorder: Recent Research and Clinical Implications', *Current Behavioral Neuroscience Reports*, Springer International Publishing, Vol. 3(1): 34-42.

Ross, M. L. (2012) *The Oil Curse: How Petroleum Wealth Shapes the Development of Nations*, Princeton: Princeton University.

Russell, G. A. (1985) 'Narcissism and the Narcissistic Personality Disorder: A Comparison of the Theories of Kernberg and Kohut', *British Journal of Medical Psychology*, Vol. 58: 137–148.

Said, E. (1978) *Orientalism*, New York: Pantheon Book.

Samuel, H. & Squires, N. (2017) 'Emmanuel Macron announces EU Plan to Launch "Concrete Military Action" to rescue African Migrants Enslaved in Libya', *The Telegraph*, available at https://www.telegraph.co.uk/news/2017/11/29/europe-promises-44bn-marshall-plan-africa-migrant-slavery-libya/.

Smith, D. (2013) 'Africa 'Ripped off Big Time' by Foreign Resource Firms, says Bank Chief', *The Guardian*, available at https://www.theguardian.com/global-development/2013/jun/18/africa-ripped-off-foreign-resource-firms, (last accessed 15 November 2017.

Smith-Spark, L. (2017) *Slavery, Security on Agenda as Merkel and Macron meet African Leaders*, CNN, available at https://edition.cnn.com/2017/11/29/africa/au-eu-summit-ivory-coast/index.html.

Spurr, D. (1993) *The Rhetoric of Empire: Colonial Discourse in Journalism, Travel Writing, and Imperial Administration*, Durham, NC: Duke University Press.

Stiglitz, J. E. (1974) 'Growth with exhaustible natural resources: the competitive economy', *Review of Economic Studies: Symposium on the Economics of Exhaustible Resources*, Vol. 41: 139–152.

The Guardian, available at https://www.theguardian.com/global-development-professionals-network/2014/jul/22/africa-rescue-aid-stealing-resources.

Trabanco, J. M. A. (2014) 'Dollar Hegemony, 'Monetary Geopolitics' and the IMF: The Symbiosis between Global Finance and Power', *Global Research*, available at https://www.globalresearch.ca/dollar-hegemony-and-monetary-geopolitics-the-symbiosis-between-global-finance-and-power-politics-2/5362357.

Tzouvala, N. (2017) 'Macron & Africa's Civilisational Problem', *Critical Legal Thinking: Law and the Political*, available at http://criticallegalthinking.com/2017/07/14/macron-africas-civilisational-problem/.

UNDP Development Report (2016) *Human Development for Everyone: Briefing note for countries on the 2016 Human Development Report: Equatorial* Guinea, UNDP.

Vamosi, S. M. (2005) 'On the Role of Enemies in Divergence and Diversification of Prey: A Review and Synthesis', *Canadian Journal of Zoology*, Vol. 83(7): 894–910.

Van der Ploeg, F. (2010) 'Aggressive Oil Extraction and Precautionary Saving: Coping with Volatility', *Journal of Public Economics*, Elsevier, Vol. 94(5–6): 421–433.

Vassalo, H. (2006) 'Economic Cannibalism', *Times of Malta*, available at https://www.timesofmalta.com/mobile/articles/view/2006012 7/opinion/economic-cannibalism.65163.

Vincent, T. (1999) 'The Myth of Development: A Critique of a Eurocentric Discourse', R. Munck, & D. O'Hearn (eds): *Critical Development Theory: Contributions to a New Paradigm*, London: Zed Books (pp.6–8).

Viscusi, G. & Gongo, S. (2017) 'Macron Says He Aims to Leave France's Colonial Past in Africa Behind', *Bloomberg*, available at https://www.bloomberg.com/news/articles/2017-11-28/macron-tells-african-crowd-he-aims-to-leave-colonial-past-behind (last accessed 15 November 2017).

Wa Wamwere, K. (2002) *I Refuse to Die: My Journey for Freedom*, New York: Seven Stories Press.

Wainaina, B. (2006) 'How to Write about Africa', *Granta*, Vol. 92, available at https://granta.com/how-to-write-about-africa/.

Wenar, L., (2008), 'Property Rights and the Resource Curse,' In *Philosophy & Public Affairs*, Vol. 36(1): 2–32.

Yancy, G. (2008) *Black Bodies, White Gazes: The Continuing Significance of Race*, Rowman & Littlefield Publishers, Inc.

Chapter 9

Consumerisation of cannibalism in contemporary Japanese society

Akira Takada

Introduction

What does it mean for human beings to engage in cannibalism? The answer to this awkward question may vary greatly according to how the responder relates to cannibalism itself, which is defined as 'the act of any life form consuming others of its own kind' (Travis-Henikoff 2008: Kindle location no. 565). The various statuses of participation (Goffman 1981) available in this act, such as that of the eater, victim, witness and bystander, entail diverse understandings of it. At the same time, widely different acts may be associated with cannibalism, depending on one's participation status. Historically speaking, 'the more we crave fulfilment through pretensions to modernity and civilisation, the greater our tendency to outsource and disguise our cannibalism' (Nyamnjoh, p. 7 in this volume). Although study of excavated bones and genetic data leads to the hypothesis that our ancestors were all cannibals (Travis-Henikoff 2008: Kindle location no. 135), cannibalism has been used to reflect the 'otherness' of modernity and civilisation in the West. In this context, cannibalism was an ethnocentric category. The imperial gaze attributed cannibalism to the peoples and societies of Africa, Melanesia and other colonised areas. The idea of cannibalism was used to justify imposing a European vision of the world and social systems on those peoples (cf. Travis-Henikoff 2008; Lévi-Strauss 2016). Scholarly activities cannot be absolved from blame here. For example, as Mbembe (2001) rightly observed, African Studies at its origin had a tendency to highlight the exotic and to characterise Africa as the negative of Western normality.

Geographical remoteness is not the only factor in the ascription of cannibalism or, more broadly, of otherness. For instance, tales of vampires, who live on the blood of living people, are a variant of cannibalism. Such tales are set within the boundaries of Europe, although vampires are depicted as living outside the residential area of normal people. These tales, which in Europe can be traced back to long ago, have diffused almost all over Europe. They have also fired the imagination of people in other parts of the world, particularly in the creative industries, with horror films involving blood-shocking bats and figures such as Count Dracula as a constant reminder of cannibalism as a source of sustenance. Tales and images of vampires and cannibalism have been regenerated in contemporary Japanese mega-hit manga and anime, such as 'Vampire Hunter D' (*Kyuuketsuki Hantaa D*), 'Tokyo Ghoul' (*Toukyou Ghoul*) and 'Attack on Titan' (*Shingeki no Kyojin*), in new and creative ways.

It should be noted that cannibalism among Japanese nationals has been reported and discussed to a considerable extent. One of the most sensational cases was the shocking murder that occurred in Paris in 1981 (see Nyamnjoh, this volume, for more details). A Japanese graduate student at the University of Paris murdered his female Dutch friend who was a fellow graduate student. He then had sex with the corpse, and subsequently consumed both raw and cooked flesh from the corpse on several occasions. After his arrest, he not only willingly talked about his deed but also confessed that he had for a long time desired to eat a beautiful young woman. He was diagnosed as criminally insane and was hospitalised in a mental asylum. However, after securing his release from the asylum, he often appeared in the media and even wrote several books about the murder and cannibalism (e.g., Sagawa 1991), which in themselves, provide sufficient material for a separate study.

Another controversial issue is that of the cannibalism that occurred among Japanese soldiers during the Second World War. On several islands of the Pacific, particularly Mindanao, Luzon and Leyte in Philippines, the soldiers were reported to have cannibalised local residents, their enemies and fellow soldiers (e.g., Ōoka 1951; Moriya 1978; Travis-Henikoff 2008; Esteban 2016). Esteban (2016) studied archived reports on cannibalism in Bukidnon Province, Mindanao, to determine the types of, and reasons for, the cannibalism from the viewpoint of the Japanese soldiers. He concluded that serious starvation, malnutrition and salt hunger led to the cannibalism, which allowed the soldiers to survive under the miserable conditions of war. Travis-Henikoff (2008: Kindle location no. 2927) argued that, in addition to the extreme hunger, the situation of war and total commitment to following the orders prompted the horrific acts associated with cannibalism. Moriya (1978), who was a surgeon in the Japanese Army, wrote about his traumatic experiences in Luzon during the war. According to him, at that time, people including himself were threatened by groups of people dubbed 'Japanese guerrillas', who actively killed people, including fellow Japanese soldiers, and ate their flesh. He inferred that some individuals from demobilised groups of the Japanese Army had initiated the deeds. As the conditions in the war became increasingly severe, it appears that cannibalism became more widespread. *Nobi* (lit. 'Wildfire') is an excellent novel written by Shohei Ōoka based on his personal experiences during the war in the Japanese Army in Leyte. In the novel, he describes in detail the profound agony of eating human flesh (Ōoka 1951).

Paying attention to cannibalism also helps us to understand the contemporary world. As Nyamnjoh (p. 5 in this volume) concludes, 'there is no reason to assume that cannibals are confined in the ancestral closets, if we were to take cannibalism seriously beyond its literal and primary connotation of eating the flesh of another human'. Indeed, if we generalise it far enough, 'the concept of cannibalism and its direct and indirect applications belong to all societies' (Lévi-Strauss 2016). Hence, the relationships that may be found between cannibalism and modern gory murder stories, and the scenes in which cannibalism is reformulated and revitalised, must be considered, along with the question of how we can assimilate the flesh of others into ourselves in the contemporary world. To address these issues, this chapter analyses three cases, namely (1) the serial murder in Zama, in which a young man was arrested following the discovery of nine dismembered bodies, (2) the success of the idol industry, in which the term 'idol' refers to young starlets, and (3) favourable use of the word *Nama* (lit. rawness, bareness and being alive) in advertisements for commodities or fashions. All of these indicate a foreshadowing of cannibalism in contemporary Japanese society, which has deepened its sense of incompleteness (Nyamnjoh 2017), in line with its rapid Westernisation and the wide reach of consumerism.

This chapter will not provide a detailed ethnography of the three cases. Instead, it examines 'a grammar of motives' (Burke 1945), revealing the strategic spots where ambiguities necessarily arise as a resource for generating social meaning, and it provides the semantic environment in which the above cases exist in practice, shown from the perspective of the Japanese. Each case represents an important component of cannibalism, namely, the temptation posed by killing or death, the desire to possess the adored other, and the allure of flesh in its various guises and disguises. Moreover, all the cases listed reflect a consumer culture that is sustained by extremely complex systems of material production, product distribution and information circulation. Seen in this way, there might be a new form of cannibalism being generated in contemporary Japanese society, one that compensates for a prevalent sense of incompleteness (Nyamnjoh 2017) throughout daily life.

Exploiting the suicidal

In late October 2017, the police found numerous dismembered bodies stored inside coolers in an apartment in the city of Zama, Kanagawa Prefecture. Parts of the bodies showed multiple cuts and some portions were already reduced to bone, according to the police. TS, a 27-year-old man who lived in the apartment, worked as a broker recruiting young women and girls into the sex industry. He was arrested the same day. He has since confessed to killing nine people: three teenage high school girls, one female teenage university student, an unemployed woman in her 20s, a woman in her 20s who was a part-time employee, a woman in her 20s employed by a company and a male and female couple, both of whom were in their 20s. The investigators have identified all nine individuals through DNA analysis of the dismembered bodies, GPS data from their mobile phones and other means. Those nine victims were residents of Kanagawa and neighbouring prefectures.

Major media outlets began reporting the case immediately after the police arrested TS.[1] This gory serial murder immediately caught the attention of the public and aroused a great deal of fear. A shock wave swept over the country. The turmoil was heightened by the private information the media released on the victims, including their names, images, ages, occupations, areas of residence, personal histories and comments from their acquaintances.[2] It is not usual for the Japanese media environment to release this kind of private information on crime victims so broadly and, not surprisingly, the news reports excited criticism.[3] The flow of reports in the major media soon ebbed. However, the information spread and was amplified through the internet, social media, email and oral communications.

Among the many distinctive features of this case that did not escape the media and the audience was the fact that the suspect targeted women had expressed suicidal thoughts on a specialised social networking service (SNS). The only exception was the sole male victim. He had never expressed that he was considering suicide, but he was the boyfriend of a female victim who did post her suicidal thoughts on the SNS where others posted about suicide. It appears that he only became a victim when he confronted the suspect to ask the whereabouts of his girlfriend. TS sought to get acquainted with his victims and earn their trust by posting his own suicidal wishes on Twitter, according to investigative sources.[4] The SNS functioned, therefore, to enable various agents to achieve their aims (e.g., the killer, the suicidal women and girls, and onlookers). It should be noted that suicide is a form of self- or auto-cannibalism. Thus, committing suicide through a facilitator can be likened to facilitated auto-cannibalism by a 'professional' cannibal.[5] Soon after the arrest, a woman who had expressed suicidal thoughts on the SNS and then directly communicated with TS just before his arrest was quoted on the media.[6] According to her, TS's voice sounded like that of a good young man. He let her unload her thoughts on him, and sometimes he unloaded on her as well (e.g., he expressed his own suicidal thoughts and distress about work). He mentioned that if she wished to die, he would like to kill her. He even mentioned that he had already killed several people. A number of media reports commented that TS exploited the deep loneliness of young people, who were losing their intimate connection with those around them.[7] Several even used phrases such as *'yowai josei wo kuimono ni suru'* (lit. 'ate the weak women'), which is a metaphor for cannibalism.[8]

In fact, this gory case of serial murder is highly relevant to cannibalism, which is related to one's concern over the boundary between the living and the dead, self and other, the realm of the idea and that of flesh. Although TS did not literally eat the flesh of his victims, it may be that he extended his self by dismembering and possessing the belongings of the victims and their bodies after their actual deaths. The media also contributed greatly to the association of the serial murder case with cannibalism in that it emphasised the extraordinary character and freakishness of the incident to attract the attention of the general public. Their reports allowed the audience to identify themselves with either the victims or the killer, letting them effortlessly fulfil the temptation of symbolic death and killing, respectively. This implies that the media not only provide us with the tools of cannibalisation but that they also cannibalise us.

Although this serial murder is an exceptional incident, it reflects the structural background of Japanese society. The desire and pressure to achieve a symbolic death among young people, which has been claimed to be a universal phenomenon of human beings as social creatures (Erikson 1959), is one that has taken a culturally distinctive form in Japanese society (Kawai 1976; Takahashi 1999) and constitutes a part of the background. Additionally, the Japanese sex industry, which prefers its young women to have an amateur aura, is a part of the background here as well. The industry has invented many 'soft' sexual services dispensed by teenage girls and young women, such as selling school uniforms and underwear to (often middle-aged and male) customers, participating in photo sessions where they wear various costumes and customers take photographs of them, doing telephone dating and walking with customers. The industry often reassures the girls and young women it is recruiting about the casualness and safety of the work they will provide, although this is not necessarily accurate (Miyadai 1994).

TS was, on the one hand, a broker who recruited girls and young women into the sex industry and, on the other, a young man seeking symbolic death. His personal history and the records he left on SNS suggest that he was an agent floating between these two worlds, showing considerable sensitivity to his victims' feelings.[9] This may be a reason why not a few, including the victims, trusted him from his messages on SNS and met up with him. When he said that he would help his victims die or would like to die together with them, he might have been seeking out what initiation rituals essentially aim for. The act of killing and the experience of dying are two sides of the same coin. Although the participation status is completely different for the killer and the victim, the imagination can connect them. That is to say, by imagining and mirroring the subjective experiences of the victims, the killer may have been attempting to experience a symbolic death. Moreover, this symbolic death may have stimulated a sense of reincarnation. Indeed, when the victims expressed their suicidal thoughts, in their vulnerability, they probably sought symbolic reincarnation rather than actual agonising death. TS as the agent of killing might also have been obsessed with such desires. However, if he killed nine people in a very short time (within two months) as the media reported, he most probably did not accomplish symbolic death but, instead, acted directly to bring about the actual death of his victims and reiterated a false initiation ritual – his wish to die was replaced by acts of living in another's death. Thus, the killer is an embodiment of the *puer aeternus* in contemporary Japanese society (Kawai 1976).

Fantasising reality and realising the fantasy

In his bestseller *The Clash of Civilizations and the Remaking of World Order* (1996), Samuel P. Huntington said that the world could be divided into eight different civilisations. In this argument, he regarded Japan as a single isolated civilisation, derived from Chinese civilisation around the second to fifth centuries. The characteristics of Japan were strengthened by rapid Westernisation, which began there in the late 19th century, before it came to other East Asian areas, and were further reinforced by the enormous influence of the US after WWII. Although Japan's reputation as a threat to Western civilisation drastically declined after Japan's economic crisis in the 1990s and 2000s, Huntington's argument still provides a constructive suggestion for our approach to the cultural distinctiveness of Japanese society. Rather than being proud of the flourishing of its unique civilisation, many Japanese today are self-flagellating, calling their islands Galapagos, with reference to the peculiar and isolated situation of its culture and society. A typical example is the Japanese cell-phone industry, which failed to appeal to the world market and has been reducing its scale, even though it had developed advanced technologies (e.g., various ringtones, camera functions, TV viewing and mobile wallets) and implemented them before the West.

Figure 1: Idol x Metal (with great respect to 'Babymetal')

Another example of the Galapagos phenomenon can be found in the Japanese pop scene, which has developed a distinctive culture and customs. Originally, idols were young popular artists in the US: Gene Austin in the 1920s and Frank Sinatra in the 1940s were the earliest artists called idols (Tyler 2007). The term was also used for those who came along more recently and recorded mega-hit songs, like Michael Jackson, the Backstreet Boys and the Spice Girls (Fairchild 2008). 'Idol' appears to have been replaced by other terms, such as 'pop star' or 'pop artist', when referring to musicians from the US and UK However, a quite a different trajectory characterises the Japanese pop scene. Idols are still frequently referred to, but this term primarily means young starlets. It is possible to find many idols who convey peculiar concepts or concept combinations, such as cute girls playing heavy metal and punk music[10] (Figure 1) or girl groups hiding their faces with hockey masks.[11] Before proceeding to its relevance to the idea of cannibalism, a brief summary of the history of the idol in Japan is necessary (for more details, see Sakai 2014).

With reference to popular musicians from the US, at the beginning of its use in 1960s, idols were young popular artists in Japan. Those artists also imitated the style of musical performances favoured in the US. However, in the 1970s, the image of idols began to transform. Starlets, who represent an ideal of immature cuteness, familiar charm and amateurish skills, which have come to constitute the fundamental features of the Japanese idol, came on the stage and were called idols. In the 1980s, idols' performances became diversified. Some exercised their relatively high levels of skill as singers and/or dancers; others mainly appeared as film actresses or actors. Large groups of idols who appealed to their audience with their familiar charms also became more common in this period. They came to their studios after school and were active on TV entertainment shows. Gravure idols or *gurabia aidoru* (the Japanese version of pin-up girls) appeared too. They did not even sing, which used to be a necessary activity of idols, and they mainly expressed their cuteness or sexiness with their photographs, which appeared in comics and other magazines for young adults. Then, in the 1990s, the Japanese idol industry faced its so-called winter, when the scale of the market for idols declined, while Japanese society at large experienced the collapse of the bubble economy and the subsequent economic crisis.

However, the Japanese idol industry has been booming again, beginning in the 2000s. A new style of management spurred its flourishing. It is increasingly common for several unknown young girls to form a large group. Such groups begin their work on a very small scale, performing a small live concert or doing an event where they shake hands with their supporters, with the purpose of succeeding in more major and established scenes. Their efforts are dramatised and documented through various agencies (e.g., in their own theatres, on TV programmes, and through other media). Their supporters, who are often associated with what are called 'otaku',[12] find a favourite individual idol and help her and her group achieve their dreams. Idols are usually prohibited any romantic relationships in their private lives. If an idol is found to have a boyfriend, it is regarded as a scandal, and she may be expelled from the group or even fired by the management company.

It is hardly surprising that not a small number of supporters seek pseudo-romances with their favourite idols or perceive an idealised self-image in them. The core admirers often buy dozens of their CDs to get a ticket to attend an event to shake hands with them, or they obtain multiple ballots to vote them into higher tiers in rallies where idols compete on the number of votes from their supporters. Each idol is ranked in hierarchical tiers based on such competitions. The higher the idol is ranked, the more opportunities she is given to achieve success. The rallies are designed to provide the admirers with scenes that facilitate their commitment to their favourite idol and fulfil their desire for being recognised and ratified as a significant individual. Some may develop the fantasy that they are dominating their favourite and adored idol (cf. Yomoda 2006). Dominating and possessing the adored 'other' is a way of extending and stabilising one's self. Paradoxically, it may bring a sense of belonging to the adored 'other'. Cannibalism, in a narrow sense, is an extreme case of acting out this desire. The logic of metonymy and analogy makes it easier and more accessible. Indeed, actual and symbolic cannibalism are two sides of the same coin, according to Travis-Henikoff (2008: Kindle location no. 1544). By gaining the belongings of the adored 'other' or products that bring the adored 'other' to mind, one can fantasise about dominating and possessing her entire existence. It thus amounts to cannibalism of the individual (Lévi-Strauss 2016). This desire can also be appeased by physically touching her at an event for shaking hands, which is an application of the logic of the index. Although she cannot fulfil all the desires of her admirers in person, various media allow her to perform for all her admirers and appeal to them. Moreover, successful performances may elicit additional desire, and the demands of the admirers may escalate without limit.

When an idol achieves her dream or finds other ways to seek it, she is expected to 'graduate' from the group, and the management company may arrange a big graduation event. When a still-popular group loses members in this way, newcomers are often brought it. In this way, the business continues. The market share of the idol industry has grown greatly in Japan. It was estimated to have reached JPY2,10,000,000,000 (approximately US$1,860,000,000) in fiscal year 2017, according to Yano Research Institute.[13] Several major groups of idols have been cast and featured in a number of TV programmes. Their live events have often filled huge stadiums and the largest concert halls in Japan.

It should be remembered that the word 'idol' is originally a term that indicates 'a statue or other object that is worshipped by people who believe that it is a god'[14]. This meaning, certainly, is reflected in the use of the term in Japan, but in a quite distinctive way. On the one hand, the core fans admire their favourite idol fanatically. They have created a jargon for describing idols, even representing them as gods, and associate themselves with their activities. They keep track of the growth and development of their favourite idol and feel as if they are nurturing her. The idols, for their part, at least in their performances in the public domain, try to behave as figures (Goffman 1981: 147) who act in ways expected of them by their admirers and fellow supporters. They wear the costumes that are preferred and speak sweetly to their admirers and cheer them on in their difficult lives, acting *as if* each individual admirer is the only one. The idols and the admirers are motivated by both desire and responsibility with respect to the imagined icons. In brief, we can find the recursive interplay between fantasising reality and realising the fantasy in their performances. Such interplay is, in general, one of the most important features of a highly industrialised and consumerised society, and it has led to the fashioning of a culturally distinctive 'world of flux, where structure is a temporary manifestation of what is otherwise a flow of constant change' (Nyamnjoh 2017).

A similar phenomenon is found in other genres of Japanese entertainment, as well as in the service industry. For example, a variety of cafés have developed, based on particular concepts (e.g., maid cafés, steward cafés, dog cafés, cat cafés, fishing cafés, military cafés and monk cafés, among others). Japanese pornography, called adult video (AV) or *adaruto bideo*, is also greatly diversified, according to the desires of its customers. It would be an interesting project to compare the history of Japanese pornography with that of the idol industry. Indeed, the heroines of pornography are often called AV idols. In these genres of entertainment and in the service industry, it seems that sexuality is associated with insatiable imagination and fantasy and, by extension, with an insatiable appetite for consumption of the object or subject of one's sexual attraction. In the next section, I will show that cannibalism, as consumption, can be achieved in yet more guises and disguises, either through direct ingestion or incorporation, or through the other senses of touch, smell, sight and sound.

Fetish to rawness[15]

In 2012, the Japanese government banned raw beef liver from restaurants as part of the Food Sanitation Act.[16] This act was a reaction to frequent occurrences of food poisoning, including fatal cases, caused by eating raw beef liver. The official reason for prohibiting it was that no methods to safely prepare raw beef liver have been found and, thus, eating it may cause serious food poisoning. If a safe preparation method is found through the progress of science, the regulation may be revised, according to the government's report.

What and how people eat is highly associated with the value system of their society. The above regulation is a reflection of the fact that raw beef liver has been commonly eaten in Japanese society since the modernisation of the country. A common preparation method for this dish is to cut a very fresh liver in pieces, quickly wash it, peel the thin skin off, and then slice it as you like. Sesame oil and salt are often used for flavouring it. Even after the ban, there seems to be no end of people secretly selling it and serving it underground.[17] Moreover, beef liver is not the only food that is eaten raw in Japan. From the cow, the third stomach, tongue and rump meat are commonly eaten raw, as is chicken meat, including its liver. These items are not prohibited by law. And of course, sashimi, namely,

320

various kinds of raw fish, crustaceans and shellfish are well known internationally. The raw meat of various fishes is also used for sushi, which is considered a national dish of Japan (Ishige 2015: 266). Eating raw meat stimulates and awakens various physical senses of the person who eats it. Looking at the wet and silky texture of the flesh, biting and chewing the thick fibre of the raw meat, and tasting and smelling its bloody juices – those who eat raw meat can enhance their imagination of subsuming the life of the creature, which is one of the central elements of cannibalism. In this context, the senses associated with cannibalism are inspired by, and integrated into, the practice of eating raw meat, thereby allowing us to be what we eat (Nyamnjoh, this volume; Lévi-Strauss 2016; Travis-Henikoff 2008).[18] From a motivational point of view there is, implicit in this context, the quality of the action that is to take place within it (Burke 1945: 6–7). In this respect, cannibalism is the embodiment of undifferentiating and the disappearance of the principle of alterity (Kilgour 1997). As Kilgour (1997) has argued, cannibalism appears horrific from the viewpoint of the individualistic formulation of self.[19] However, it also offers an attempt to strengthen our conviviality with animals and things.

Raw meat is called *nama niku* in Japanese. *Nama* is a noun or adjective that indicates the state of being raw, bare or nude, or alive, while *niku* is a noun that designates meat or flesh. The processing of meat by heating, marinating or fermenting are the basic forms of cooking. It is thought-provoking to contemplate why people appreciate eating meat raw, which is the opposite of cooked. Moreover, it is interesting that *nama* is also favourably used in advertisements for commodity or fashion items that are not meat. For instance, undiluted alcohol is called *nama zake*, in which *zake* or sake, designates alcohol. *Nama zake* is appreciated for its fresh flavour and taste, although it cannot be preserved long. Similarly, draft beer is called *nama biiru*, where *biiru* means beer. *Nama biiru* is one of the most popular alcoholic beverages, served at the beginning of dining in most Japanese restaurants.

Another interesting and peculiar use of the term *nama* is in *nama ashi*, which literally means bare legs. In this usage, not the Chinese character 生 but the katakana term ナマ is usually used, because katakana expresses the casualness or novelty of the term. *Nama ashi* indicates bare or naked legs without stockings or tights. Usually this phrase is only used for women, although both males and females can use the phrase. Feet without socks are designated by *suashi* or *hadashi*, both of which mean bare foot. *Nama ashi* as a fashion is often combined with the miniskirt or short pants. It has been a popular fashion in Japan since the 1990s. Consequently, the market share of stockings has been reduced to about one ninth of what it was at its height.[20] One study reported that males overwhelmingly like *nama ashi*, because it looks healthy, cute, attractive and sexy. It appears that the bareness of *nama ashi* invites the gaze of the perceiver directly onto the bare skin. Women do not always value this, because it requires them to be more careful in their grooming and skin care.[21] This indicates that the bareness in *nama ashi* fashions is rendered pleasing by the daily efforts of women. It is noteworthy that this use of the term *nama* is also seen in the phrases *nama sex* and *nama ecchi*; in both phrases, the word *nama* indicates having sex without wearing a condom.[22] Remember that sex where bodily fluids are exchanged is a form of cannibalism (Lévi-Strauss 2016).

Nama also means live in Japanese. Live music is called *nama ensou*, where *ensou* means music performance. A number of pubs, museums, restaurants and, of course, music clubs advertise that they have *nama ensou*. Similarly, *nama housou* indicates live broadcasting. Direct comments by customers or audience members are called *nama no koe*, which literally means 'live voice'. Contingent exchanges of actions in live music performance and talk events stimulate listening and invoke a sense of participation in the course of interactions.

A commonality to the above uses of *nama* is that people have developed fetishes for *nama* items and admire them greatly. It appears that rawness, nudity or bareness and the quality of being live or alive, all subsumed into the concept *nama*, increase the symbolic value of things in Japan's highly industrialised and consumerised society, while also invoking various senses associated with cannibalism as a mode of consorting with others. Additionally, *nama* is associated with the sense of wildness, often connected with otherness in the West. We could say that, rather than outsourcing a sense of wildness, contemporary Japanese society internalises and reproduces it by admiring *nama*.

Consumerisation of cannibalism

Each of the above cases is taken to represent an important component of cannibalism; the temptation to kill or to effect one's own death, the desire to possess the adored other, and the allure of flesh. These components are not here integrated into a unified form. Rather, divergent agents, who are ramified and distributed in different strata of contemporary Japanese society, are engaged with them. However, all of them are relevant to the logic and framework that enable a 'life form consuming others of its own kind' (Travis-Henikoff 2008: Kindle location no. 565). It is not difficult to imagine that outsiders could attribute a cannibalistic character to the Japanese and their society based on some or all of these features, as Westerners did to Africans and Melanesians. Moreover, it deserves serious consideration that all of these cases reflect a consumerist culture, sustained by the massive and complicated capitalist system of material production, product distribution and information circulation in contemporary Japanese society. In that sense, it is possible to say that these cases feed on each other. Thus, let us move on to discuss the relationships between the three cases and the consumer culture of contemporary Japanese society.

In the case of the serial murder at Zama, the SNS that specialised in providing a platform for expressing suicidal thoughts, suicide being a form of self- or auto-cannibalisation, functioned as a way for young people to express their thoughts in a less threatening manner than via face-to-face communication. The SNS is widely known, because it had been reported on in the media, along with the criminality associated with it, before the serial murder case.[23] On that SNS, anyone can post their suicidal thoughts online without addressing any particular individual. Then, after receiving twitter responses, they can choose those whose responses seem favourable to them and get in touch through the SNS account or other means.

This provides us with the tools of cannibalism and, at the same time, it also cannibalises us. In fact, SNS played an important role in connecting the suspect with his victims, who lived at some distance away. Zama is located about 50 km from the centre of Tokyo and about 20 km from the centre of Yokohama. It is a bedroom community for those two mega cities. The greater Tokyo area has a population of about 35 million, and it is almost impossible for anonymous and highly mobile people to meet without online communication media such as an SNS. SNS enable people like TS to reiterate a false initiation ritual as a form of cannibalism. TS was experienced in the communication style of that SNS, which is a necessary skill for a broker who recruits girls and young women to the sex industry. It is easy to imagine that, in view of his past achievements, he could put together the appropriate words to elicit a favourable response from the victims and propose meeting offline, which is how people who become acquainted with each other in online communication meet and cultivate their relationship. Offline meetings change the mode of communication and, thereby, offer the opportunity or risk of transforming the nature of relationships among SNS users.

The prosperity of the idol industry is correlated with the national economic situation: epoch-making idols often appear as the economy declines, become popular while the economy is expanding and then fall soon after the economy reaches its peak.[24] This is at least partly explained as follows. The decline of the economy sends many people fleeing from their real affairs to the idol industry. As the economy grows, more and more investments flow into the idol industry, which can inspire the desire for purchases in broader economic activity. Consequently, the idol industry amplifies and symbolises minute differences among idols, which provides their supporters with various customised means of obtaining access to the idols. A variety of goods (e.g., photographs, movies, CDs, character goods, autographs, and belongings) are produced for the idols' supporters to buy online, in shops and at performance venues. Their activities are also diversified. They do shaking-hands events, events to sell their CDs and other goods, live music performances outside, at live houses, in concert halls, on various TV programmes, and in films.

Moreover, their activities and products are designed to have synergistic effects: Through documenting and dramatising the efforts of idols, the management company, on the one hand, is trying to nurture amateur girls into becoming popular icons and, on the other hand, it is attempting to cultivate the market that appreciates them. For instance, as mentioned in a previous section, admirers can buy multiple CDs to obtain a ticket to participate in a shaking-hands event or to find multiple ballots for a rally. The purchase of multiple CDs provides the core admirers with a quantified indicator of their commitment to, and affection for, their favourite idols, which is difficult for them to express verbally in their limited opportunities to have face-to-face communication with the idols. On the one hand, communication online or through product purchases enables the admirers to possess and dominate the idol as a form of cannibalism and, on the other hand, it allows the idols and the management companies that choreograph them to shape and control their image by highlighting only their most favourable features. The dramatised image of the idols is copied and pasted through the various media, where the wide market consumes it. Consequently, not only the core admirers but also a range and variety of people are exposed to the realised fantasy, which is the product of an insatiable appetite for consumption of the object or subject of one's attractions. Those people make responses *as to* what they have seen, rather than replying to what they have seen (cf. Goffman 1981: 10) and, thus, the image of the idols is transformed beyond its original purpose, as arranged by the idols and their management companies.

The development of effective and large-scale transportation systems allows many people to eat raw meat, which used to be accessible only to those few who lived close to the animals. For instance, eating sushi with raw fish and sashimi became prevalent nationwide only recently. Although sushi has more than a thousand-year history in Japan, it long indicated aged fish, fermented with salt, rice, lees and vinegar. Around the 15th century, half-fermented sushi appeared. Only in the 19th century, just before Japan opened the country to the West, was there sushi with fresh raw fish on vinegared rice (Shinoda 1980: 185–259; Sakurai 2002). From that time, it became a more and more common dish, as techniques developed to preserve raw fish and the transportation system grew. In this way, the culture of sushi with raw fish, with an appreciation of the quality of the food materials, cooking tools, cooking skills, service treatment and style of the restaurant was established (Shinoda 1980: 91–98; Kitaoji 1980: 147–159; Ishige 2015: 265–268). Now, it stimulates the senses of people worldwide and augments the concept of cannibalism as consumption.

Since the 7th century, when the emperor implemented an act banning the eating of meat, beef has been largely and officially avoided, except for medicinal uses in nutrients and tonics. However, when Japan was opened to the West in the 19th century, people were astonished at the differences between Western physiques and their own. A number of people ascribed the differences to the food culture of the Western people, particularly the custom of eating beef and drinking milk (Ishige 2015: 63–67, 174–187). Yukichi Fukuzawa, one of the most influential scholars of the time, criticised the custom of avoiding beef as having little valid reason (Fukuzawa 2001[1870]). The national policy of Japan at that time was to increase wealth and military strength against the modern and 'civilised' Western powers. Thus, the government, wishing to establish a nation state, promoted the custom of eating beef (Majima 2002). Hence the custom of eating beef went hand in hand with the nationalistic movement at the time of the modernisation and 'civilising' of the country. In other words, at that time, the Japanese tried to be Western by eating beef, among other ways, believing that one is what one eats. The custom of eating raw beef became common later, after Japan occupied Korea and colonised it in the course of their own modernisation and 'civilising' of the country and, as a result, Korean food culture dominated the Japanese palette.

The system of circulating information has also greatly developed. In contemporary Japanese society, there are various TV programmes, comics, magazines and internet sites featuring and appreciating appetising and delicious foods. In these media, raw meat is often advertised with well-articulated words and pictures and is, thereby, given additional value. Thus, the media contributed significantly to facilitating the concept of cannibalism as consumption in various guises and disguises. Not only is the wildness associated with raw meat marked but it is also actively invoked or even created for the purpose of attracting customers. The concept of *nama* has rapidly penetrated the consumerism found in the ever-changing Japanese society. The allure of flesh constitutes a central element of this consumerism.

Similar to the idea of raw meat, nudity or bareness appears to have gained additional value in our consumerised society, which is overflowing with countless artificial goods, through invoking the various senses as a form of cannibalism. It should be noted that, as a result of the consumerisation of cannibalism, nudity is often the product of careful image control by the relevant agents in various ways. As mentioned in the previous section, the nudity in *nama ashi* fashions is rendered attractive by the daily efforts of women. Additionally, a number of fashion magazines, TV programmes, and YouTube content have shown the detailed process of make-up that facilitates supposed natural beauty. A similar argument can be used with regard to the concept of 'being live' as well. The selling point of live music or live comments is that of its contingency, according to circumstances. However, it is often the case that what seems to be an improvised musical performance or unscripted comment is often a carefully designed product built up through mass media. For example, although we can find a number of live music programmes broadcast on Japanese TV shows, many of them often use lip-synching.

Concluding remarks

Japanese society was thoroughly imbued with the spirit of 'civilisation' and modernisation, which led to rapid Westernisation and the dissemination of consumerism. I believe, however, that cannibalism has not been expelled, even now, from society as a result of that process. Rather, it may have even flourished as part of the process of rapid Westernisation and the dissemination of consumerism, which makes us constantly aware of the incompleteness of our everyday life. Contemporary Japanese society is composed of infinitely incomplete beings, constantly in need of activation, potency and enhancement through relationships with incomplete 'others' (Nyamnjoh 2017). Captivated by the magic of civilisation and modernity, we might have endogenously generated a new form of cannibalism, one that allows us to surmount the pervasive sense of incompleteness we feel in our daily lives.

Endnotes

[1] https://digital.asahi.com/articles/ASKB05G0FKB0UTIL037.html, last accessed 22 January 2018.

[2] http://www.sankei.com/affairs/news/171113/afr1711130003-n1.html and
https://digital.asahi.com/articles/ASKCB142FKC9UTIL08B.html, last accessed 22 January 2018.

[3] http://biz-journal.jp/2017/11/post_21377_3.html, last accessed 22 January 2018.

[4] https://digital.asahi.com/articles/ASKCP5QN7KCPUTIL051.html and https://digital.asahi.com/articles/ASKCK4VQJKCKUTIL02K.html, last accessed 22 January 2018.

[5] See Nyamnjoh (this volume) for the famous case of a German who placed an advert online for a victim, and then ate parts of the victim together with the victim, before killing him off.

[6] http://gendai.ismedia.jp/articles/-/53452, last accessed 22 January 2018.

[7] https://mainichi.jp/articles/20171104/ddm/041/040/059000c, last accessed 22 January 2018.

[8] http://news.livedoor.com/article/detail/13857514/ and https://www.tokyo-sports.co.jp/entame/entertainment/814549/, last accessed 4 March 2018.

[9] http://gendai.ismedia.jp/articles/-/53452, last accessed 22 January 2018.

[10] http://www.babymetal.jp/home/, last accessed 22 January 2018.

[11]. http://www.alice-project.biz/kamenjoshi/jp, last accessed 22 January 2018.

[12] *Otaku* is a Japanese word that indicates people with obsessive interests, commonly in anime and manga fandom. Such people tend to avoid committing themselves to real interpersonal relationships in the highly industrialised and consumerised Japanese society. For a detailed analysis of the relationship between *otaku* and Japanese society, see Miyadai (1994: 153–274). This group is comparable to nerds in the US.

13 https://news.mynavi.jp/article/20171207-553131/, last accessed 22 January 2018.

14 Collins Cobuild Advanced Learner's English Dictionary (5th ed.)(2006) Glasgow: HarperCollins Publisher.

15 I owe the inspiration for this section to informal discussions with my dear friend, Matthias Brenzinger, who is a distinguished linguist at the University of Cape Town.

16 http://www.mhlw.go.jp/stf/seisakunitsuite/bunya/kenkou_iryou/shokuh in/syouhisya/110720/, last accessed 22 January 2018.

17 https://www.47news.jp/802399.html, last accessed 22 January 2018.

18 As Nyamnjoh (this volume) indicated, beliefs in transmutation and transubstantiation between humans and animals and things are widespread among non-Western cultures around the globe (Bourguignon 1959; Zulaika 1993; Miller 1995; Ellis 1999; Thornton 2003; Podruchny 2004; Richards 2009; Fardon 2014).

19 Vegetarianism can be seen as another polar idealisation of the relationships between humans and animals: if we extend the view of individualistic self to animals and then respect their autonomy and self-determination, it is a logical consequence to decide not to eat them. The question is where do we draw the line between creatures with a respectable self and others?

20 http://www.js-hosiery.jp/data.html, http://trendy.nikkeibp.co.jp/atcl/coltop/15/121104/111600034/?rt=noc nt, last accessed 22 January 2018.

21 https://woman.mynavi.jp/article/150603-35/, last accessed 22 January 2018.

22 http://www.fuzoku.sh/teaches/0056/, last accessed 22 January 2018.

23 https://digital.asahi.com/articles/ASKB02Q6ZKB0UTIL006.html, last accessed 22 January 2018.

24 https://style.nikkei.com/article/DGXNASFK1203C_S4A210C1000000, last accessed 22 January 2018.

References

Bourguignon, E. (1959) 'The Persistence of Folk Belief: Some Notes on Cannibalism and Zombies in Haiti', *The Journal of American Folklore*, Vol. 72: 36–46.

Burke, K. (1945) *A Grammar of Motives*, New York: Prentice-Hall Inc.

Ellis, S. (1999) *The Mask of Anarchy: The Destruction of Liberia and the Religious Dimension of an African Civil War*, London: Christopher Hurst.

Erikson, E. H. (1959) *Identity and the Life Cycle*, New York: International Universities Press.

Esteban, R. (2016) 'Cannibalism among Japanese Soldiers in Bukidnon, Philippines, 1945–47', *Asian Studies: Journal of Critical Perspectives on Asia*, Vol. 52(1): 63–102.

Fairchild, C. (2008) *Pop Idols and Pirates: Mechanisms of Consumption and the Global Circulation of Popular Music*, Aldershot: Ashgate Publishing, Ltd.

Fardon, R. (2014) *Tiger in an African Palace and Other Thoughts about Identification and Transformation*, Bamenda: Langaa.

Fukuzawa, Y. (2001) *A Theory of the Custom to Eat Meat*, Aozora Bunko, (Kindle version; originally published in 1870 in Japanese).

Goffman, E. (1981) *Forms of Talk*, Philadelphia, PA: University of Pennsylvania Press.

Huntington, S. P. (1996) *The Clash of Civilizations and the Remaking of World Order*, New York: Simon & Schuster.

Ishige, N. (2015) *The History of Japanese Food Culture: From Old Stone Age to Nowadays*, Tokyo: Iwanami Shoten, (in Japanese).

Kawai, H. (1976) *Pathology of Japan as a Materialistic Society*, Tokyo: Chuokoronsha, (in Japanese).

Kilgour, M. (1997) 'Cannibals and Critics: An Exploration of James de Mille's "Strange Manuscript"', *Mosaic: An Interdisciplinary Critical Journal*, Vol. 30(1): 19–37.

Kitaoji, R. (1980) *The Realm of Cooking: Essays of Rozanjin*, Tokyo: Bunkashuppankyoku, (in Japanese).

Lévi-Strauss, C. (2016) *We Are All Cannibals and Other Essays*, New York: Columbia University Press.

Majima, A. (2002) 'Meat is Modern: Food and Power in Meiji Japan',

International Christian University publications, 3-A, Asian Cultural Studies, Special Issue 11: 213–230, (in Japanese).

Mbembe, A. (2001) *On the Postcolony*, Berkeley, CA: University of California Press.

Miller, L. (1995) 'Southern Silk Route Tales: Hospitality, Cannibalism and the Other', *Merveilles & contes*, Vol. 9(2): 137–169.

Miyadai, S. (1994) *The Choice of School Girls*, Tokyo: Kodansha, (in Japanese).

Ōoka, S. (1951) *Wildfire*, Tokyo: Shichobunko, (in Japanese).

Moriya, T. (1978) *Humans in the battlefront of Philippines*, Tokyo: Keisoshobo, (in Japanese).

Nyamnjoh, F. B. (2017) 'Incompleteness: Frontier Africa and the Currency of Conviviality', *Journal of Asian and African Studies*, Vol. 52(3): 253–270.

Podruchny, C. (2004) 'Werewolves and Windigos: Narratives of Cannibal Monsters in French-Canadian Voyageur Oral Tradition', *Ethnohistory*, Vol. 51(4): 677–700.

Richards, P. (2009) 'Dressed to Kill: Clothing as Technology of the Body in the Civil War in Sierra Leone', *Journal of Material Culture*, Vol. 14(4): 495–512.

Sagawa, I. (1991) *Cannibalism Illusion*, Tokyo: Hokusosha, (in Japanese).

Sakai, M. (2014) *Idol's Wealth of Nations: Analyzing the Idols from the Era of Seiko and Akina to that of MomoClo*, Tokyo: Toyo Keizai Inc, (in Japanese).

Sakurai, S. (2002) 'Sushi of Ancient Japan', *Shoku Nihongi Kenkyu*, Vol. 339: 19–38, (in Japanese).

Shinoda, O. (1980) *A Book of Sushi*, Tokyo: Shibatashoten, (in Japanese).

Takahashi, Y. (1999) *Lectures in Sociology: A Perspective from the Theory of Emotions*, Kyoto: Sekaisisosha, (in Japanese).

Thornton, J. (2003) 'Cannibals, Witches, and Slave Traders in the Atlantic World', *The William and Mary Quarterly*, Vol. 60(2): 273–294.

Travis-Henikoff (2008) *Dinner with a Cannibal: The Complete History of Mankind's Oldest Taboo*, Santa Monica, CA: Santa Monica Press LLC.

Tyler, D. (2007) *Hit Songs, 1900–1955: American Popular Music of the Pre-rock Era*, Jefferson, NC: McFarland & Company, Inc, Publishers.

Yomoda, I. (2006) *Minding 'Kawaii (cuteness)'*, Tokyo: Chikuma Shobo, (in Japanese).

Zulaika, J. (1993) 'Further Encounters with the Wild Man: Of Cannibals, Dogs, and Terrorists', *Etnofoor*, Vol. 6(2): 21–39.

INDEX

A

abattoir 52, 172, 177

abomination 180

academic texts 62, 100, 102

access 1, 69, 107, 199, 234, 238, 242, 256, 273–4, 276, 278, 325

act of compassion 225

administration 170–1

    colonial 139, 162, 164, 166, 170, 175, 178–9

Obama 54

traditional 172

Trump 54

admirer 67, 318–20, 325

adultery 180

African Christianity 64, 191

African converts 161

African life-forces 138

African nationalistic regimes 144

African religions 184

after-tears parties/celebrations 232

agency 6, 45-6, 62, 119, 121, 129, 202, 214, 271, 289

age-old indigenous traditions and cultures 162

alterity 16, 29, 45, 47, 127, 321

ambivalence 20, 46, 51, 77

animalism 6

animal-like person 289

anthropological enquiry 59

anthropologist 7–10, 14, 62, 99-101, 103, 105, 108–13, 117–22, 159–60, 180, 187, 230

    man-eating 109–25

anthropology 10, 19, 99–100, 105, 108-11, 115, 117–20, 140, 267

cannibalism and colonial violence 101–3

cannibalism: beyond the modern world and towards a new 120–2

anthropophagy 13, 19, 73, 76, 224, 246

Anti-Retro Virals (ARVs) 241

antisemitism 50

apartheid 65, 197–206, 231, 235, 248, 267–77

aposematic prey 295–6

appetisers 265–8

Araweté 43

archaeologists 7, 14

archaeology 140

Aretsebaneng 237

ashes 28, 65, 79, 226, 234, 246

    the saga of human 240–5

Average Effective Tax Rate
(AETR) 286
Aztec human sacrifice 226

B

background 54, 67, 120, 190, 257,
271, 314
on black middle class in South
Africa 198–202
Bamenda Grassfielders 63
Christianity and the cannibalisation
of the 157–95
banquet of Moctezuma 226
baptism 163, 173, 177, 181
barbarism 1, 17, 19–20, 22, 70, 99
Basel Missionary 157–9
being human 2–3, 9, 18, 22, 39, 43,
57, 60, 68, 71, 73
as eating and being eaten 39–41
Biafra war warriors 226
Bible 32, 70, 133, 158–160, 164,
171, 173, 175–6, 181–2
biomedical fraternity 229
biomedical practitioners 229
biomedical procedures 228
black diamonds 199–200
Black Economic Empowerment
(BEE) 66, 256, 266–8, 278
black middle class 64–5, 197–8,
205–15, 235, 269
background on 198–202

cannibalising 202–5
black tax 64, 197, 202–3, 207, 215–6
media on cannibalising
208–12
block societies 238
blood of Christ 182
bodily fluids 28, 31, 79, 262, 295,
322
body harvesters 24
body of Christ 157, 181–2
bone-ash cannibalism 226
British South African Company
137, 139
British Southern Cameroons 157,
160
burial 20, 225, 232, 238–9
location 236
place 236
preparations 232, 239
societies 208, 236–7
soft 48

C

cannibal democracy 5
cannibal feast 121, 226
humans and animals as
two sides of the same 41–52
Cannibal Tours 116–117
cannibalisation 2–12, 25, 51–4, 62,
64, 69, 146–8, 197, 255, 314, 324
of Africans 131–2

of the Bamenda
Grassfielders 63, 157–95
of the non-Western
(Other) 2, 12
of Zimbabwe 130, 133–
42
cannibalising
black middle class 202–5
obligations 205–7
systemic obligations 214–5
cannibalism
under the ANC 201–2
in camouflage 52–62, 69
out of control 53
metaphorical 231, 245
beyond the modern world and
towards a new anthropology 120–2
there is more meat to 4–18
mortuary 36, 77, 224
problematic notion of 104–9
symbolic 8, 32, 110, 319
cannibalistic practices 99, 110–3,
122
capitalism 2, 5, 46, 54, 58–61, 71,
100, 103–4, 117, 120, 206, 214,
255–6, 278–9
capture
and cannibalisation of Zimbabwe
133–42
deterrence 294–8
Cecil John Rhodes 132–3

celebrities 11, 74, 237
Christianisation 12, 60, 183
Christianity 63–4, 133
and the cannibalisation of the
Bamenda Grassfielders (Cameroon)
157–95
domestication of Western 183–90
Christmas 206
church compounds 160, 176–7
consuming and being
Consumed: 'Love' and 'Sex' in the
178–83
citizenship 41, 53
and cannibalism 212–4
racialised 5
civilisation 3–4, 7, 18–24, 34, 39–40,
47–53, 59–60, 68–72, 99, 105, 139,
148, 159–61, 309, 315–6, 328
civilised society 1, 107
collective success 64–5, 198, 203,
206, 214
collectivities 5, 203, 205
colonial logics 129
colonial project 41, 99
colonialism 2, 12, 14, 18, 38, 49, 51,
59–66, 71, 100–20, 137, 160–4,
173–5, 182, 190–1, 197, 284–97
colonialist conquest 100, 104
colonialists 56, 117, 134, 137, 139–
40

colonisation 12, 107, 131, 133, 139, 183

coloniser 114, 159

commodification 2, 23, 228, 255, 278

common humanity 1, 38, 50, 57, 133–4

communion 31, 120, 181–3

compassion 20, 23, 31, 34, 39, 48, 122, 225, 232, 246

compassionate cannibalism 18–39, 71, 76, 270

consumer 11, 20, 32, 41, 57, 66–7, 99–100, 177, 200–2, 231, 235, 238, 246, 255–8, 278–9, 312, 324

    capitalism 255–6, 278–9

consumerisation 327

of cannibalism 323–7

of cannibalism in contemporary Japanese society 309–32

consumerism 2, 120, 199, 202, 214–5, 235, 258, 312, 327–8

consuming and being consumed: 'love' and 'sex' in the church compounds 178–83

consummation 12, 37

contagion 26, 262

convert 58, 160–3, 167, 172–5, 181, 188

corporate cannibalism 55, 213

corpse medicine 29

cosmology/ies 2, 17, 42–4, 57, 71, 68, 139

cremated human ashes 242–5

criminals 26, 52, 147

culture 2, 4, 8–9, 16, 19–21, 43, 45, 47, 51, 54, 62, 66–7, 102, 105, 109–10, 114, 118–21, 187–8, 213, 240, 258, 264, 270, 312, 316, 323–7

cultural relativism 8, 29, 110–1, 114

cultural translation 100, 118

cynosure 175–6

D

defence 110, 163, 294, 297

delegitimisation 157, 164, 190

    argument 164–70, 189, 203

delicacy/ies 37, 131, 142, 146–7

dependency 5, 129, 202, 215

depredation 138–139, 147–8

dessert 132, 144, 271–2

dichotomy/ies 42, 99, 104, 111, 264

dictatorship 143–4

dignity 1, 6, 57, 203, 215, 235–6, 246

direct violence 101

diriyankes 257–8

discourse 19, 22, 30, 63, 75, 99–120, 128–9, 142–5, 148, 161, 163, 182, 209, 215, 231, 265, 267, 270

disquettes 257–8

domestication 12, 63
of Western Christianity by the
Bamenda Grassfielders 183–90
dominance 4, 7, 19, 50–1, 59–61,
73, 76, 102–4, 161, 186, 203, 255
domination 103, 184, 200, 230–1,
255, 297
drug abuse *see* substance abuse

E
eaten, the 1, 33, 39, 41, 231
eater 1, 4, 21, 33, 40–4, 57, 157,
224–5, 231, 309
eating   and being eaten 4, 39–42,
50, 60, 62, 68, 72–3
eating up traditional rulers 164–70,
189, 203
Ecclesia in Africa 186
economy 56, 70, 138–9, 145, 198,
201, 203, 207, 227, 257, 262, 318,
324–5
endocannibalism 35–6, 76, 246
enhancement 261, 328
Enlightened Man 66–7, 283–307
Enlightened Soil 66, 283, 285
Enlightenment 12, 19–20, 52, 60,
66, 99, 103, 105–6, 109, 111, 116,
285, 296
enslavement 2, 12, 16, 41, 66, 145,
147, 284, 288, 290, 297
entertainment industry 11, 37

entitlement 6, 215
epistemology/ies 17, 47, 63, 129,
138
ethics of vulnerability 63, 128–9,
140, 148
ethnographic praxis 10
ethnography/ies 20, 42, 71, 103,
120–1, 270, 312
        of cannibalism 109–18
        and the violence of
making a text from data 118-20
Eucharist 31, 84, 163
Eurocentric background 190
Eurocentric idea 17
Eurocentric index of consumption
1
Eurocentric understanding 18
Eurocentrism 17–8
evangelisation 185–9
exclusion 199, 203–5
exotic other 104–5, 109, 112, 116,
121, 270
exploitation 12, 61, 67, 100–4, 116,
118, 121, 130, 142, 145, 148, 209,
257, 270–1, 285, 288
exploiting the suicidal 312–5
ex-servicemen 172, 175–7, 179, 181
        and cannibalism 175–7
ex-soldiers or 'Fernando Po
Repartees' and the licence to
consume Grassfielders 171–5

extended family 199, 224, 239

extraction 6, 27, 117, 227–8, 271, 284, 291, 293, 297–8

    pale tale of 285–91

Extractors 284–7, 290–2

F

fantasising reality and realising the fantasy 67, 315–20

feasting 16, 256, 258, 262, 278

Fernando Po 170–5, 177–81

fetish 67, 163–4, 187, 323

to rawness 320–3

flavour 267, 272–3, 278, 321–2

flesh 21, 25, 183, 223, 284, 310–4, 321–3, 327

    human 5–8, 11–4, 19–66, 73, 99, 105–6, 113, 122, 129, 137, 140, 159, 163, 190, 224–31

    naked 261

    rainbow nation of the 255–81

fluidity/ies 3, 41, 68, 114

Fondoms 164–6, 170, 172–3, 175–7, 179

Fons 164–5, 171, 176, 178, 180

Fore 20, 26–7

fulfilment 4–5, 7, 231, 235, 257, 309, 246

funeral 35, 65, 100, 111, 122, 231–2, 234–9

insurance 65, 238–9

cover packages 237

G

Galapagos 316

genocide 50, 53

mobility 2, 49-51, 53, 72, 161, 168, 175, 199–200, 204, 206, 235, 257

ghu-ghelli-wong 175

ghu-i-wo-fyi 170

global consumerism 214–5

global market 24, 228

global south 17, 145

globalisation 2, 138

gluttony 272–8

gourmandise of an enlightened man 283–307

H

hair 34

hallucinogenic effects 241

Harvey Weinstein 6

Herero 51

hierarchy/ies 7, 33, 44, 50, 54–5, 62, 68, 72, 77, 102, 131, 138, 167, 170, 173, 198, 261, 269, 278, 318

historical disadvantage 207

HIV 242, 258

Holocaust 50

holy supper 182–3

honour 235–6, 243

How High 244

human ashes

the saga of 240–5

human body parts 140, 227–30

human organs 31

humanity 1–2, 6–7, 17–8, 38–43, 49–53, 57, 62–77, 99–103, 109, 133–4, 181, 197–8, 203, 209, 213–6, 271

humans and animals as two sides of the same cannibal feast 41–52

human sacrifice 31, 226

hunger cannibalism 224

hunhu/unhu 63, 128

I

idols 67, 104, 316–20, 324–6

impunity 16, 174, 179

in lieu of a conclusion: after dinner mint, coffee & brandy 278–9

incompleteness 2–3, 67, 312, 328

incorporated or cannibalised by posthuman others 127–55

indigenous religions 63–4, 184

ingestion 12, 20, 28–31, 36–8, 56, 132, 228, 230–1, 246, 320

inheritance dynamics 65, 233

initiation 31, 315, 324

insurance policy 234, 246

investment of 'life' 235–40

i-wong-a-wo 175

J

Japanese pornography 320

jujus 171, 181

K

Kabaka 170

King Lobengula 127, 130, 132–3

kitchen 177, 258–65

Kom 161, 165–81, 188

kraals 137

kuru 26, 111, 113

L

labour 2, 5, 12, 22, 48, 54, 56, 58–59, 61, 137–8, 162, 198, 200–6, 212–3

Lancaster House Constitution 134

land redistribution 134–5

lap dancing 66, 255–9, 266, 273, 278

law of survival 106

legitimation 160, 170, 172

Lehu la gago le ya mphidisha 65, 223–54

liberation

movements 231

struggle 201

war of 31

life chances 5–6, 54, 199

life-force 137–8

literal meaning 64, 224

literary cannibalism 40

luring and incorporating 'delicious' Africa in a cannibalistic world 142–8

M

main course 268–71

Maka 14, 56, 107–8, 114–5, 117, 120

Mane community 226

man-eating anthropologists 99–125

Maori 8, 14, 120

matrilineal descent line 234

Mbaya dance 172

media 12, 32, 64, 131, 135–6, 138, 143, 197, 205–7, 213, 215, 227, 241–2, 310, 312–5, 318–9, 324–7

on cannibalising black tax 208–12

social 10, 31–2, 205, 210, 212–3, 313

medicinal cannibalism 23, 29–31, 228–9, 246

Melanesia/n 35–6, 224, 309, 323

metaphoric consumption 132, 259

metaphorical cannibalism 231, 245

mimesis 142–8

missionary/ies 15, 19, 49, 60, 64, 108, 111, 114, 133, 157–74, 180–90

modernity 1–2, 7, 22, 49, 51, 53, 59, 68–70, 109, 115, 170, 179, 202–3, 214–5, 309, 328

monetary revenue 285–6

moral/s 133, 139–40

agency 129

assessment 209

commitments 34

community/ies 58–60

compasses 3

debates 57

dilemma 3

discourse 111

duty 284

economy 70

excuse 108

high ground 17

imperative 127, 130

implications 2

insensitivity 55

judgment 102, 105, 111, 113–4

myopia 283

norms 108

obligations 229

order 3, 7, 62, 68

particularism 54

philosophy 106

pretence 104

quandary 32

resources 9

revulsion 255

science 108

sensibility 59

sensitivities 59

subscriptions 34

superiority 53, 111

sympathies 3

universalism 54

values 255

morality 2–3, 8, 24, 41, 53, 62, 72, 136, 141

mortuary cannibalism 36, 77, 224

mortuary rites 232–3

Movement for Democratic Change (MDC) 135

muti 227

killings 65, 227–30, 244–7

mutual eating 258

my African heart 283–307

N

naked flesh 261

nama 67, 311, 321–3, 327

narcissistic predator 293–7

nationalistic regime 144

natural law of survival 106

natural man 106

natural resources 66, 107, 284–7, 291

necrophilia 36

neo-cannibalism 25

neoliberalism 2, 136, 200–1, 211, 215

niku 67, 321–2

nkwifoyn 173, 181

non-governmental organisations (NGOs) 135–6, 143–4, 291, 297

non-people people 283, 288

non-Western 99

context 19, 41

critic 1, 27

culture 44

hemisphere 44

intellectual 18

other 2, 12, 110, 202

people 16

societies 15, 29, 226

world 16, 162

nourishing transactions 262

nudity 67, 323, 327

nyaope 240–244

boys 234, 241–6

Nyongo 219

O

obligations 2, 28, 34, 46, 135, 229, 235

    cannibalising 205–7

    cannibalising systemic 214–5

customary 162

to home and host communities 64

to relations and kin 64, 213

researching cannibalising 197–222

obscure gourmandise of an enlightened man 283–307

occult

  beliefs 39, 69

practices 31, 38–9, 69

ontology/ies 2, 17, 44–7, 57, 63, 68, 71, 129, 230, 278

oppression 113, 117, 230, 232

Orient 161

otaku 318

otherness 47, 309, 323

outsourcing 3, 52, 60, 70, 207, 214–6, 323

P

paganism 162, 168, 188–90

pale tale of extraction 285–91

paradox 23, 30, 49, 58, 103, 109, 160

Paradox of Plenty 286

path of the dying heart 291–8

patriarchal ideologies 233

patriarchal phenomenon 55

performance 263–5, 270, 277, 317, 319–20, 322–7

personhood 6, 45, 59, 61, 74, 120, 202–4, 214–5

Phakathi 213

placenta 27, 116, 226

placentophagy 226

places of birth 206, 209

political correctness 1, 8

political buffer 203, 214

political rhetoric 53

polygamy 163–5, 175

pornography 32–3, 320

posthuman ethics 63

posthuman others 127–55

posthumanism 63, 128, 130

power relations 40–1, 74, 119, 203

power sharing 256, 277–8

predator 11, 33, 43, 176, 225, 289, 291, 293–7

prey 5–6, 11, 13, 32–3, 38, 42–3, 50, 79, 143, 181, 225, 284, 289–90, 292, 294–9

primitive 32, 101–2, 106, 108, 111–7, 159, 183, 189–90, 205, 283

culture 19

savage 7, 10, 32, 69, 107, 120

savagery 1, 21

society 20

primitivism 1, 108, 116–7

principle of alterity 47, 321

problematic notion of cannibalism 104–9

projection and delegitimisation argument 164–70

R

racial difference 276

racial dominance 51

racial exclusion 199

racial hierarchies 198

racial oppression 113

racial stratification 213

racial supremacy 51

racialised citizenship 5

rainbow nation of the flesh 255–81

raw beef liver 320–1

raw meat 67, 321, 326–7

regime 17, 62, 114, 135, 141, 143–5, 231, 256, 261

relativism 8, 29, 110–1, 114

religion 46, 51, 54, 57–8, 63–4, 133, 138–40, 157, 168, 171–3, 179, 183–4

repartees 171–2

    and the licence to consume Grassfielders 171–5

reproduction 2–3, 17, 33, 46, 53, 62, 183

researching cannibalising obligations in post-apartheid South Africa 197–222

Resource Curse 286

resurrection 31, 182

retrenchment 202, 204

revenue 285–6

rhetoric 53, 57, 117

rite

body-tearing 9, 26

funeral 100, 122

mortuary 232–233

ritual 6, 16, 26–7, 34, 36, 38, 66, 110, 131, 147, 187, 224–7, 230, 232, 236–7, 243, 246, 260, 263, 315, 324

cannibalism 8, 16, 31, 51, 69, 109, 148

Robert Mugabe 134, 136, 144

Robinson Crusoe 13, 40–1, 44, 49, 285, 287

royal wives 160, 164, 175

S

Saartjie Baartman 255, 270

sacrament 31, 163–4, 176–7, 181, 189–90

sacrifice 31, 48, 64, 70, 74, 77, 104, 197, 208–9, 215, 226, 258

saga of human ashes 240–5

sanctions 63

    and witchcraft in contemporary Zimbabwe 127–55

        Zimbabwe and 142–8

secret societies 31, 69

seduction 142–8

self-worth 6, 202

serial monogamy 163

serial murder 311, 313–4, 324

sexual commerce 257

sexualised cannibalism 257

shared humanity 40, 198, 216

slave trade 56–7, 137, 170, 183

social status 162, 231

'soft' sexual services 314

specialised social networking service (SNS) 313–5, 324

static

    actors 114

    image 117

    notion of space and time 120

object 109

representations 118

stereotypes 16, 52, 267

stereotypification 68

stereotyping 16

Stonehenge 79 n 27, 243

street society 238

structural violence 62, 100–3, 108, 116–7

struggles for succession 136

substance 9, 23–30, 35–6, 71, 258

abuse 240–1

subversive liberators 177

suicidal

    exploiting the 312–5

thoughts 315, 324

superiority 2, 7, 12, 16, 51, 53, 57, 60, 71, 73, 111, 133, 202, 215

supremacy 2, 40, 51, 57, 202, 205, 215, 277

surgical enhancements 261

surgical procedures 228

survival 27, 56, 77, 106, 232, 287, 289, 291–8

of the fittest 3, 130

survivalism 3

survivors 234, 236

symbolic cannibalism 8, 32, 110, 319

symbolic death 67, 314–5

T

Ten Commandments 176

The Texas Chainsaw Massacre 46

there is more meat to cannibalism than meets the eye 4–18

'thing-ification' 115

Thiofs 257–8

tolerance 1, 8

tombstone unveiling 232–3

Tooro 163, 182

tradition 13, 31, 36, 49, 108, 179–80, 224

traditional administration 172

traditional authority/ies 160, 172–3, 190

traditional beliefs 176

traditional capital 172

traditional custom 181

traditional dress 185, 257

traditional framework 110

traditional healer 227, 230

traditional healing 228

traditional hierarchy 173

traditional law 181

traditional medicine 31, 34

traditional mores 162, 172–4

traditional musical instruments 187

traditionl norms 175

traditional pedigree 180

traditional practitioners 229

traditional religion 157, 172–3

traditional rulers 157, 163–4, 171

      eating up 164–70

traditional world 6

traditional worldview 181

trafficking 2, 25, 31, 140, 229

transaction 257, 261–3, 270–3

transformation 44–5, 47, 201, 203, 263, 277

transnational boundaries 50

transnational corporations 63, 128, 137, 139, 144

transubstantiation 31, 44

U

Ubuntu 4, 63, 131

unemployment 137, 204, 211, 241–2

United Nations Development Program's (UNDP) Human Development Index (HDI) 287

universal attribute 4

universal ethics 62

universal humanism 62

universal humanity 17, 99

universal phenomenon 56, 314

universal reality 68, 70

universal status 223

universal terms 19

universality of sameness 53

universe 2, 45–6, 50, 57, 72, 160

upwardly mobile black South Africans 197, 202–7

V

vampire 26, 59, 118, 310

violence 7, 16, 18, 20, 22, 47, 51, 58–60, 62, 76, 101–3, 108, 115–7, 121, 141–2, 231

      of making a text from data 118–20

of translating people into cannibals 99–101

virgin 265

      canvas 265

territory/ies 12, 265

vulnerability 49, 63, 128–9, 136, 140, 148, 204, 262, 315

W

Wally Hope 243

warfare cannibalism (exocannibalism) 225–6

Wari' 20, 23, 34–5, 37, 42–3, 48, 71, 122, 224, 270

weapon 287

bible as 173, 175

licensed 159

of mass destruction 13

of the weak 14

Western Christianity 64, 157, 164–5, 168, 175, 183, 190–1

domestication of 183–90

Western domination 184

Western thought 44, 100, 105

Westernisation 12, 312, 315, 328

winner takes all 3, 6, 60

witchcraft 22, 38, 42, 47–8, 63, 115, 163, 182–3, 209

in contemporary Zimbabwe 127–55

Y

Yanomami 42

Z

zero-sum games 130

Zimbabwe African National Union (Patriotic Front) 135–6

www.ingramcontent.com/pod-product-compliance
Lightning Source LLC
Chambersburg PA
CBHW050626280326
41932CB00015B/2542